THE CARIBBEAN POLICY OF THE
UNITED STATES
1890—1920

THE ALBERT SHAW LECTURES ON DIPLOMATIC HISTORY, 1942
THE WALTER HINES PAGE SCHOOL OF INTERNATIONAL RELATIONS

THE CARIBBEAN POLICY OF THE UNITED STATES, 1890—1920

BY

WILFRID HARDY CALLCOTT

1966

OCTAGON BOOKS, INC.

New York

Reprinted 1966
by special arrangement with The Johns Hopkins Press

OCTAGON BOOKS, INC.
175 FIFTH AVENUE
NEW YORK, N.Y. 10010

LIBRARY OF CONGRESS CATALOG CARD NUMBER: 66-28374

Printed in U.S.A. by
NOBLE OFFSET PRINTERS, INC.
NEW YORK 3, N. Y.

To

GEORGE
NANCY
FRANK
THOMAS
MARY

APOLOGY

The purpose of this study is to focus attention on what the author feels to be the central theme of the foreign policy of the United States for the years indicated in the title. For the first half century or more of the existence of the new nation it was inevitable that the chief interest after organizing its government should have been in westward expansion and the security of its own borders. Once these had been accomplished tentative gestures were made in the direction of oversea possessions but all such received a severe setback by the Confederate War and its aftermath.

With the re-birth of national pride and the renewed energies springing in part from a rapidly growing economic system it was inevitable that ambitions should again expand and that they should now be fixed on the region which was obviously important both for the sake of defense and because of economic possibilities. The result was the development of a definite program to bring the said region under the aegis of the Stars and Stripes. Just how it was to be done, or just what was to be done in any given case, was not at all clear in the minds even of the national authorities of the time. The main fact, however, continued to stand out—something had to be done.

A noteworthy fact, also, is that the actions taken were not the result of applying the policies of any particular political party, for the settlement of a long series of incidents took place under varied administrations and under the guidance of men who professed different political creeds and advised different international policies. But slowly incidents occurred and their solutions had cumulative effects. Regardless of party platforms these settlements had many features in common and the whole program fell into a pattern and somewhat unconsciously formed a policy for the nation.

After the end of the First World War it is true that the Caribbean no longer occupied the unique position it held during the preceding third of a century. The reason was simple. Improved communications and the increasing demands of trade and of international rivalries demanded the formation of a larger policy: one that would consider the world in general and the whole Western Hemisphere in particular.

Thus the evolution of the foreign policy of the United States falls conveniently into four periods, each dominated by a central theme.

1. Mainland Development, 1776-1890.
2. Evolution of a Caribbean Policy, 1890-1920.
3. Evolution of a Hemisphere Policy, 1920-1940.
4. Evolution of a World-Wide Policy, 1940—

Of course incidents arose in each period that were not a part of the main theme, but still the central idea of each remained. Certainly after the Revolution there arose complications arising from the earlier European contacts and relationships. Likewise no one would deny the significance of the Hague Conferences and the League of Nations in the development of a world-wide policy. No more would the present writer deny that the basis of a hemisphere policy was developing throughout the second period. To say this is simply to point out the continuity of history and the fact that each new departure had its roots in the past, and by no means eliminated the predominant features of the past and the fact that it vitally conditioned what was to follow.

Thus, once its mainland territories were acquired and its national unity secured by dint of the trial of war, the nation began again to reach out. It is this first successful overseas program with its trials and errors that is here examined as the prototype of the larger program of the next two decades and the still larger one of to-day. As such the Caribbean Policy of the United States from 1890 to 1920 is believed to have real significance and importance.

ACKNOWLEDGMENT

In preparing this manuscript the author has been the recipient of an unusual number of privileges. Chief among the benefactors to be noted are the Administration and Board of Trustees of the University of South Carolina for a reduced teaching load while the manuscript was being prepared for the press, and the Social Science Research Council of New York City for a Grant-in-Aid of Research to help in the collection of material.

The following persons responsible for important sets of private letters and papers have assisted materially: President Charles Seymour of Yale University for permission to use the E. M. House Papers; Professor J. F. Manning for permission to use the W. H. Taft Papers; Mrs. Woodrow Wilson for permission to use the Woodrow Wilson Papers, and Professor St. George L. Sioussat and Dr. T. P. Martin of the Division of Manuscripts of the Library of Congress for permission to use a number of collections in their charge. Further, Mr. R. G. Pruden, Assistant Curator of the House Papers, and Miss Katherine Brand, the able supervisor of the Wilson Papers, gave most courteous and valued assistance in the efficient handling of large quantities of material.

The following publishers have kindly given permission to quote from volumes to which they hold copyrights:

Columbia University Press for Miner, *The Fight for the Panama Route.*
Dodd, Mead and Company, for Jessup, *Elihu Root.*
Doubleday, Doran and Company, for Baker, *Woodrow Wilson, Life and Letters.*
Houghton, Mifflin Company, for Seymour, *Intimate Papers of Colonel House.*

Alfred A. Knopf, for Bemis, *American Secretaries of State*.

Similarly, Professor John Bassett Moore has kindly given permission to use material from the famous Moore Memorandum to Theodore Roosevelt of August, 1903, and the Honorable Sumner Welles, has given permission to quote from his *Naboth's Vineyard*.

Finally, personal thanks are due to President Charles Seymour for his reading of the manuscript and for valuable suggestions, especially in connection with the period from 1913 to 1920; to Professor R. H. Wienefeld of the University of South Carolina who helped the author avoid errors in referring to the European contacts of the study and who patiently pursued irregularities of language and style throughout the manuscript, and to Professor Owen Lattimore of the Walter Hines Page School of International Relations for appreciated editorial comments. In addition, my wife, Rebecca A. Callcott, has made suggestions as to style and organization, and Mrs. Sara Q. Anderson has done much of the meticulous work of typing. To all these and others unnamed I extend very sincere thanks and express hearty appreciation.

W. H. C.

TABLE OF CONTENTS

CORRECTIONS TO 1942 EDITION

Page   25, line   8:   for "of" read "by".

"   32,   "   6:   for "assertain" read "ascertain".

"   93,   "   20:   for "last" read "previous".

"   120,   "   10:   for "disapproved" read "hostile".

"   132, to footnote 47 add "On the other hand the Atlantic fleet had been held intact, hence in itself
constituted something of a threat."

"   137, line 21:   for "how" read "lest".

"   150,   "   1:   for "protest" read "protect".

"   191,   "   14:   delete "then".

"   197,   "   9:   delete "a".

"   197,   "   13:   for "vessels" read "vessel".

"   210,   "   3:   for "lost" read "lose".

"   242,   "   21:   for "Cartegena" read "Cartagena".

"   315,   "   22:   footnote No. "15" in text should read
"18".

"   323, footnote 43, line 1: For "Mc" read "MS".

"   359, line 17:   for "Through" read "Though".

"   412,   "   13:   for "hasted" read "hasten".

"   414,   "   24:   for "no" read "on".

"   448,   "   19:   insert "is" between "these" and "out".

"   457,   "   16:   for "Sanvador" read "Salvador".

"   459,   "   17:   for "Ticonos" read "Tinocos".

"   471,   "   18:   for "invasion" read "denial".

"   491,   "   16:   for "simply" read "originally".

"   504,   "   10:   delete "(".

CHAPTER I

PORTENTS: RECOGNITION OF SPHERE OF INFLUENCE

Men of foresight and political leaders of ability from colonial times onward have shown a steadily rising interest in the Caribbean area. True, at first the interest was primarily because of the early Spanish trade through the region to Mexico and Panama. Rivalry developed for the sake of the trade itself and for the loot that could be secured from piracy and privateering which made use of the numerous islands as hiding places and supply bases.

As early as 1700 the strategic value of Cuba was urged in England, and half a century later the island was actually captured by the British in the Seven Years' War. About the same time Benjamin Franklin advised that Britain take the island for the sake of its value in connection with the mainland colonies.[1]

This somewhat tentative and mild interest waned or was never very widespread as can be seen from the fact that Cuba was returned to Spain in the peace agreed to in 1763 even though England was in a position to secure about what terms it wished in the negotiations. At the moment control

[1] Russell H. Fitzgibbon, *Cuba and the United States, 1900-1935* (Menasha, 1935), pp. 67-8.

Author's note: In a background chapter it is impossible to give full references to source materials because of publication difficulties. Hence very few are listed here. Instead an effort has been made to list the best secondary studies which may be used as a guide by students of various phases of the subject.

of Florida, which meant completion of the control of the whole of the whole east coast of North America, was more to be desired than another Caribbean island, however important.

With the acquisition of independence by the United States the fundamental need was the organization of a government that had some hopes of permanence. The next step was to secure the back-door of the new nation and the outlet for inland trade west of the Alleghenies. Next came the southwest trade through Mobile and the region known as West Florida. The results were the acquisition of Louisiana and progressive steps in the acquisition of Florida during the first two decades of the new century. Thus, by 1820, the United States found itself a nation with steadily growing interests on the Gulf of Mexico. With the exception of a small volume of overland traffic the trade of the newly acquired districts had to pass through New Orleans or Mobile and thence along the shores of Cuba on its way to market. As a result it was more or less at the mercy of the nation owning that island and responsible for the use or abuse of its waters for legitimate or privateering purposes.

Meanwhile, some had been considering the Caribbean for its inherent values. Thomas Jefferson, for example, while United States Minister to France in 1787-1788, was much interested in watching the European powers as they considered the possibilities of a canal at Panama.[2] A more direct and practical interest was shown in the appointment by Congress, in 1781, of one Robert Smith to act as the first

[2] Miles P. DuVal, Jr., *Cadiz to Cathay. The Story of the Long Struggle for a Waterway across the American Isthmus* (Stanford University Press 1940), pp. 18-9.

United States consular agent to Cuba. With the outbreak of war between Spain and France in 1793 French privateers in the West Indies so crippled Spanish trade with Cuban ports that the officials of the island opened their trade to the United States and active contacts were thus established. By 1795, however, the scence changed and Spain became the ally of France in the war against Great Britain. Then, indignant over the Jay Treaty and other incidents, the allies captured and condemned as prizes thirty United States ships taken in the Caribbean just prior to 1797.[3] The recently rising interest inevitably declined.

As the century closed there also arose considerable interest in the island of Santo Domingo where the Negroes were struggling to secure their independence. It would seem that at this point Great Britain made its first effort to have the two Anglo-Saxon nations adopt a common program for a part of the Caribbean when it instructed its new agent to Santo Domingo to proceed to his post via the United States so that a common policy could be arranged for the two nations to follow.[4] The friendly relations that ensued with the Negro republic were interrupted when Jefferson became president and the United States adopted a policy of actively cultivating the French.[5]

By the end of his administration Jefferson's interest in Caribbean revolutions against Spain was actively aroused and word was sent to United States agents in both Mexico and

[3] R. F. Nichols, "Trade . . . and United States Consulates in Spanish America," *Hispanic American Historical Review,* XIII, 289 ff.

[4] Joseph Byrne Lockey, *Pan-Americanism, Its Beginnings* (New York, 1926), p. 139.

[5] C. L. Lokke, " Jefferson and the LeClerc Expedition," *American Historical Review,* XXXIII, 322 ff.

Cuba that they should intimate to leading personages that the United States was quite willing for both regions to remain in the hands of Spain but would oppose the transfer of either to France or Great Britain.[6] In a letter to Madison the President calmly reasoned that in case of war Napoleon would give up Florida to the United States quite readily and to prevent United States aid to Mexico would allow it to take Cuba, adding:

... I would immediately erect a column on the southernmost limit of Cuba, and inscribe on it a ne plus ultra as to us in that direction. ... Cuba can be defended by us without a navy, and this develops the principle which ought to limit our views.[7]

Meanwhile spasmodic interest was shown by certain adventurers or enthusiasts for the cause of Latin American independence. Thirty-six such had been captured and imprisoned in Colombia. A vigorous debate arose in Congress over a proposal to help the hapless creatures. Caution predominated and it was even decided in 1809 not to send an agent to Caracas for, in the opinion of Randolph and others, this would amount to a premature recognition of independence which might be construed as a declaration of war by Spain. Three years later Secretary of State Monroe still took the position that for the United States to recognize the neighboring Venezuela might injure the United States without rendering the rebels any assistance.[8]

---

[6] Lockey, *op. cit.*, p. 264; Henry Merritt Wriston, *Executive Agents in American Foreign Relations* (Baltimore, 1929), pp. 530-1.

[7] Quoted by John Holliday Latané, *Diplomatic Relations of the United States and Spanish America* (Baltimore, 1900), p. 90.

[8] Frederick L. Paxson, *The Independence of the South American Republics, A Study in Recognition and Foreign Policy* (Philadelphia, 1916), pp. 106-7; W. S. Robertson, "Recognition of Hispanic American Nations," *Hisp. Amer. Hist. Rev.*, I, 243.

Even as late as 1817 the United States was anxious to postpone any decisive action with regard to New World rebels and it has been stated that the sending of a commission to investigate the qualifications of the Latin American rebellious states with a view to recognition was inspired as much by a desire to postpone action as by any other consideration.[9] Only Clay, at the head of a " factious opposition," could afford to be a little more decisive in his stand for he could rely upon the expansionist West for support of his program.[10]

However, with the exception of occasional acts of Congress to suppress piracy in the Caribbean, the incidents occurring were mere straws showing the direction of a few wind currents. No policy had been adopted and the general attitude of the country until the 1820s remained that of Representative Rhea who stated in 1811 that he would not be in favor of annexing West Indian territory unless " it would please the Almighty Maker of worlds to move the foundations of the West India islands and place them alongside of the United States." [12] The imaginations of some were stimulated when word came that the province of San Salvador of the Federal States of the Center of America had asked to be annexed to the United States in preference to being swallowed up by the Empire of Iturbide which had just been established in Mexico. But this, too, was forgotten

[9] Watt Stewart, " The South American Commission," *ibid.*, IX, 36-7.

[10] Paxson, *op. cit.*, pp. 132-4; H. L. Hoskins, " Hispanic American Policy of Henry Clay," *Hisp. Amer. Hist. Rev.*, VII, 466.

[11] Milton Offutt, *Protection of Citizens Abroad by the Armed Forces of the United States* (Baltimore, 1928), p. 152.

[12] Albert K. Weinberg, *Manifest Destiny, a Study of National Expansion in American History* (Baltimore, 1935), p. 65.

for with the overthrow of Iturbide the request was withdrawn and only a sentimental interest remained.[13]

Any general discussion of the origin of the Monroe Doctrine is of course out of place here. It has been so thoroughly covered by numerous authorities that it only remains to mention the pronouncement in passing. Jefferson, in 1820, expressed a kind of "pious hope" with regard to two spheres of influence, one of which would be the western world with the United States as its leader. J. Q. Adams and President Monroe, taking full advantage of European complications, announced this in the well known proposal that was at first considered as merely the policy of the party in power.

With regard to the Caribbean, though, more definite ideas were developing, and as was natural Cuba was still the center of attention. Jefferson warned Monroe that it would never do for the island to fall into the hands of Great Britain but hastened to add that an excellent procedure would be to get Great Britain to join with the United States in guaranteeing Spanish sovereignty. Even if this failed and Britain did take over the island he felt that it would not be advisable for the United States to go to war about it because "the first war on other accounts will give it to us, or the island will give itself to us when able to do so." [14]

Meanwhile a warning had already been sent to the United States Minister to Spain that his country would disapprove the transfer of Cuba to Great Britain,[15] and detailed instructions were sent to Mr. Randall, a special agent to Cuba, to observe and report carefully on foreign influences in the island and foreign naval activities in the vicinity. He was

[13] Wriston, *op. cit.*, pp. 435-6.   [14] Latané, *op. cit.*, p. 98.

instructed that the United States preferred Spanish ownership of the island but was not to commit himself in any way
on the position his country would be likely to assume in connection with any proposed changes in the form of government of the island.[15] The fact is that the idea of annexation
was being considered by a number of people and Jared
Ingersoll recorded in his diary that leading Cubans wished
annexation and considered it so important that " I have
long tho't that whenever Cuba presents herself, without
any forcing or manoeuvering on our part, we must e'en
take the goods the Gods provide us." He continued that
the western states wanted it because Cuba in the hands of
England would be intolerable, doubtless because of trade
interference; the southern states had no objection, and the
middle and eastern states would consent though perhaps a
bit reluctantly.[16] Adams thought that the annexation of
Cuba in the course of half a century would be " indispensable
to the continuance and integrity " of the Union, and said
that though annexation was not immediately in order:

. . . there are laws of political as well as physical gravitation;
and if an apple, severed by the tempest from its native tree,
cannot choose but fall to the ground, Cuba, forcibly dis-
joined from its own unnatural connection with Spain, and
incapable of self-support, can gravitate only towards the
North American Union, which, by the same law of nature,
cannot cast her off its bosom.[17]

But Adams was also looking still further afield and was
fully impressed with the tremendous possibilities of Colombia

[15] John Bassett Moore, *A Digest of International Law* (Washington, 1906), VI, 383-5. Hereafter referred to as " *Digest.*"

[16] Quoted in *op. cit.*, I, 583.

[17] Quoted by Harry F. Guggenheim, *The United States and
Cuba; a Study in International Relations* (New York, 1934), p. 4.

which he was convinced was destined to be one of the "mightiest nations of the earth" because of its strategic location between the oceans, its proximity to the great river systems of the Amazon, Orinoco and Magdalena, the fertility of its soil and its spendid climate. In fact, both he as Secretary of State and the British seemed to consider the future of Colombia more promising and potentially important than that of Mexico.[18]

When the Monroe Doctrine was announced it is well known that Adams intended to speak for the time only [19] and had no idea of binding the actions of his country for future generations. To forestall such a possibility Canning urged the British Cabinet that his country follow the course initiated by the United States and recognize the new republics of America. In this way the British could guarantee that "The deed is done. The nail is driven. . . . Spanish America is free, and if we do not mismanage our affairs sadly, she is English," as he proudly boasted in December, 1824.[20]

Throughout the Caribbean the announcement attracted little attention. Haiti was disgruntled that it was not mentioned as one of the rising nations of the New World; Central America applauded the pronouncement but the president in announcing the fact to the provincial governors had introduced it with the statement: "England protects our

[18] Lockey, *op. cit.*, p. 39; Paxson, *op. cit.*, pp. 206-7.

[19] Dexter Perkins, *The Monroe Doctrine, 1823-1826* (Cambridge, 1927), p. 260. This is the first part of the excellent and detailed three-volume study of the Monroe Doctrine that brings the story down to 1907. Detailed references provided.

[20] R. B. Mowat, *Diplomatic Relations of Great Britain and the United States* (London, 1925), p. 94; see also Chester Lloyd Jones, *The Caribbean since 1900* (New York, 1936), p. 280.

just cause." [21] Mexico was probably jealous of the United States and that may partially account for the insignificant amount of attention paid to the Monroe message, but certainly President Guadalupe Hidalgo gave it no special comment in his public utterances and the historians of the time largely ignored it.[22] On the other hand, when a French fleet appeared in the waters off Martinique in 1825 with apparent instructions to watch the situation in Haiti and possibly to help suppress insurrection in Cuba, as well as to be in position for eventualities elsewhere, the Mexican Minister promptly invoked the Monroe pronouncement insisting that under it the United States was "virtually pledged" to action.[23] Joel R. Poinsett, the Minister of the United States, formally protested the interpretation much to the chagrin of Mexico. Henry Clay was able to speak more freely and insisted that the United States "could not consent to the occupation of those islands by any other European power than Spain under any contingency whatever." [24]

In Colombia the Liberator, Simón Bolívar, was little interested in the Monroe Doctrine but public approval was considerable. The Colombian Minister in Washington cordially endorsed the doctrine and asked that the northern republic enter into a treaty of alliance to guarantee the independence of his home nation against the machinations

---

[21] Lockey, *Pan-Americanism*, pp. 236-9. True, a permanent West Indian squadron was organized with an initial complement of eight vessels in 1822, but its activities were chiefly directed against piracy at this time. Arthur Preston Whitaker, *The United States and the Ind. of Lat. Amer.* (Baltimore, 1941), pp. 293 ff.

[22] Perkins, *op. cit.*, pp. 156-7.

[23] *Ibid.*, p. 201.

[24] John Holliday Latané, *The United States and Latin America* (Garden City, 1920), p. 88.

of the Holy Alliance.[25] Secretary of State John Q. Adams in his answer minimized the danger and stated that the ultimate decision as to resisting such aggression belonged exclusively to the legislative department of the Government. Further, the United States would not be willing to sign a blanket agreement for defense of any area but must consider each actual case of aggression as it arose.[26] Perkins comments: " Put in plain and blunt terms this means that the United States, in spite of its brave words, would not act unless Great Britain did, and, to all appearances, would not act except in the event of a ' general European intervention.' " [27]

In 1825 came an opportunity to clarify the attitude of the United States toward New World problems. Though Bolivar had not desired the attendance of the Anglo-Saxon republic at the Panama Conference proposed by him, the insistence of others secured the presentation of an invitation to this country which was delivered in Washington by the ministers of Mexico, Colombia and the United Provinces of Central America.[28] In the United States the press, especially in the northern states, was enthusiastic in support of the idea

[25] Perkins, *op. cit.,* pp. 157; 187-8; President Santander in Alejandro Alvarez, *The Monroe Doctrine, its Importance in the International Life of the States of the New World* (New York, 1924), pp. 122-3.

[26] For discussion of this see C. W. Hackett " Development of J. Q. Adams' Policy," *Hisp. Amer. Hist. Rev.,* VIII, 509-10; and Gaston Nerval (pseudonym for Raul Díez de Medina), *Autopsy of the Monroe Doctrine; the Strange Story of Inter-American Relations* (New York, 1934), pp. 117-8; Whitaker, *op. cit.,* pp. 555 ff.

[27] Perkins, *op. cit.,* p. 192. For an analysis of pro and anti British feeling in the Monroe and Adams Cabinets see Whitaker, *op. cit.,* pp. 432 ff., 492 ff.

[28] Hackett, *op. cit.,* VIII, 514-5; Lockey, *op. cit.* pp. 393 ff.

because of the trade possibilities involved as well as for other reasons. Adams exulted that the period of isolation which Washington had advised had now elapsed as a result of the magnificent growth and development of the nation.[29] However, both he and Clay were very circumspect in framing the actual instructions to the delegates and advised that their nation was not willing to go beyond a general endorsement of the non-colonization idea for New World territory. The enthusiasm of Poinsett and others was not reflected among the politicians as a whole and the long and acrimonious debate in Congress over sending delegates to the Conference soon reached the point where it was recognized as being more the product of politics than of principles.

With the actual sending of the abortive mission this study is little interested since its accomplishments were purely negative—in truth its effects rather tended to discourage Latin American and Caribbean enthusiasm for cooperation with the United States. Great Britain, however, was more awake to the possibilities of the conference than the United States Congress and took note of the potential danger. George Canning early sought to obviate the adverse influences upon British interests that might arise from the meeting by endorsing the conference " if England was to be invited." [30] After the fiasco was over the London *Times*, in 1829, was still concerned over the fact that the American states were interested in forming a " community of their own " and stated further that if this were done " the first

[29] Frances L. Reinhold, " New Research on First Pan-American Congress," *Hisp. Amer. Hist. Rev.*, XVIII, 363; 356-7; Perkins, pp. 209-10; James Brown Scott, *The International Conferences of the American States, 1889-1928* (New York, 1931), pp. x-xi.

[30] Reinhold, *op. cit.*, XVIII, 354-5.

obvious consequence . . . would be to place the United States at the head of the new federation." [31]

Meanwhile as the third decade of the century closed events forced the United States to commit itself in repeated isolated cases so that its conduct began to assume a rather definite pattern for the Caribbean area. The first point of interest was, as usual, Cuba. Colombia and Mexico were showing an active interest in revolutionizing the island with the idea of making their own trade safer and for the sake of expansion. The protest of the United States through Poinsett, in 1826, is well known and possibly served to cool somewhat the ardor of the enthusiastic new republics of the south. Incidentally, they must have known that Great Britain wished to commit the United States to a non-aggression pact as to Cuba.[32] If Great Britain felt thus it was inexpedient for Colombia and Mexico to meddle.

The United States was afraid of the situation and repeated that Cuba in the hands of Spain (Clay's instructions to the Panama delegates) was the guiding principle of its policy.[33] It did send an executive agent to Cuba but remained very cautious as to any action that might involve intervention and carefully instructed its representatives in Colombia, Mexico and Chile in 1829 and 1830 to take no action which might be interpreted as interference with local or domestic issues.[34]

[31] Quoted by Lockey, op. cit., p. 420.

[32] Elbert J. Benton, International Law and Diplomacy of the Spanish-American War (Baltimore, 1908), p. 15.

Of course this idea was dropped when France declined to become a party to the agreement in 1825.

[33] See Alvarez, op. cit., p. 166; Albert Bushnell Hart, The Monroe Doctrine; an Interpretation (Boston, 1920), pp. 106-7.

[34] Offutt, op. cit., pp. 150-1; Wriston, op. cit., pp. 698 ff.; Moore, Digest, VI, 14.

A temporary interest in the neighboring country of Santo Domingo was aroused by a proposal to transfer Negroes from the south to that island in the 1830s. However, the movement failed and interest waned. Similarly, interest lapsed as to Haiti for the quite flourishing trade of the 1820s was seriously handicapped by the opposition of the slave holding members of Congress who prevented opening diplomatic relations with the Negro republic.[35] Trade with and through the islands had been protected by active efforts to suppress piracy but for some twenty-five years after 1830 there was no case of United States troops landing in the area.[36]

On the other hand, interest in an isthmian canal continued and as early as 1823 one Colonel William Duane, a relative of Benjamin Franklin, visited Bogotá with the idea of securing a concession. Though his efforts came to nothing the instructions to the Panama delegates again showed a direct interest in the subject. At about the same time, 1826, one Aaron H. Palmer was actually securing a concession for the construction of a canal in Nicaragua by English and United States capitalists. This, too, failed of realization but served to maintain interest in the projects. With both regions, however, diplomatic relations had become difficult. The Indian fighter William Henry Harrison with his vociferous endorsement of democracy was hardly a representative to establish cordial relations as Minister with a dictator such as Bolivar who was possibly hankering

[35] Sumner Welles, *Naboth's Vineyard, the Dominican Republic, 1844-1924* (New York, 1928), pp. 53-4. For early trade see Stephen Bonsal, *The American Mediterranean* (New York, 1913), p. 413.

[36] Offutt, *Protection of Citizens Abroad*, pp. 157-8.

for a crown.[37] Further, the constant upheavals in Central America caused the United States to close its legation there in the 1830s even though good relations were desired because of the canal interests of United States citizens.[38] In truth the early enthusiasm declined and there was little interest displayed by either British or United States citizens in the idea of constructing a canal.[39] By 1836 the Congress of the Central American republics tried to revive the issue and offered the United States prior canal rights over all other nations. The United States Senate passed a resolution showing interest and the President appointed an investigator. In 1837 he reported to Congress that the proposals were premature. This, it is true, misrepresented the views of the agent who had practically secured a concession for a company which he hoped to form, but it did reflect the President's opinion.[40] By 1839 some business groups showed interest and another agent was sent down but he reported adversely because of the revolutionary conditions.[41] Thus the matter dropped and general apathy ensued on the subject for some time to come. Perkins not inappropriately remarks:

. . . there is no evidence to show that the American government desired to control any canal that might be built, or even to exclude European capital, or European governments, from a share in the undertaking. With regard to a Dutch

[37] Lockey, pp. 130-1; Dexter Perkins, *The Monroe Doctrine, 1826-1867* (Baltimore, 1933), pp. 34-5.

[38] Wriston, p. 636.

[39] W. W. Pierson, "Political Influences of an Interoceanic Canal," *Hisp. Amer. Hist. Rev.*, VI, 211-2.

[40] J. Fred Rippy, *The Capitalists and Colombia* (New York, 1931), pp. 38-9.

[41] Harmodio Arias, *The Panama Canal, A Study in International Law and Diplomacy* (London, 1911), pp. 14-5.

project, for example, in 1829, there seems not to have been the slightest hostility, the only interest of the United States being in the principle of absolute equality of treatment for the vessels using the canal.[42]

As for Cuba, a kind of a dog in the manger policy is to be noted but little interest was shown in the other countries except Mexico. With it relations were badly strained due to the rising complications over settlements in Texas. That, however, was still a part of the story of western expansion and does not apply directly to the Caribbean story or policy as it is being developed here. In fact, negotiations of the period do not place Mexico in the setting of Caribbean complications except for the possible exception of the French invasion connected with the "Pastry Cook War." In that, the advice of the British and their mediation secured the desired result of keeping the French out, while the United States, probably in part because of strained relations with Mexico over Texas, contented itself with an expression of sympathy for Mexico in its hour of danger.[43]

About 1840 something of a change began to come over the foreign policy of the United States. The young nation was now fully conscious of its strength and had transferred leadership from the old conservative tidewater to the expansionist frontier. There the demand for new lands grew with what it fed upon until Texas was acquired in 1836, as well as lands west to the Pacific at the end of the Mexican War. Indeed, the question at that time in the minds of many was not whether California should be annexed but

[42] Perkins, *op. cit.,* p. 157.

[43] A discussion of this may be found in standard Mexican histories while the author's own treatment and references may be found in Wilfrid Hardy Callcott, *Santa Anna, the Story of an Enigma who once was Mexico* (Oklahoma University Press, 1936).

whether this only, or the whole of Mexico, should be acquired in the name of democracy and progress. Increasingly after 1845 the idea of Manifest Destiny seized on the popular fancy until it was the general conviction of the man in the street. Of course, it was Polk who carried this idea into the White House and made it the admitted policy of an administration.[44] From the " swelling periods " of Walt Whitman to the New Jersey State Democratic Convention ran the theme:

Land enough—land enough! Make way, I say, for the young American buffalo—he has not yet got land enough; he wants more land as his cool shelter in summer—he wants more land for his beautiful pasture grounds. I tell you, we will give him Oregon for his summer shade, and the region of Texas as his winter pasture. (Applause.) Like all of his race, he wants salt, too. Well, he shall have the use of two oceans—the mighty Pacific and turbulent Atlantic shall be his. . . . He shall not stop his career until he slakes his thirst in the frozen ocean. (cheers.)[45]

Naturally enough, such ideas were only encouraged by the events of a successful war.

The Monroe Doctrine as such was still considered merely a party policy of the Democrats [46] which the Whigs were quite free to denounce but in view of the events of the times it is not surprising that the countries to the southward were perturbed. Even from far away Chile Juan Bautista Alberdi in 1844 urged a Hispanic American League which would secure its sanction or force from European support by way

---

[44] E. G. Bourne, "United States and Mexico, 1847-48," *Amer. Hist. Rev.*, V, 492 ff.; Weinberg, *op. cit.*, cir. p. 144.

[45] Quoted by Weinberg, p. 119. Also see discussion on following pages.

[46] Perkins, pp. 181-2.

of protection against the advancing menace from the north.[47] The dictator, Antonio López de Santa Anna in Mexico sent a special Minister to Caracas, Venezuela, to attempt to organize a Latin American movement to offset the Yankee. Venezuela proved lukewarm, however, and when the agent's salary was not paid regularly he returned to Mexico instead of prosecuting his mission in other countries.[48]

Just beyond the active range of the land-hunger of the moment lay Central America and the tempting prizes of trans-isthmian traffic. Even though Polk was preoccupied with Oregon and Mexican complications he was interested in the isthmus also. British activity around Belize or British Honduras was undoubtedly increasing [49] while United States leaders felt that the region was of increasing importance to the Stars and Stripes. After some preliminary negotiations [50] an agreement was finally reached with Colombia, or New Granada, by which the United States guaranteed the integrity of the isthmus in return for the right of free transit of its goods. In the United States the chief discussion regarding the treaty was whether it constituted a violation of the no-entangling-alliance idea which was so popular. In fact, Polk in his message to the Senate on the treaty, seemed to consider this the chief objection that would be raised to the document.[51] But explain as he would the fact remained that the treaty provided for the right of the

[47] W. W. Pierson, "Alberdi's Views on the Monroe Doctrine," *Hisp. Amer. Hist. Rev.*, III, 371-4.

[48] Carlos A. Echanove Trujillo, *La vida pasional e inquieta de Don Crecencio Rejón* (México, 1941), chapter xxiii.

[49] Perkins, pp. 16-9.

[50] J. B. Lockey, "A Neglected Aspect of Isthmian Diplomacy," *Amer. Hist. Rev.*, XLI, 296-8.

[51] Moore, *Digest*, III, 8-10.

United States to transport troops across the isthmus and would almost certainly require the frequent landing of expeditionary forces within the boundaries of a friendly state.[52] Soon after the treaty was ratified Polk showed his increasing interest by a message to Congress dated April 18, 1848, in which he presented the Yucatán question to that body and specifically denounced the idea that the peninsula could be transferred from Mexico to any European power such as Great Britain or Spain. By implication at least it was to be inferred that the United States should annex the province itself in order to prevent such a transfer.[53]

Suspicions are usually mutual and so the rivalry of the Anglo-Saxon nations developed apace when United States capitalists secured concessions in both Nicaragua and Panama. The United States representative in Nicaragua wrote to Secretary of State Clayton, in 1849: " . . . I beg . . . that you will not . . . think me afflicted with Anglo-Mania. Far from it. Still, I must repeat that no person, not on the spot, can credit the extent and intricacy of these intrigues." [54] The Central American republics themselves were becoming worried as may be seen by the fact that the Nicaraguan legislature adopted a report, unanimously accepted by the congresses of El Salvador and Honduras, denouncing European interference with the domestic affairs of " Republican American States." [55] Whether the British

[52] *Ibid.*, II, 390; Arias, *The Panama Canal*, pp. 16-7; Jones, *Caribbean and the U. S. since 1900*, pp. 319-20.

[53] Perkins, p. 174 ff.

[54] Mary W. Williams, " Letters of George E. Squier . . . ," *Hisp. Amer. Hist. Rev.*, I, 427-8; J. Fred Rippy, *The Caribbean Danger Zone* (New York, 1940). pp. 83-4.

[55] Perkins, pp. 200-1.

foreign minister Palmerston was seriously concerned by fear of United States influence in the region may be open to debate [56] but certainly his agent in Central America was quite popular with Guatemala and Costa Rica while the countries less amenable to his wiles were subjected to no little pressure. Indeed, Palmerston himself definitely decided that Britain needed a naval base on the Pacific Coast of Central America and that the Central American states should be reunited under British direction with Belize as a center of influence.[57]

Over the Caribbean islands there was more active apprehension. Webster feared British designs as early as 1851 and Polk, while he was president, instructed Secretary of State Buchanan to try to purchase Cuba.[58] Calhoun was outspoken in his desire for the island and trade interests were growing, but as a whole the old policy of supporting Spanish ownership of the Pearl of the Antilles was still held by the Government. As an offset to this there was a growing conviction that the island must never fall into the hands of a strong country and that the United States would fight even Britain itself rather than allow such a loss.[59]

Doubtless the French were tempted to intervene in Santo Domingo about 1844 because of the local disturbances which menaced French investments and provided excuses and opportunities for such an action. However, the certain knowledge that Britain would object strenuously if not

[56] R. W. Van Alstyne, "Central American Policy of Lord Palmerston," *Hisp. Amer. Hist. Rev.*, XVI, 346-7.

[57] Perkins, pp. 198-200; Van Alstyne, *op. cit.*, XVI, 351-2.

[58] Guggenheim, *U. S. and Cuba*, pp. 8-9; Latané, *U. S. and Span. Amer.*, pp. 269-70.

[59] *Ibid.*, pp. 104-5; Arnold Bennett Hall, *The Monroe Doctrine and the Great War* (Chicago, 1920), p. 48.

forcibly was a great deterring influence and the opportunity was allowed to pass. In 1848 the United States commercial agent reported that France had recently been asked to establish a protectorate but that England still objected.[60] In fact, protectorates by both of these countries over the island were declined, probably because of mutual fear and because of the dislike of each of them for the complicated racial and economic conditions that existed there. The next step of the islanders was to offer a protectorate or annexation to the United States. Lacking instructions, the United States agent returned a non-committal answer and the offer was withdrawn though the northern republic maintained a careful watch on the country as may be inferred from the fact that six executive agents visited the island in the years from 1845 to 1854. A similar watch was being maintained on Haiti from time to time though the efforts had a comical aspect in view of the lack of diplomatic recognition by the United States. For instance, Duff Green was sent there in 1849 to see if he could secure the payment of some claims of United States citizens against Haiti without extending the recognition which the Haitians desired. He was instructed " to conceal his character in order to preserve the dignity of the home government." [61]

Thus on the mainland south of Mexico though the United States was not as yet aspiring to dominate the area it had reached the point of insisting that its growing interests be protected. Up to the middle of the century it would have been well pleased with some arrangement by which the proposed canal route would be guaranteed on a free basis

[60] Perkins, pp. 257-60; Welles, *Naboth's Vineyard*, I, 91-3.
[61] *Ibid.*, I, 99-102; Wriston, *Executive Agents*, pp. 444; 722-5.

for all.[62] In the Caribbean islands the United States was increasingly interested: Cuba was not to be interfered with, that much was certain; the free republics were a problem their northern neighbor did not want to handle but at the same time it could and would not allow them to escape beyond its influence.

By the 1850s the United States was more convinced than ever that it was the child of destiny and was intrusted with a God-given duty to dominate the areas it thought needful for its own development. This idea found official expression in a Senate report of 1859:

The law of our national existence is growth. We cannot, if we would, disobey it. While we should do nothing to stimulate it unnaturally, we should be careful not to impose upon ourselves a regimen so strict as to prevent its healthful development.[63]

In general it can be said that the Democrats were the expansionists but the fact is also to be noted that no powerful group dared to express opposition to the idea very vigorously and that every successful Whig candidate for the presidency had a definite personal record of expansionism.

Of course, the two major problems of the 1850s were centered in Cuba and Central America but there were some remaining items to be noted in regard to Mexico. There was still interest in some quarters, definitely encouraged by Daniel Webster, in securing transportation concessions

[62] Arias, *The Panama Canal,* pp. 20-1.

[63] Weinberg, *Manifest Destiny,* p. 202.

An interesting parallel development, outside of this study, is that of the United States traders who developed the guano trade of the Pacific Islands at the same time and who received full support of the administration for their activities. For references see Hart, *Monroe Doctrine,* pp. 136-7, and Moore, *Digest,* index volume.

across the Tehuantepec Isthmus,[64] though this interest slowly faded. Filibustering was active and though official efforts were made to curb it apparently not too much was accomplished by the federal officers.[65] During the decade the unfortunate republic south of the Río Grande suffered the orgy of the Santa Anna dictatorship, discussed proposals of an European monarchy and suffered from miscellaneous other suggestions and rumors. Not surprisingly, the people of the United States lost all respect for the Mexican Government and calmly considered whether they should take some, all, or none of the area for themselves. Gadsden in 1855 and Buchanan in 1858 endorsed a program calling for a protectorate or active intervention in the whole of Mexico, but nothing came of the idea.[66] However, this was still primarily the story of western expansion so is not to be discussed here except to comment that the only outcome was the Gadsden Purchase which clarified the international boundary and gave the northern republic a good route for a southern railway to the Pacific.

Similarly the quandary continued as to what should be done about the island of Haiti and Santo Domingo. While officials were unable to adopt a policy conditions in both republics were notoriously irregular and adventurers of the type of the somewhat unsavory William L. Cazneau had a good opportunity to operate and added confusion to the disorder.

Webster, as Secretary of State in 1851, clearly sympa-

---

[64] Frederick Sherwood Dunn, *Diplomatic Protection of Americans in Mexico* (New York, 1933), pp. 63-4.

[65] J. F. Rippy, "Anglo-American Filibusters," *Hisp. Amer. Hist. Rev.*, V, 175-6.

[66] Dunn, *op. cit.*, pp. 77; 87-8; H. L. Wilson, "Buchanan's Proposed Intervention in Mexico," *Amer. Hist. Rev.*, V, 689 ff.; Perkins, pp. 336 ff.

thized with the Dominicans.[67] Thus with just a little encouragement, it is not surprising that the islanders, who always feared foreign intervention, made the suggestion that the United States, France and Great Britain should adopt a tri-partite agreement to handle the situation. When this promised to involve coercion, however, the United States representative found himself without instructions so the two European powers had to proceed virtually alone.[68] Another complication was the rising interest of the United States in naval bases. In 1854 Captain George B. McClellan of the United States Army made a survey of the harbor of Samaná Bay with the idea of its acquisition. Naturally enough the French and British promptly moved to block this.[69] To add another element to the confusion Spanish ambitions were again awaking in regard to Santo Domingo and the Spanish Government was actively stirring the devil's broth of intrigue and insurrection to see if by some means it could not reacquire its one-time possession. Thus, to use again an old phrase, it would seem to be the fact that the Dog in the Manger policy was being ever more actively extended to the dusky republics in the 1850s.[70]

In Cuban matters the United States began to find out that it had some very concrete opinions by that time. True,

[67] Welles, *op. cit.*, I, 112-3.

[68] Jones, *Caribbean and the U. S.*, pp. 77-8; Perkins, pp. 263-6.

[69] Melvin M. Knight, *The Americans in Santo Domingo* (New York, 1928), pp. 4-5.

[70] At about the same time the United States refused to take any part in a controversy between Venezuela and France when the South American Republic dismissed the French Minister for alleged interference in domestic affairs. In fact a mere expression of appreciation for the Venezuelan request for support was as far as the United States Minister was allowed to go in responding to the application (Moore, *Digest*, VI, 17.)

they were being blundered into and cannot be said to have been too consistent, but just the same private individuals were reaching conclusions and national policies were growing. Sugar trade with the island was increasing steadily [71] and the general spirit of confidence of the time had its effects. To stimulate this feeling there were the Narcisco López expeditions; first attempted out of New York in 1849, and actually undertaken out of New Orleans a short time thereafter. The active and financially substantial interest shown by some officials and numerous prominent men in the southern states began to give the matter a sectional atmosphere but there were still many men throughout the nation who were interested in seeing the United States grow regardless of the direction of the territory involved. Efforts to suppress the expeditions failed and attempts to bring violators of neutrality laws to justice likewise failed. [72]

To the outsider the appearance of the whole affair smacked of collusion, and Cuba was by this time unquestionably valuable both strategically and economically. So it was inevitable that Great Britain and France should have been perturbed by the developments. A short time after the López expeditions these two nations reported that they had ordered their navies to repel any attempted invasion of Cuba. Spain then asked them to secure a triple statement from themselves and the United States to the effect that none of the three would acquire the island. The proposal was duly made to the United States in 1852. [73]

[71] Leland H. Jenks, *Our Cuban Colony, a Study in Sugar* (New York, 1928), pp. 19-20.

[72] Latané, *U. S. and Latin America*, pp. 92-3; Rippy, *op. cit.*, V, 173-4.

[73] Latané, *U. S. and Spanish America*, pp. 113-5.

In response Secretary of State Edward Everett made one of the few early and positive statements of policy of the United States with regard to the island. He foresaw that it was possible that Cuba might become a part of his country but he restricted himself to a general statement of public morality as to intention. He declined to enter into an agreement with the European nations on the ground of the uniform disapproval of his nation of alliances with foreign powers. At the same time he pointed out the importance of Cuba to the United States since it controlled the entrance to the Gulf of Mexico and the trade of five states of the Union. Then he skillfully suggested that if such an island lay in the entrance of the Seine the European powers would scarcely entertain a proposal from the United States of the type which they had just made to his country. On the contrary they would consider it a problem for European consideration and settlement primarily.[74] In other words, the United States made it clear that it had no intention of acquiring the island but also stated that it considered the problem of its disposal as one to be settled in the New World. Now, not only the free republics, but even an existing European colony was a proper problem for the United States to consider.

Interest mounted steadily. Pierre Soulé was selected as United States Minister at Madrid at a time when the appointment of such a bitter critic of Spain could only mean that a positive, if not drastic, policy was to be expected. Support could be relied upon both from those who wanted Cuba for its strategic value and from the slave holders of the south who were feverishly seeking for more slave states

---

[74] Mowat, *Great Britain and the U. S.*, pp. 143-4; Hall, *The Monroe Doctrine and the Great War*, pp. 49-50.

to bolster their voting power in Congress. A direct United States offer to buy Cuba for $100,000,000 was brusquely declined. Soon thereafter Mr. Soulé took advantage of a semi-smuggling, semi-filibustering complication known as the *Black Warrior* affair to present what amounted to an ultimatum at Madrid. This crisis having been imperfectly weathered the United States Ministers to Great Britain, France and Spain were advised to meet in Ostend to talk matters over. The strong minded Soulé seems to have dominated the meeting and the outcome was a recommendation for their country to acquire Cuba by purchase— or force. When the cautious Secretary of State Marcy declined to support the proposal the diplomatic career of Soulé quickly came to an end. Members were now saying that Cuba was a " political necessity of the United States " [75] while some British diplomats were freely expressing the opinion that there was actual danger of war with this country over expansionism and that it would be well for the British to force it on the grounds of the Cuban and Dominican situations rather than over Central America.[76] Fear in the Caribbean was widespread and even in Jamaica there were those who felt that that island too was likely to be a victim of the expanding Yankee.[77] But in spite of the serious potentialities of the situation nothing happened for the domestic differences between the North and South soon sidetracked all discussion of overseas acquisitions.

Meanwhile the tempo of events had accelerated in Central

[75] John Bigelow, *Retrospections of an Active Life* (New York, 1909-13), I, 530.

[76] R. W. Van Alstyne, "Anglo-American Relations, 1853-57," *Amer. Hist. Rev.*, XLII, 497-8.

[77] Welles, *Naboth's Vineyard*, I, 162.

America. The Panama Railway was completed in 1855 [78] and soon proved to be a most profitable enterprise, thanks in part to a rapidly rising trade between the Atlantic seaboard and the recently acquired California and its gold diggers. But this only attracted more attention to the Clayton-Bulwer treaty which had been negotiated at the direct request of the United States—not of Great Britain [79]— in 1850 and which provided that in case either country undertook to construct a transisthmian canal it would operate the project under joint ownership, or on an equal partnership basis. In addition the two countries expressed their intentions of limiting expansion in Central America though the British negotiator at the time of the exchange of ratifications made it clear that Britain did not give up its claims to Belize.[80] This sanctified the recent expansion in which the British were most interested, but it is noteworthy that it was the first time Great Britain had agreed to even this much of a restriction in Central America. On the other hand, some point out that this was actually a case, as Buchanan claimed, of "reversing the Monroe Doctrine" and of applying it against the United States for the first time in its history.[81]

Beyond doubt the agents of both Anglo-Saxon nations in Central America were fearful of each other and were eager to encourage their nationals to acquire property rights and to expand in general. As a natural result feelings soon became seriously strained. Up to this time Britain had been the dominant foreign power in the region [82] and now it:

---

[78] Rippy, *Capitalists and Colombia*, pp. 39 ff.

[79] Elihu Root, *Addresses on International Subjects* (Cambridge, 1916), pp. 210-11.

[80] Moore, *Digest*, III, 136-7.   [81] Perkins, p. 211.

[82] Van Alstyne, "Cent. Amer. Policy of Palmerston," *Hisp. Amer. Hist. Rev.*, XVI, 356-7.

ex-colony was respectfully but firmly entering its bid and gave notice of the fact that it intended to forestall further British expansion of territory or power in the neighborhood. Soon the United States felt that the next object to be secured was the withdrawal of Britain from Belize and the Mosquito Protectorate adjoining, but this was a case of taking matters much too far and too fast for the Court of St. James. Aggravating the situation were the constant intrigues of both British and United States citizens in Central America as they strove to secure advantages over each other. In the eyes of the British the activities of William Walker were especially alarming for it was understood that he had the support of financial leaders of the United States, and probably the moral encouragement of some officials. His abortive movement and the futile efforts to bring him to justice in the United States for violations of neutrality laws helped to convince a suspicious British sentiment that here was an active effort to oust Britain completely from a region properly hers—and such a feeling the Britons have never entertained kindly. In the United States, on the other hand, there was a similar suspicion of British expansion in the Bay Islands.[83]

Bulwer had written to Clarendon in March, 1854:

Central America is no longer what it was & is daily becoming the most important spot of earth in ye whole world: to us especially with Australia [and] New Zealand in our hands & the Chinese empire falling to pieces. We cannot, we must not see it American, I mean belonging to the U. S.[84]

[83] Perkins, pp. 215-30.
[84] Van Alstyne, "Anglo-American Relations, 1853-57," *Amer. Hist. Rev.*, XLII, 495-6.

And the United States was convinced that because of its California interests it must view control of the isthmus in the hands of any foreign power as essentially a menace. A quiet and sensible conclusion of the trouble was reached when, in the middle 1850s, it was agreed that both countries would keep hands off, that Britain would restrict its claims extending from Belize, and that local problems would be settled locally in Central America. Thus mutual suspicion was given a chance to wane, while the ensuing Confederate War allowed it time to be largely forgotten.

On the Isthmus of Panama itself there were a few complications resulting from local disorders but these did not threaten international complications of a serious nature. In 1856, and again in 1860, on the latter occasion with the aid of a British force, there were landings of United States troops to maintain peace and protect property. This was with the approval of local authorities and beyond showing the growing recognition of the United States and its interest in the region is of no particular importance in this study. Probably the most interesting feature of the affair is the attempt of the United States to secure the five small islands of Taboga, Ilenao, Perico, Flamingo and New Granada as bases for the purpose of proper protection of the isthmus. The special mission sent to secure the cession was unsuccessful [85] and the matter was dropped.

With the outbreak of the Confederate War the new administration of Abraham Lincoln with William H. Seward as Secretary of State found its hands fully tied with the domestic situation and for the next four years used its

---

[85] Moore, *Digest*, I, 590; *Use by the United States of a Military Force in the Internal Affairs of Colombia* ([Washington, n. p., n. d.], Senate Document No. 143, 58th Cong., 24 sess.), p. 90.

foreign policy as the tool of, or merely as supplementary to, domestic events. This was clearly seen in the Secretary's well-known *Thoughts for the Consideration of the President* when he proposed to go to war with a promiscuous assortment of European nations in order to create a diversion that might help avert the war at home. Naturally a bitter reaction was the result, especially in Spain, since he had specifically made a point of the Dominican situation, in which Spain was dabbling, as a point of departure for provoking the expected European protest.

This use of foreign affairs as the football of domestic issues had already been begun by the Buchanan administration in connection with Mexico. In 1859 foreign relations were becoming complicated for the administration of Benito Juárez which was unable to meet its debt payments. The Mexican finally agreed to a treaty proposal by which the United States was to be given transportation rights over three great Mexican highways in perpetuity. The proposal further included the right of intervention and troop transportation in a fashion that probably would have resulted in the absorption of the whole country in the course of a relatively short time.[86] To the disappointment of Buchanan the treaty was rejected by his Senate, and the bitterness of the slavery controversy prevented its later consideration. Now, in connection with his insults to Spain over Santo Domingo, Seward began to show definite expansionist sentiments with regard to Mexico and went so far as to authorize the United States Minister to that country to negotiate a

---

[86] W. Stull Holt, *Treaties defeated by the Senate, a study of the Struggle between President and Senate over the Conduct of Foreign Relations* (Baltimore, 1933), pp. 92-4; H. L. Wilson, Buchanan's Proposed Intervention," *Amer. Hist. Rev.*, V. 696-7.

treaty by which the northern nation would guarantee the interest at 3% on the Mexican funded debt (largely held in Europe) if the European nations would agree not to collect the sums by force. In return Mexico was to mortgage four of its states as security and to surrender these if it failed to pay the moneys involved within six years after the initial five years for which the interest was to be advanced. Of course, this was presented as a help to Mexico and such *may* have been the chief motive. Needless to say, however, the British and French were far from pleased with the proposal and were duly relieved when domestic difficulties precluded its serious consideration by Congress.[87]

Seward's bellicose utterances with regard to Santo Domingo were obviously, as already seen, for the purpose of creating a diversion and when Lincoln declined to endorse them they were not followed up except for a somewhat formal protest when Spain proceeded to re-occupy its old colony. To be consistent in an anti-slavery war, and partly also because of trade interests, Haiti was recognised officially for the first time in 1862. In general Seward's official attitude toward the Latin American states while the war continued was expressed in his instructions to the United States Minister to Nicaragua, June 5, 1861, when he said that everybody wished the Spanish-American states well but was a bit restless at their lack of wisdom, constancy and stability. He instructed the Minister to inform the Nicaraguan president that his nation would deal justly, fairly and in a friendly spirit with them and that its desire

---

[87] James Morton Callahan, *The Evolution of Seward's Mexican Policy* (Morgantown, 1908), pp. 19-27; Latané, *U. S. and Latin America,* pp. 200-2.

was for true cooperation based on trade rights and privileges equal to those granted to any other foreigners.[88]

A little later when there was a threat to the Isthmus of Panama from rebels and when Colombia asked the United States to send troops, Lincoln and Seward sounded out Great Britain and France to assertain their views. The responses indicated that the European powers hardly thought intervention was necessary.[89] Possibly this was caution born of the war situation but it is worth mentioning in passing. Certainly in 1865 Seward probably came nearer to expressing his actual opinion when he wrote:

The United States have taken and will take no interest in any question of internal revolution . . . but will maintain a perfect neutrality in connection with domestic altercations. The United States will . . . protect the transit trade across the Isthmus against invasion of either domestic or foreign disturbers of the peace of Panama. . . . The purpose of the stipulation was to guarantee the Isthmus against seizure or invasion by a foreign power only.[90]

Meanwhile the Mexican situation was developing in a menacing fashion. The French, Spanish and British governments took advantage of Mexico's failure to pay its debts and sent naval units to bring pressure to bear. Preliminary notice to the United States of this intention brought the response that this country would not cooperate with such a move but would not oppose the right of nations to collect the just debts of their nationals. At the same time a note of caution was sounded with regard to the danger of such a proceeding lest it result in territorial acquisitions in an area that would be of serious concern to the United States.

[88] Moore, *Digest*, V, 409-10.
[89] Latané, *U. S. and Spanish America*, pp. 183-5.
[90] Quoted by Jones, *Caribbean and the U. S. since 1900*, p. 319.

When the French policy proved to be one of active intervention the Spanish and British naval units withdrew rather than be party to the affair. The French, meanwhile, gloated over the fact that the Monroe Doctrine was innocuous because of the Confederate War, and feeling reasonably safe they set up a puppet state under Maximilian of Hapsburg as emperor.

The patriot government of Juárez received cordial sympathy and encouragement from Washington but for the time being that was all that could be extended. With the collapse of the Confederate cause the way was opened for a more active program. This involved sending troops and supplies to the Mexican border—so that at least part of the supplies could reach Juárez—and increasing diplomatic pressure on France. To overlook no possibilities Seward even went so far as to contact the old adventurer, Santa Anna, with the object, apparently, of using him as an agent in case Juárez proved to be unsuitable.[91] Thanks in part to the menace of the United States, in part to a rising set of complications in Europe, to the heavy expenses of the intervention to the French and rising resentment of the French people, and to a surprising and steady resistence of the Mexican people to the intervention, the affair terminated in the withdrawal of the French troops and the double tragedy of the insanity of the Empress Carlota and the execution of the Emperor Maximilian. In the eyes of the people of the United States it was the Monroe Doctrine—which, incidentally, Seward never endorsed by name for he was an old Whig—which had been gloriously vindicated.

During the Mexican intervention both the Peruvian and Chilean governments suggested general New World co-

[91] Callcott, *Santa Anna*, p. 337 ff.

operation to drive out the French. Seward avoided committing himself on the question. When Costa Rica proposed
a Latin-American conference to protest Seward let the Mexican Minister Romero know that he considered that " an
alliance with the states of Latin America would have many
more disadvantages than advantages " for the United
States.[92]   Here the matter rested.

While thus avoiding forming foreign obligations for the
United States Seward was turning his attention more and
more to some way to accomplish his old " Arctic to isthmus "
idea. His interest in the far north finally culminated in the
purchase of Alaska but it was the Caribbean and the south
that still attracted with its romance and promise. He dismissed Mexico from his mind for the time feeling that it
would be secured by absorption if in no other way,[93] and
turned his attention to a direct disapproval of Spanish
control of Santo Domingo. This may have been a desire to
vindicate his early proposal to Lincoln to make Santo
Domingo the point of departure for invoking a European
war. However, the fact was that the old Mother Country
had about decided that the disgruntled and troublesome
ex-colony was not worth the trouble and expense of occupation and control. Hence, with the victory of the United
States in the Confederate War and the rising protests against
Spanish expansion in the New World it is not surprising
that Spain permitted the island to return to its recent status
of revolutionary peace and doubtful independence. By 1868
there was a plan on foot between the agent of the United
States in Santo Domingo and the president of that country
to provide for the acquisition of Samaná Bay by the United

[92] Latané, *U. S. and Latin America,* p. 297; Perkins, pp. 459-61.
[93] Callahan, *op. cit.,* p. 52.

States and the virtual establishment of a protectorate over the whole country. Seward wrote saying that this was too much like the recent action of Spain; though there is reason to believe that such consideration of international morality did not restrict Mr. Seward's interest and conduct very long.[94] More likely it was the local resentment at the negotiations and prospective loss of sovereignty that brought about the dismissal of the project by Seward and the transfer of his interests to other areas,[95] though not before President Johnson had notified Congress in his annual message of December 9, 1868:

It cannot be long before it will become necessary for this Government to lend some effective aid to the solution of the political and social problems which are continually kept before the world by the two Republics of the island of St. Domingo. . . . The subject is commended to your consideration with all the more earnestness because I am satisfied that the time has arrived when even so direct a proceeding as a proposition of annexation of the two Republics of the island of St. Domingo would not only receive the consent of the people interested, but would give satisfaction to all other foreign nations.[96]

Johnson was so definitely *persona non grata* to his own Congress by this time that his recommendation carried little weight, but at least it is interesting in passing for certainly Grant was to take up the proposition promptly on his accession to the executive office.

Seward's direct interest was now transferred to the Virgin Islands because of their strategic value. The events of his trip to the West Indies and his negotiations for the purchase of the Danish West Indies are well known. However, with enormous war debts to be paid, a currency

[94] Welles, I, 350-3.
[95] Jones, *op. cit.*, pp. 88-90.   [96] Quoted by Welles, I, 355.

none too stable, and the dissipation of national energies in the war now resulting in real reaction and national lassitude, it is not surprising that there was little enthusiasm for the expenditure of even modest sums for the acquisition of a few small islands in the lower Caribbean when they were inhabited chiefly by Negroes and obviously cursed by earth-quakes and hurricanes. This was reflected by a House Resolution, introduced September 23, 1867, and passed by a vote of 93 to 43 denouncing "any further purchase of territory" as inexpedient.[97] When Grant proved lukewarm to the idea the negotiations finally lapsed.

But Seward had still other strings to his bow and sounded out Spain as to the acquisition by the United States of the remaining Spanish islands in the Caribbean, named Culebra and Culebrita. When this project failed he glibly turned to the ever interesting possibilities of isthmian transit. His first effort was to secure a treaty with Honduras in order to acquire transit rights. The treaty was negotiated but came to nothing since no transcontinental route developed. His next effort was to secure Tigre Island as a naval base; this failed. A third effort was in connection with a more com-plete control over the Nicaraguan route; this was ratified in 1868. The last was an effort to secure sole canal rights in Panama; this too failed.[98] But the persistent efforts had attracted considerable attention and there were now to be heard those who said that the whole of the West Indies ought to be acquired and that the defense of the United States demanded control of the Caribbean.[99] The contrast

---

[97] Charles Callan Tansill, *The Purchase of the Danish West Indies* (Baltimore, 1932), p. 90.

[98] Hart, *The Monroe Doctrine,* pp. 156-7.

[99] Weinberg, *Manifest Destiny,* pp. 235; 392-3.

of this with the strict neutrality applied to, if not lack of interest in, the Spanish expansionist program in Chile and Peru is striking to say the least.

Following Seward came the diplomatic doldrums that were to last until the strong hands of Cleveland and Olney guided the country into a recognition of new issues that were to be faced with an expanding economic and political system.

Grant, the new president in 1869, aspired to become known as a nation builder as well as a national savior. When scarcely seated in the White House he began his activities either directly or through agents looking to the acquisition of naval bases or territory in the island of Santo Domingo.[100] This promptly developed into a question of annexing the Dominican Republic outright. The ethics involved in the drafting of the treaty and its submission to the Senate are not a part of this story. Certainly there was inept handling of the whole matter and this, together with the reaction already noted, the tainted if not mephitic atmosphere of the negotiation, and the spectacular opposition of the powerful Sumner prevented senatorial approval. Finally, after bitter personalities had developed the matter dropped.[101]

Grant, however, made an unqualified statement to the effect that the United States endorsed the Monroe Doctrine, which he defined specifically to mean that there should be no transfer of European colonies from one of them to another in the American hemisphere.[102] This was done

[100] Rayford W. Logan, *Diplomatic Relations of the United States with Haiti, 1776-1891* (Chapel Hill, 1941), pp. 333-4.

[101] Welles, I, 400.

[102] Hart, *op. cit.*, p. 164; Perkins, p. 25.

by way of inveighing against the Spanish intervention that had recently taken place in Santo Domingo.[103] The President did not propose to protect New World states from European intervention resulting from their sins and it is to be noted that " France in 1869, Spain in 1871, Germany in 1872, Great Britain in 1877 . . . resorted to force or to the threat of force against the black politicians of Port-au-Prince without a word of protest from the State Department." [104]

Meanwhile the Cuban problem arose again as usual. Unrest in the island culminated in the Ten Years War which started in 1868. As was to be expected agents were active in sending supplies from the United States.[105] Grant early repeated his no-transfer idea with regard to the island and urged six European governments to bring pressure on Spain to avoid such a contingency. However, the nations proved reluctant to act,[106] Congress was unable to make up its mind, and the President and his Secretary of State could

[103] Archibald Cary Coolidge, *The United States as a World Power* (New York, 1909), p. 112.

[104] Perkins, p. 118.

A most interesting application of the no-transfer principle as applied to the protection of a Caribbean region as against the United States and not as against Europe, is to be seen in the treaty of 1874 which Haiti tried to force on the Dominican Republic. This was to prevent the transfer of Dominican soil to the United States and not surprisingly had the support of British and French agents on the ground. In such disordered times and places nothing permanent came of the attempt but it is of decided interest in passing. See Logan, *Diplomatic Relations of U. S. and Haiti*, p. 351.

[105] James Morton Callahan, *Cuba and International Relations. A Historical Study in American Diplomacy* (Baltimore, 1899), pp. 370-1.

[106] Perkins, p. 13; Guggenheim, pp. 28-9.

not agree on the question of recognition of the rebels. In this state of uncertainty Fish proposed joint intervention in Cuba by the United States and several European powers.[107] True, there was a distinct repercussion in Congress as soon as the suggestion became bruited abroad, and Fish resorted to a quibble to avoid having the facts published; but the fact remains that this is one of the very interesting reversals of policy of the now commonly accepted interpretations of the Monroe Doctrine that went to make up the composite of the Grant administration. The final episode in the affair came in February, 1876, when Fish reported to the Spanish Minister of Foreign Relations:

In the first place the President desires emphatically to disabuse the mind of the government and people of Spain of the existence of any desire on the part of the government of the United States for the acquisition of Cuba. . . . Whatever grounds may be supposed to have existed in the past evincing such desire, there are at this time no considerations, moral, social, political, or financial, which are regarded . . . as making the acquisition of Cuba by the United States either desirable or convenient.[108]

Thus for a million and a half Cubans the period of uncertainty was prolonged. Times were not yet ripe for a general adoption and recognition of a Caribbean policy by their powerful neighbor of the north.

To the south of the Río Grande there was little of serious concern to Washington while Grant was in the

---

[107] Latané, *U. S. and Latin America*, pp. 123-5; Hart, *Monroe Doctrine*, p. 167.

[108] French Ensor Chadwick, *The Relations of the United States and Spain. Diplomacy* (New York, 1909), p. 389. See also Moore, *Digest*, I, 107-8, for Grant's message to Congress of December 7, 1875, in which he advised against recognition.

White House. Border incidents, protection of foreigners south of the line, the rise of Protestant missionary activity, claims payment and such items provided substance for diplomatic correspondence and some material to continue to feed the suspicion with which the Yankee was regarded. However, for the general survey of policy formation there is little to be noted, even though the minister of the United States was generally considered now as the unofficial spokesman of the diplomatic corps at Mexico City.

In the isthmian region there were other problems of real import to the would-be nation builder. Instructions were issued to the United States Minister at Bogotá in 1869 to secure a canal treaty with Colombia which would ignore the Clayton-Bulwer agreement and place the proposed canal under the auspices of the Stars and Stripes. Some leaders in Colombia feared the result of an entangling alliance with the United States,[109] and supported European interests in securing modifications of the proposed treaty so as to provide for a joint protectorate feature. In this form the document was unacceptable to Washington.[110]

During the year 1873 two landings of troops were undertaken for the protection of the isthmus under the treaty of 1846 but this was clearly considered something of an unpleasant duty and was not for the purpose of policy making. This was probably the more true because of the rising interest in the Nicaraguan route where two surveys were undertaken; the one in 1872 and the other in 1876.[111]

[109] Arias, *The Panama Canal,* pp. 38-9.

[110] Perkins, *The Monroe Doctrine, 1867-1907* (Baltimore, 1937), p. 68.

[111] Foreign Policy Association Information Service, *The United States and the Nicaraguan Canal,* IV, No. 6, p. 107.

And now Venezuela entered the Caribbean picture because of its financial difficulties. For the first time apparently, a suggestion was seriously made that the United States should control and administer the customs of the country.[112] The idea was premature for such policies were to be reserved until the twentieth century but in view of the existing complications the young and ambitious German Empire inquired in 1871 what the United States thought of joint intervention to guarantee rights for foreigners. The answer of Fish was nebulous: "On the one hand, he declared that the United States could not object to war on the part of Germany against Venezuela. On the other hand he does object to the common action of several European states."[113] Nothing definite was done and two years later the good offices of the United States composed a dispute between Holland and Venezuela[114] and so the position of priority or at least active interest of the United States was mildly asserted.

Meanwhile a general watch was being kept on the Caribbean and occasional suggestions that Germany might acquire territories there were promptly investigated. Thus appeared for the first time that *bête noire* which was to give later administrations so much concern. In truth it would seem that as yet there was little to fear though it is also true that as early as 1868 Germany was judiciously sounding out Costa Rica, at least, with regard to securing a possible naval base there.[115] In general, for a decade or so the new empire

---

[112] Rippy, *Caribbean Danger Zone*, pp. 42 ff.
[113] Perkins, p. 114.   [114] *Ibid.*, p. 50, note.
[115] Count Otto zu Stolberg-Wernigerode, *Germany and the United States during the Era of Bismarck* (Reading, Pa., n. d.), pp. 210-2.

hardly knew what it needed or wanted but was sure that it did not want to pass up any chances and was determined to investigate all possibilities carefully while building up national prestige by a generally aggressive foreign policy— especially when it was possible to do so against small countries such as Venezuela and Haiti.

In March, 1877, after a hectic election and fears of renewed civil disorders if not war, Rutherford B. Hayes took office as President and selected as his Secretary of State W. M. Evarts. These two men were to preside over the foreign relations of their government whenever time could be spared from the pressing domestic issues that beset them on every side. Under such circumstances it is not surprising that there was little protest when the Government of Norway and Sweden ceded the small island of St. Barthélemy to France without even consulting the United States or informing it of the negotiations until it was a *fait accompli*. Fish had protested just such a proposed transfer some years earlier but now in direct violation of the no-transfer idea the deed was done even though it was for the purpose of strengthening the naval position of France in the West Indies at the time that De Lesseps was proceeding with the construction of the Panama Canal.[116] This incident, small as it was, serves to give a fair idea of the policy that was to be followed, i. e., avow few policies except where one's hand was forced, and then ignore specific incidents if advisable and politic. No. A Caribbean policy had not yet evolved.

In the West Indies in general there was little interest though trade was rising. The Ten Years' War wore itself

[116] Tansill, *op. cit.*, pp. 180-1; Coolidge, *U. S. as a World Power*, p. 113; Perkins, p. 33.

out in Cuba and interest in that problem waned too though there were still revolutionary juntas in the United States to agitate for annexation, or for aid to the friendless,[117] and to protest Spanish trade restrictions.[118] Revolutions continued with surprising regularity in Santo Domingo but were no longer of news value and for the most part were ignored by the administration at Washington.

There was still a hankering for the sweets of Mexican acquisitions and it would seem that Evarts was not immune to the cravings. However, if the report of the able young United States Minister in Mexico, John W. Foster, is to be trusted this appetite soon faded when his confidential agents became discredited because of injudicious conduct and undue publicity.[119] Some little pressure was exerted on the new Mexican president, Porfirio Díaz, who was just coming into power for his long and able reign but recognition was finally extended in 1878 and it soon became evident that the southern republic had met its master. Washington breathed something of a sigh of relief and turned its attention elsewhere as it realized that its citizens were being encouraged to invest their money south of the Río Grande with a maximum of opportunity and a very modest risk indeed.

Farther to the south the United States was due to wake up with quite a shock when it realized that the boasted Clayton-Bulwer treaty had overlooked a vital something. It had presumably guaranteed the control of the proposed

[117] Herminio Portell Vilá, *Historia de Cuba en relaciones con los Estados Unidos y España* (Havana, 1938-9), III, 24 ff.

[118] C. E. Chapman, *A History of the Cuban Republic, a Study in Hispanic American Politics* (New York, 1927), pp. 70-1.

[119] John Watson Foster, *Diplomatic Memoirs* (Boston, 1909), I, 89-93.

canal to the joint ownership of Great Britain and the United States. Now, Ferdinand de Lesseps had completed his conquest of the Suez Isthmus and had quietly turned his attention to Panama. A concession had been secured from Colombia and the first thing the two signatories of the old treaty knew was that the Frenchman was about ready to begin work—and they were left out in the cold. Each had tied the hands of the other but had paid no attention to the country whose national was to prove the most dangerous after all. The protest of the American public was emphatic for it felt that it was just " not right " for things to develop thus. Business interests, politicians and the public were all concerned for somehow all had taken it for granted that the route would ultimately belong to the United States. There was even wild talk of a protectorate over Nicaragua while the United States constructed a canal there in competition.[120]   Meanwhile Hayes reported to Congress that it was the policy of the United States to have a canal between the oceans under such supervision and authority as would protect our national interests.[121] This perforce satisfied the public for after all it was very convenient to throw the responsibility on the national government which had made a very " nice " statement about it all and had relieved John Doe from responsibility about a situation which he did not know how to mend anyway—and one which was slowly to take care of itself thanks largely to the mismanagement of the French company.

[120] J. F. Rippy, " Justo Rufino Barrios and the Nicaraguan Canal," *Hisp. Amer. Hist. Rev.*, XX, 190 ff.

[121] Charles Richard Williams, *Life of Rutherford Birchard Hayes, Nineteenth President of the United States* (Boston and New York, 1914), p. 222.

Further south still was another disconcerting problem in the Venezuela-British Guiana boundary. After steady obstructionism in securing a settlement for nearly half a century, Venezuela awoke to the fact that its neglect was resulting in steady absorption of the disputed area by the British. Now the South American Republic urged that the United States come to the rescue for the sake of the defense of the continent. Fish had shown little interest in the matter and now Evarts displayed interest but no activity. This aroused no public response and no political reaction. Its prophet had not yet arisen.

Thus another quadrennium passed but in March, 1881, the brilliant and egotistical nationalist James G. Blaine entered the State Department for a nine months incumbency. With much éclat and dash he " threw his weight about " and announced plans and ideas for everyone in general and the New World in particular—always privately bearing in mind the fact that he was an active presidential candidate and that international recognition might be flattering to his egotism but that domestic popularity could lead to the White House. One student of his foreign policy comments that in his letter of acceptance of the nomination as Secretary of State " Blaine showed himself as first and foremost the party man, a political leader of congressional stamp and training, and only potentially the statesman. . . ." [122]

With his business contacts the new Secretary was well aware of the growing economic development of the Latin American nations and soon determined to make the New World his chief field of foreign activity as Secretary of State. A benevolent protectorate for Latin America under

[122] Alice Felt Tyler, *The Foreign Policy of James G. Blaine* (Minneapolis, 1927), p. 15.

the guidance of the United States was highly desirable for this could be used to emphasize the cultivation of friendship which in turn would bring a large increase in United States exports and trade.[123] A first step in the accomplishment of this program was the determination to curtail foreign influence in the Caribbean. About this time an agreement was reached between Costa Rica and Colombia to submit a long-standing boundary dispute to the arbitration of the King of Belgium, the King of Spain, or the President of Argentina. Here was Blaine's chance; the two European monarchs were informed that the United States disapproved their acting in view of the rights of the United States under the treaty of 1846 with New Granada. Naturally both monarchs promptly informed the United States that they would decline the honor.[124]

But this was negative and Blaine was too good a leader to rely on negatives. A general positive approach to the subject was proposed in the invitations issued in the fall of 1881 for a Pan-American meeting to take place in Washington the following year. Nine acceptances were received forthwith but at this point President James A. Garfield died. The new president, Chester A. Arthur, named F. T. Freylinghuysen as his Secretary of State and the plan for a conference was dropped.[125] One interesting detail in the invitations was the omission of the Negro Republic of Haiti which caused no little feeling in that state.

[123] James G. Blaine, *The Foreign Policy of the Garfield Administration* (Reprint from *Chicago Weekly Magazine* of September 16, 1882), pp. 1-8.

[124] Tyler, *op. cit.*, pp. 69-70; D. Y. Thomas, *One Hundred Years of the Monroe Doctrine* (New York, 1927), p. 185.

[125] David Saville Muzzey, *James G. Blaine, a Political Idol of Other Days* (New York, 1934), p. 217.

In other ways also Blaine got his policies started before he was to leave office. For instance, he was concerned in acquiring naval bases on the western coast of South America,[126] as well as in efforts to settle the boundary dispute between Mexico and Guatemala.[127] He likewise extended his approval to the idea of a Central American Union, but this, too, came to naught, chiefly because of difficulties inherent in the region concerned.[128]

His treatment of the troublesome question of Venezuelan debts was to endorse the proposal that the United States install an agent there to collect the customs revenues and distribute the sums on a fair basis among local and foreign claimants.[129] This was an interesting forerunner of Roosevelt's later action in Santo Domingo, but it like the other proposals, was dropped by Freylinghuysen.

The popular disapproval of the French activities in Panama had resulted in numerous petitions to Congress to which that body responded by a joint resolution urging the abrogation of the Clayton-Bulwer treaty. A policy thus demanded by his master, the great *vox populi*, was not to be ignored by Secretary Blaine who promptly notified the diplomatic agents of the United States that the treaty of 1846 with New Granada did not need reinforcement by any European guarantee of the neutrality of the isthmus [131] (this to forestall possible complications). The next step was to send his later well-known dispatch in which he indicated the reasons why the Clayton-Bulwer treaty was essentially null

---

[126] Tyler, pp. 90-1; Moore, *Digest,* III, 28.

[127] Robertson, *Hispanic American Relations,* pp. 154-5; Callahan, *American Policy in Mexican Relations,* pp. 413 ff.

[128] Tyler, pp. 47-9.   [130] Arias, p. 42; DuVal, pp. 95-7.

[129] *Ibid.,* pp. 75-9.   [131] Moore, *Digest,* III, 189.

and of no effect. Other European governments declined to commit themselves and the British with tantalizing slowness responded with the calm statement that they stood upon their treaty rights. Thus nothing was accomplished at the time and one imagines Freylinghuysen rather gladly allowed the issue to die out. However, it had been raised and brought out into the open where facts were to be faced and the problem solved eventually. Further muttering and quarreling in a corner was about ended and there was a definite popular feeling that Blaine was right when he disapproved such foreign investments as those of De Lesseps.[132] Thus the Secretary's policy may be summed up as one to make his country economically preeminent in the New World, the arbiter of its disputes, and the master of its isthmus transit.

So it was that the new Secretary inherited a score of public acts and pronouncements that had committed the United States to various positions. Not surprisingly, he seems to have felt that what the country needed was rest and peace. As one commentator observed: " Mr. Freylinghuysen is understood to hold that the American eagle should not strain his naturally fine voice by shrill and prolonged screaming on small occasions." [133] Caution and conservatism was to be the order of the new day. The invitation to the nations to attend a Pan-American conference was in effect withdrawn,[134] and the Secretary stated that the maximum proposal of this type that he would endorse was to

[132] T. A. Bailey, " The Lodge Corollary of the Monroe Doctrine," *Political Science Quarterly*, XLVII, 227-8.

[133] Quoted by P. M. Brown, " Freylinghuysen " in S. F. Bemis, *The American Secretaries of State and their Diplomacy* (New York, 1929), VIII, 3.

[134] Scott, *International Conferences*, p. 449.

consider the wisdom of organizing a " consultative council " whose views would have the " respectful heed " of its New World member nations.[135]

Relations with Santo Domingo were resumed and Haiti was assured that in case any general meeting of the American nations was called by the United States it would be invited to attend. When reports circulated that France was again interested in intervening in Haiti an immediate protest was forwarded by the United States to which France made the response that it had no interest in the island.[136] Thus issues were consistently side-stepped and even Cuban problems which were becoming serious were largely disregarded.

In the field of commerce the new administration was more at home and under an act of Congress of 1884 a commission was appointed to visit Latin American countries and to report on means of fostering trade with them. The President showed an active interest and reciprocity treaties were signed with Mexico and the Dominican Republic, and with Spain on behalf of its colonies, Puerto Rico and Cuba. These all failed to secure Senate approval however, partly because of the change of administrations in 1885 and partly because of opposition in Congress.[137]

As for naval bases, the administration definitely refused

[135] Brown, *op. cit.,* VIII, 23.

[136] Welles, I, 463 ff.; Logan, *Diplomatic Relations,* pp. 382-3; Perkins, pp. 35-6.

[137] United States Tariff Commission, *Reciprocity and Commercial Treaties* (Washington, 1919), pp. 139; 141; John Ball Osborne, " Reciprocity in American Tariff System," *The Annals of the American Academy of Political and Social Science* (hereafter referred to as " *The Annals* "), XXIII, 76-7; Foster, *Diplomatic Memoirs,* I, 239-40.

offers of such in Haiti [138] even though this did not mean complete renunciation of the idea of expansion, for Frey-linghuysen entered into negotiations for canal rights and a naval station in Nicaragua.[139] The fact that such a canal would prove a direct violation of the Clayton-Bulwer treaty does not seem to have caused Washington much concern, though it was to be gravely protested by Cleveland early in 1885. The Senate declined to advise ratification and the treaty was saved from immediate death only by a motion to reconsider.[140]

In Venezuela the boundary dispute was becoming more serious as a deadlock developed between that country and Great Britain. To make matters worse the South American country had made substantial grants to two United States citizens in the disputed area so their property was now involved. This the British resented.[141] The Secretary of State in a dispatch to Minister Lowell at London pointed out the concern of the United States in " all that touches the independent life of the Republics of the American conti-nent " and instructed the Minister " to let Lord Granville know that we are not without concern as to whatever may affect the interest of a sister Republic of the American continent and its position in the family of nations." [142] But events moved slowly, Great Britain was not unduly

[138] Logan, pp. 371-7; Moore, *Digest,* I, 432-3.

[139] *Ibid.,* III, 197; Wriston, *Executive Agents,* p. 794.

[140] Perkins, pp. 103-4; Samuel Pasco, " Isthmian Canal Ques-tion as affected by Treaties and Concessions," *The Annals,* XIX, 31-2.

[141] Charles Callan Tansill, *The Foreign Policy of Thomas F. Bayard* (New York, 1940), p. 628; Perkins, pp. 47-8.

[142] Grover Cleveland, *The Venezuela Boundary Controversy* (Princeton, 1913), p. 65.

perturbed over the affair, and this matter too lay over until the next administration.

Beyond doubt there was a rising tendency toward renewal of the old program of expansionism but this was, with the possible exception of the short incumbency of Blaine in the State Department, the result of a more or less impulsive or opportunistic utilization of incidents that occurred to make political capital at home or to strike a blow for liberty without much thought of the implications of the individual act. Just at this point, however, came the first Democratic administration for a quarter of a century when Grover Cleveland entered the White House. Not a man trained in diplomacy or foreign affairs, he thought slowly but on the whole thoroughly. Given the disturbed condition of the nation and his own background there was a natural tendency to keep one's " horns drawn in " on foreign affairs. " Jingoism and imperialism " were out and " a quiet and unadventurous foreign policy " was the new standing order of the day.[143]

The immediate problem was what to do with the reciprocity treaties pending with Mexico and the Spanish colonies in the West Indies. Lacking active endorsement, though Cleveland did give mild support, the Mexican treaty failed to secure proper enabling legislation in the House of Representatives, the Cuban treaty failed to come to a vote in the Senate and the other treaties were withdrawn by the President for further consideration.[144] Other negotiations with Great Britain on behalf of its West Indian colonies were

[143] Allan Nevins, *Grover Cleveland. A Study in Courage* (New York, 1932), p. 404.
[144] Foster, *op. cit.*, I, 259-60.

suspended [145] and the whole matter lapsed as the Democrats professed to be concerned about the disturbance of revenues and the balance of trade as a result of special treaties with small areas.

In general time passed quickly and few issues arose. With Mexico relations continued quite happy as foreigners were welcomed and the efficient Mexican Minister Romero graciously conducted his office, made himself popular and avoided personal and international complications.[146] Unwise United States representatives in Mexico had caused unfortunate scandals so Bayard wrote a rather careful exposition of his views to the new Minister, General E. S. Bragg:

> . . . Fate has placed the two very dissimilar peoples in contiguity, and great good sense, constant forebearance, and careful self-control are indispensably requisite to keep matters in pacific train between them. The overflow of our population and capital into the bordering states of Mexico, must, sooner or later, saturate these regions with Americanism, and control their political action, but until they are prepared for our laws and institutions, we do not want them, and when they are fit they will find their way to us. In the meantime we must deal amicably with them, and avoid, as far as possible, all occasions for friction.[147]

No specific stand on the Cuban question seems to have been assumed though the President was later stated to have been in favor of annexation.[148] Some English travellers

[145] H. Parker Willis, "Reciprocity with Cuba," *The Annals,* XXII, 131; 133.

[146] For instance, he curtly declined to be caught in an indiscretion such as tripped the veteran Sackville-West into expressing a most unfortunate opinion on domestic politics.

[147] Tansill, *op. cit.,* p. 610.

[148] Portell Vilá, *op. cit.,* III, 87: James Anthony Froude, *The English in the West Indies, or, the Bow of Ulysses* (New York, 1888), p. 333.

feared this but certainly no such attitude was adopted publicly so Cleveland's later statements on Cuba were not embarrassed by unwise commitments at this time.

The President likewise refused to get excited about Haiti and the reported British invasion of La Tortue; and again time proved his policy wise.[149] However, when complications arose due to varying claimants for the presidency of Haiti the matter was settled so far as the United States was concerned by applying the *de jure* principle rather than the *de facto* one.[150] Thus it might be noted that Cleveland, not Woodrow Wilson in 1913, initiated such a procedure as a part of United States foreign policy. True enough, a wholesome reservation was made until it was obvious that the man about to be recognized would not turn his country over to the French, who had meanwhile been warned that the United States could not approve such a step even if attempted.[151] When a direct offer reached Washington from Santo Domingo to lease Samaná Bay to the northern republic under absolute temporary sovereignty the communication was not even answered by Cleveland.[152]

When a dispute arose between Italy and Colombia Secretary of State Bayard cooperated with Great Britain and France in getting the contestants to agree that the matter should be arbitrated by Spain. This is not the complete reversal of Blaine's position on the Colombia-Costa Rica dispute that appears at first glance for Bayard himself com-

---

[149] Logan, pp. 392-3.

[150] H. L. Stimson, "The United States and Other Latin American Republics," *Foreign Affairs,* IX, No. 3, supplement, pp. v-vi; John Bassett Moore, *Candor and Common Sense* (Address before New York City Bar Association, December 4, 1930), p. 22.

[151] Logan, p. 397; Perkins, p. 38.

[152] Welles, I, 468-9.

plained of an Anglo-Nicaraguan agreement of 1880 which submitted the settlement of the boundary of Belize to the Emperor of Austria as arbitrator. In this Bayard invoked the interest of the United States as provided in the Clayton-Bulwer treaty somewhat as Blaine had invoked the treaty of 1846 with Colombia or New Granada.[153] In addition a dispute between Italy and El Salvador was resolved through the good offices of the United States Minister to Central America. Also Cleveland handed down an award in the arbitration of the Costa Rica-Nicaragua boundary that was to prove more than a little awkward for extreme United States claims under the Bryan-Chamorro treaty of the new century.[154] Likewise the United States Minister in Central America was quite active in maintaining or securing peace in the troubled middle section of the continent. The idea of a Central American union was encouraged but Bayard made it plain that his country would not endorse any union based on the coercion of any of the independent states.[155]

The Freylinghuysen-Zavala canal treaty, giving the United States canal rights in Nicaragua, was promptly repudiated as a violation of the Clayton-Bulwer treaty and as creating dangerous entangling alliances.[156] Yet when Colombia sought to take advantage of the situation to present some old claims to Nicaraguan territory orders were issued for a United States warship to proceed to the region to prevent hostilities. Likewise disturbances on the Isthmus of Panama in 1885 caused United States troops to be landed to protect

[153] Tansill, *op. cit.*, pp. 668 ff.

[154] *U. S. and the Nicaragua Canal*, F. P. A., IV, No. 6, pp. 109-10.

[155] Graham H. Stuart, *Latin America and the United States*, pp. 335-6.

[156] Perkins, p. 104.

the railroad transit when Colombia confessed it could not provide proper protection. The troops were withdrawn as soon as order was reestablished.[157]

In his first annual message to Congress, December 8, 1885, the President defined his canal policy saying: " I do not favor a policy of acquisition of new and distant territory or the incorporation of remote interests with our own." He insisted that any highway across the isthmus must be for the world's benefit as a trust for mankind " to be removed from the chance of dominion by a single power." [158] And this regardless of the fact that the State Department had certainly been warned of the threat of a German-French bargain as to the isthmus area.[159] Meanwhile the attention of special groups remained fixed on Panama and H. H. Bancroft speculated in 1887:

What is to be the future status of the Isthmus? A strong government is doubtless a necessity, and must be provided from abroad. Shall it assume the form of a quasi independent state under the protection of the chief commercial nations, eliminating Colombia from participation therein? Or must the United States, as the power most interested in preserving the independence of the highway, take upon themselves the whole control for the benefit of all nations? [160]

The old aching tooth that was the Venezuela-British Guiana boundary dispute continued its gnawing pain but no definitive stand was taken. The United States Minister

[157] John H. Latané, " Treaty Relations of the United States and Colombia, *The Annals,* XXII, 125-6.

[158] Moore, *Digest,* III, 198. See also L. B. Shippee, " Bayard," in Bemis, *Secretaries of State,* VIII, 91; Arias, *Panama Canal,* pp. 50 ff.

[159] Stolberg-Wernigerode, *Germany and U. S.,* pp. 308 ff.

[160] Quoted by DuVal, *Cadiz to Cathay,* p. 130.

at Caracas had agreed with the British Minister that a joint presentation of claims by the two countries would probably have beneficial results but Mr. Bayard at once sent word that his government would not endorse a " joint " proposal even when such action arose " from an act equally invading the common rights of American citizens and the subjects of another state residing in the country to whose government complaint is made." A " coincident and even identical representation " was as far as he would go. Relations between the two disputants were broken off by action of Venezuela in February, 1887.[161] Still no solution was in sight. The Secretary of State merely received communications on the subject as information and in one memorandum commented that he did not " even feel inclined to form an opinion " on Venezuelan claims of British aggression since " it had been suggested that the United States might become the arbitrator " and he could not afford to " form an opinion in advance." [162]

A year later the Secretary had apparently become convinced that Great Britain was unduly delaying matters so he sent the famous " undelivered dispatch " in which he earnestly protested through Mr. Phelps, the United States Minister, to Lord Salisbury against the indefiniteness of British claims saying:

If . . . it should appear that there is no fixed limit to the British boundary claim, our good disposition to aid in a settlement might not only be defeated, but be obliged to give place to a feeling of grave concern.[163]

[161] Grover Cleveland, *Presidential Problems* (New York, 1904), pp. 217 ff.
[162] Tansill, *Foreign Policy of Bayard,* p. 639.
[163] *Ibid.*, pp. 641-2.

Mr. Phelps did not deliver this forceful statement thinking that it would do no good unless the United States was ready to employ force. He notified Bayard of his action and the Secretary seemed to acquiesce in his conduct and even failed to protest further when Great Britain had its officials in Guiana create a new colonial district which incorporated part of the disputed territory. However, the protest was published in the official correspondence while the letter showing the non-delivery was forgotten and unpublished. Thus during the second Cleveland administration the President and his new Secretary of State apparently thought the British had simply ignored the United States protest. This may help in part to explain the later intransigent attitude of Cleveland.[164]

When Congress by act of May 24, 1888, authorized the calling of a Pan-American conference (the old Blaine idea) Cleveland allowed the act to become law without his signature. Four and a half months later invitations were issued for the conference to meet in October, 1889. The purpose was declared to be the fostering of peace, of trade and communications through better transportation and a customs union, standardization of weights, measures, coins and the like; while arbitration was sponsored for all questions except those affecting national honor or independence.[165]

Thus drew to a close the period during which the United States was finding for itself a Caribbean program. Republican

[164] R. B. Mowat, *The Life of Lord Pauncefote, First Ambassador to the United States* (Boston and New York, 1929), p. 175; Tansill, *op. cit.,* pp. 644-5.

[165] Scott, *International Conferences*, pp. 3-4. For congressional action in the United States on these recommendations see Tyler, *op. cit.,* pp. 174-5.

leaders had drifted into a policy of rising activity based on genuine interest in the region. The Democrats, too, even under the leadership of a domestic minded and stubborn Cleveland, were showing more and more of a tendency to take a hand. The ship of foreign policy had obviously about passed through the diplomatic doldrums for repeated gusts of wind clearly presaged the coming change. This did not mean an immediate and consistent policy of expansionism or absorption of the area involved but clearly did mean that foreign monopolies or undue influence were not to be tolerated in Venezuela, Haiti or the canal area. The United States was beginning to play with the idea that it was " nation enough " to see that any policy it might adopt for the region would be enforced. While the term Monroe Doctrine was now frequently heard and generally accepted by the public as incorporating all that was desirable in the way of a foreign policy the fact remained that the activity and pronouncements that had taken place were essentially based on the Caribbean area. The public had begun to conceive of this region as economically and morally a United States problem since nature had placed it geographically adjacent to this country. Ideas as yet were vague and only occasionally expressed but they were generally widespread and were only waiting for vigorous leadership and concrete expression to cause them to crystallize.

CHAPTER II

ASSUMING THE BURDEN OF EMPIRE:
IMPERIALISM THROUGH WAR

In 1889 the Republicans again returned to power and once more installed the old political veteran, James G. Blaine, in the office of Secretary of State. Yet he was a chastened Blaine compared to the ebullient Secretary of eight years before. Defeats in inter-party and intra-party fights had taken something of the old irresponsibility. Further, he had that able wheel-horse and steady adviser, A. A. Adee, as Assistant Secretary of State, whose potent influence was to be felt in that position so consistently from 1882 to 1924. Adee knew the rules of the game thoroughly and did much to keep the prancing feet of successive inexperienced superiors on the narrow path of diplomatic decorum and precedent.[1] Yet though somewhat subdued the Secretary of State was still Blaine and as such he could always qualify under Ferrara's description of the United States diplomat at the end of the nineteenth century as

brilliant at times, audacious as befits the agent of a democracy, a stranger to the beaten paths of international politics, easily vanquished in routine matters but capable of smashing all the rules of form and convention and winning success

[1] Whatever the source of Blaine's new conservatism it is seen in his frowning on the Portuguese proposals forwarded by Minister Whitelaw Reid at London by which the United States was to have secured trade and naval bases in the Indian Ocean, in Angola, and the Azores as an offset to the British.

in a day, almost violent when confronted with an obstacle which the skill of others had put in his way.[2]

Many writers have pointed out the poetic justice of the fact that soon after taking office the new Secretary was called on to preside over the first Pan-American conference which he had originally proposed when Secretary of State under Garfield. All nations of the New World except the Dominican Republic (which was piqued because the reciprocity treaty of 1884 was still unratified) sent delegates and Blaine was able to welcome them in an address in which he pled for justice, equality, cooperation, friendship and good will in the Americas, while he decried the idea of a balance of power and of extensive armed forces in the New World.[3] Thus was launched, at least in its modern form, the Pan-American program, which was to be centered in the Pan-American Union as it is now known.

The resolutions adopted bore a decided economic emphasis and called for: acceptance of the decimal system of weights and measures as standard; standard nomenclature for business invoices etc.; endorsement of a Pan-American railroad; acceptance of the sanitary convention of Rio de Janeiro or that of Lima; treaties for the protection of patents and trademarks; better steamship connections with Mexico and the Caribbean; better communication facilities between the Atlantic and Pacific oceans; standardization of consular fees and customs regulations, and an international American bank.[4] On the subject of international difficulties

[2] Orestes Ferrara (William E. Shea, translator), *The Last Spanish War. Revelations in " Diplomacy "* (New York, 1937), pp. 10-11.

[3] Lockey, *Pan-Americanism,* pp. 4 ff.

[4] Moore, *Digest*, VI, 600-1.

and quarrels that might lead to hostilities there were two resolutions of importance: a plan of arbitration which was later signed by eleven nations including the United States, in spite of only mild congressional interest indeed, and Guatemala, Haiti, Honduras, Nicaragua, Salvador and Venezuela of the Latin states of the Caribbean; [5] and a resolution which announced that there existed no right of conquest in the Americas " whether the object or consequence of war." [6] Needless to say in this last the Caribbean was especially interested.

Also close to Blaine's heart was the question of reciprocity which he also conceived of as a weapon of diplomacy. With Latin America the United States had a trade which amounted to $170,000,000 of imports annually, but exports were a mere $68,000,000.[7] This, naturally, was irksome to any trader especially when it was coupled with the fact that some 87% of the imports from Latin-America to the northern republic were admitted duty free, whereas most of the trade in the other direction was taxed by customs regulations. When the committee failed to incorporate Blaine's ideas in the new tariff bill as passed by the House of Representatives the Secretary took the fight to the Senate where his ideas were accepted at least in part. Sugar, molasses, coffee, hides and some other commodities imported from the Caribbean and Latin America were still to come in free, but if products of the United States shipped to those countries did not receive what the executive considered to be proper treatment he was authorized to apply penalty duties that were listed

[5] *Ibid.*, VII, 70-1; Scott, *International Conferences,* pp. 11 ff.

[6] Moore, I, 292.

[7] Muzzey, *Blaine,* pp. 443-4; Benjamin H. Williams, *Economic Foreign Policy of the United States* (New York, 1929), pp. 257-8.

in the bill.[8] This was a part of Blaine's program for he frankly said that the best results of the Pan-American conference would not be realized if the State Department were not given a sugar tariff with which it could bargain.[9]

Of the Caribbean countries Haiti, Venezuela and Colombia failed to make trade concessions and were promptly penalized. They protested: Haiti on the ground that it was protected from such discrimination by the most-favored-nation provision in its treaty of 1864; Colombia that it was protected similarly by the treaty of 1846, and Venezuela on more general principles though its position was weak since it had cancelled its commercial treaty with the United States.[10] How serious was the injury may be seen from the fact that trade with the penalized countries was reduced to about 25% of its earlier volume.[11] John W. Foster, who acted as the agent of the State Department in the reciprocity negotiations, soothed Spanish feelings and secured a treaty for Cuban and Puerto Rican products. Salvador, Nicaragua, Honduras, Guatemala and Santo Domingo fell in line at once,[12] as did most of the British islands in the West Indies.[13] But the program was reversed by the Democrats after 1893 so it is difficult to determine effects except in the case of Cuba where the results were prompt and startling because of the single outstanding commodity—sugar—

[8] Robertson, *Hispanic American Relations,* pp. 214 ff.

[9] Foster, *Diplomatic Memoirs,* II, 2-4.

[10] Tariff Commission, *Reciprocity and Commercial Treaties,* pp. 421-2.

[11] *Ibid.,* p. 172.

[12] W. R. Castle, "Foster" in Bemis, *Secretaries of State,* VIII, 191; Foster, *op. cit.,* II, 9.

[13] J. E. Osborne, "Reciprocity in the American Tariff System," *The Annals,* XXIII, 57-8.

involved in the sales of the island to the United States. United States exports to the island doubled from 1891 to 1893 but with the termination of the agreement the total dropped almost to the original figures by 1895.[14] The potentialities of this for the whole of the Caribbean were obvious. All in all some twenty reciprocity treaties were negotiated with Latin America and only the three, Haiti, Venezuela and Colombia declined to make any special arrangements.[15]

In taking up the problems of the Caribbean Blaine early became interested in the Venezuela boundary question and tentatively considered it. However, he was deeply involved in the Bering Sea controversy with Great Britain so his views were probably colored by that problem. He instructed Mr. Robert T. Lincoln, United States Minister at London, to use his good offices to bring about the resumption of diplomatic relations between Venezuela and Great Britain as a preliminary to a boundary settlement and then to propose an informal conference of representatives from Great Britain, Venezuela and the United States in either London or Washington to consider terms of a settlement.[16] The South American republic was delighted at the prospect but Britain preferred direct negotiations and returned a polite answer that amounted to a postponement of a decision.[17] On October 28, 1891, Blaine showed his restlessness be-

[14] *Ibid.*, pp. 65-6.

[15] Tyler, *Foreign Policy of Blaine*, p. 188.

[16] Cleveland, *Presidential Problems,* pp. 244 ff.; Tansill, *Foreign Policy of Bayard,* p. 648; Henry James, *Richard Olney and his Public Service, with Documents Including Unpublished Diplomatic Correspondence* (Boston and New York, 1923), pp. 100-1.

[17] P. R. Fossum, "Anglo-Venezuela Boundary Controversy," *Hisp. Amer. Hist. Rev.,* VIII, 319-30.

cause of British expansion at the expense of Venezuela and suggested to Minister Scruggs at Caracas that " at an early date " the United States should " take an advanced and decisive step " in support of the claims of Venezuela. However, other matters pressed for attention, Blaine was far from being a well man, and the defeat of the Republican party at the polls the next year forestalled any decisive action for the time.

In other matters Blaine's expansionist tendencies reasserted themselves. Because of the opposition to a cession of territory in Haiti the able colored minister of the United States, Frederick Douglass, and Admiral Gherardi were to cooperate to secure the lease of a naval base. The local government was to be assured that this would mean a more or less constant presence of a substantial part of the United States navy which would extend material protection [18] to the local authorities. Negotiations lagged, possibly in part because of jealousy between the minister and the admiral, and finally expired when the two violently disagreed on the advisability of United States occupation of the Môle St. Nicholas by force. The admiral insisted this would remove a local incitement to revolution and that later negotiations could settle the international complications. Douglass disagreed.[19]

The next step was to urge the cession of Samaná Bay. However, reports of the negotiations were published in newspapers in this country and the Caribbean government took fright at the disapproval that ensued. Heureaux complained:

---

[18] Tyler, *op. cit.*, pp. 93 ff.

[19] L. M. Sears, " Frederick Douglass and the Mission to Haiti, 1889-1891," *Hisp. Amer. Hist. Rev.*, XXI, 222 ff.

The great difficulty is your American press. Whenever a Dominican editor writes anything objectionable or puts my picture in his paper as a caricature I put him in prison. That settles it. In the United States, the writers abuse their privileges and your ruling men do nothing. That article in the *Gaceta Oficial* [a denial that negotiations were in progress] will quiet the people. Then Mr. Blaine can send instructions. We can go to work some months in the future secretly. If we succeed it will be done before anybody can make any noise. If we obtain no good result, there will be no bad feeling.[20]

In 1892 Heureaux again opened the question, for he needed cash badly. His offer was for an offensive and defensive alliance with the northern republic in which the latter would get one naval base at least, and in case war ensued between Haiti and Santo Domingo there would be the chance to take others. By mid-summer Blaine had retired from the State Department and John W. Foster carried on his plans by instructing the United States Minister to secure a ninety-nine year lease on Samaná Bay on the basis of a cash payment of $250,000, plus a rental of $50,000 per year for five years and of $25,000 annually thereafter; the lease to be renewable. Heureaux wanted a large amount of the cash in advance. The reply was that the United States President could not advance money until Congress had appropriated it. The Dominican answered: " You know my situation. I cannot ask insurgents to wait until I receive money from the United States with which to fight them." [21] But again negotiations failed because another news leakage caused trouble and because the dictator had secured money from private sources in New York which enabled him to

[20] Welles, *Naboth's Vineyard,* I, 479-80.
[21] *Ibid.,* p. 487.

feel too independent to risk his position by increasing the popular clamor over the alienation of territory.[22]

Incidentally, it should be noted that President Harrison probably acted as something of a brake on his secretaries Blaine and Foster. Just before he became President, in January, 1889, he had written Blaine of his special interest in relations with Central and South American states saying: " We must win their confidence by deserving it. . . . Only men of experience, of high character and of broad views should be sent to the least important of these States." [23] In his inaugural address he had stated that in obtaining naval and coaling stations his administration would not coerce powers, however feeble, into making concessions.[24] Such statements would be a slight deterrent though there is no proof that the secretaries would have used force, nor indeed was there much need for it in view of the chronic state of indigence and disorder of the regions in question.

On the subject of the immediate needs for new territory Blaine wrote to Harrison: " I think there are only three places that are of value enough to be taken, that are not continental. One is Hawaii, the others are Cuba and Porto Rico. Cuba and Porto Rico are not imminent and will not be for a generation." So he turned his major attention to Hawaii but watched all Caribbean possibilities carefully. With regard to the Virgin Islands he said that they were destined to belong to the Stars and Stripes anyway but that

[22] Rippy, *Caribbean Danger Zone*, pp. 121-3.

[23] Albert T. Volweiler, *The Correspondence between Benjamin Harrison and James G. Blaine, 1882-1893* (Philadelphia, 1940), p. 44.

[24] James D. Richardson, *A Compilation of the Messages and Papers of the Presidents, 1789-1897* (Washington, 1896-9), IX, 10.

they lacked both strategic value and commercial value and that in case of war they would be a liability.[25] Foster was more optimistic and welcomed the possibility of acquiring them but did not have time to secure action in the short period of his incumbency at the State Department.[26]

Mexico too, continued to feel the danger of *El Fantasma* for periodically there were wild schemes hatched by those who would have brought about friendly or forcible annexation of parts of Mexican territory.[27] The two governments, however, maintained cordial relations. Business flourished, northern capital flowed steadily into Mexico and every consideration continued to be shown to the foreign investor south of the Río Grande. Occasional questions of border raids and even of Chinese immigration to the northern republic through Mexico in essential violation of United States laws merely aroused diplomatic correspondence and were not the subject of serious misunderstandings.[28] Indeed, with the growing strength of the Díaz government there developed a tendency to cooperate with Mexico on Central American questions. Thus, joint pressure was brought to bear on Guatemala and Salvador to accept the good offices of their northern neighbors to secure peace in their controversies. This was finally accomplished in 1895.[29] Questions

[25] Volweiler, *op. cit.*, p. 174.

[26] Tansill, *Purchase of Danish West Indies*, pp. 194-5.

[27] W. R. Shepherd, "The Monroe Doctrine Reconsidered," *Political Science Quarterly*, XXXIX, 63. See also Callahan, *Amer. Pol. in Mex. Relations*, pp. 430 ff.; Henry Cabot Lodge, *Selections from the Correspondence of Theodore Roosevelt and Henry Cabot Lodge, 1884-1918* (New York and London, 1925), pp. 44-5.

[28] W. R. Castle, "Foster" in Bemis, *Secretaries of State*, VIII, 203-4.

[29] Callahan, *op. cit.*, pp. 432-4.

of the shipment of arms and supplies from the north were involved, but on the whole these were disposed of without much trouble even though Guatemala did feel aggrieved.[30] Disturbances in Nicaragua leading to the ascension to power of the later objectionable José Santos Zelaya were watched with apprehension but questions of neutrality and petty issues as to the right of asylum and trade were muddled through.

By this time the expansionists were in full cry. The influential Captain Mahan turned expansionist [31] and commanded increasing attention as he urged acquisitions in the Pacific and the construction of a big navy that would enable his country to construct and protect an isthmian canal. He frankly believed that backward nations should not be allowed to monopolize areas which they could not develop [32] and in justification quoted Blaine: " It is not an ambitious destiny for so great a country as ours to manufacture only what we consume, or produce only what we can eat." [33] Overseas lay the destiny of the nation and he was fond of referring to our " natural, necessary, irrepressible expansion " [34] which in his eyes again justified a navy strong enough to control completely the Caribbean and the approaches to the canal which would revolutionize the economic life of the United States.[35] In line with this idea the United States Minister to Ecuador was told to protest the rumored cession of the

[30] Moore, *Digest,* VII, 659; Tyler, *op. cit.,* pp. 99-100.

[31] W. D. Puleston, *The Life and Work of Captain Alfred Thayer Mahan, U. S. N.* (New Haven,1939), pp. 129 ff.

[32] *Ibid.,* p. 334.

[33] Alfred Thayer Mahan, *The Interest of America in Sea Power, Present and Future* (Boston, 1918), p. 5.

[34] *Ibid.,* p. 36.

[35] *Ibid.,* pp. 12-4; 99-100.

Galapagos Islands to Great Britain as a coaling station,[36] while German and British trade throughout the New World was being most carefully watched. All in all the people were interested in commerce whose concrete terms they appreciated, but obviously it was strategy that was to guide much of the policy of new administrations. In fact, for many years to come Dollar Diplomacy was to be the stalking horse of strategy in the popular appeals of politicians.[37]

Inevitably so much discussion of various possible acquisitions created foreign suspicions so it is not surprising that there were occasional suggestions for the formation of a Caribbean confederation of the British possessions for the sake of mutual trade advantages and for political protection.[38] Latin America, too, took fright at the situation and engaged in increasing talk of Pan-Hispanism as an offset to Pan-Americanism or any movement that the Republic of the North might dominate. The plea was for some organization based on the needs, social, economic and strategic, of Latin America.[39]

With the stage thus set for a general advance on all fronts came the election of 1892 when the eloctorate, profoundly concerned about domestic politics, again repudiated the administration in office since it had not brought the desired

[36] Rippy, *op. cit.*, pp. 129-30.

[37] Benjamin H. Williams, *American Diplomacy, Policies and Practice* (New York, 1936), pp. 66-7.

[38] C. S. Salmon, *The Caribbean Confederation . . .* (London, New York, etc. [1888]), pp. 129-41.

[39] Clarence H. Haring, *South America Looks at the United States* (New York, 1929), pp. 111-13; 180-1; J. Fred Rippy, *Latin America in World Politics; An Outline Survey* (New York, 1928), pp. 205-7.

prosperity. The return of Cleveland to power meant another cautious four years, or at least this was the anticipated effect on foreign affairs. Even though Cleveland was now more clearly affiliated with big business than before, the fact remained that he was innately cautious and conservative and was determined to be reasonably consistent in his foreign policy, especially since this was not his primary interest. What the American people wanted was bread and work, and that was what he was to try to give them.

This renewed caution was at once visible in regard to Hawaii and Samoa.[40] Manifest Destiny again became a phrase on the lips of the people. Carl Schurz protested this in *Harpers Magazine* and the new Secretary of State, Roger Q. Gresham, promptly congratulated him on presenting the matter to the public.[41] On the other hand, Theodore Roosevelt was constantly thinking and talking war: war with Mexico, with Japan, with England over Venezuela, with Germany, or with Spain, were all possibilities, if not probabilities.[42] Roosevelt's crony and confidant, Henry Cabot Lodge, was only slightly less bellicose though he decried promiscuous expansionism and advised the immediate construction of the isthmian canal, whose defense would then mean that the " island of Cuba . . . will become to us a necessity." [43] This narrowed the Roosevelt conception and focussed attention on a politician's immediate objective when an election was in sight. Mahan, arguing from the stand-

[40] Julius W. Pratt, *Expansionitsts of 1898. The Acquisition of Hawaii and the Spanish Islands* (Baltimore, 1936), pp. 200-2.

[41] Gresham to Schurz, October 6, 1893, Library of Congress (hereafter referred to as " LC "), Gresham MS.

[42] Leland H. Jenks, *Our Cuban Colony*, pp. 151-2.

[43] Quoted by Pratt, *Expansionists of 1898,* p. 207.

point of strategic advisability and largely ignoring politics, insisted that the Caribbean was the crux of the problem:

In the cluster of island fortresses of the Caribbean is one of the greatest nerve centers of the whole body of European civilization; and it is to be regretted that so serious a portion of them now is in hands which not only never have given, but to all appearances never can give, the development which is required by the general interest.[44]

True, his ideas of expansion did not include areas south of the Caribbean and in this Roosevelt and Lodge thought him entirely too modest [45] but his articles in *Atlantic Monthly, Forum, North American Review, Harpers Magazine* and *McClures Magazine* appealed to an enormous proportion of the thinking public and to the policy-making classes of the nation. An Englishman commented that it would seem that Mahan had remade the spirit of the United States and continued that his teaching:

was as oil to the flame of " colonial expansion " everywhere leaping into life. Everywhere a new-sprung ambition to go forth and possess and enjoy read its sanction in the philosophy of history ennobled by the glory of conquest. . . . I doubt whether this effect of Mahan's teachings has gone deeper anywhere than in the United States.[46]

In short, the national wealth of $30,000,000,000 of 1870 had become $88,000,000,000 by 1900 and exports trebled in the single decade after 1890,[47] but the owners remained queerly unconscious of the possibilities overseas. This wealth had been created at home and only occasionally did one of

[44] Mahan, *op. cit.*, p. 261.

[45] Lodge, *op. cit.*, pp. 486-7.

[46] Pratt, pp. 21-2.

[47] Achille Viallate, *Economic Imperialism and International Relations During the Last Fifty Years* (New York, 1923), p. 31.

its possessors catch a vision of foreign profits. Mahan and the theorists forthwith determined that more should see such visions and dream such dreams so that their own objectives of imperialism and strategic defense could be un-obtrusively accomplished as an accompaniment of profits.[48] The next step was to offset the religious taboo on indiscriminate expansion that existed in the minds of the masses. To this end Darwin's theories, denounced but generally believed, as to superiority of certain groups was made to appeal skillfully to those very people who were in reality peeking through the fingers of hands ostentatiously held in front of their eyes so that they would not see the forbidden fruit. They were already taking unction to their souls over the idea of their own superiority—regardless of how they got that way—so it was an easy step to convince them of their obligation to assume the " White Man's burden " on behalf of the unfortunate and at the same time acquire the needed supplies and territories for the continued prosperity of their own superior kind.[49] Not to do this would be to fly in the face of that Providence which had obviously thus planned for them since it had given them this ability.

True, Schurz deplored the tendency but the denunciation only attracted attention to the idea. Woodrow Wilson wrote his biting criticism of the imperialism of the United States in the days of the forties [50] but most of those who read his splendidly rounded sentences applauded, not their applications and implications in their own day but merely to enjoy a feeling of superiority that the new generation was obviously more righteous than that which had gone before.

[48] Pratt, p. 22.   [49] *Ibid.,* pp. 18-9; 154.
[50] Harley Notter, *Origins of the Foreign Policy of Woodrow Wilson* (Baltimore, 1937), p. 55.

In spite of all this the Democrats reversed the reciprocity program of Blaine and Latin America hoped the step portended good and not ill for them.[51] Next Gresham stated that Great Britain had a right to discipline Nicaragua, short of territorial acquisitions, for misconduct [52] and further proved indifferent to a chance to acquire the Danish West Indies.[53] But the fact was that public opinion had been aroused to the point where a boundary dispute in far away Venezuela and continued disturbances in Cuba justified a later writer in commenting that:

suddenly in 1895 the Caribbean hove into sight. . . . What we had fancied peculiar to the expansive tendencies of European nations in the remoter parts of Africa, Asia and the archepelagoes of the Pacific had become a reality in our own career. A region near in space but hitherto isolated in thought has been converted into a sphere of influence for this country. The Caribbean Sea has become an American Mediterranean, if not altogether an American lake.[54]

The region involved amounted to an area in islands and on the mainland of approximately 1,300,000 square miles or more than one-third as large as the continental United States itself.

Immediately to the south relations with Mexico continued cordial, especially since Gresham was more *simpático* with Minister Romero than with most of the representatives from the New World.[55] For the most part correspondence be-

[51] Nevins, *Cleveland*, pp. 549-50.

[52] J. B. Moore, "The Monroe Doctrine," *Pol. Sci. Quar.*, XI, 28-9; M. Schuyler, "Gresham" in Bemis, *Secretaries of State*, VIII, 261.

[53] Tansill, *Purchase of Danish West Indies*, pp. 197-8.

[54] W. R. Shepherd in George Blakeslee, *Mexico and the Caribbean* (New York, 1920), pp. 184-5.

[55] Matilda Gresham, *Life of Walter Quintin Gresham, 1832-1895* (Chicago, 1919), p. 697.

tween the two countries dealt with bandit chasing on the border, an occasional report of a filibustering expedition, or something of the kind. The settlement of a troublesome boundary dispute between Mexico and Guatemala was facilitated at least in part by United States efforts.[56] Indeed, so cordial were the relations that in the acute period of the Venezuela controversy Mexico maintained discreet silence and when the matter was resolved President Díaz reported to his Congress: ". . . the Mexican government cannot but declare its partiality for a doctrine which condemns as criminal any attack on the part of the Monarchies of Europe against the Republics of America, against the independent nations of this continent, now all subject to a popular form of government." However, he continued that no one nation should have the obligation of protecting the whole hemisphere, but that this should be the duty of each of the republics who should issue a Monroe Doctrine of its own and stand ready on call of an endangered fellow republic to go to the rescue.[57]

In this connection the proposed Pan-American conference should be noted. Ecuador had suggested that the conference be held and presented the proposal to Olney early in 1896 but received no encouragement,[58] probably because it had specified that a primary purpose of the conference would be a discussion of the Monroe Doctrine. Incidentally, the Mexican Minister reported from Washington that Olney felt that Ecuador did not have enough prestige to call such

[56] Callahan, *Amer. Pol. in Mex. Relations,* pp. 439-40.

[57] Alvarez, *The Monroe Doctrine,* p. 186.

[58] Genaro Estrada, editor, *La Doctrina de Monroe y el fracasado de una conferencia panamericana en Mexico* (Mexico, 1937), pp. viii-ix.

a conference.[59] Mexico at last agreed to issue the invitations but the United States so effectively frowned on the enterprise that when the date of meeting arrived there were only seven states represented. A very significant fact, however, is that delegates were present from Mexico, Venezuela and the five Central American states. These delegates formally urged that the Monroe Doctrine be made a general policy of the Americas but beyond the presentation of the resolution to this effect nothing was accomplished for the assembly rapidly disintegrated. The one significant fact was the fear of the United States that was displayed.

With Colombia there were occasional negotiations concerning the protection of the transit across the isthmus and for the prevention of filibustering expeditions, but again there were no complications of importance.[60] In fact, Cleveland was asked to act as arbitrator in a claims dispute between Colombia and Italy,[61] and in the case of the long-standing dispute between Costa Rica and Colombia it was urged that the matter be settled by arbitration either by the Queen of Spain (page Mr. Blaine!) " or by resort to any impartial arbitrator." [62]

The last question that the personally décolleté and some-what idiosyncratic Gresham had to handle with the Caribbean countries was a hang-over from earlier days; that of British interests on the Nicaraguan border. Secretary Foster had protested British expansion,[63] and now further

[59] *Ibid.,* pp. xii-xiii.

[60] For reports on United States commercial interests in Colombia and a request for visit of the warship to secure " moral " effects see Coolidge to Olney May 3, 1893, October 8, 1894, and October 26, 1898, LC, Richard Olney MSS.

[61] Moore, *Digest,* VII, 42-3.

[62] *Ibid.,* III, 32-3.   [63] *Ibid.,* III, 238-41.

difficulties were in sight if Harrison's scheme to have his country underwrite the Maritime Canal Company with funds for the completion of the canal by a company chartered in the United States was to be carried out. This of course violated the spirit, if not the letter, of the Clayton-Bulwer treaty. Cleveland ended the second difficulty promptly by reversing his predecessor's attitude and by dismissing all idea of dominance of the canal through Harrison's scheme and the Maritime Canal Company. As for the trouble that was brewing at Bluefields between Nicaragua and the Mosquito Protectorate officials of the British Foreign Office assured Ambassador Bayard at London that Great Britain had " no intention or desire . . . to exercise a protectorate in any form over any portion of Nicaraguan territory, but to act thoroughly in concert with the United States for maintaining safety of the citizens and property of both countries, continuing our treaty of 1850 in unbroken force and effect." [64] Such an attitude mollified the State Department which in spite of the repeated Nicaraguan protests now insisted that the British demands were legitimate and must be met. [65]

Interestingly enough, the United States Minister in Nicaragua seemed to favor the Mosquito government in its expansionist program and certainly United States business interests in the area did so. However, the two governments had chosen their positions so it only remained to hold a " farcical vote " in the territory concerned so that the people could publicly avow an undesired wish to be incorporated into Nicaragua. [66] Later efforts of British and United States

[64] *Ibid.*, III, 246.

[65] Tansill, *Foreign Policy of Bayard,* cir. p. 687.

[66] R. L. Morrow, . " Conflict between Commercial Interests," *Hisp. Amer. Hist. Rev.,* X, 7 ff.; Stuart, *Latin Amer. and U. S.,* pp. 258-9.

citizens in the area to reverse the decision could not hope for support from abroad and so died aborning.[67] In the whole of the discussions the United States was clearly assuming increasing responsibilities for the conduct of its southern neighbor. For instance, when the British Ambassador Sir Julian Pauncefote suggested that under the existing treaty his country was bound to see that Nicaragua did not oppress the Mosquito Indians, Mr. Gresham responded: " We will see that she does not." [68] And in June, 1895, the Nicaraguan Minister affirmed the same opinion when he wrote to Olney:

My country looks upon this powerful nation as the natural protector of all the small republics of America, and has always cherished, in the highest degree, the friendship of the United States. No better proof of this could be presented than our traditional policy in the canal question, which has been essentially an American policy in the truest sense of the word.[69]

As a matter of fact there was a surprising public reaction to the whole affair. British conduct was freely denounced in the press and the Assembly of Cleveland's home state of New York criticized the lack of patriotism " which has characterized the Administration at Washington in dealing with this complication " in Nicaragua. The Senate of Massachusetts took much the same position.[70] Indeed, as Tansill points out, this protest from his home state and the public may have influenced the President not a little in his later stand on Venezuela.

Meanwhile foreign countries were increasingly recognizing

[67] L. M. Keasbey, " The Nicaraguan Canal and the Monroe Doctrine," *The Annals,* VII, 24-5.

[68] Gresham, *op. cit.,* p. 782.

[69] Guzman to Olney, June 27. 1895, LC., Olney MS.

[70] Tansill, *op. cit.,* pp. 689-90.

this position of the United States, and China requested Washington to protect its nationals in both Salvador and Nicaragua. This was done and a special form of certificate of Chinese citizenship was prepared which would entitle the bearer to the good offices of United States consular and diplomatic officers.[71]

As the Administration drew to its close and Richard Olney had become Secretary of State at the end of May, 1895, there arose the question of the formation of another of those transitory unions of the Central American republics. Great Britain asked what attitude Washington would take, implying that Queen Victoria would follow Cleveland's lead with regard to recognition. Olney responded that his government would receive the minister accredited to it.[72] This was done December 24, 1896. Unfortunately, only Nicaragua, Costa Rica and El Salvador had agreed to the union and before this could be made effective revolutionary movements had wrecked it.[73] However, the United States had followed its custom of *de facto* recognition and there could be no criticism that undue efforts had been made to influence events. Also, Great Britain had voluntarily implied that it expected the United States to guide the policy of foreign nations in regard to recognition and all that it implied.

A rising popular interest in the Nicaraguan, hence in the Panamanian, canal was to be noted and in January, 1896, the *Annals of the American Academy of Political and Social Science* devoted three articles to the historical background,

[71] Moore, *Digest,* IV, 590-1.

[72] Pauncefote to Olney, December 1, 1896, and Rodríguez to Olney, December 23, 1896, LC., Olney MS.

[73] Edward Perry, " Central American Union," *Hisp. Amer. Hist. Rev.,* V, 35.

the arguments in favor of, and the economic advantages of a canal. In Congress the interest was reflected by periodic discussions and in 1895 that body appropriated $50,000 to investigate the practicability of the Maritime Canal Company's plans which Harrison had endorsed.[74]

Among the miscellaneous items considered by Olney was the acquisition of the Virgin Islands. He showed interest so long as there was danger of a sale by Denmark to some foreign power, but as soon as he was reassured on the subject he turned to more important issues in spite of the prodding of Lodge and others.[75] A welcome bit of recognition was extended to Haiti and Santo Domingo when the representatives of the United States stationed there were advanced to plenipotentiary rank;[76] and an even more welcome and very substantial aid was extended to Santo Domingo on the occasion, in 1895, of the somewhat exorbitant demands of the French consul on the government of President Heureaux. These demands were supported by the arrival of a French warship—whose effect was as promptly nullified by " the simultaneous arrival of three American war vessels . . . which entered the harbor of Santo Domingo ostensibly for gun practice in the waters near the Republic." " The open support so rendered by the Government of the United States necessarily forced a peaceful settlement of the disputes." [77]

---

[74] Dwight Carroll Miner, *The Fight for the Panama Route. The Story of the Spooner Act and the Hay-Herran Treaty* (New York, 1940), p. 28.

[75] Lodge to Olney, March 23, 1896, LC, Olney MS.; Tansill, *Purchase of Danish West Indies,* pp. 201-2.

[76] Moore, *Digest,* V, 582.

[77] Welles, *Naboth's Vineyard,* II, 506.

Naturally when the administration took office in 1893 one of its immediate problems was the perennial one of Cuba. The cancellation of the reciprocity agreements forthwith produced economic disaster in the island and that in turn meant revolution against Spain. During the preceding period of prosperity, however, the amount of United States capital had increased to approximately $50,000,000. This had been invested under the Spanish flag and hesitated to endorse any disturbance of relations that might lead to war. Typical of these investors was E. F. Atkins, friend of Secretary of State Olney, who constantly urged that Cuba be given autonomy under Spanish rule. This, he felt, would avoid war yet would give the Cubans satisfaction and the right to key their trade to the United States market. In fact this group, having ready access to the State Department, was also in direct touch and was advising with the Spanish Minister, Dupuy de Lome, in Washington, and had apparently converted him to its ideas.[78]

As conditions became more disturbed in the island the annexationists became more and more active in the United States. The Lodge-Roosevelt group wrote and orated. Chauncey Depew bluntly stated: " . . . this country ought to own Cuba. . . . The United States is too conservative as far as annexation of property is concerned." [79] In Administration circles also there were friends of the idea in the person of the wealthy William C. Whitney and other conservatives of his type. Eager and amply able to support the activities of this powerful group was the Cuban junta

[78] Edwin F. Atkins, *Sixty Years in Cuba. Reminiscences of Edwin F. Atkins* (Cambridge, 1926), pp. 157; 142-3; Portell Vilá, *Historia de Cuba,* III, 134 ff.

[79] Quoted by Portell Vilá, Ill, 127.

in New York with branches in various parts of the country. They collected money and supplies, broadcast propaganda and in general agitated public opinion. True enough, a definite line of cleavage began to develop among the agitators in the fact that the juntas wanted independence and were not willing to endorse annexation to the United States as urged by the annexationists. The public, however, did not make such fine distinctions. It simply heard of mortality rates in Cuba, of taxation abuses and deviltry in general; then blamed the whole situation on the Spanish authorities and endorsed anything that would eliminate them. With the increase of disturbances in the island the number of Spanish troops was increased, health conditions became worse and military expenditures—which were charged against the Cubans—rose until they consumed practically half of all Cuban taxes collected.[80] In turn, the efforts of the juntas increased until at the opening of 1895 they were estimated to have a fund of a million dollars with which to support their activities.[81] Spain felt that the situation would long since have been under control had it not been for support from the United States.[82] The Cuban rebels adopted ruthless methods of destruction of private property, frankly announcing: " there remains no other solution but to triumph, it matters not what means

[80] As for taxation abuses it might be noted that in 1894 Cuba was paying about 27% of all taxes collected for the maintenance of the army and navy in the island, while about 49% went to pay interest on the debt assigned to Cuba by Spain, and less than 3/4% was used for public instruction. French Ensor Chadwick, *Relations of U. S. and Spain,* pp. 403-4.

[81] Benton, *International Law and Diplomacy of the Spanish-American War,* p. 25.

[82] Ferrara, *Last Spanish War,* pp. 35 ff.; Moore, *Digest,* VI, 114-5.

are employed to accomplish this." [83] Business interests in Cuba, of course, resented such procedure and Olney and Cleveland definitely sympathized with them. In an unofficial interview with members of the Cuban junta the Secretary of State was informed by each of them that they were proud to be able to state that they were United States citizens. In answer to direct questions they admitted they had endorsed the destruction and burning of property in Cuba. Olney replied: " Well, gentlemen, there is but one term for such action. We call it arson." [84]

The President, as well as the Secretary of State, was keeping a careful watch on developments.[85] Slowly the leaks through which arms had been shipped to Cuban rebels in spite of the neutrality laws were plugged so that after May, 1896, considerable care and skill were required to avoid detention.[86] In all, seventy-one such expeditions were fitted out, twenty-seven reached their destination, and forty-four failed. Of the latter United States authorities blocked thirty-three, the Spaniards five, storms four, and the British two.[87]

In the island itself, it should be noted, the authorities were most considerate of United States susceptibilities in the handling of cases. Despite the alarming reports current in the yellow journals the fact remained that at the end of 1897 there was not a single United States citizen held as a prisoner in the island. In fact, Benton concludes: " The testimony of American official sources exonerates

[83] Chadwick, pp. 408 ff.

[84] Atkins, p. 214; also pp. 185-6; 233.

[85] Cleveland to Olney, October 8, 1895, LC., Olney MS.

[86] Chadwick, pp. 414-5; Benton, p. 58; Moore, *Digest,* VII, 965-6.

[87] Chadwick, pp. 418-9; Benton, p. 42.

Spain from injustice, and proves her most liberal and conciliatory in the treatment of Americans involved." [88]

In addition to seeing that the application of neutrality laws was tightened, Olney did not hesitate to warn quite sternly those who sought his advice as to unneutral conduct,[89] and when he left office both the Spanish Minister of Foreign Affairs and the Spanish Ambassador at Washington sent most cordial notes and personal good wishes which were cordially reciprocated.[90]

This does not mean that the Administration was living in a sealed vacuum. The public was thoroughly aroused by atrocity stories and was demanding action. Congress responded with resolutions and debates. On June 12, 1895, Cleveland had recognized Cuban insurgency [91] and now the clamor led by the able John Sherman was for the recognition of belligerency at least. As pressure increased and there was a move to force the Administration to act through the passage of a joint resolution directing the recognition of the rebels Cleveland burst out: " If it [the resolution] comes, it will give me an opportunity to tell the American people some plain truths, and d——d if they don't get them." [92] However, opposition leaders at the time were too wise to give the President such an opening.

Conditions in the island were regularly reported by the United States consul, Fitzhugh Lee, who insisted: " There has been no change here in the situation and no prospect,

[88] *Ibid.*, p. 64.

[89] For an example of this see Olney to Massey, June 18, 1895, LC, Olney MS.

[90] Dupuy de Lome to Olney, March 6, 1897, and Olney to Dupuy de Lome, April 1, 1897, *ibid.*

[91] Benton, *op. cit.*, p. 34.

[92] Nevins, *Cleveland,* p. 716.

in my opinion, unless the United States stops this horrible war." [93] Also, one Charles E. Akers writing on stationary carrying the letter-head of *The* [London] *Times,* who gave his Havana address " c/o British Consulate," sent Olney many details of the Spanish army, the condition of the rebels and miscellaneous information, and definitely urged the need for United States intervention as the " only salvation for Cuba." He insisted that if Washington did not intervene some European power would have to do so and the United States would have to protest. The idea of Cuba as an independent republic he frankly could not entertain as a possibility.[94] That full and accurate information was sought is evident from the following letter from Olney to Lee, dated June 29, 1896:

Private and Confidential

My dear General:

Your confidential notes to me regarding the situation in Cuba have been perused by both the President and myself with great interest. They fulfill our anticipations—which were that we should get from you an account of matters as full, intelligent and satisfactory as the difficult circumstances of the case would admit. Please communicate freely in the same way as often as any changes in conditions occur.

I observe that you have hardly been out of Havana and presume the interior of the island will continue to be practically closed to you—so that the knowledge of affairs there will have to be derived second hand, from persons living in the interior and visiting Havana, or writing from there. Nevertheless, from such sources as are available it is quite material to ascertain what sort of civil government and administration, if any, prevail in that large part of the

---

[93] Lee to Olney, February 18, 1897, LC, Olney MS.

[94] Akers to Olney, May 13, 1896 and November 7, 1896, *ibid.*

island which is under the control of the insurgents. Is there any civil government *de facto?* Has it any fixed seat? Are there any elections of legislators or other civil officers? Is there any legislature which convenes and enacts laws? Are the insurgent forces under the control of any such civil government? What does the civil government, if any, do in the way of protecting life, liberty and property? Has it established courts which are actually administering justice and whose judgments are executed by the ordinary civil processes? Does this civil government, if there is any, lay and collect taxes in accordance with general and special laws? Or is each military commander a law unto himself . . . in each particular case? Does this civil government, if there is any, provide any mail service, have any currency, do anything in the way of furnishing roads or of providing for the poor or of supplying the youth of the country with educational facilities? In short, what of the ordinary functions of civil government, if any, does the so-called Cuban Republic exercise? Or is it a mere government on paper? [95]

The line of thought and the wishes of the writer are quite patent from this.

When Congress did take the bit in its teeth and pass a joint resolution recognizing the insurgents and tendering the good offices of the United States to end the trouble on the basis of the independence of the island, the matter was presented to the President by a committee who bluntly informed him that they were about to declare war on Spain. He as bluntly replied that they might declare it but that there would be no war for " I will not mobilize the army." He continued that he was considering the purchase of Cuba for $100,000,000 and that " It would be an outrage to declare war." Incidentally this idea of purchase was entertained for quite some time and there was much reason

[95] Olney to Lee, June 29, 1896, *ibid.*

to feel that Spain would consent.   In fact, McKinley's Minister to Spain, Woodford, later wrote that the Queen had been advised to sell and that he thought she would agree.   However, for some at present unknown reason Day or McKinley, or both, came to the strange conclusion that the United States did not want Cuba, and so ended the matter.[96]   To the Congressional resolution Cleveland responded that it was an opinion only, expressed for no more than advisory purposes and that the handling of foreign relations and the recognition of foreign states was solely a matter for executive decision.

But the constant agitation of the interventionists had begun to have its effects and Mr. Olney at least was showing the strain. He reported to the President on December 7, 1896: " the time may not be far distant when the United States must seriously consider whether its rights and interests as well as its international duties in view of its peculiar relations to the island do not call for some decided change in the policy hitherto pursued." [97]   The good offices of the United States had been offered to Spain as early as April, 1896, in a communication of the Secretary that carried more than a hint of sternness.[98]   Likewise, in his last annual message to Congress the President reviewed the affair carefully and again urged autonomy for the island in no uncertain tones. He stated that patience was about exhausted and that it was quite possible " our obligations to the sovereignty of Spain " might be " superseded by higher obligations." [99]

[96] Shippee and Way, " Day " in Bemis, *Secretaries of State,* IX, 44-5.

[97] Moore, *Digest,* VI, 122.

[98] *Ibid.,* VI, 108-10.   [99] *Ibid.,* VI, 129.

Thus the matter was to carry over to the next administration with both Cleveland and Olney thoroughly disgusted with the jingo press [100] and the thoughtless imperialists who were trying to rush the country into war; but both remained aware enough that the situation was acute. Before leaving the subject of Cuba a few comments are necessary as to the European point of view. There can be no doubt that London was watching the situation carefully, especially since the Venezuelan dispute was steadily approaching the point of crisis. However, the United States Ambassador wrote to Olney, June 17, 1896, that he had just had an interview with Lord Salisbury in which the deplorable conditions in Cuba were discussed and in which the Ambassador remarked that he had " assumed . . . that it would be a matter of indifference to Great Britain whether we were to annex the island or not, to which he at once replied. ' It's no affair of ours [England's]; we are friendly to Spain and should be sorry to see her humiliated, but we do not consider that we have anything to say in the matter whatever may be the course the United States may decide to pursue.' " An independent Cuba the British statesman feared would likely become another Haiti, though he realized it would be difficult to bring it into the United States system. However, he did not attempt to give advice of any kind.[101] And the very fact that he did refrain constituted a much cherished form of recognition.

Another situation is that revealed by the work of Orestes Ferrara, *The Last Spanish War*. He carefully examined the efforts of Spain to bring about an organized European intervention to block the expansion of United States territory or influence at the expense of Spain. It is sufficient for

[100] Nevins, *op. cit.*, p. 744.   [101] James, *Olney*, pp. 240 ff.

this study to remark that the interplay of European rivalries was so keen that after two strenuous efforts the attempt
had to be dropped. Ferrara concludes with the interesting
statement:

authentic documents exist to prove that, although O'Donnell had the memorandum written out and ready for trans-
mittal in July 1896, the Washington government did not
learn of its existence, until considerably later. President
Cleveland's reiteration of the neutrality of the United
States, in his proclamation of July 27, had therefore no
connection whatever with O'Donnell's plan for promoting
European intervention, its purpose being solely to place on
the United States Government the reproach of failing to
take a stand against its citizens giving aid to the Cuban
rebellion.[102]

The remaining major issue of the second Cleveland administration has been so often belabored and discussed that
the facts of the case will be largely taken for granted here,
except for the barest summary. In his annual message to
Congress, December 3, 1894, Cleveland urged the resumption of diplomatic relations by Great Britain and
Venezuela and strongly urged settlement of the dispute by
arbitration saying that this was a means of settlement
" which Great Britain so conspicuously favors in principle
and respects in practice, and which is earnestly sought by
her weaker adversary." On February 22nd following Congress passed a joint resolution seconding the President's
suggestion.[103] By shrewd press-agenting Venezuela was
getting its interpretation of the dispute before the United
States public and imperialists such as Lodge were glad of
new grist for their mill.[104] In the early days of the ad-

---

[102] Ferrara, *Last Spanish War,* p. 31.

[103] Cleveland, *Presidential Problems,* p. 251.

[104] Perkins, pp. 143-51.

ministration Cleveland, Gresham and Ambassador Bayard
at London, were taking much the same cautious and conservative view of the problem that they, and Olney too,
were to practice with regard to Cuba.

The reasons for the later change in the point of view
are obscure. The unconventional Gresham seems to have
begun a study of the case with the possible idea of bringing matters to a head though his wife later declared:
"there was to be no ultimatum as my husband had prepared it [the dispatch]." [105] Be that as it may, Gresham
fell ill and died on May 23, 1895. The President at once
elevated Olney to the headship of the Cabinet. Olney, in
some ways was more popular with the Latin American
diplomats than his predecessor [106] but beyond doubt was a
far more aggressive character. His truculence in the Pull-
man Car Strike had earned him and the administration
bitter criticism and the stock of the Democratic Party was
certainly at a low ebb both because of this and because of
Cleveland's stand on gold and his reported subservience to
the moneyed interests when party success depended on
votes from the West and South. Some would say that this
situation demanded a strong hand on selected foreign issues
so as to recoup the prestige lost at home. Others point out
that Mr. Cleveland was a sternly honest man whose whole
career indicates that he would disdain such a trick—and
the present writer rather subscribes to that interpretation
but he is not so sure but that Mr. Olney might have been

[105] M. Schuyler, "Gresham" in Bemis, *Secretries of State,* VIII,
266; also Perkins, pp. 141-2.

An interesting article published after this study was written is
that of N. M. Blake, "Background of Cleveland's Venezuelan
Policy," *Amer. Hist. Rev.,* XLVII, 259 ff.

[106] James, *op. cit.,* p. 79; Nebins, *op. cit.,* pp. 512-3.

willing for a fortunate bit of party and possibly personal advertising to ensue if events so fell out. The Venezuela authorities in pressing their case had certainly at times resorted to rather " sharp " practices, and for long periods they had been grossly negligent of the areas now so ardently claimed. On the other hand the President had become convinced that Great Britain was merely rendering lip service to the idea of arbitration by agreeing to submit unimportant and extreme claims only for adjudication while it reserved the major portion of the territory rightfully in dispute. This called for the " firm " policy of Olney and the new Assistant Secretary Rockhill, rather than the attitude of the deceased Gresham, Ambassador Bayard and the recent adviser of the State Department, J. B. Moore.[107]

Also it should be remembered that the President and Secretary were under the impression apparently that the protest of Cleveland to the British Foreign Office toward the end of his first administration had been ignored when in reality it had not been delivered at all. Long afterwards (January, 1912) Olney wrote to Secretary of State Knox a letter marked " Personal " in which he complimented Knox on a recent address to the New York State Bar Association and then continued:

The words you quote . . . from the dispatch to Lord Salisbury have been severely criticized on both sides of the Atlantic. They were undoubtedly of the bumptious or-der—as are some other parts of the same communication— and were felt to be so at the time. The excuse for them was that in English eyes the United States was then so com-pletely a negligible quantity that it was believed only words the equivalent of blows would be really effective.[108]

[107] Tansill, *Foreign Policy of Bayard,* p. 732.

[108] Olney to Knox, January 29, 1912, LC., Philander C. Knox MS.

Feeling thus Olney indicted a proposed dispatch to be sent to Great Britain. This was read by Cleveland, admittedly carefully studied, slightly changed and then generally endorsed. It was sent on its fateful way July 20, 1895. Of the expressions " undoubtedly of the bumptious order " one only needs to recall those which asserted that the United States was " practically sovereign " on this continent and its fiat was law upon those subjects in which it interposed, and the one which ended with a thinly veiled threat that sounded like a " do this—or else " attitude. Though the dispatch contained a worthwhile suggestion presented in a statesman-like fashion, this was, unfortunately, the core of the matter and was surrounded by the bombast that smacked strongly of an ultimatum. With the ensuing negotiations as such this study has no interest; suffice it to say that the British rejoined with an immediate delay of four months while active pressure was continued on Venezuela. The response that finally arrived rather casually brushed aside the applicability of the Monroe Doctrine to the case in hand and patronizingly continued in a tone of self-confidence, if not of condescension, that completed the disturbance of the equanimity of the Washington spokesman. Cleveland admitted that he was mad " clear through " and forthwith prepared a statement for Congress, dated December 17, 1895. He again lauded the Monroe Doctrine, asked Congress to authorize him to appoint a commission to determine the proper boundary between the disputants and then to apply the findings of the commission, stating bluntly that he was aware that this might require the use of force. His statement staggered the English-speaking world as two great nations in fundamental ignorance of the issue between them were brought to the brink of war.

At once the best elements in both countries began to work to find a peaceable way out of the impasse.

The clamor of the public was deafening. The Lodge and Roosevelt crowds were hilarious [109] and their raucous cries of "A Daniel come to judgment! A Daniel come to judgment! ", added to the somewhat bewildered joy of the yellow journalists and threatened to sweep the nation into war hysteria overnight. On the contrary there were equally surprised but even more determined protests from sources whose judgment demanded consideration. Ambassador Bayard in London, though discredited with administration leaders, still had considerable influence.[110] The stock exchange and business leaders were greatly perturbed—and it will be remembered that Cleveland was close to them, especially during his second term. In fact, Theodore Roosevelt said: " The antics of the bankers, brokers and anglomaniacs generally are humiliating to a degree. . . . Personally I rather hope the fight will come soon. The clamor of the peace faction has convinced me that this country needs a war." [111] But there was another side to the picture. Professor Burgess' protests against this pseudo-Monroeism appealed to many and some seriously wondered if his suggestion might not have merit when he argued that British dominance of South America might be better for democracy, the region involved, and the United States, than existing conditions.[112] Then there was a protest from a per-

[109] Roosevelt to Olney, December 20, 1895, LC., Olney MS.; Jennie A. Sloan, "Anglo-American Relations and the Venezuela Boundary Dispute," *Hisp. Amer. Hist. Rev.,* XVIII, 490-1.

[110] Perkins, pp. 187-8.

[111] Quoted by Walter Millis, *The Martial Spirit* (Boston and New York, 1931), p. 38.

[112] J. W. Burgess, " The Recent Pseudo-Monroeism," *Pol. Sc. Quar.,* XI, 60-1.

son whom Cleveland and Olney had recently rated as worthy of serious consideration. John Bassett Moore in a letter
to the Post Master General pointed out that the course recently taken by the President and Secretary of State involved the destruction of traditions of the United States
and involvement in numerous quarrels; that the Venezuelan claims were not reasonable and as a result " Instead
of asserting that arbitration is the only reasonable way of
settling the question, I should say that it would be a very
unsatisfactory way of attempting it. . . . " He further
accused Venezuela of trying to make its northern neighbor
a catspaw for its unethical conduct.[113]

Just as the Administration was doubtless indulging in a
period of sober second thinking a not dissimilar process was
being followed in Great Britain, because both of natural
reaction and the arising of a counter-irritant in the South
African situation and the Krueger telegram, to say nothing
of complications in the Far East. The result was a very
conciliatory despatch from the Foreign Office which was far
different from the last response in its tone and which indicated willingness to submit the dispute concerning most of
the region involved to the commission suggested by the
President in his message to Congress. The substantial qualification was made that fifty years' undisputed occupancy of
any area should constitute preemption. This avoided, for the
British, a possibly disastrous compromise decision of the tribunal yet was in line with the private law of both countries.
It saved the face of all parties and provided a way out.
As is well known the whole matter was finally submitted
to an international arbitral court with the United States

[113] Robert McElroy, *Grover Cleveland, the Man and Statesman*
(New York, 1923), II, 184.

acting as a friend of (really on behalf of) Venezuela instead of as arbitrator.[114] The decision rendered was that Great Britain should retain some two-thirds of the disputed area though Venezuela secured control of the important trade route through the mouth of the Orinoco river.

For this study the important fact lies not in the award nor even in the fact that arbitration was agreed to, but in the fact that the great European nation had recognized the right of the United States to speak for Venezuela and to present its case. In other words, Great Britain admitted the sphere of influence of the United States in the whole Caribbean area since Venezuela was the most distant of all the countries bordering that sea. Uncle Sam was pleased to use the term " Monroe Doctrine " and had made something of a fetish of the phrase so John Bull was actually willing to brook the use of the term though it took no stretching of the imagination to realize that this was felt to apply to the Caribbean only and not to the whole New World. In using the term the stubby fingers of John Bull were definitely crossed for regions not specifically within the direct sphere of influence of his New World colleague. On the other hand the term " sphere of influence " caused no qualms in Great Britain; it was one that the great nations of the world were quite familiar with and which they had long since used to explain their conduct in so-called backward quarters of the globe.

The continental nations of France, Germany and others

[114] The arbitral court was composed of two members chosen by the United States Supreme Court (Chief Justice Fuller and Justice Brewer actually named) ; two by the British Supreme Court of Justice (Lord Hershell and Sir Richard Collins named), and F. de Martens chosen by the above four. (Tansill, *Foreign Policy of Bayard*, pp. 775-6.)

simply could not understand all this. They definitely disapproved the rise of a nation in the New World to which they would have to extend the courtesies due to a real equal as a first class power. The excellent study by Stolberg-Wernigerode points out the situation and laments the shortsightedness of Germany during these years. He comments: " Great Britain, by recognizing the Monroe Doctrine in the spring of 1896, took the last decisive step " which would result in an entente of the Anglo-Saxon powers and which would leave Germany out in the cold.[115]

As for the Caribbean countries they could only applaud the actual settlement of the dispute though they had serious misgivings as to the method employed. The Secretary of State had used the term " sovereign on this continent." Just where did that leave them? Was this a father, or the proverbial step-father, who had stepped into the picture? In either case they objected. If it was the step-father they felt they ought to resent him; and before recognizing the father they wanted further proofs of paternity. They felt the least they could do was to request or demand the right of jointly endorsing the so-called Monroe Doctrine so that they would automatically have a voice in its applications. This view was, as already seen, expressed very clearly at the conference attempted at Mexico City but was in fact nullified by the disapproval of the United States.

From this it may be concluded that Cleveland had not played an imperialistic role and his conduct with regard to annexation amply proves the statement. Also he was willing for disputes to be settled by arbitration by this or other countries so long as they were settled peaceably. When it

[115] Stolberg-Wernigerode, *Germany and the U. S. in the Era of Bismarck,* p. 275.

came to the possibility of the use of force by an outsider in any part of the Caribbean, however, another subject had been broached and he had absolutely no intention of allowing anything of the kind if it could be averted. Obviously, consciously or unconsciously, he had reached the conclusion—and the people of the United States were willing to support that conclusion—that this was the United States backyard and it intended to be responsible for international activities therein. Caribbean responsibility had been accepted by the actively non-expansionist administration of Cleveland (and it will be noted that there was no remote suggestion of territorial expansion of the United States itself involved). It remained to be seen what a change of parties in power would bring forth.

Once more in 1896 the American public relieved its pent-up feelings based on distressing domestic conditions with a hectic orgy of emotionalism in the national election. Once more the electorate showed that it was at a loss and for the fourth successive time changed the party affiliation of the president. With such an uncertain domestic support and such a tenuous grasp on power it is not surprising that an executive of the type of William McKinley, whose principles and intentions were good but whose stamina was frankly and openly questioned by members of his own party at the time, finally chose the path pointed out by the obstreperous clamorings of a small group. These men were admittedly trying to use him the while they, behind his back, belabored him as a man with a " chocolate eclair " backbone. However, they were always careful to point out that the path they advocated would lead to national glory and private prosperity, that elusive thing for which the masses had been seeking these many weary years and for which all good politicians had been earnestly hoping while they were in power.

That the President was primarily interested in domestic affairs and party consolidation, as well as the repayment of political debts, was painfully obvious in the selection of his new Secretary of State. John Sherman had for years been a fiery critic of Spain, even though McKinley argued that he wanted to maintain peace with that nation. To make matters worse the Secretary was already reported to be beyond his prime in strength and physical, if indeed not also in mental, ability. All too obviously the appointment was a political one and the Assistant Secretary, John Day, who was later to take active charge for a time, was the man who actually carried the burden of the office through the war. When he went to the peace conference the thoroughly trained and able cultured scholar and imperialist John Hay took his place.

The Republican platform had underwritten all expansionist ideas then current by calling for a reassertion of the Monroe Doctrine " in its full extent "; independence of Cuba; control of the Hawaiian Islands; ownership of the Nicaraguan Canal; purchase of the Virgin Islands; union of all English-speaking peoples of this continent and the withdrawal of the European powers from this hemisphere.[116]

The new President himself doubtless hoped to avoid war and in this he was supported by most of the business men of the nation who wanted peace and who felt that war would disrupt rising prosperity. But the President was also convinced of the advisability of following popular demands and little dreamed of stemming them. No wonder the

[116] Pratt, *Expansionists of 1898*, pp.213-4.

Spanish Minister took leave of Olney with regret.[117] Sherman was convinced that war would soon come with Spain,[118] Theodore Roosevelt was Assistant Secretary of the Navy, and, with Henry Cabot Lodge, had access to headquarters. Clearly, the great need of this group was to make their imperialistic program conform to humanitarian interpretations. If that could be done the people would endorse it, the President would follow suit and all would be happy. True, Spain was sounded out as to the possibility of purchasing Cuba but when the response was in the negative the matter was dropped at once.[119] The autonomists, represented by Atkins in Cuba, were also in touch with the State Department and the President himself (Atkins asserts that he had a long interview with the President and some members of the Cabinet) so there can be no doubt but that the various phases of the problem were presented to the Administration.[120]

The humanitarian feature was emphasized by the message of the President to Congress of May 6, 1897, in which he urged a congressional appropriation of $50,000 for the destitute in Cuba, many of whom were reported to be American citizens. This was followed by a vigorous protest of Sherman to the Spanish Minister dated June 26, 1897, against the "uncivilized and inhumane conduct of the campaign in Cuba." [121] In his annual message to Congress the following December the President said: " I speak not of forcible annexation, for that cannot be thought of.

[117] Dupuy de Lome to Olney, March 21, 1897 [?], LC., Olney MS.

[118] Chadwick, *Relations of U. S. and Spain,* p. 550.

[119] Portell Vilá, *Historia de Cuba,* III, 295-6.

[120] Atkins, *Sixty Years in Cuba,* p. 263.

[121] Quoted by Moore, *Digest,* VI, 131.

That, by our code of morality, would be criminal agression." [122] In truth, the war was a little difficult to get started because of this hesitance and because of the situation which Olney mentioned in a " strictly personal " letter of March 9, 1897, to Rockhill of the State Department in answer to a request for advice as to a detail of Cuban relations. Said Olney: " The truth is . . . Spain, while theoretically not conceding the American contention, practically concedes it in every case of emphatic insistence." [123] 'Twas hard to make war under such conditions especially when the most ardent protests against violations of the laws of humanity by Spanish officials in Cuba met with such barbed retorts as those indulged in by the Spanish Minister of State who with no little pertinence referred to the destruction wrought by the heroes of the Confederate War:

Hunter's and Sheridan's invasion of the valley of the Shenandoah, of which it was said, to show its total ruin, that ' if a crow wants to fly down the valley he must carry his provisions with him ' . . . ; the expedition of General Sherman, that illustrious and respected General [brother of the Secretary of State], through Georgia and South Carolina; the taking of Atlanta and the subsequent expulsion of non-combatants—women and children—and their concentration at remote distances; the shootings at Palmyra; the burning of Columbia; the horrors connected with the treatment of prisoners and peaceable suspects who were confined together in the warehouses and prisons at Richmond and Danville, and, more particularly, in the prisons at Andersonville, where, according to official data, more than twelve thousand perished; and many other incidents of that struggle, . . . which . . . furnish an eloquent, though mournful, example of the distressing but unavoidable severity which accompanies war.[124]

[122] Richardson, *Messages and Papers*, X, 131.
[123] Olney to Rockhill, March 9, 1897, LC., Olney MS.
[124] Quoted by Chadwick, *op. cit.*, p. 500.

Thus did the devil impertinently quote scripture—and the McKinley administration was one that did not enjoy it. In addition word came that there were no United States citizens held as prisoners in Cuba [125] in spite of the popular belief that large numbers were so held as a result of the filibustering expeditions which were known to have gone out.

However, events developed rapidly. There was the publication of the Dupuy de Lome letter which with unfortunate aptness characterized the hesitant nature of McKinley, the minister's unwise newspaper interview, the sinking of the *Maine*, and the constant agitation of the war party whose policy was expressed in a letter of Mahan to Roosevelt. In referring to Hawaii the naval officer said: "Do nothing unrighteous, but as regards the problem, take the islands first and solve the problem afterwards." Roosevelt responded: "I suppose I need not tell you that as regards Hawaii, I take your views absolutely, as indeed I do on foreign policy generally." He continued that he wanted the United States to construct the Nicaraguan canal at once, and that he wanted Spain out of the West Indies. [126] Dennis sums up the matter when he says that "A study of the documents drives home the conviction that the war with Spain was, from the standpoint of technical diplomacy, an unnecessary war," but that it is difficult to see how it could have been averted because of the turgid domestic politics, the awakened nationalism of the time, the humanitarians demanding armed intervention, the property interests in-

---

[125] Woodford to Sherman, December 4, 1897, *Papers Relating to the Foreign Relations of the United States* (Washington, varying dates), 1898, p. 644. (Hereafter cited as "*Foreign Relations*," with year.)

[126] Puleston, *Mahan*, p. 182.

volved in Cuba, the newspapers inflaming an aroused popular passion and a politician as President.[127]

Thus Spanish concessions, reluctantly made, whether in good faith or not, came too late. The President gave Congress the signal in his war message of April 11, 1898, and after technicalities had been cared for the war was on. The expansionists chortled with glee as they envisioned the acquisition of the outlying possessions of the Spanish empire in the Far East and the West Indies as well as miscellaneous naval stations to protect these, with ample justification now for a navy to occupy the stations and to gain prestige the world around. It was in vain that Cleveland wrote to Olney the day after war was declared:

> With all the allowance I can make . . . I cannot avoid a feeling of shame and humiliation. It seems to me to be the same old story of good intentions and motives sacrificed to false considerations of complaisance and party harmony. McKinley is not a victim of ignorance, but of amiable weakness not unmixed with political ambition. He knew, or ought to have known, the cussedness of the Senate and he was abundantly warned against Lee, and yet he has surrendered to the former and given his confidence to the latter.[128]

---

[127] Alfred L. P. Dennis, *Adventures in American Diplomacy, 1896-1906* (New York, 1928), p. 63.

[128] Millis, *op. cit.*, p. 161.

It will be remembered that the Cleveland administration had become quite disgruntled with Mr. Lee as consul-general in Cuba. However, when the new administration came in, Lee apparently became one of its chief advisers. On March 1, 1898, the United States Minister in Spain, Woodford, cabled that Spain was much concerned about the conduct of Mr. Lee in Cuba and considered that he was sending "misleading and untrustworthy" reports to his home government. Acting Secretary of State Day responded: "The President will not consider any proposal to withdraw General Lee. Even a suggestion of his recall at this time would be most un-

Business interests that had looked askance at the expenses and interruptions of war, loyally supported the government and made the best of the situation by demanding as many new possessions and markets as possible; while the humanitarians too saw the silver lining in the opportunity to Christianize the heathen and to assume the White Man's Burden. Further, the incidents of the war in the West Indies proved to all concerned the great need for a trans-isthmian canal and for West Indian naval bases.

In the short days of the actual conflict the United States promptly advanced in Cuba and then proceeded to occupy Puerto Rico. By this time the idea of Cuban autonomy was naturally forgotten and the only question remaining was whether the United States would take it outright, as Spain was now inclined to suggest so as better to protect Spanish investments there than would be possible under a new government, or whether it should be left independent as had been the demand of the United States at the opening of hostilities.

The President showed every desire to keep his hands free. He did not want any recognition of a rebel government that would put his government in the position of having to ask permission for such action as this country might see fit to take.[129] The protocol signed as preliminary to an armistice simply provided that Spain would withdraw immediately from " Cuba, Puerto Rico and other islands under Spanish

---

fortunate from every point of view. Our information and belief is that throughout this crisis General Lee has borne himself with great ability, prudence, and fairness." (Quoted by Moore, *Digest,* VI, 187.)

[129] Jones, *Caribbean and the U. S. since 1900,* p. 26; Moore, *Digest,* VI, 109-10.

sovereignty in the West Indies." [130]   The Caribbean was freed from one of its non-American owners.

The Cuban leaders themselves were not at all sure what the outcome of the situation would be. Many feared that the United States expeditionary force would not return home leaving an independent nation behind; and such a view a study of United States history tended to confirm.[131] Not surprisingly there were those who were willing to use bribery to secure recognition—and there has been a suggestion that some congressmen were not averse to the idea.[132]

The imperialists knew what they wanted: all they could get. On his way to Cuba Rough Rider Theodore Roosevelt (Ex-Secretary of the Navy it will be remembered) had written to Senator Lodge, June 12, 1898: " You must get Manila and Hawaii, you must prevent any talk of peace until we get Porto Rico and the Philippines as well as secure the independence of Cuba." Lodge thus expressed himself on May 24: " Unless I am utterly and profoundly mistaken the administration is now fully committed to the large policy that we both desire "; then on July 23: " I had a long talk with the President before leaving Washington and he was very clear and strong about both Cuba and Porto Rico." [133]

But the general feeling of the nation was that the word and honor of the nation had been pledged and that there were ample spoils to be had elsewhere than in Cuba. The

[130] Benton, *International Law and Diplomacy of Span.-Amer. War*, p. 225.

[131] Guggenheim, *U. S. and Cuba*, pp. 48-9.

[132] Portell Vilá, *op. cit.*, pp. 359 ff.

[133] Roosevelt to Lodge, June 12, 1898, Lodge to Roosevelt, May 19, 1898, and July 23, 1898, Lodge, *Roosevelt-Lodge Correspondence*, pp. 309; 300; 330.

result was a general support of the understanding announced at the opening of the war; i. e., that Cuba was to be an independent nation under the protection of the United States. What such a status would amount to only time could determine. For the moment Cuba was to be an island handled as " foreign territory . . . under the control of the United States. . . . A citizen of Cuba (was) a citizen of a foreign state." [134] Private property was to be respected, and if taken for the use of the army of occupation was to be paid for, while trade was to be interfered with as little as possible. This was conquered territory, but territory " held in trust for the inhabitants." [135]

With Cuban sovereignty in a state of suspended animation what would the conquerer do in the island? The treaty of peace provided simply " The civil rights and political status of the native inhabitants of the territories hereby ceded to the United States shall be determined by the Congress," similarly Washington could determine when and how Cuba would be returned to the inhabitants.[136] Leonard Wood as military governor was put to work on a combined political-sanitation program. With magnificent energy the problems of street sanitation, yellow fever control, disarming of insurgents, calling of a constitutional convention, determination of who could vote, reopening of local courts, truancy problems of reopened schools, ownership problems of church property, and a score of other questions were attacked. Doggerel punsters soon adopted a rhyme that has been translated thus:

---

[134] Benton, *op. cit.,* p. 258.
[135] Moore, *Digest,* VII, 261-3.
[136] Benton, p. 262.

RULES OF THE OFFICES

Don't eat, don't spit;
Don't scratch, don't smoke;
Arrive very early;
Depart almost by night.
There is no time for lunch
Nor anything other than writing [i. e., working]
He who wishes to work here
Is he who wishes to die.[137]

By using three millions of dollars originally appropriated for war purposes the nondescript veterans of the Cuban army were paid and—far more important—demobilized and sent to their homes.[138] This was in spite of the fact that many Cubans wished to hold them under arms so as to have a means by which to bring pressure on the United States to leave the island. Thus the way was cleared but a long range policy had yet to be adopted.

The amazingly short and decisive course of the war had naturally attracted a great deal of attention in Europe. Desperate last minute efforts were made by Spain to secure some kind of aid on the continent. Germany encouraged the idea but felt that France must first be induced to act— and this France declined to do. Queen Victoria personally sympathized with Spain but the officers of her Government felt otherwise and the British people openly applauded the United States victories and took a kind of paternal pride in the resounding naval successes secured. It was a kind of " chip off the old block " feeling of smug enjoyment, especially when there was no danger of the conquests inter-fering with British empire needs. In fact Chamberlain, May 23, 1898, commented in an address at Birmingham:

---

[137] Fitzgibbon, *Cuba and the U. S.,* p. 31, note.
[138] Chapman, *Hist. of Cuban Republic,* pp. 102-3.

I don't know what the future has in store for us; I don't know what arrangements may be possible with us; but this I do know and feel, that the closer, the more cordial, the fuller, and the more definite these arrangements are, with the consent of both peoples, the better it will be for both and for the world—and I go even so far as to say that, terrible as a war may be, even war itself would be cheaply purchased if, in a great and noble cause, the Stars and Stripes and the Union Jack should wave together over an Anglo-Saxon alliance.[139]

Henry White, United States Ambassador at Berlin, analyzed the situation with remarkable accuracy when he reported on January 7, 1898, that there had probably never been a time when continental ill-will had been as strong as then, but that the numerous cross-currents of European politics and interests were such that he did not think that a coalition could or would be formed against the United States.[140] A threatened protest by foreign ministers at Washington was softened and discounted when either Pauncefote's " experience and judgment " or Balfour's " instinct," or both, came to the rescue and Britain formally withdrew from the threatened movement.[141] It must be remembered that the British leaders had Gibraltar to consider, Russia to watch, Germany to offset, as well as home opinion to bear in mind In view of all this it is not surprising that Chamberlain was able to sway the balance of power in favor of doing nothing and letting the war take its course while the United States acquired the spoils of victory. Beyond doubt, in reaching such a conclusion the influence of the able and popular John

[139] Quoted by Dennis, *op. cit.*, p. 122.

[140] Ferrara, *op. cit.*, p. 97.

[141] J. L. Garvin, *Life of Joseph Chamberlain* (London, 1932-4), pp. 298-300; Mowat, *Life of Lord Pauncefote,* pp. 218-9; Ferrara, *op. cit.,* pp. 129-30; 144 ff.

Hay, Ambassador at London, must be given real credit.[142] He was in close touch with Chamberlain and may even have inspired some references in the address mentioned above.

The last specific effort to intervene seems to have resulted in the German inspiration back of the Papal offer of mediation. When Spain absolutely refused to consider Cuban independence, Germany washed its hands of the proposition. The Spanish Ambassador at Berlin was warned that there was no real prospect of intervention in Spain's behalf, and reported that he had been informed by the German Foreign Minister Bülow:

You are isolated, because everybody wants to be pleasant to the United States, or, at any rate, nobody wants to arouse America's anger; the United States is a rich country, against which you simply cannot sustain a war; I admire the courage Spain has shown, but I would admire more a display of practical common sense.[143]

Meanwhile, what of this " nigger in the woodpile," Germany in the Caribbean, that was so perturbing to the statesmen of the time? On every side the matter was mentioned with bated breath, and carried the implication of deep and dark chicanery and mysterious plots. That Germany had taken the initiative in a number of the efforts made to organize a coalition in Europe hostile to the United States there can be little doubt, and that its emissaries had dabbled in the Philippines is likewise well known.[144] They had resented the Monroe Doctrine and scoffed at it as " a spectre that would vanish in plain daylight " and as a policy

[142] Stephen Gwynn, editor, *Letters and Friendships of Sir Cecil Spring Rice* (Boston and New York, 1929), I, 253.

[143] Ferrara, p. 127. See also *ibid.,* pp. 113 ff.

[144] Grand Admiral Von Tirpitz, *My Memoirs* (New York, 1919), I, 241-2.

that was inconsistent with United States expansion in the Far East.[145] Not surprisingly, John Hay in England and Roosevelt, Lodge and others on this side became seriously worried.[146]

Even the level headed Elihu Root commented in a public address on April 27, 1900: " No man who carefully watches the signs of the times, can fail to see that the American people will within a few years have either to abandon the Monroe Doctrine, or fight for it, and we are not going to abandon it." [147] However, the Kaiser frankly said that he thought that Britain was over-anxious for an alliance with the United States and was likely to be " sold short " by the New World nation which only wanted friends while the war was on.[148] As for German hopes of what would happen in the New World there can be little doubt, for the Wilhelmstrasse felt that this was the largest and most attractive region of the globe still in the control of weak governments and hence more or less available for conquest. But at the moment it was far too shrewd to become implicated in serious plots or plans. The Berlin archives have been thoroughly searched with negative results in this connection. If any instances arose where pressure or force could be applied to secure recognition of German might or prominence, both would be used to the full, but the German navy was needed elsewhere, the European situation was too threatening, and all German officialdom could do was to grumble at the monstrosity of a thinly veiled protectorate

[145] Gwynn, op. cit., I, 248; Perkins, pp. 301-3.

[146] Dennis, Adventures in American Diplomacy, p. 98.

[147] Quoted by Perkins, p. 307.

[148] G. P. Gooch and Harold Temperley, British Documents on the Origins of the War, 1898-1914 (London, 1926-36), I, 34-5.

under the name of the Monroe Doctrine which it felt was merely a way of keeping Europe out of the New World until the United States had become strong enough to gobble up all the desirable areas for itself. As Spring-Rice wrote, to Roosevelt, European nations were in the position where each "would like someone else to bell the cat."[149] And how Roosevelt must have later enjoyed feeling that he was the cat!

The Administration in Washington was, at least for the time being, fully converted to the principle of imperalism, and humanitarian considerations were not too carefully weighed in every case. The President wanted the "full results of victory," and was none too enthusiastic even about such a self-denying ordinance as the Open Door policy in China which Hay was endorsing. As Hay told John W. Foster, he had discussed the idea with the President who replied: "I don't know about that. May we not want a slice, if it is to be divided?"[150]

In the New World program there was also a definite swing away from the program of reciprocity treaties. Under the Dingley Tariff at least four such treaties were signed for the Caribbean (for Nicaragua, Santo Domingo, the Danish Islands and the British Islands) but they had been blocked in the Senate in spite of Presidential approval.[151] But regardless of this business interests were investing large sums in Mexican petroleum and mines, in tropical fruits (the United Fruit Company was organized in 1899 with an

[149] Gwynn, I, 233.
[150] Foster, *Diplomatic Memoirs*, II, 257.
[151] Tariff Commission, *Reciprocity and Commercial Treaties*, pp. 29-30.

authorized capital of $20,000,000), and in other countries.[152] And the holders of such investments favored a strong foreign policy.

The public felt the same way. Nothing succeeds like success and the public was delighted at the new far-flung empire of the Republic. The Washington *Post* editorialized:

A new consciousness seems to have come upon us—the consciousness of strength—and with it a new appetite, the yearning to show our strength. It might be compared with the effect upon the animal creation of the taste of blood.

Ambition, interest, land-hunger, pride, the mere joy of fighting, whatever it may be, we are animated by a new sensation. We are face to face with a strange destiny.

The taste of empire is in the mouth of the people even as the taste of blood in the jungle. It means an imperial policy, the Republic, renascent, taking her place with the armed nations.[153]

One shrewd observer remarked:

Most striking of all, perhaps, is the way in which we have forgotten what we set out to accomplish and have become engrossed in new interests. Starving reconcentrados and struggling Cubans are crowded quite into the background of our imagination to make room for our own larger prospects and ambitions.[154]

Simultaneously, the Bureau of the American Republics was growing and by 1899 could boast for the first time that all the republics south of the United States were represented

---

[152] Samuel Crowther, *Romance and Rise of the Tropics* (Garden City, 1929), p. 185; Cleona Lewis, *America's Stake in International Investments* (Washington, 1928), p. 588.

[153] Quoted by Weinberg, *Manifest Destiny*, p. 289.

[154] H. H. Powers, "The War and Manifest Destiny," *The Annals*, XII, 173-4.

in it.[155] Plans were also going forward for a new Pan-American conference to meet in 1901—and this the United States was endorsing. Europe might look on with latent suspicion, fearing United States domination of the meeting,[156] but the fact was that this nation was not using its opportunity to anything like its full value. The Latins in their fear of the great power to the north with its insatiable appetite, were sending representatives to the Bureau and conferences but were spiritually huddling together in something that closely resembled fright. Unfortunately, the State Department under Mr. Hay was hardly calculated to inspire much of a change in this attitude. Hay cordially disliked and bitterly resented pressing unsavory claims on Latin America, and could protest angrily that senators were besieging him to fill diplomatic vacancies in posts to the southward with their friends whom they appeared to be combing the Keeley cures to find for the posts. But still the fact remains that Hay and his associates themselves too often dismissed the Latin American representatives at Washington as " Dagoes " while with almost supercilious disdain they looked to Europe for culture and civilization.[157] Misunderstanding and apprehension were the inevitable results of such an attitude.

While Franklin H. Giddings was boasting of the inevitability of United States expansion and was crying out for tropical possessions,[158] and while Henry Adams was coming

---

[155] Message of McKinley to Congress, December 5, 1899, *Foreign Relations,* 1899, p. xxxiii.

[156] J. Fred Rippy, *Latin America in World Politics,* p. 112.

[157] Tyler Dennett, *John Hay, from Poetry to Politics* (New York, 1934), p. 264.

[158] F. H. Giddings, " Imperialism?," *Pol. Sc. Quar.,* XIII, 586; 599-600.

to the conclusion that his nation would " sooner or later have to police " the West Indies,[159] the State Department had again become involved in the question of the purchase of the Virgin Islands, or Danish West Indies. Lodge still urged the idea and McKinley wanted them but the War delayed consideration [160] though more or less unsavory activities in connection with them and involving the ubiquitous and somewhat questionable Captain Walter von Christmas Dirckinck-Holmfeld continued spasmodically.[161]

Meanwhile in Haiti the exorbitant demands of Germany because of the alleged abuse of one of its nationals had created serious antagonisms and caused repercussions in the United States. However, the demands were met and the issue passed.[162] When a protectorate by the northern neighbor was suggested to prevent such happenings in the future Secretary Sherman responded in January, 1898, that such a proposal was contrary to the practice of his country and quite inadvisable.[163] Probably the rising complications with Spain in part accounted for the restraint expressed. Certain it is that when a kind of extra-territorial court was proposed to settle suits of foreigners in the island, Secretary John Hay disapproved the idea as " an essential interference with the sovereign rights of Hayti." [164] On the other hand United States business interests were receiving protection for their activities in Haiti. When that Republic threatened to reduce the value of bonds held by United States citizens the act was

[159] Henry Adams, *Education of Henry Adams* (Boston and New York, 1918), pp. 363-4.
[160] Transill, *Purchase of Danish West Indies*, pp. 215; 216, note.
[161] *Ibid.,* pp. 221 ff.
[162] Moore, Digest, VI, 474-5; Tansill, *op. cit.,* pp. 379-80.
[163] Moore, *Digest;* VI, 475-6.
[164] Dennis, *Adventures in Amer. Diplomacy,* p. 278.

protested as were efforts to charge discriminatory fees for the licensing of business concerns of Yankees.[165] Also, in at least one case a claim for damages by United States citizens against the Haitian Republic was submitted to the arbitration of ex-Secretary of State, William R. Day, in 1899.[166]

The widespread fear throughout the Caribbean of an overwhelming United States victory in the war with Spain was nowhere better illustrated than in the Dominican Republic. In spite of the harsh treatment accorded Haiti by Germany just at this time the Dominicans actually applied to that country for intervention to protect them against the United States and as an inducement offered the cession of a naval base to Germany. The Foreign Secretary cabled his ambassador at Washington to know what the local reaction would be to such a step. The response was that it would make the " worst conceivable impression " and that the step should only be taken after careful consideration of the inevitable consequences.[167] The matter was dropped, for Germany did not want trouble with the leader of the New World, as has already been stated. The Dictator Heureaux was reaching the end of his popularity, his funds and his career so he again approached Washington with a proposal for the lease of Samaná Bay, and finally for a direct protectorate.[168] However, the northern republic had all the new complications on its hands in 1898 and 1899 that it wanted and so the suggestions were not followed up.

[165] Moore, *Digest*, V, 730-1; VI, 729.
[166] *British and Foreign State Papers* (London, 1841–), XCII, 461-3.
[167] Tansill, *op. cit.*, p. 396.
[168] Powell to Hay, September 1, 1899, *Foreign Relations*, 1899, pp. 247-8; Welles, *Naboth's Vineyard*, II, 528-34.

On the mainland there was general peace and prosperity in relations with Mexico. That republic remained strictly neutral during the war and had sometimes been accused of very strict applications of its neutrality laws, but there could be no complaint of the matter.[169] Friendly amenities were exchanged by business men and officials, the Mexican Government appropriated $30,000 for the relief of sufferers of the Galveston Flood in 1900 [170] and the United States paid indemnities for Mexican citizens lynched north of the Río Grande.[171]   When an over-enthusiastic United States minister in Guatemala expressed himself too freely on a local boundary dispute with Mexico a prompt and sharp reprimand was sent from the State Department.[172] Thus matters continued with mutual satisfaction.

Farther southward, in Central America, the policy of the United States was to avoid all complications, at least until emergencies arising from the war were over. The outstanding question that could not be much longer avoided was the demand for something to be done about a canal. The actual negotiations involved, however, belong predominantly to the subject of Imperialism by means of Diplomacy and so will be discussed in the next chapter.

In local disorders and revolutions in Venezuela the northern republic wished to have no part. Caution was displayed in recognizing the rising star of General Cipriano Castro [173] but finally on November 8, 1899, John Hay sent the fol-

---

[169] *British and Foreign State Papers,* XC, 370; Benton, *op. cit.,* p. 394.

[170] Callahan, *Amer. Policy in Mex. Relations,* p. 445.

[171] Moore, *Digest,* VI, 851-2.

[172] *Ibid.,* VI, 30-1.

[173] *Ibid.,* I, 153-4.

lowing cable to Mr. Loomis, United States Minister at Caracas:

If the provisional government is effectively administering government of nation and in position to fulfil international obligations, you will enter into de facto relations.[174]

This was done on the 20th. Efforts of the Minister to bring about a substantial loan to provide for refunding operations and to be guaranteed by a limited customs control again came to nothing between 1898 and 1900, apparently because the bankers were not yet awake to the possibilities of such investments, or because the State Department was not endorsing the venture. Facts are as yet uncertain in the affair.[175]

In truth the war had brought the United States an overseas empire of some proportions and varied complications. The result was an enormous increase of pride and of a sense of self-importance. But the necessity to protect that empire was obvious so further obligations were not immediately sought after. Wars cost money and a sense of caution, plus the indisputable fact that the chief rival in Central America was the doughty Great Britain supported by the Clayton-Bulwer treaty, led to the sensible conclusion that imperialism via diplomacy could well be employed. Publicists were fond of sweeping generalizations about a world empire and world responsibilities, but the fact remained that the immediate cause of the war had been a Caribbean problem and most of the ensuing problems were to center in the same area.

[174] Hay to Loomis, November 8, 1899, *Foreign Relations,* 1899, p. 809.
[175] Rippy, *Caribbean Danger Zone,* p. 49.

Chapter III

IMPERIALISM VIA DIPLOMACY: ASSUMPTION OF
NEW POSITIONS; CANAL

Once more the position of the chief actors on the stage must be noted as the scene opens on the continuation of the expansion drama. McKinley was assassinated and Theodore Roosevelt became President in 1901. With a queer mixture of boyish enthusiasm, Don Quixotism, and the bullying of the adolescent the new executive eagerly seized the idea from Darwin that certain races—especially his own— were superior, hence had a God-given duty to rule the less well endowed. Most fortunately for the nation over which he presided there had already been called to the State Department that scholarly, lovable, imperialist by conviction but humanitarian by instinct, John Hay, who was also a thoroughly trained diplomat. He it was who would soften some of the harshest blows, and direct some of the otherwise promiscuous strokes of the Roosevelt Big Stick. Then, just at the end of the period covered by this chapter, after a thorough apprenticeship in the War Department where he had been called to organize the new found dependencies of the United States, Elihu Root became Secretary of State upon the death of John Hay.

Roosevelt was the schoolboys' hero, for his glamor so bedazzled the eyes that his ruthlessness was the less noticeable to the casual observer. Hay possessed the additional element of pity but dwelt in a cold, aloof plane of conscious superiority and dealt with the affairs of Caribbean diplomacy with an attitude of condescension. Elihu Root, however, with his splendidly trained legal brain, brought a fellow feeling and a spirit of actual cooperation into the dealings of the State Department with the Latin American members of the diplomatic corps for the first time in recent history.

For the United States, priority in the Caribbean was a definite fact but it was necessary to secure further European recognition of the fact. As it happened two events at the opening of the new century went far to provide the recognition desired: the Hay-Pauncefote treaty and the Venezuela debt settlement.

The Hay-Pauncefote treaty was a most satisfactory arrangement and the natural outgrowth of time although when the arrangements were finally completed there was considerable reluctance on the one hand and much pride on the other. Fortunately the British were forced to admit that the conditions under which the Clayton-Bulwer treaty had been signed no longer existed: the relative financial and naval strength of the contracting powers had changed; the possessions of at least one of them had greatly increased in the Caribbean and the possessions of the other had relatively declined in that area while they had greatly increased in other parts of the world. In fact, Ambassador White reported that Lord Salisbury told him that this region was of "comparatively little importance to England now that they [the English] have the Suez Canal." [1]

It will be remembered that the old Clayton-Bulwer treaty had provided that any canal constructed through the isthmian region was to be a joint British-United States enterprise.

[1] Dennett, *John Hay*, p. 249.

The blundering rough-shod methods of Blaine had appealed to the egotism of some but did not appeal to those who took pride in considering themselves bound by both the spirit and the letter of their international obligations and to whom repudiation of a treaty had an ugly sound. Also the idea that the treaty had lapsed through inapplicability was not too convincing so President Hayes' earlier suggestion of securing release from the treaty by negotiation was again seriously considered now that the people of the United States had become convinced that the acquisition of a canal route and the construction of the waterway had become a necessity of their new empire.[2]

Here was the very kind of situation that most appealed to John Hay. The chance of negotiating with his good friends and doughty opponents, the British, on a matter of world wide significance to both nations on the basis of strategy and trade, the while parallel negotiations had to be carried on with the annoying and worrisome little Central American countries appealed to his sense of dexterity. It was the very field for a statesman and worthy of his mettle. To add a further filip for the taste, or spice for the wine, was the fact that Great Britain was inclined to connect the settlement with the troublesome Canadian boundary dispute, thus clearing the boards of both complications at the same time. Professor R. B. Mowat claimed that Britain was especially reluctant to add the substantial advantage of an isthmian canal to the United States navy until it was certain that war, which was considered by some as imminent over

[2] L. M. Keasbey, "Terms and Tenor of the Clayton-Bulwer Treaty," *The Annals*, XIV, 22-3 G. L. Rives, "Problems of an Inter-Oceanic Canal," *Pol. Sc. Quar.*, XIV, 201 ff.; Mowat, *Lord Pauncefote*, pp. 267-8.

the Canadian boundary dispute, was completely averted.[3]
To add to the complications was the rising pride of Canada
that insisted nothing be done by the Mother Country in the
settlement of the boundary without Canadian approval—and
that was very difficult to secure. Finally, however, Canada
agreed, and by a judicious mixture of delays and pressure
the two projects were separated.[4]

On December 7, 1898, the question of ownership of the
canal was formally opened by the State Department in a
communication to Ambassador White at London. On the
22nd White reported that this had been cordially received
and added: " I do not believe if it [the canal] is to be open
to all nations on equal terms that there will be any serious
difficulty in effecting an agreement satisfactory to both
nations." [5] McKinley himself was anxious to bring matters
to a conclusion and in his annual message to Congress
stated:

All these circumstances [concerning the Nicaraguan Canal]
suggest the urgency of some definite action by the Congress
at this session if the labors of the past are to be utilized and
the linking of the Atlantic and Pacific oceans by a practical
waterway is to be realized. That the construction of such a
maritime highway is now more than ever indispensable to
that intimate and ready intercommunication between our
eastern and western seaboards demanded by the annexation

[3] *Ibid.*, pp. 277-8.
[4] Allan Nevins, *Henry White. Thirty Years of American Diplomacy* (New York and London, 1930), pp. 145-6; Dennett, *op. cit.*, p. 238; Mowat, *Diplomatic Relations of Great Britain and the U. S.*, p. 287.
[5] White to Hay, December 22, 1898, *Diplomatic History of the Panama Canal. Correspondence . . .* (Senate Document No. 474, 63d cong., 2d sess.), p. 3. (Hereafter cited as *Dip. Hist. of Pan. Canal.*)

of the Hawaiian Islands and the prospective expansion of our influence and commerce in the Pacific, and that our national policy now more imperatively than ever calls for its control by this Government, are propositions which I doubt not the Congress will duly appreciate and wisely act upon.[6]

Such a blunt statement of the case aroused enthusiastic comment in the United States but was unfavorably received in Great Britain where popular reaction to any retirement of the Union Jack, unless a careful educational program had proved its advisability, was sure to be disapproved.[7] Meanwhile Congress followed the lead of the President and threatened to take the bit in its teeth.[8]

It is not pertinent here to go into a detailed discussion of the negotiations that followed. Hay had a real feeling for the British mentality and thought processes at the same time that he was determined to secure this great boon for his own people. He was ably supported by Ambassador Joseph H. Choate at London and Elihu Root who was to be his own successor in the State Department. Lord Salisbury, Lord Lansdowne and Sir Edward Grey in London, and the British representatives at Washington, Lord Pauncefote and James Bryce, were likewise men who knew the world, diplomacy, and John Hay as a man. The result of the negotiations was the document known as the First Hay-Pauncefote treaty. This amended the old Clayton-Bulwer agreement and authorized the United States to construct, manage and control the proposed canal. The waterway was to be neutralized and open both in peace and war,[9] while foreign powers were to

---

[6] *Foreign Relations,* 1898, pp. lxxi-lxxii.

[7] Mowat, *Pauncefote,* p. 272.

[8] Dennett, *Hay,* pp. 251-2.

[9] *Ibid.,* pp. 250-1.

be invited to subscribe to the treaty in a kind of joint guarantee.

When the document was sent to the Senate for its consideration the protests began. Two points of attack were that the old treaty had not been expressly abrogated, hence could still be a nuisance, and that the joint guarantee arrangement would provide an entrance into New World affairs for any country that wanted to meddle therein.[10] Likewise there were those who wanted to fortify the canal. True enough most of the Central American powers through their Ministers expressed sincere approval of the idea of neutralization rather than of fortification,[11] and some military men pointed out that the defense of the canal would be based on naval control of the approaches and not on defense works actually placed on the waterway.[12] However, public opinion did not hesitate and senatorial response to the question was equally prompt. Both demanded a more specific statement than this vague document that tried to make an old, admittedly outworn treaty fit an entirely new situation.

Much to Hay's chagrin the treaty was returned to the State Department and negotiations had to be resumed, taking into consideration the Senate amendments that the Clayton-Bulwer treaty be cancelled and that other nations be not invited to adhere to the convention. To abrogate the old treaty formally would be something of a shock to British public opinion, but after all it had become rather accus-

[10] See Roosevelt to Hay, February 18, 1900, in William Roscoe Thayer, *Life and Letters of John Hay* (Boston and New York, 1915), II, 339-41.

[11] *Ibid.*, II, 224.

[12] Peter C. Hains, "An Isthmian Canal from a Military Point of View," *The Annals*, XVII, pp. 397 ff.

tomed to the idea by this time and the fact was that the action was so patently desirable to obviate future difficulties that there was not too much opposition to it. The question of fortification was more serious for it was one thing for Britain to give up its right to half control and something else again, even on paper, for it to allow such an important waterway of the world's trade to be fortified, possibly against British trade itself. After much discussion it was decided to resort to a " diplomatic " treatment of the matter by simply providing that the United States might maintain such military police along the canal as might be needed to protect it from lawlessness and disorder.[13] The provision as to neutralization, of course, no more took away from the United States the right to defend that canal than did the neutralization of Belgium and Switzerland take away their right to defend themselves from aggression.[14] The omission of the definite statement was understood not to handicap the United States for the reason that for generations it had been the proud boast of Englishmen that " a man's house is his castle " and that he had a right to defend his own.

McKinley had continued to press the matter in his annual message of 1899 [15] and with his death the accession to the presidency of Roosevelt materially strengthened the demands for revision. This was accomplished much as desired by the Senate and the finished treaty submitted to that body once more.[16]

In passing it is interesting to note that the negotiators

[13] Dennett, *op. cit.*, p. 262.

[14] Cf. Arias, *The Panama Canal*, pp. 132; 143.

[15] *Foreign Relations*, 1899, p. xvii.

[16] Hay to Cullom, December 12, 1901, *Dip. Hist. Pan. Canal*, pp. 53 ff.

thought that they were providing for a Nicaraguan canal and not for one at Panama. Hay wrote to Choate a " confidential " letter of September 29, 1901, in which he said:

I think it hardly conceivable that any other route than Nicaragua will be chosen. The House of Representatives has declared for it by a vote of two to one, and the Senate is apparently of the same mind; but whatever route shall be chosen I think our draft of treaty pledges us to adopt the principle of neutralization therein set forth, as you will observe that no particular route is mentioned.

And again on October 2nd in a " confidential " communication:

Our intention is that the treaty shall cover all isthmian routes, and we consider that this object is attained by our draft. I am authorized by the President to say this.[17]

One final comment must be made as to why the United States was so surprisingly successful in obtaining its desires in both the canal negotiations and the Canadian boundary settlement. Certainly the British statesmen were not of the kind to be at all " softened up " by the Rooseveltian bluff or the bombast with which he approached the latter problem. On the other hand it is quite surprising that the United States showed so little interest in the efforts of the Boers who were struggling against such heavy odds in South Africa when this nation had always boasted of its aid to the oppressed. The fact is that each nation was primarily interested in that which most nearly touched it rather than in more abstract principles and in distant problems. As Dennis says:

---

[17] Hay to Choate, September 29, 1901, and October 2, 1901, *ibid.*, p. 45.

All of these matters [problems as to China, Canadian disputes and Central American problems] were in progress at
the same time as the Boer war and each was of far greater
importance to the United States than the South African
question. Each of them was settled to the advantage of the
United States, which would have been impossible had
America acted in any belligerent way in aid of the Boers.[18]

The other major Caribbean problem that involved European nations was the Venezuela Debt controversy. During
the last few years the control of the dictator Castro had become more and more complete. Foreign governments had
become restless and even the United States had been forced
to send a curt reprimand in connection with the abuse of a
consular officer.[19] The United States Minister at Caracas
had confidentially reported, January 26, 1901:

> The talk about the constitution is bosh. It is used as a
> convenience. When either it or the law can be quoted to
> advantage they are brought forward and referred to with a
> good imitation of solemn pride. When the constitution
> stands in the way of any course the Government desires to
> pursue, it is remorselessly and regularly ignored. This is not
> a constitutional government. General Castro is a dictator,
> and does pretty much as he pleases.[20]

As is well known the basis of the trouble was the fact
that the Dictator Castro was refusing on various pretexts to
pay or approach reasonable settlement of many foreign
claims. That many were grossly padded is obvious from the
fact that they amounted to nearly 188,000,000 *bolivars* while
the arbitral court awarded less than 33,000,000 *bolivars*

---

[18] Dennis, *Adventures in Amer. Diplomacy*, p. 130.
[19] Hay to Loomis, June 7, 1900, *Foreign Relations*, 1900, p. 952.
[20] Quoted by Howard C. Hill, *Roosevelt and the Caribbean*
(Chicago, 1927), p. 108.

(The *bolivar* being worth slightly less than twenty cents).[21]

Since so much of the discussion that followed revolved around the German claims it might be well once more to examine the extent to which Germany had evolved a New World and Caribbean policy. At the time of the Venezuela Boundary Dispute the semi official *Norddeutsche Allgemeine Zeitung* probably expressed the opinions of many German leaders when it said:

And now England willingly acknowledges the Monroe Doctrine. . . . We wish, however, to state right here that England stands perfectly isolated in the establishment of this precedent. Germany at least will never permit a foreign power to interfere if she finds it necessary to defend German interests in South and Central America.[22]

And Bismarck's protests and sputterings about an international " impertinence " are well known.

However, the fact was that Germany found its rivalry with Great Brtain was becoming increasingly acute and actually serious, hence felt it advisable to cultivate the leading nation of the New World. Early in 1901 rumors reached the State Department that Germany was about to acquire Margarita Island on the coast of Venezuela. April 10th Hay instructed the United States chargé at Berlin to notify the Foreign Office that in view of the well known and long established policy of the United States he was to " intimate, with like discretion and informality but with distinctness, that any attempted realization of the scheme would be a source of concern to this government, if not tending to the embarrassment of the cordial and frank relations we are so

[21] Jones, *The Caribbean since 1900*, p. 233, gives a list of these claims and awards by countries.

[22] Quoted by Rippy, *Latin Amer. in World Politics*, p. 144.

desirous to maintain with the German Empire." [23] The matter was dropped with no German aggression but Roose-velt, about to become president, was writing to Lodge urg-ing a stronger army and navy because of danger from Germany.[24]

And this was just as the Venezuela Debt affair was com-ing to a head. December 11, 1901, Germany notified the State Department of its determination in a promemoria which outlined its position but specifically disclaimed any intention of " acquisition or of permanent occupation of Venezuelan territory." [25] Then a year was allowed to lapse before anything more was done. Count Von Bülow, the German Chancellor, was ready to act but the Kaiser was apparently aware of the suspicion in the United States and determined to cultivate the New World power by sending his brother on a good-will tour; [26] something of a pre-view of the custom that was to become such a popular sport for political leaders who yearned for a Latin-American tour a quarter of a century later.

The aim of this journey was, in the main, to please the Americans and win their sympathies. . . . Nor was the Prince to speak on his own initiative of conditions in Cen-tral and South America, and on no account to let any German aspirations in regard to these countries to come to light. If the Americans displayed uneasiness on the sub-ject of German plans to gain a foothold in these regions, the Prince could assuage all such fears by pointing to the peacefulness of our policy and the many other urgent tasks

[23] Joshua Ruben Clark, *Memorandum on the Monroe Doctrine* (Senate Document No. 114, 71st cong., 2d sess.) (Washington, 1930), p. 174.

[24] Roosevelt to Lodge, March 27, 1901, in Lodge, *Roosevelt-Lodge Correspondence*, pp. 484-5.

[25] Jones, *op. cit.*, p. 220.   [26] Hill, *op. cit.*, p. 113.

that demanded our attention elsewhere in the world, while dismissing thoughts of military conquest as quite absurd.[27]

It is extremely doubtful if this " pulled any wool " over the eyes of such an experienced diplomat as John Hay. Would it not rather tend to confirm his already aroused suspicions? As for the President, he went through the proper social amenities but in his own words felt that he had been engaged in " teaching the Kaiser to ' shinny on his own side of the line ' " [28] from the time he entered the White House. That he was a bit disingenuous in all this appears from a letter of October 11, 1901, to Baron H. S. von Sternburg, soon to be German Ambassador at Washington:

I most earnestly desire to have Germany and the United States work hand in hand. I regard the Monroe Doctrine as being equivalent to the open door in South America. That is, I do not want the United States or any European power to get territorial possessions in South America but to let South America gradually develop on its own lines, with an open door to all outside nations, save as the individual countries enter into individual treaties with one another.[29]

During the year 1902 matters steadily approached a crisis. In the disturbances then in progress between Colombia and Venezuela Great Britain had become involved in serious controversies about English vessels trading with the troubled areas.[30] In May Germany was demanding set-

[27] *Memoirs of Prince Von Bülow. . . . From Secretary of State to Imperial Chancellor, 1897-1903* (Boston, 1931), I, 660-1.

[28] Henry F. Pringle, *Theodore Roosevelt* (London, 1932 and 1934), p. 288.

[29] Joseph Bucklin Bishop, *Theodore Roosevelt and his Time Shown in his own Letters* (New York, 1920), I, 158.

[30] *The Venezuelan Arbitration before the Hague Tribunal, 1903* . . . (Senate Document No. 119, 58th cong., 3d sess.) (Washington, 1905), pp. 515-89.

tlement of claims but suggesting arbitration. Venezuela responded that it was busy with an insurrection at the moment and insisted that the cases at issue be settled in its own courts. On July 29 Great Britain telegraphed a vigorous protest at Venezuelan treatment of half a dozen British vessels and at the deportation of British subjects and threatened to " take such steps as may be necessary to obtain . . . reparation " therefor. Venezuela, felt London, was only stalling for time.[31] Italy, meanwhile, was also protesting abuse of its properties and nationals and asked Great Britain to make the undertaking of a settlement a joint proposition.[32] The British, not too long suffering where their commercial interests were involved, determined to take matters in hand firmly. So, with Germany determined that no one should get ahead of it and Italy anxious to get its share, the intervention was launched.[33]

Great Britain had really taken the initiative but the Germans were constitutionally inclined to use forceful methods and so promptly agreed to the British suggestion of a war blockade instead of a peace blockade (the Italians said " me too ") but hastened to reassure the United States that this was as far as they intended to go.[34] Lord Lansdowne in the House of Lords gave similar assurances that the British had no intention of landing an expeditionary force or of occupying territory.[35] In truth, a reading of the

[31] *Ibid.,* pp. 613-4; 127.

[32] Hill, *op. cit.,* p. 116.

[33] Von Tirpitz, *Memoirs,* I, 242-4; *Venezuelan Arbitration,* pp. 1166-7.

[34] Tower to Hay, December 14, 1902, *Foreign Relations,* 1903, p. 421.

[35] White to Hay, December 16, 1902, *ibid.,* p. 453.

English and German despatches to the United States gives the impression that each wished Washington to feel that the other was taking the more emphatic stand.[36] On December 8th German and British ministers withdrew from Caracas leaving their legations in charge of the United Sates minister who had recently agreed to act for Colombia also in the disputes between that nation and Veuezuela.

The next day the blockade was established and certain Venezuelan vessels were seized. Two of these were sunk after capture by the Germans, and in the ensuing week the blockade was extended to other ports of the Republic. The Dictator retaliated by ordering under arrest all citizens of Great Britain and Germany whom he could apprehend and their release was only secured after considerable effort on the part of the United States Minister.[37] And now, with a loud voice Castro called for arbitration. This was relayed to the intervening powers by the United States which again automatically assumed the position of spokesman for the New World troublemaker. The British felt that Castro was " cracking his fingers at Great Britain " while safe among his mountains;[38] the Germans wanted world recognition and dreaded the merest suggestion of weakness which might entail a smile of ridicule, but they likewise feared criticism especially if it arose from the United States and caused the British to leave them in the lurch.[39]

[36] For example see Tower to Hay, December 14, 1902, *ibid.*, p. 421; Marquess of Lansdowne to Buchanan, November 26, 1902, Gooch and Temperley, *op. cit.*, II, 157-8.

[37] Perkins, pp. 337-8.

[38] Dennis, *Adventures in American Diplomacy*, p. 287.

[39] Count Bernstorff, *My Three Years in America* (New York, 1920), pp. 16-7.

In Great Britain the response to the establishment of the blockade and the capture of the Venezuelan vessels was far from satisfactory, and criticism appeared in both Parliament and the press.[40] In the United States public opinion had been sensitive to Venezuela ever since the boundary settlement caused this country to take a paternal interest in the affairs of its southern neighbor. It was probably well expressed by the British Ambassador Sir Michael Herbert when he wrote to the Marquess of Lansdowne, December 17:

Although I have, so far, no reason to believe the United States Government will change their attitude, there is a growing feeling of irritation in Congress, especially in the House of Representatives against the action of the two Powers, chiefly owing to the bombardment and the sinking of Venezuelan ships. The administration is not suspicious of us, but it is undoubtedly apprehensive as to German designs. The impression prevails in Washington that Germany is using us, and our friends here regret, from the point of view of American good feeling towards us, that we are acting with her.[41]

The State Department now had time to take second thought on the matter. Significantly enough, in view of his later career, Secretary of War Taft had busied himself in trying to secure funds for Venezuela and while in touch with Speyer and Company had also approached the President and the Secretary of State on the subject.[42] Seligman and Company were also reported to be interested,[43] but all the suggestions and efforts of the " dollar diplomats " came

[40] Gooch and Temperley, III, 413; Jones, *op. cit.,* pp. 238-40.

[41] Herbert to Marquess of Lansdowne, December 16, 1902, Gooch and Temperley, II, 162.

[42] Tweed to Root, December 19, 1902, LC., Root MS.

[43] Rippy, *Caribbean Danger Zone,* pp. 203 ff.

too late to prevent the trouble or to solve it. Another element in the second thinking was the warning that came from men of experience to the effect that Castro was attempting to use his northern neighbor to rake his chestnuts out of the fire.[44] Then there was always the possible alternative course by which the United States would actively intervene and attempt to force a settlement by direct means.[45]

The ambiguous and somewhat disingenuous offer of Venezuela for arbitration, dated December 13th, found the British in a conciliatory mood, so they informed the protesting German Ambassador at London, Count Metternich, that they would arbitrate.[46] There was nothing left for Germany and Italy but to agree as soon as the suggestions should become reasonably specific. Great Britain then hit upon the, for it, happy idea of asking Roosevelt to arbitrate the matter. This appealed to the President's vanity but greatly perturbed John Hay. Quickly the Secretary found an insuperable obstacle in the fact that the United States Minister at Caracas had been asked to act as Venezuela's agent in the arbitration. This Hay pointed out would make for endless complications if Bowen, as agent for Venezuela but a member of the State Department, had to appear before his own President as arbitrator. Also Hay felt this was an excellent opportunity for showing the sincerity of the United States in support of the Hague Court by advising that the case be referred to that tribunal. This was done with the Venezuelan case actually presented by the United States.

[44] Jones to Root, December 15, 1902, LC., Root MS.
[45] Stephen Bonsal, *The American Mediterranean* (New York, 1913), pp. 175-6; 186; Perkins, pp. 388-90.
[46] Hill, *op. cit.,* pp. 120-1; Nevins, *Henry White,* pp. 210-11.

A passing comment is all that it needed on the now pretty well exploded claim that Roosevelt forced Germany into arbitration by use of a direct ultimatum. This claim, not advanced until August, 1916, seems to have been largely a figment of the imagination insofar as its details are concerned; probably invoked by the man's intense nature under the excitement of the First World War psychology. That he had been suspicious of Germany for years prior to 1902 is clear, and his enthusiastic mind, later possibly clouded by age and disappointments, appears to have fed his craving for fame and popularity by this bombastic claim that once more placed him in the role of protector of the downtrodden. Those who have carefully examined the documents have arrayed such evidence that any other conclusion is largely precluded until more information has been amassed by the Roosevelt apologists. In fact, in Chicago, early in April, 1903, Roosevelt commented in a public address: "Both powers assured us in explicit terms that there was not the slightest intention on their part to violate the principles of the Monroe Doctrine, and this assurance was kept with an honorable good faith which merits the fullest acknowledgment on our part." [47]

Now comes the important question of the significance of the whole affair. Germany with poor grace had submitted to the idea of arbitration just a little too late and had accepted the spokesmanship of the United States just a bit too reluctantly to offset the growing suspicion in Washington. It again missed the opportunity which the British so skillfully seized.[48] In England statesmen were glibly using

[47] Arnold Bennett Hall, *The Monroe Doctrine and the Great War* (Chicago, 1930), p. 74.

[48] Bernstorff, *op. cit.*, p. 20.

the term Monroe Doctrine in a way that was balm to sensitive souls across the Atlantic: Lord Cranborne before the House of Commons; the Duke of Devonshire before the House of Lords; the Marquess of Lansdowne and Mr. Chamberlain, all in effect endorsed the words of Mr. Balfour when he said:

The Monroe Doctrine has no enemies in this country that I know of. We welcome any increase of the influence of the United States of America upon the great Western Hemisphere. We desire no colonization. We desire no alteration in the balance of power, we desire no acquisition of territory. We have not the slightest intention of interfering with the mode of government of any portion of that continent. The Monroe Doctrine, therefore, is really not in the question at all.[49]

The United States had been recognized as spokesman of the New World by Great Britain, Germany and Italy, and it was only logical that with the new recognition of responsibility it was understood there went a commensurate authority and willingness to exercise both the responsibility and authority simultaneously. This the British Ambassador made quite clear in an interview with Roosevelt—and Roosevelt with equal frankness acknowledged it.[50] In this the President was the typical nationalist. He suspected German intentions and by no means was enthusiastic about the British. As he wrote to a friend, December 3, 1904:

. . . the average Englishman is not a being whom I find congenial or with whom I care to associate, I wish him well, but I wish him well at a good distance from me. . . . England has been friendly with us since we have grown so strong as to make her friendship a matter of more moment to her than to us. If we quit building our fleet, England's friendship would immediately cool.[51]

[49] Quoted by Alvarez, *The Monroe Doctrine*, p. 92.
[50] Perkins, p. 364.   [51] Pringle, *Roosevelt*, p. 281.

After the whole matter was settled Roosevelt informed Germany that the United States President had no objection to, in fact endorsed, the idea of an independent German state in south Brazil as the best means of developing that section.[52] One can only wonder. Does this mean that Roosevelt's ebullient nature had reacted and that he had said more than he meant in his relief of the moment? Or did he really have no ambitions for the United States south of the Caribbean? Be that as it may Germany increasingly believed that the United States eagle was a potential menace but that it was the British lion that effectually barred Germany's growth while the lion paid court to the eagle.[53] In fact, the Kaiser even began to consider the possibilities of a German-French-Russian-United States alliance to accomplish his ends.[54] As for the British they confidently pursued their course in a way calculated to bind the United States to their own program while themselves withdrawing from active policies in the Caribbean. The Earl of Selborne in the House of Commons, March 22, 1904, stated that the birth of the United States navy had revolutionized the British naval policy in the West Indies and that the great naval base of St. Lucia was no longer needed in the old sense, hence had been allowed to decline.[55] In brief, the British

[52] Rippy, *Latin Amer. in World Politics*, p. 198.

[53] Cartwright to Grey, August 20, 1906, in Gooch and Temperley, III, 371-2; Trench to Lascelles, January 6, 1908, *ibid.*, VI, 109-10; *Documents Diplomatiques Francais, 2e serie (1901-1911)* (Paris, 1934-7), VI, 172-3.

[54] Isaac Don Levine, editor, *Letters from the Kaiser to the Czar, copied from Government Archives in Petrograd, unpublished before 1920* (New York, 1920), pp. 193-5.

[55] Chester Lloyd Jones, *Caribbean Interests of the United States* (New York, 1916), pp. 314-5.

effectually withdrew their West Indian squadron and left the patrol duty to the United States.

In Latin America these developments were viewed with mixed approval and alarm. Of course all were delighted at the idea of protection from threatened aggression, but in the minds of many there was a question if the cure was not worse than the disease. Venezuela was not a little embittered by the fact that the boundary settlement of the 1890s was actually negotiated by the United States and Great Britain while it, as the party most concerned, had merely been given the privilege of looking on while its interests were determined.[56] The new agreement was more or less of the same nature, and many were saying that the conduct of the United States merely constituted an " act of conceit and ambition " and was purely selfish in both purpose and intent.[57] Now that the danger was past the Caribbean countries forthwith forgot the fear that had once beset them and which the United States agent before the arbitral court expressed when he pointed out that Great Britain and Germany had blockaded Venezuela, seized its gunboats and announced that if that proved not to be sufficient " ' then they must consider what should be the next step.' It is because one such step is only too likely to lead to another and another, that we are here representing the Government of the United States and the Government of Venezuela." [58]

Officials of the State Department had repeatedly made it very clear that their policy did not forbid European nations to collect debts actually due but was only intended to secure

[56] *Venezuelan Arbitration*, p. 1129.

[57] Letter of Marcial Martínez in Alvarez, *Monroe Doctrine*, pp. 303-4.

[58] *Venezuelan Arbitration*, pp. 1163-4.

territorial integrity in the New World.[59] If this was the case then had not these small countries swapped their bauble for a gewgaw? They had little more than a bauble of fancied independence from European intervention in the first place, but how was their new status any better? They were still subject to European pressure to pay their debts and, in addition, were menaced by what now appeared to be a titular right of the United States to speak and act for them whenever it saw fit. To clarify the situation on December 29, 1902, while the controversy was still in its acute stages, the Argentine Minister at Washington, Sr. Luis M. Drago, proposed what amounted to a New World statement of policy on debt collection by force. He stated, in part:

> The collection of loans by military means implies territorial occupation to make them effective, and territorial occupation signifies the suppression or subordination of the governments of the countries on which it is imposed.
>
> Such a situation seems obviously at variance with the principles many times proclaimed by the nations of America, and particularly with the Monroe Doctrine, sustained and defended with so much zeal on all occasions by the United States, a doctrine to which the Argentine Republic has heretofore solemnly adhered.[60]

This posed a rather delicate question. Would the United States approve such a joint proposal which would naturally be hailed throughout the New World and more particularly in the tropical regions where there was most probability of its application? On February 17th Secretary Hay sent a thoroughly diplomatic and non-committal response in which he stated:

---

[59] F. B. Loomis, "Position of the United States in the American Continent," *The Annals,* XXII, 11-2.

[60] *Foreign Relations,* 1903, p. 3; also, Moore, *Digest,* VI, 592-3.

Without expressing assent or dissent from the propositions ably set forth in the note . . . the general position
of the Government of the United States . . . is indicated
in recent messages of the President.

The President declared in his message to Congress, December 3, 1901, that by the Monroe Doctrine " we do not
guarantee any State against punishment if it misconducts
itself, provided that punishment does not take the form of
acquisition of territory by any non-American power."

In harmony with the foregoing language, the President
announced in his message of December 2, 1902:

" No independent nation in America need have the
slightest fear of aggression from the United States. It behooves each one to maintain order within its own borders
and to discharge its just obligations to foreigners. When
this is done they can rest assured that, be they strong
or weak, they have nothing to dread from outside
interference." [61]

The United States as a rising creditor nation with a business
man's administration in Washington of course had to be
careful how the right to protect its own investments abroad,
and its preeminent strategic needs in the Caribbean, might
be sacrificed. In plain language " if the Drago Doctrine
were to be accepted, then the Monroe Doctrine would lose
its terror for Central and South America." [62] The sequel to
the interchange came at the Second Hague Conference when
the United States sponsored some kind of self-denying ordinance of this type for creditor nations. The result was
the eminently just agreement that the nations of the world
would renounce the right of collection of debts by force
unless the debtor had first refused arbitration by a reasonable and fair international tribunal—and with the Hague

[61] Memorandum of Hay to García Merou, February 17, 1903,
Foreign Relations, 1903, p. 5.
[62] H. E. Nettles, " The Drago Doctrine," *Hisp. Amer. Hist.
Rev.,* VIII, 223.

Court in operation such a tribunal was available at all times on the mere working out of details on the case in point and the selection of the justices to preside.

During this period while Europe was coming to recognize, however willingly or reluctantly, the priority of the United States in the Caribbean and New World, what was the policy that the Republic was evolving for itself in the area concerned? Three incidents or series of incidents showed rather clearly what was happening. First, there was the all important question of the trans-isthmian canal; second, there was the question of organizing governments for newly acquired dependencies (Cuba and Puerto Rico); and finally, there was the question of a general Caribbean policy to be adopted toward the independent nations of the region.

In the first place during the middle nineties efforts had been made to organize a so-called Greater Republic of Central America, with Honduras, Nicaragua and El Salvador cooperating in the movement. This culminated on August 27, 1898, when a constitution was proclaimed for the United States of Central America. However, a revolution promptly developed in El Salvador and the movement collapsed before the year was over. In the whole affair the United States seems to have maintained the role of interested observer and to have exercised no special supervision or pressure.

Following this there were the more or less customary revolutionary activities that had long been endemic in Central America. Washington watched these carefully but for the most part refrained from interference. It merely issued instructions to prevent filibusters from the United States taking advantage of the disorders.[63] Foreign governments

---

[63] *Foreign Relations*, 1899, pp. 364 ff.

at times asked the United States to present the cases of their nationals to the local authorities and this was usually done, as in the case of Chinese citizens in Guatemala in 1903 and Danish interests in El Salvador in 1902.[64] The rights of United States citizens in the disturbed countries frequently called for diplomatic representations as in the case of the shooting of a man in Honduras in 1899,[65] damages claimed in Nicaragua in 1900,[66] protection of miscellaneous rights in Costa Rica in 1901,[67] and the questions of settlement of the Guatemalan debts in 1902.[68] These, however, were for the most part routine affairs and called for little special attention though they did show that the interests and investments of the Northern Republic were of increasing importance.

Central America as such was apparently of little concern to Roosevelt except in connection with its potential availability as a canal route and insofar as the securing of an organized government there might cater to such an objective.[69] In spite of this specific cases developed and demanded attention. Disorders in Nicaragua in 1899 forced some attention. A revolt by one General Juan Pablo Reyes had the support of United States citizens locally resident and of " Rough Riders " who went from Cuba to join the fracas. Officially the United States remained entirely neutral, and its consul together with the consular representatives of

[64] Loomis to Combs, March 16, 1903, and Merry to Hay, February 29, 1902, *ibid.*, 1903, p. 573 and 1902, pp. 836-7 respectively.
[65] Moore, *Digest,* VI, 762-4.
[66] Award of Arbitrator, *Foreign Relations,* 1900, pp. 826 ff.
[67] Hill to Merry, May 7, 1901, *ibid.,* 1901, p. 421.
[68] Hay to Hunter, April 10, 1902, and Bailey to Hay, July 24, 1902, *ibid.,* 1902, pp. 578; 579.
[69] Hill, *Roosevelt and the Caribbean,* pp. 196-7.

Great Britain, Norway and Sweden advised that customs payments should not be made to the rebels. Marines were landed from United States and British warships on the scene and the rebellion soon collapsed. But in spite of the official advice foreigners sympathetic to the rebels had paid them customs dues and so now ensued a diplomatic correspondence as to the rights of re-collection by the legitimate government. Foreigners actually involved in the disorders were sent to New Orleans and Mobile in accordance with arrangements made by the local authorities and the British and United States naval authorities on the ground. These numbered thirty-two Americans, seven English, six Norwegians and a half dozen of scattered nationalities.[70] At the same time the United States consular agent was instructed to inform the remaining residents from the United States that they must appear before the local courts and give such information as they had in connection with the recent rebellion.[71] Thus the position of the Northern Republic was strictly correct even though the dictator of Nicaragua was no little irritated by the conduct of those foreign residents contemptuously referred to as of Yankee nationality.

With regard to the Panama Isthmus proper there was a more direct contact and a somewhat more active interest due to the fact that the old treaties of the middle of the century and the obvious narrowness of the isthmus at that point made the construction of a canal there an ever present

[70] Merry to Hay, July 25, 1899, *Foreign Relations,* 1899, pp. 583-4. See also Milton Offutt, *Protection of Citizens Abroad by the Armed Forces of the United States* (Baltimore, 1928), pp. 82-3; Anna I. Powell, " Relations between the United States and Nicaragua," *Hisp. Amer. Hist. Rev.,* VIII, 46.

[71] Moore, *Digest,* VI, 686-7.

possibility. The railroad across the isthmus had made money for United States stockholders for years and the efforts of the French company to construct the canal had also attracted attention and kept the subject alive. In addition some of the shrewdest propagandists Washington has known appeared on the scene. One was the dexterous P. Bunau-Varilla, Chief Engineer and heavy stockholder in the bankrupt French enterprise. In order to save something from the wreck it was essential for the company to sell its holdings to some other company or nation to finish the work.[72] As time passed it became increasingly obvious that if this was to be done the Government at Washington was the one most likely purchaser.

To assist Bunau-Varilla there was the able lawyer-politician Nelson Cromwell who was later to claim $800,000 for fees for his services and who, as agent, did not hesitate to contribute $60,000 to the Republican campaign fund, charging the sum as necessary expense to the canal company which had retained his services.[73] Whenever it appeared that the idea of construction at Nicaragua was imminent it became the duty of these men to see to it that the Panama route was advertised and the way kept open for a substitution of the Panama project for the more northern and nearer one. Railroad companies fearing competition for their transcontinental rates from cheap water freight also lobbied actively against any trans-isthmian undertaking regardless of location. But the idea appealed to the nation

[72] The French Company was estimated to have completed about one-third of the work of the canal undertaking though at a cost of approximately $400,000,000 in actual construction, waste and hard luck.

[73] Pringle, *Roosevelt*, p. 304.

at large with a great deal of force: the navy men wanted it, shippers clamored for it, the west coast was eager for it and the man in the street liked the idea for its economic, nationalistic and romantic appeal.

Sentiment developed steadily after 1900 when President McKinley reported to Congress " the Nicaragua Government shows a disposition to deal freely with the canal question either in the way of negotiations with the United States or by taking measures to promote the waterway." [74] In the same year tentative agreements were made with Costa Rica and Nicaragua with regard to a canal via Lake Nicaragua.[75] In Colombia, however, it was thought that no other route than that at Panama could be seriously considered. Had not the French company chosen it and could not any simple minded person see that a canal located there would be much shorter and better? As a result Colombian officials did not realize the actual competition they were facing. When Secretary Hay and President Roosevelt showed impatience this was discounted in Bogotá as just another illustration of their much resented attitude to " Dagoes," or as diplomatic bluff from which the small nations had suffered all too often.

In the United States the struggle to determine which of the two routes to exploit was a real contest with Senator Morgan of Alabama supporting the Nicaraguan project opposed by his colleague Mark Hanna of Ohio who had been ably coached by Bunau-Varilla and Cromwell for his part as a protagonist of Panama. The debate has been

[74] Message of December 3, 1900, *Foreign Relations*, 1900, p. xxv.

[75] *Dip. Hist. Pan. Canal*, pp. 572-3. See also Isaac J. Cox, *Nicaragua and the United States* (Boston, 1927), pp. 856-7.

often and ably discussed and needs no repetition here since it was based, not on a question of national policy as to a canal (the type of issue of concern to this study) but on a detail as to method, or the advisability of one route as compared with the other.

It will be remembered that Congress had authorized the Walker Commission to investigate and report on the practicability of the various routes. This report was presented to Congress and showed that the Nicaragua route would be the cheaper and better, unless the holdings of the French Company could be purchased for $40,000,000 or less. Since the French were asking much more than this a bill was introduced into Congress to proceed with negotiations looking to the construction of the more northern enterprise. Promptly the French decided that half a loaf was better than no bread and so agreed to sell their holdings for the price set in the report. The result was the now famous Spooner Amendment that changed the bill and provided for construction at Panama. This did not end the matter but did give the Panama advocates a great advantage. In truth, it left the United States in a splendid position to play off the interests of one small country against those of another and to secure the best possible bargain. And many presidents would have done just that. However, Roosevelt did not possess a bargaining disposition even though at first he apparently had no particular choice in the matter and was inclined to follow the lead of his Congress.

It was well known that since the date of the signing of the treaty giving the United States free transit across the isthmus in 1846 there had been frequent interventions to maintain the neutrality of the district. Half a dozen times or more such landings had taken place (almost every writer who surveys the diplomatic correspondence seems to find a different number varying up to eight or ten).[76] In addition, to give the administration a recent unfavorable impression there was disorder on the isthmus in 1900-1901 and troops again had to be landed. The fighting actually took place along the line of the railroad and trains wishing to use the road had to have a United States army captain notify the contesting parties. With seeming courtesy " The soldiers stepped off the track for the train to pass and at once after we cleared them the fighting began again." [77]

Hay now undertook the negotiation of a treaty with Colombia, but still tried to keep Nicaragua " on the string." Both proved refractory and Hay found his impatience getting the better of him.[78] The chief trouble lay in Colombia. There the profound ignorance of tempers in the United States was aggravated by serious local opposition to the Colombian President. And of this the United States was generally ignorant. What to the Colombian were political maneuverings based on necessity, in the United States appeared to be sheer opportunism and sharp dealing. The Colombian Minister in Washington well knew the situation but was unable to do anything about it. He finally had to assume authority and submit a treaty draft so as to placate Washington temporarily and to procrastinate a bit longer hoping that his country would act. He wrote a friend:

The past six months have been virtual torture for me; pressed and harried day after day at various critical mo-

[76] Hill, Roosevelt and the Caribbean, pp. 45-6; W. W. Pierson, " Political Influences of an Interoceanic Canal." Hisp. Amer. Hist. Rev., VI, 215-6.

[77] Quoted by William D. McCain, The United States and the Republic of Panama (Durham, 1937), p. 11.

[78] Dennett, Hay, pp. 367-8.

ments to express categorically the propositions of the Government of Colombia, I have had to resort to every manner of delay without compromising the outcome of the negotiations.[79]

And again:

If the Colombian government would only give up playing the Sphinx and adopt intelligible business methods, I would hopefully look forward to an easy victory in the near future; but as matters now stand, I fear our friends more than I do our enemies.[80]

The fact was that President Marroquín of Colombia did not dare to submit concrete terms for his popularity was waning dangerously at home and Panama had long been considered to be the chief source of revenue of the nation. To alienate it was more than the people of Colombia were willing to stand for. His position was well shown in his letter to his general at Panama, dated July 26, 1902:

Concerning the canal question, I find myself in a horrible perplexity; in order that the North Americans may complete the work by virtue of a convention with the Government of Colombia, it is necessary to make concessions of territory, or sovereignty and of jurisdiction, which the Executive Power has not the power of yielding; and if we do not yield them and the North Americans determine to build the canal, they will open it without stopping at trifles, and then we will lose more sovereignty than we should lose by making the concessions they seek.

History will say of me that I ruined the Isthmus and all Colombia, by not permitting the opening of the Panama Canal, or that I permitted it to be done, scandalously injuring the rights of my country.

I would only be able to free myself of (my) responsibilities if I should succeed in transferring them to the con-

[79] Quoted by Miner, *The Fight for the Panama Route,* p. 128.
[80] Quoted by DuVal, *Cadiz to Cathay,* p. 157.

gress and, as for that, God knows when it can be convened. I think that it would be unwise to call for elections until all the municipalities of the Republic are under control of proper authorities.[81]

There were also blunders in the transmission of the text of the proposed treaty [82] but at last the document was completed providing for the cession of a six mile canal zone, Colombia to retain sovereignty but the lease to be indefinite in length with revision of the money rentals each hundred years. It was also stated that the French company would have the right to transfer its holdings to the United States, and as amended at the insistence of Washington, provided that Colombia was not to charge the company anything for the privilege.[83] This document was signed by the Colombian Chargé d'affaires, Tomás Herrán, and by Secretary Hay.

In the Southern Republic there ensued one of those periods of strenuous political activity which to the Anglo-Saxon looked like mere fuss, feathers and furore. President Marroquín knew full well that immediate ratification of the treaty was highly advisable but the recent landing of United States troops on the isthmus had had a most unfortunate effect on public opinion and in view of the President's weakened popularity it was gravely doubtful if his recommendation on the treaty would be accepted.[84] But the passage of time found the Colombian Congress more and more factious. It finally reached such a frame of

[81] Quoted by Miner, *op. cit.*, p. 233.

[82] *Ibid.*, p. 162.

[83] Dennett, *op. cit.*, p. 369; Pringle, *Roosevelt*, p. 310.

[84] For diplomatic correspondence see Senate Document No. 143, 58th cong., 2d sess.

mind that almost any terms proposed would have been considered inadequate, and so after numerous delays the treaty was rejected in August, 1903.[85] Efforts to secure a reconsideration likewise came to naught on October 30th.[86]

The delays and rejection infuriated Roosevelt for he and Hay had not realized and probably never did realize the actual position of the Colombian President in his own country. Instead Roosevelt was fully convinced:

> President Marroquin, through his Minister, had agreed to the Hay-Herran treaty of January, 1903. He had the absolute power of an unconstitutional dictator to keep his promise or break it. He determined to break it. To furnish himself an excuse for breaking it, he devised the plan of summoning a Congress especially called to reject the canal treaty. This the Congress—a Congress of mere puppets—did, without a dissenting vote; and the puppets adjourned forthwith without legislating on any other subject.[87]

Hay had long since lost his patience and in connection with the amendment referred to above had written on August 14, 1903, to the President protesting against Colombia making the United States a party " to the gouge " involved in the payments, if any, of the French company to Colombia in return for which the company would have the right to sell its holdings to the United States verified.[88] In spite of the amendment the Colombians felt that such a payment was in order since the French had failed to fulfill their contract either during the original term of years or during the first extension thereof, and that now Colom-

---

[85] Beaupré to Hay, August 12, 1903, *Dip. Hist. Pan. Canal*, p. 426.

[86] Miner, *op. cit.*, p. 333.

[87] Theodore Roosevelt, *Theodore Roosevelt, an Autobiography* (New York, 1919), pp. 561-2.

[88] DuVal, *op. cit.*, p. 261.

bia would in a short space of time be able to exercise the right of foreclosure, thus partially recouping losses due to French incompetence and blundering. In their exasperated frame of mind Hay and Roosevelt viewed this as little better than theft.

Once thwarted by Colombian rejection of the treaty the President had no further doubts as to the route to be used. Colombia had sinned and must be punished.[89] In letters from July to October the President exhausted his versatile vocabulary in the use of epithets describing the Bogotá politicians as "contemptible little creatures," "jack rabbits," "foolish and homicidal corruptionists" and the like.[90] Meanwhile in a letter to his Chief Hay sounded a more ominous note, September 13, 1903:

It is now perfectly clear that in the present state of Colombian politics we cannot now, nor for some time to come, make a satisfactory treaty with Colombia.

It is altogether likely that there will be an insurrection on the Isthmus against that government of folly and graft that now rules at Bogotá. It is for you to decide whether you will (1) wait the result of that moment or (2) take a hand in rescuing the Isthmus from anarchy, or (3) treat with Nicaragua.

Something we shall be forced to do in case of a serious insurrectionary movement in Panama, to keep the transit clear. Our intervention should not be at haphazard, nor, this time, should it be to the profit, as heretofore, of Bogotá. I venture to suggest that you let your mind play about the subject for two or three weeks before finally deciding. For my part, I think nothing can be lost, and something may be gained, by awaiting developments for a while.[91]

[89] Dennett, *op. cit.,* p. 379.

[90] Pringle, *Roosevelt,* p. 311.

[91] A. L. P. Dennis, "Hay" in Bemis, *Secretaries of State,* IX, 163-4.

Thus was the question of intervention " not . . . to the benefit, as heretofore, of Bogotá " squarely raised. And this was a new departure for it was well known—or at least should have been to both Hay and Roosevelt—that the earlier interventions on the isthmus had, with one exception that was promptly explained if not apologized for, been at the request of the Colombian authorities.[92] Mark Hanna was much more conciliatory and wrote the President on October 4th: " It is not surprising that a treaty made in our interest should find opposition . . . so we should not be impatient under present conditions. . . . Meanwhile we can handle the matter in Congress, so as to save the situation and I feel certain in the near future effect a satisfactory settlement with Colombia." Roosevelt's answer smacked strongly of a retort when he wrote: " I think it well worth considering whether we had not better warn these cat-rabbits that great though our patience has been, it can be exhausted." [93]

Meanwhile that master politician, Bunau-Varilla, was preparing his greatest *coup*. Probably dropping a hint of German interest in securing the rights of the French company in the right places (such a hint had certainly reached the State Department from the United States Minister at Bogotá [94] and apparently perturbed Roosevelt no little) he proceeded with his schemes. Later investigation has provided no evidence that a German move was on foot [95] but the President was not in a mood to await evidence. True,

[92] Pringle, *op. cit.,* p. 330.

[93] Quoted by DuVal, *op. cit.,* p. 296.

[94] Theodore Roosevelt, *Fear God and Take Your Own Part* (New York, 1916), p. 324.

[95] Dennis, *Adventures in Amer. Diplomacy,* p. 338, note.

Germany had asked the United States to protest its interests in Panama during the troubles of 1902 [96] but that might be another red herring.

To aggravate matters Colombia's attitude remained thoroughly impractical so that once Panama was determined on as the route practical and imperial minded observers felt there were two alternatives only: a revolt in Panama such as that with which Bunau-Varilla had threatened Colombia in November, 1902,[97] or direct intervention and occupation. Neither procedure would have surprised those experienced in diplomacy. For instance, the King of Italy remarked: " I should think your President [Roosevelt] would send a fleet down there and take possession of the isthmus. It would create an excitement for a week, but then all would be over and in the end it would be a benefit to the whole world." [98]

As early as May, 1903, Minister A. M. Beaupré at Bogotá reported that there was great local excitement because large numbers of United States citizens were reported to be entering Panama.[99] This was at once denied by the State Department but the rumors persisted and by October had become alarming. In an effort to quiet the excitement in the Colombian Senate the Minister of Foreign Affairs called attention to the fact that there was no danger, stating that the treaty of 1846 bound the United States to protect

[96] *Use by the United States of a Military Force in . . . Colombia* (Senate Document No. 143, 58th Cong., 2d sess.) (Washington, n. d.), pp. 322; 325.

[97] Philippe Bunau-Varilla, *Panama, the Creation, Destruction and Resurrection* (London, 1913), p. 255.

[98] Quoted by Dennis, " Hay " in Bemis, *Secretaries of State,* IX, 160-1.

[99] Beaupré to Hay, May 28, 1903, *Dip. Hist. Pan. Canal,* p. 391.

Colombian control of the isthmus and that this had been amply proven from time to time by actual experience.[100]

While Bunau-Varilla was actively attempting to organize prospective rebels on and for the isthmus, and while Hay and Roosevelt were toying with the idea of using the Big Stick there came to their hands a powerful weapon in the way of legal justification for their proposed conduct. The able international lawyer, John Bassett Moore, talked matters over with Acting Secretary of State Loomis on an occasion when Hay was absent. The conversation so impressed Loomis that he asked for a written opinion which he then forwarded to the President. In this Moore argued:

> In view of the fact that the United States has for more than fifty years secured to Colombia her sovereignty over the Isthmus, for the mutually avowed purpose of maintaining a free and open transit, the United States is in a position to demand that it shall be allowed to construct the great means of transit which the treaty was chiefly designed to assure. In reality, the Panama canal, so far as built, has actually been constructed under the protection of this very guarantee. The persons that undertook it failed to finish it. The United States would be justified in asserting and maintaining a right to finish it.

> The position of the United States is altogether different from that of private capitalists, who, unless expressly exempted, are altogether subject to the local jurisdiction, and who, before invoking their government's protection, may be required to tread the paths of ordinary litigation and establish their rights before the tribunals of the governments against which they assert them. Under such conditions, the private capitalist must have everything before nominated in the bond. The United States is not subject to such disabilities, and can take care of the future.[101]

---

[100] Beaupré to Hay, October 21, 1903, *Foreign Relations*, 1903, p. 214.

[101] Miner, *op. cit.*, pp. 431; 432. For Moore Memorandum in full see *ibid.*, pp. 427-32.

Apparently arguing from this thesis the President wrote the first draft of his annual message to Congress (before the revolution broke out in Panama) and in it bluntly stated: "we should purchase all the rights of the Panama Company and, without further parley with Colombia, enter upon the completion of the canal which the French company has begun." [102]

But events in Panama developed before the message was sent to Congress. In September Lodge had written that he was in strong hopes "that either under the treaty of '46 or by the secession of the Province of Panama we can get control of what is undoubtedly the best route." [103] Meanwhile it was inevitable that there should be unrest on the isthmus. On events actually transpiring obviously depended the prosperity or depression of the region for years to come. Hopes had been high while the French were digging, then came despondency. Hopes revived with the reports of the Hay-Herrán negotiations but were crushed by news that Bogotá was stalling and likely to ruin this new chance for prosperity on the isthmus. The unrest was reported from too many sources and was too logically explained to be dismissed as nothing but a figment of the imagination.[104] However, it was preposterous for Panama to revolt unless powerful outside aid was forthcoming. Whatever might have been the internal dissensions in Colombia the nation would have been a unit in opposing revolution in the sparsely settled but income producing transit route.

[102] Hill, *Roosevelt and the Caribbean*, p. 59.
[103] Lodge to Roosevelt, September 5, 1903, Lodge, *Roosevelt-Lodge Correspondence*, II, 54.
[104] Dennis, *op. cit.*, pp. 319-32; McCain, *U. S. and Panama*, p. 13.

President Roosevelt had long been interested and three days before the Senate approved the Hay-Harrán treaty in March had ordered the Secretary of War to send two or three army officers in civilian dress " to map out and gather information concerning the coasts of those portions of South America which would be of especial interest . . . in the event of any struggle in the Gulf of Mexico or the Caribbean Sea." [105] Pringle in his biography of Roosevelt states that these men reported confidentially to the President and emphasized the prospects of a revolt on the isthmus. To them it was clear that the Government was planning some action but they did not know just what. Incidentally, they were cautioned to say nothing of having seen the President.[106]

As the month of October passed the French agent, Bunau-Varilla was straining every nerve to get the revolution under way, but the prospective rebels hesitated to move unless they were positively assured of foreign aid. Yet for the United States to send aid before the revolt started would never do. Finally about the 18th of October the Frenchman went to see Mr. Hay and they together deplored the " blindness of Colombia " to its own best interests. When the Secretary asked what the outcome of the whole affair would be the latter replied, "the whole thing will end in a revolution. You must take your measures, if you do not want to be taken by surprise." The Secretary responded: "Yes, . . . that is unfortunately the most probable hypothesis. But we shall not be caught napping. Orders have been given to naval forces on the Pacific to sail

[105] Pringle, *Roosevelt*, p. 315.
[106] *Ibid.*, pp. 320-1.

towards the Isthmus." [107] Bunau-Varilla states that he forthwith instructed the would-be rebels to start their activities. In naval circles a very fever of activity broke out at this time. Between October 21 and 31 seven war vessels of the United States began to converge on the about-to-be troubled zone while only one was withdrawn.[108] The Colombian Chargé at Washington was well aware of the danger and on September 10th had cabled his government: "Hostile attitude will consist in favoring indirectly a revolution in Panama." By letter he amplified the statement and commented on "the promptness with which the independence of our department of Panama will be recognized." [109]

When the rebels remained loath to commit themselves Bunau-Varilla was convinced from an apparently casual meeting with the Acting Secretary of State Loomis that the U. S. S. *Nashville* was on its way to Colón and that this was the actual guarantee desired.[110] Mr. Loomis' famous telegrams of inquiry to the isthmus on November 3rd show that he was far from satisfied in his own mind [111] as to the conditions there, but in truth events were now actually moving rapidly. The revolution did break out; troops were landed from the *Nashville* to protect the transit; the railroad was seized by United States forces so that Colombian troops on the opposite side of the isthmus could not dis-

[107] Bunau-Varilla, *op. cit.*, p. 318. In the account written in his old age the Frenchman reiterates the claim made earlier that he mentioned the possibility of a revolution in Panama to Roosevelt himself on October 19. Bunau-Varilla, *From Panama to Verdun* (Philadelphia, 1940), pp. 131-2.

[108] DuVal, pp. 516-7.

[109] Jones, *Caribbean since 1900*, p. 300; see also DuVal, p. 287.

[110] Bunau-Varilla, *op. cit.*, p. 331.

[111] Pringle, *Roosevelt*, pp. 326-7.

turb the peace of the region by putting down the rebellion on their own soil; and other Colombian troops on their way to the troubled zone by sea were refused the right to land.

The formal rebellion had broken out late on the 3rd of November and early the next day Bunau-Varilla was at the State Department. His statement to Mr. Loomis (Hay was reported not in) that he would soon appear as the official delegate of Panama seemed not to cause Mr. Loomis " any great surprise " though he reported conditions on the Isthmus confused, saying that the United States would not tolerate " armed conflict " along the right of way of the railroad and added: "Provided the new Government [which only claimed to have come into existence the night before] takes no step contrary to the interests and to the duties of the American Government you may be assured that its acts will be regarded with benevolence." The Frenchman was further assured that the United States would dispose of all troops necessary " on both sides of the Isthmus." [112]

As has been frequently pointed out this meant a clear reversal of the policy of Washington as to the transit area. Heretofore interventions had been for the purpose of maintaining Colombian sovereignty while protecting the open transit, and no disturbances had been allowed to disturb the sovereignty on the isthmus. Now the program was reversed and Colombia was not to be allowed to disturb the peace of the isthmus by suppressing disorders thereon. Heretofore the Mother had been supreme. If the child protested maternal conduct a firm hand was promptly placed over its mouth to stifle its cries even when the

[112] Bunau-Varilla, pp. 343-4.

desired candy had been curtly refused. Now the child again began to cry and the maternal activities were sternly repressed while the child was given its candy and dandled on the knee of the stern uncle who up to this time had ignored the child except to repress it.[113]

Roosevelt in Washington was convinced that action was taken in the nick of time and that otherwise there would have been a bloody massacre and grave disorders on the isthmus.[114] John Hay said: "the only alternative would have been an indefinite duration of bloodshed and devastation through the whole extent of the Isthmus. It was a time to act and not to theorize, and my judgment at least is clear that" the President "acted rightly."[115] Root, who had been abroad, returned to Washington after the affair was over. He confessed to being "much troubled" about the situation while it was in progress but on reaching Washington and talking with Roosevelt and Hay he whimsically dismissed the whole matter as already settled saying that Colombia now found itself in the position of the girl who kept refusing a suitor, thinking all the while that she would marry him ultimately, only to wake up one morning to find that he had married another girl.[116] And this was about the verdict of a majority of the American people. The President's explanation that Colombia was acting the "dog in the manger" (it could not build the canal itself and would not let the United States do it); that it was trying to blackmail the French Company and the United

[113] Williams, *Economic Foreign Policy of the U. S.*, p. 159.
[114] Roosevelt, *Fear God and Take Your Own Part*, pp. 327-8; Roosevelt, *Autobiography*, pp. 566-7.
[115] Jones, *op. cit.*, p. 334.
[116] Philip C. Jessup, *Elihu Root* (New York, 1938), I, 402.

States; that it was holding up the prosperity of the world in general, and the prosperity and actual safety of the United States in particular, caused a feeling in this country that the end justified the means. In short, the rights of " collective civilization " were superior to the legal claims of one selfish nation.

In view of all the known facts an impartial observer of the record must come to the conclusion that Mr. Roosevelt's disclaimers of responsibility for the events as they transpired sound extremely thin even though his skirts may have been technically clean. The debate, however, rapidly drifts away from the major purpose of this study. Actually, the fact remains that this was simply another step in the imperial program for the control of the strategic connection between the coasts of the United States—and the step involved the establishment of a canal in the Caribbean region whose importance was thereby enormously enhanced in all policies that could possibly be adopted in Washington from that time onward.

As soon as the revolt was an accomplished fact the government of Colombia became panic stricken at the prospect of losing its prize province. As early as November 5th Secretary Hay notified the authorities at Bogotá of the " apparently unanimous movement " by which the people of Panama had " resumed their independence." He further stated that the United States had entered into diplomatic relations with the new republic and that the President of the United States " earnestly commends to the Governments of Colombia and Panama the peaceful and equitable settlement of all questions at issue between them." [117] That same day the troops that were supposed

[117] Bunau-Varilla, *op. cit.*, p. 350.

to maintain Colombian sovereignty on the isthmus were persuaded—some say in part by financial considerations probably supplied by Bunau-Varilla—to leave for home. Appalled at the prospect of losing everything the Government at Bogotá began to make excited offers and pleas for a chance for reconsideration of the Hay-Herrán treaty. The news of the actual revolt in Panama did not reach the Colombian capital until the 6th,[119] the day Hay actually entered into diplomatic relations with the new republic. At 6 P. M. Minister Beaupré telegraphed Washington:

> Knowing that the revolution has already commenced in Panama, General Reyes says that if the Government of the United States will land troops to preserve Colombian sovereignty and the transit, if requested by the Colombian chargé d'affaires, this Government will declare martial law, and by virtue of vested constitutional authority, when public order is disturbed, will approve by decree the ratification of the canal treaty as signed; or, if the Government of the United States prefers, will call extra session of Congress with new and friendly members next May to approve the treaty. . . . There is a great reaction of public opinion in favor of the treaty, and it is considered certain that the treaty was not legally rejected by Congress.[120]

This was confirmed by a telegram the next day stating that the Government of Colombia was anxious to cooperate in full with the United States in the isthmus, and that Colombia had requested the President of Mexico to ask his northern neighbor and all countries interested in the Pan-American Union to aid Colombia to preserve its territorial

---

[118] Dennis, *Adventures in Amer. Diplomacy*, pp. 324-5; J. Fred Rippy, *The Capitalists and Colombia* (New York, 1931), pp. 97-8.

[119] Miner, *op. cit.*, p. 371.

[120] Beaupré to Hay, November 6, 1903, *Foreign Relations*, 1903, p. 225.

integrity.[121] From Washington, however, came word that if Colombia sent a representative to Panama he would be courteously received but that the landing of troops would not be permitted.[122]

Naturally the death-bed repentance of Colombia materially weakened its case for the feeling arose that if the authorities had the power to secure the ratification of the treaty now they had had it earlier.[123] However, it should be recognized that there was some plausibility and reason in the Bogotá statements for the opposition to the Government in Colombia had been materially weakened by the events that had occurred and ratification of the treaty was actually more probable now than before.

On November 13th Bunau-Varilla was received as Minister Plenipotentiary of the Republic of Panama but first an interesting exchange took place between him and John Hay on the 12th. Hay wrote in his own hand that the discourse that the Frenchman proposed to read on the occasion was " admirable as literature " but " not quite in the usual form " and added that Mr. Loomis would talk it over with him. To leave no doubt Mr. Bunau-Varilla writes on the bottom of the letter in his collection of papers:

The discourse of which Sec. Hay speaks is the one prepared by me for the ceremony of the reception by the President of the U. S. of myself as Minister of Panama on the 13th of November.[124]

[121] Elihu Root, *Addresses on International Subjects* (Cambridge, 1916), pp. 198-9.

[122] Hay to Beaupré, November 11, 1903, *Dip. Hist. Pan. Canal*, p. 358.

[123] Roosevelt, *Fear God and Take Your Own Part*, pp. 317-8.

[124] Hay to Bunau-Varilla, November 12, 1903, LC., Bunau-Varilla MS.

Apparently the pupil learned his lesson and the reception took place without novelty in spite of the extremely recent French nationality of the new official. On November 14th word was sent to all United States diplomatic representatives that their country had fully recognized the Republic of Panama.[125]

Meanwhile the new Minister Plenipotentiary was finding himself in a difficult position.[126] As a newspaper man he had always sought publicity and popular applause. Now he was besieged by reporters, munitions salesmen [127] and all the hangers-on that beset the path of a man raised to notoriety or prominence by spectacular events. Naturally he was inclined to talk somewhat too freely in the exuberance of the moment as to the brilliant accomplishments achieved and the prospects ahead. His advisers urged caution,[128] old John Bigelow praised him as surpassing the feats of Cortez, Iturbide and Bolívar but added in familiar vein " lend your ears only and not your tongue to news mongers." " Give the public now some eloquent flashes of silence."[129] Three days later Bigelow again wrote deploring the loquacity which had informed the newspapers that

---

[125] *Foreign Relations,* 1903, pp. lxxxiii.

[126] It should be noted that Bunau-Varilla endeavored to secure the services of John Bassett Moore as Washington counsel for the new Republic. However, the offer was declined by Mr. Moore in view of the fact that his name had been associated in the press with the determination of the President to go ahead and construct the canal under the treaty of 1846 and he did not wish to embarrass anyone. Pavey to Bunau-Varilla, November 11, 1903, *ibid.,* and Moore to Loomis, November 11, 1903, LC., Root MS.

[127] For example see Georg Grutstuck to Bunau-Varilla, LC., Bunau-Varilla MS.

[128] Pavey to Bunau-Varilla (telegram), November 11, 1903, *ibid.*

[129] Bigelow to Bunau-Varilla, November 14, 1903, *ibid.*

Morgan had extended the Republic of Panama a credit of $350,000. So small was the figure that it would have been better not to publish the details and the old diplomatic warrior compared the publication of such a fact with the famous comment on the décolleté dresses of the French court under Louis Phillippe when he said "How much better men's imaginations would have done for them [the wearers] than [the scanty dresses] had done."[130]

It soon became evident that the Latin American nations sympathized with Colombia but were unable to do anything about it beyond sending expressions of friendship.[131] In response to a direct question as to what the United States would do in case Colombia invaded Panama the forthright response was:

. . . I am instructed to say to your excellency that the Government of the United States would regard with the gravest concern any invasion of the territory of Panama by Colombian troops, for the reason that bloodshed and disorder would inevitably result throughout the whole extent of the Isthmus, and for the broader reason that, in the opinion of the President, the time has come, in the interest of universal commerce and civilization, to close the chapter of sanguinary and ruinous civil war in Panama.[132]

The attitude of European governments was about what might have been expected. Early attention turned to France because of the interests of the French business world in the old construction efforts at Panama. The United States Ambassador reported on November 11th that the French peo-

[130] Bigelow to Bunau-Varilla, November 17, 1903, *ibid.*

[131] Loomis to Bunau-Varilla with enclosures from Presidents of Colombia and Ecuador to each other, December 30, 1903, LC., Bunau-Varilla MS.

[132] Hay to Reyes, December 11, 1903, *Foreign Relations,* 1903, pp. 279-80.

ple " generally are much pleased with events in Panama " [133] and the Government showed its attitude in being the first foreign power to extend formal recognition to Panama in less than a week after the United States received Bunau-Varilla as Minister. As usual there was the rumor that Berlin was dabbling in the affair and that it had offered to extend protection to Colombia in exchange for territorial cessions in the region. An inquiry sent to Berlin was answered on November 10th with the positive assurance that there was no truth at all in the report.[134] This was followed by formal German recognition of the new nation on the last day of November. France, China and Austria had already acted, and Denmark, Russia, Norway and Sweden, and Belgium followed promptly, so there was no reason to feel that European nations were especially surprised at imperialism in practice. In truth, they were accustomed to take such things in their stride as a matter of course.

However, no country in the New World had committed itself in spite of the great importance they must have attached to the events. Finally, between the 15th and 23rd of December Nicaragua, Peru and Cuba took action, to be followed on the 24th by Great Britain and Italy. Then Costa Rica, Guatemala and Venezuela followed suit along with four other European and Asiatic powers. A second glance shows that only three Central American republics and only five in the whole Caribbean area had acted but that Mexico, El Salvador, Honduras, Santo Domingo and Haiti, as well as Colombia, held aloof.[135]

[133] Porter to Hay, November 11, 1903, *Dip. Hist. Pan. Canal*, p. 360.

[134] Tower to Hay, November 10, 1903, *ibid.*, pp. 359-60.

[135] List sent by Hay to Root in letter of February 15, 1904, LC., Root MS.

Now that the grapes had been gathered there remained the question of how they were to be used. Would they be eaten raw (as Puerto Rico) or made into some strange new wine (as Cuba)? The treaty signed with Panama would give at least an inkling of the intentions of the administration. Bunau-Varilla, advised by ex-Senator Frank D. Pavey who was acting as adviser to the Panama legation, and Secretary Hay at once went to work. In the document signed a canal zone ten miles wide was leased to the United States on a ninety-nine year, renewable contract. Ample provisions were made for the protection of the enterprise by the United States, as well as for its sanitation and for the acquisition of additional lands for construction or defense purposes. The details of the agreement have been printed so often it is unnecessary to list them here. Probably more significant from the standpoint of policy were provisions that appeared in the Panama Constitution that was adopted immediately after the revolt. Article I stated that " the United States guarantees and will maintain the independence of the Republic of Panama. Article III stated that the territory of the new nation was established subject to the jurisdictional limitations stipulated " or that are to be stipulated " in the public treaties with the United States. In commenting on this one writer says: " This is, probably, the only time in contemporary history in which a sovereign state establishes at birth the paramount rights of an alien power. It was so, at least, until newly born Manchukuo turned to the Rising Sun for nurture and paternal care." [136] But of course, this was written before Quisling and his ilk made their unsavory appearance on the contemporary stage.

[136] Nerval, *Autopsy of the Monroe Doctrine*, p. 226.

This and the Cuban treaty (the Cuban document was signed May 22, 1903, and the Panamanian on November 18, 1903) were the first experiments of the United States at government making for quasi-dependencies in the Caribbean. Up to this time a debtor and not a creditor nation, there was little experience available for use in drafting the financial provisions of the basic treaties. Not surprisingly, both showed weaknesses of a serious nature in connection with the fact that the borrowing power of the new nations was practically unsupervised. Actual experience was to show that supervision was needed and so the State Department had to fall back on the provisions of the first article of the treaty by which the guarantee of the independence of the new Republic was provided in order to control the financial activities of the nation. This, as was the case in Cuba, proved so awkward that later documents dealing with the Dominican Republic and Haiti were made far more specific and in the long run eliminated much petty friction.[137]

Inevitably relations with Colombia were strained to the verge of war itself and there were many who expected actual hostilities. Roosevelt himself, probably given pause by the storm of criticism throughout the nation, and the very mild indorsement of even such strong Republicans as Root,[138] wrote to the Secretary of the Navy on December 21:

Would it not be well to issue instructions down at and around Panama that under no circumstances must they fire

[137] C. L. Jones, "Loan Controls in the Caribbean," *Hisp. Amer. Hist. Rev.*, XIV, 144.

[138] DuVal, *Cadiz to Cathay*, pp. 439-40.

unless fired upon. If there should come a brush with Colombia I want to be dead sure that Colombia fires first.[139]

Relations between the two countries had been broken off but Colombia was not in a condition to fight its powerful neighbor. If it attempted to do so it was certain to lose additional territory for the departments of the mother nation adjacent to Panama were contemplating the advantages of climbing on the Panama bandwagon.[140] So Bogotá wisely refrained from overt hostile acts and resigned itself to vociferous demands for arbitration of pending issues by the Hague Court. The United States refused to consider such a basis of settlement on the ground that national honor was involved and that such a question, consequently, could not be arbitrated.[141]

In a single sentence then, in meeting concrete and emergency cases the United States continued successful in a striking fashion but there were already those who, even under the impetus of the spectacular and in spite of the glamor of the leadership of Roosevelt, were beginning to hesitate on both ethical and practical grounds.

[139] Quoted by *ibid.*, pp. 373-4.
[140] *Ibid.*, p. 370.
[141] *Foreign Relations*, 1903, pp. 229; 313-4.

CHAPTER IV

IMPERIALISM VIA DIPLOMACY, 1899-1905:
ORGANIZATION OF DEPENDENCIES;
GENERAL POLICY

From the treatment of the concrete and specific emergency cases arising at the opening of the new century it thus appears that a rather definite pattern was developing for a Caribbean policy during the administration of John Hay and Theodore Roosevelt. However a second major problem of the administration was the question of new governments for Puerto Rico and Cuba. The one had been ceded outright to the United States, and would naturally be looked upon as the model for regions that might be acquired later by the rapidly expanding Nation of the North—and this was definitely a possibility in the thinking of small countries in the Caribbean. The other was in many ways the first protectorate of the United States in the Caribbean, and similarly was to be considered as the model for areas brought under the less direct control of the Stars and Stripes. The story has been repeated that an official of the old Austrian government, just prior to the first World War made the statement that Austria wished to " Cubanize " Serbia. What was this process of " Cubanizing " and what did it portend for the future?

First as to Puerto Rico. A primary question was that concerning the application of the United States Constitution, its bill of rights, and the principles of government generally understood to apply in the states of the Union. This problem was considered by both the Congress and the Supreme Court of the United States. With the expected increase of trade the actual question of revenue to be derived from tariffs was of some significance in general and was of vital importance to certain business interests of the United States and of the islands themselves. On the important question of sugar a test was made in the case of *De Lima vs. Bidwell.* Not surprisingly many conservatives had held that the laws of the United States did not apply to the new possessions unless specifically extended thereto by acts of Congress. In the case cited, however, the court held that tariffs collected from shippers in the new possessions were to be returned since the island of Puerto Rico was no longer a " foreign country " under the terms of the Dingley tariff act then in force. The broader question as to whether Congress could legislate special tariffs to be applied to imports from the said possessions was settled in the same term of court in the decision in the *Downes vs. Bidwell* case announced May 27, 1901. By this it was decided that the island was a " territory appurtenant and belonging to " the United States, even though it did not become a part of the United States as understood in the revenue sections of the Constitution.[1] This meant that special revenue producing laws might be applied by particular acts of Congress.

In other decisions as to citizenship rights the court displayed a variety of opinions and divided with disturbingly equal votes. However, the general idea developed that the rights in the United States bill of rights applied in some

[1] A convenient discussion of this is found in John Holliday Latané, *America as a World Power* (New York and London, 1907, pp. 143 ff.

cases, and in some cases did not, depending on what was considered advisable in the special case and at the moment. This was disconcerting to precedent loving souls but was not so surprising in the Caribbean countries where such liberties had long been considered privileges and where their enjoyment was not automatically taken for granted. If the program adopted was followed with reasonable consistency there would not be too much actual discontent or criticism except as it developed later as a result of education to abuses whose existence had theretofore been accepted as a matter of course, but which now were complained of. In truth, political happiness is all too often the relative thing that is so familiar to all peoples in the economic realm.

When the United States took possession of Puerto Rico the population was about 890,000, eighty-one per cent of whom were estimated to live in the country[2] though the total area was only a little over 3,400 square miles. Pending the establishment of a civil administration the Military Governor, George W. Davis, stated in a personal letter to Secretary Root that he was having serious trouble maintaining order, due to the restlessness of groups who clamored for rights and privileges of which they knew nothing.[3] These groups were naturally supported by the old Spanish sympathizers and were able to secure ample publicity in the United States through the lively opposition press then preparing for a general election.

As soon as possible a civil governor, Charles H. Allen, was sent out. He worked hard, visited the adjacent islands

[2] Report of United States Commission to Porto Rico to President McKinley, November 26, 1899, LC., Root MS.

[3] Davis to Root, April 5, 1900, *ibid.*

owned by the British and French to get new ideas, and constantly attacked the problem of installing the new government with a minimum of opposition.[4] He was so successful that the Federal (opposition) party in June, 1901, formally endorsed his program and pledged cooperation.[5] Of course this did not end troubles over systems of taxation and over numerous petty issues, and for many doubtless represented a decision to " make the best of a bad job " but just the same it was a substantial accomplishment.

One real trouble was the lack of understanding between the two peoples and the lack of experience of the United States in colonial management. The government as set up eliminated the old Spanish citizenship of the natives but did not provide United States citizenship at the same time. The result was that many proud people felt themselves international outcasts, and probably resented this far more than they did the fact that the President of the United States appointed a Governor's Council which also acted as the Puerto Rican Senate and so had the power to defeat undesired legislation. Roosevelt asked Congress in 1905 to confer citizenship on the islanders saying there was " no excuse " for the restriction [6] but Congress did not see fit to act for another decade. The lack of trained colonial administrators likewise appeared in the fact that by 1906 the federal judge in the island was proved guilty of demanding and accepting a loan from litigants [7] before his

---

[4] Allen to Root, February 15, 1901, August 14, 1900, and May 28, 1901, *ibid.*

[5] Allen to Root, June 19, 1901, *ibid.*

[6] Message of December 5, 1905, *Foreign Relations,* 1905, p. lix.

[7] See Taft to Roosevelt, April 22, 1906, LC., William Howard Taft MS.

court. A flagrant matter like this was corrected promptly but a more difficult situation was that arising from the snobbishness of untrained administrators. The journalist Richard Harding Davis wrote to Secretary of War Root saying:

He [Governor W. H. Hunt] also seems to be the only American official on the island, either military or civilian, who endeavors to treat the native as an equal. He consults with him, invites him to his house, and makes no social distinctions. To the other officials the native no matter how well bred and educated he may be, is a " Speakitte " and a " dago."

It is most unfortunate, and Hunt's good work is often undone overnight by the impertinence of some foolish woman to a native's wife, or by the insolence of one of our own officers.[8]

Further good impressions were made by private and public philanthropy on behalf of the needy islanders. The Central Porto Rican Relief Committee was an example of this. Its funds, collected from the public and amounting to tens of thousands of dollars, were handled by the banks expense free and with a good interest rate allowed on deposits,[9] and were then distributed with reports made to the Secretary of War. In addition the need of a school system was widely recognized and soon a program was adopted for the double purpose of general education and of " Americanizing " the people.[10] One W. G. Brumbaugh

[8] Davis to Root, April 27 [1902], LC., Root MS.

[9] Bliss and others to Root, November 5, 1902, *ibid.*

[10] Allen to Root, May 12, 1900; Report of War Department to Senate and House of Representatives (corrected MS.), January 30, 1900; Davis to Root, February 24, 1900, *ibid.*

The following letter in the Root MS throws some light on Mr. Root's approach to his problem:

was selected to install the new system and by January, 1902, he could report that there were 1000 schools in actual operation with 50,000 pupils in attendance.[11]

Roosevelt's ubiquitous interest in all that happened in the World was coupled with a real ability to inspire confidence on the part of his subordinates. In colonial matters this arose in part at least from this type of letter which he wrote to Governor William H. Hunt of Puerto Rico, September 26, 1901:

In dealing with the Philippines, Cuba and Porto Rico my purpose is to give Taft and Wood and yourself the largest liberty of action possible, and the heartiest support on my part.[12]

CHARLES SCRIBNER'S SONS,
Publishers, Importers and Booksellers,
153-157 Fifth Avenue,
Between 21st and 22nd Streets.

New York, Aug. 4th, 1899 [?].

Mr. Elihu Root,
The Arlington,
　　Washington, D. C.

Dear Sir:—

On your order of August 1st, we send you to-day the following books, viz:—

Dilke's Problems of Greater Britain.
Warner's Protected Princes of India.
Chesney's Indian Polity.
Life of Sir Henry Maine.
Life of George Higinbotham.

The balance are all English books and we have been unable to find copies in the city. We have, therefore, made a special import order and trust to fill the same within the month.

Yours truly,
CHARLES SCRIBNER'S SONS.
C. K.

[11] Brumbaugh to Root, January 6, 1902, *ibid.*
[12] Bishop, *Roosevelt and his Time*, I, 153.

Such support at times doubtless meant overriding strict legality—which was never too much of an obstacle to the redoubtable Teddy—if he felt there was a chance of securing results.

The details of financial administration of the island need not detain this account for it is well known that affairs were managed with efficiency and that there was a minimum of criticism from the standpoint of the policy adopted by the United States. Interesting accounts of this early work may be found in the personal letters of the Treasurer J. H. Hollander to Secretary of War Root.[13]

The trade of the Island responded splendidly to a systematic administration and peace, as well as the new trade opportunities opened in the United States. From 1901 until the outbreak of the World War in 1914 the exports rose every year over the preceding one (except for one occasion when there was a drop of less than 1%) so that in 1913 the exports were $49,104,000 as compared with $8,584,000 in 1901. Imports likewise had risen from $8,918,000 to $36,900,000.[14] Such results carried significance throughout the Caribbean so that the question in the minds of increasing numbers was " Self-government or Profits, Which? "

But in Cuba the situation was far more complicated. At first, as in Puerto Rico, the island was under the military control of the United States, with General Wood in charge. The number of the occupying forces was steadily reduced as can be seen from the fact that on December 5, 1899, McKinley reported that there were only 334 officers and

---

[13] Hollander to Root, April 24, 1901, and May 28, 1901, *ibid.*

[14] Victor S. Clark and Associates, *Porto Rico and Its Problems* (Washington, 1930), pp. 401-2.

10,796 enlisted men in the island; [15] by 1902 this was further reduced to 26 officers and 858 men.[16]

Naturally both army and navy were interested in the strategic value of the island in connection with the Caribbean. That this was not overlooked is evident from the report signed by George Dewey, President of the General Board of the Navy, and addressed to the Secretary of the Navy, calling for certain strategic positions to be under the control of the United States as important for " a possible war situation in the West Indies " " whether the cause of war be an isthmian canal or a question of the Monroe Doctrine." [17] Similarly, detailed and extensive mapping operations " intended solely for the use of the War Department of the United States Government " were undertaken costing over $60.000.

The data for this latter work is to a certain extent available for Cuba as well as the United States. Nevertheless, the United States is possessed of a very detailed and complete information concerning the most important area in Cuba; information which she could not have obtained, except under the condition existing during the Military occupation.[18]

Then for a permanent program Wood advised:

Permit me to call attention to the advisability of continuing some of our officers in as close touch as possible with the Cuban armed forces. They want to start a military school for the training of some of their young men and are especially anxious to have Captain Aultman with them. I don't know of any other way in which we can

[15] *Foreign Relations,* 1899, p. xxxviii.

[16] Fitzgibbon, *Cuba and the U. S.,* p. 89.

[17] Dewey to the Secretary of the Navy, December 7, 1900, LC., Root MS.

[18] Wood to the Secretary of War, November 18, 1902, *ibid.*

keep better informed or more in touch than by keeping one of our officers as an instructor attached to their armed forces.[19]

But there were also immediate activities of far reaching importance. As a surgeon of the army Wood's interest in health improvement and sanitation became a famous and major chapter in the world's fight on tropical diseases. Educational conditions were most unsatisfactory for some claimed that there was not a single actual school house on the island in 1898. Alexis E. Frye, a graduate of Harvard, was asked to inaugurate a school system.[20] This was done and Harvard University was induced to give a special summer training course to a selected group of Cuban Teachers in 1900.[21] As a result of the novelty and advertising and because it was the proper thing to do children flocked to the schools until 256,000 pupils were enrolled. Then came the natural reaction as the numbers settled down to an actual attendance of about 125,000 out of 160,000 enrolled[22]— a real contribution to say the least. Another problem was the use of Church property which had long been used for governmental purposes and for which the Spanish Government had made varying arrangements with the ecclesiastical authorities; for the most part paying rent. After an investigation and extended negotiations it was decided that the property should be bought by the military administration on behalf of the Cuban Government. This was approved by the War Department,[23] and was carried into effect in 1901.

[19] Wood to the Secretary of War, March 25, 1903, *ibid.*
[20] Fitzgibbon, *op. cit.,* p. 45.
[21] Eliot to Root, July 4, 1900, and July 9, 1900, LC., Root MS.
[22] Chapman, *History of Cuba,* p. 114.
[23] See undated memorandum, and Wood to Root, June 10, 1901, LC., Root MS.

Local governmental problems were also in need of attention. The number of municipalities or units of government were excessive with the result that taxes needed to support the number of local officers were entirely too high. After some delay while studying the problem the number of units was reduced by one-third in spite of protests from the abolished units and office holders who represented a not negligible group in the island. The elimination of the " consumo " taxes, mostly placed on necessities, was to seriously cripple the remaining municipalities so that such public services as sanitation, police, public education and charities had to be taken over at least for a time by the Military Government. Such local functions as were discharged were under the direction of officials appointed by the Military administration for it was feared that locally elected officials would not be efficient. Though complaints ensued results were secured.[24] Reforms with regard to imprisonment without trial, the use of the writ of *habeas corpus*, classification of prisoners as to types of crimes, ages and length of terms were also undertaken,[25] as was the organization of the judiciary. The fee system was abolished and salaries instituted, competitive examinations installed for minor court officials and a standard set of court records established;[26] at the same time that lawyers for the defense of the poor were provided.[27] Such innovations were sure to meet criticism but in the long run were approved.

[24] L. S. Rowe, " Reorganization of Local Government in Cuba," *The Annals,* XXV, 311 ff.

[25] Fitzgibbon, *op. cit.,* pp. 32-3.

[26] Chapman, *op. cit.,* p. 108.

[27] Fitzgibbon, pp. 34-5; for Wood's own summary of his administration in Cuba see Leonard Wood, " Military Government of Cuba," *The Annals,* XXI, pp. 29 ff.

With such wholesale developments in progress it was inevitable that some unsavory contracts would slip through and that real pressure would be used to guarantee their completion. So far as he was able it seems that General Wood did his best to suppress them and to cancel them when necessary.[28] Secretary Root by no means closed his eyes to what was going on and made every effort to get reports from all angles of the issues that arose.[29] When the criticism reached serious proportions Root fully supported his appointee as an efficient and honorable officer whose work deserved great praise.[30] The President himself endorsed the publication of a memorandum ending with the statement: "The Secretary, by direction of the President, thanks General Wood and the officials, civil and military, serving under him, upon the completion of a work so difficult, so important and so well done." [31]

Unquestionably the Government was somewhat autocratic, but in the long run the chief question was, did it train the Cuban people for self-government while it was in charge? Chapman quoting a critic comes to the conclusion that Wood

had no Congress to restrain him, he dominated the judiciary by force of character, and he accomplished his results primarily by such methods, making little effort to elicit the cooperation of the people. The result was that the

[28] Wood to Root, December 19, 1900, and December 10, 1901, also Platt to Root, December 24 and December 28, 1900, LC., Root MS. A suggestive later account is Beals, *The Crime of Cuba* (Philadelphia, 1933), pp. 170-2.

[29] Rubens to Root, August 24, 1900, July 28, 1901 [?], and March 17, 1902, LC., Root MS.

[30] See his nine-page letter to Abbott, December 19, 1903, *ibid.*

[31] Memorandum with corrections and postscript in the hand of Roosevelt, *ibid.*

ground was not prepared by him for institutional government, but rather he employed the autocratic government which had preceded and was to follow him. All else about Wood's record was good, and speaks for itself.[32]

However, as Chapman then points out it is doubtful if any other type of administration could have succeeded at that time, given conditions as they existed in Cuba at the close of a war and among a people who had never been taught to respect any other type of government.

Meanwhile, what about Cuban efforts and preparations for the establishment of their own government? Certainly some desired statehood in the United States [33] but this was inadvisable for obvious reasons and plans went forward for the calling of a constitutional convention. Root had made a careful study of the situation. He even made three trips to Cuba himself and was convinced that the best procedure had been adopted. Men who paid taxes on a nominal amount of property, who could read and write, or who had served in the Cuban army were allowed to vote for the delegates who, when elected, were called to order by General Wood. Root's conceptions (and he spoke for the plans of Washington at the time) were clear. He wrote:

Three things are of vital importance:

1. To secure a conservative and thoughtful control of Cuba by Cubans during the formative period, and avoid the kind of control which leads to the perpetual revolutions of Central America and the other West India Islands.

2. To make the suffrage respected so that there will be acquiescence in its results.

3. To stimulate the people to thrift and education.

[32] Chapman, *History of Cuba,* p. 150.
[33] Nickles [*sic*] to Root, April 15, 1901, LC., Root MS.
[34] Jessup, *Elihu Root,* I, 287.

I do not believe any people, three-fourths of whom are contented to remain unable to read and write, can for any long period maintain a free government.[35]

Unfortunately, either the Cubans did not know how to practice self-government as yet or were convinced that the election would be a farce for only about 30% of the qualified voters went to the polls. Unquestionably leaders of the people were sent to the convention, but they were the liberal "if not radical" leaders and there was only one bona fide conservative in the group.[36] Wood commented: " I hoped they would send their very best men. They have done so in many instances, but they have also sent some of the worst agitators and political rascals in Cuba." He continued that he was sure many of the best people desired continuance of United States control or actual annexation,[37] though it is probable that in this opinion the wish was the father to the thought. By January 19th Wood pled for prompt action and consistency by the United States but still hoped satisfactory results might be obtained and stated that he was going to use every means at his disposal to bring the conservatives to the front.[38]

As the Constitutional Convention proceeded with its work it was increasingly evident that scant attention was to be paid to General Wood and Secretary Root though the latter made clear the position of his Government to the Cuban leaders.[39] Wood wrote in June: " After the Convention had been in session some time I received thoroughly reliable information from various members to the effect

[35] Root to Dana, January 16, 1900, LC., Root MS.

[36] Fitzgibbon, *Cuba and the U. S.,* p. 72.

[37] Jessup, *op. cit.,* I, 307.

[38] Wood to Root, January 19, 1901, LC., Root MS.

[39] Chapman, *op. cit.,* pp. 138-9.

that the spirit of the Convention was to entirely ignore the question of relations with the United States." [40] Conservative Cubans were much concerned [41] and the people of the United States, as they became informed of developments, were first surprised, then resentful. Of the Constitution itself, as signed by the delegates February 21, 1901, Root wrote in his annual report:

I do not fully agree with the wisdom of some of the provisions of this constitution; but it provides for a republican form of government; it was adopted after long and patient consideration and discussion; it represents the views of the delegates elected by the people of Cuba; and it contains no features which would justify the assertion that a government organized under it will not be one to which the United States may properly transfer the obligations for the protection of life and property under international law, assumed in the treaty of Paris. [42]

Evidently, the dissatisfaction that existed was due to the provisions dealing with the relations of the new nation to its protector.

In the Congress of the United States there was much discussion that finally crystallized around the Platt Amendment, as it has been called. Senator Orville H. Platt sponsored the proposal and has generally been credited with its authorship, and indeed he specifically claimed the credit himself, in spite of the fact that many would insist that Root and others provided the ideas. [43] This proposal took

[40] This is a ten-page "Personal and Confidential" report to Root, dated June 9, 1901, LC., Root MS.

[41] Odoardo to Root, June 13, 1901, *ibid.*

[42] Quoted by Chapman, p. 35.

[43] Louis A. Coolidge, *An Old-Fashioned Senator; Orville H. Platt of Connecticut* (New York, 1910), p. 351; Jessup, *Elihu Root*, I, 310-11; Hill, *Roosevelt and the Caribbean*, pp. 73-4.

the form of an amendment to the army appropriation bill for the fiscal year 1902 and provided:

1. No contracts alienating Cuban territory for colonization, military or naval purposes should be made with foreign powers by Cuba.
2. The Cuban Government was not to contract any public debt whose retirement could not reasonably be provided for from the current revenues.
3. The United States was to have the right of intervention in Cuba to preserve Cuban independence, to maintain an adequate government for the protection of life and property, and to fulfill the provisions of the Treaty with Spain ending the war.
4. The acts of the Military Government of the United States were to be specifically endorsed and maintained.
5. The continuance of the sanitation program of the Military Government was guaranteed.
6. Title to the Isle of Pines was to be settled later.
7. Lands for naval bases were to be ceded to the United States.[44]

This amendment provided that the agreement was to be incorporated into the Cuban constitution but to prevent its elimination by later constitutional amendments after the Military Government had ceased to function, it was also to be signed as a treaty between the two countries.

One writer comments that this is "probably the first international agreement formally defining a right of forcible intervention." [45]   Inevitably there were many who called these provisions both too weak and too strong. However, the comments of Senator Platt might well be considered,

[44] For a convenient discussion and summary see Dana G. Munro, *The United States and the Caribbean Area* (Boston, 1934), pp. 11 ff.

[45] Benton, *International Law and Diplomacy of the Span.-Amer. War*, p. 290.

for whether he was the sole author of the provisions or not he was certainly a leader in the movement. He wrote June 11, 1901:

Personally, I was in favor of very much more stringent measures requiring much more as to our future relations, but in legislation you have got to consider the preponderance of public sentiment. As you say, it is difficult enough to bring those Cuban delegates to an acceptance of the terms we propose. If we had proposed more stringent terms, we would not only have had that difficulty vastly increased but we would have had a party in the United States and in Congress giving aid and comfort to the Cuban radicals. My own judgment is that when they conceded to us the right of intervention and naval stations, as set forth in the Amendment, the United States gets an effective and moral position which may become something more than a moral position and which will prevent trouble there. It is easy to say that we ought to insist on more, it was impossible to pass through Congress anything more drastic than we did.[46]

It might be noted in passing that there was no official demand for repayment by Cuba of any part of the war expenses of the United States though there were numbers who advocated this.[47] A good index to feeling in the United States is seen in the vote in the Senate on the provision giving the Northern Republic the right of future intervention in Cuba. A motion to eliminate this was defeated 43 to 20. Those who favored the provision were Republicans who supported the Administration while the opposition came from Democrats and two Republicans who genuinely feared this international police power idea. A similar alignment was seen in the House.[48]

[46] Coolidge, *op. cit.*, pp. 348-9.
[47] *Ibid.*, pp. 338-40.
[48] Perkins, *Monroe Doctrine, 1867-1907*, pp. 402-3.

When the provisions were sent to the Cuban Constitutional Convention there were serious protests. A local cartoon showed Cuba nailed to a cross between two thieves, General Wood and President McKinley, while Platt as a Roman soldier offered the Amendment as a sop on the end of a spear. More sensible Cubans, however, urged caution. They doubtless knew that Wood himself had reached the point in his thinking where he was advocating outright annexation for the good of both Cuba and the United States.[50]   Root spoke the definitive word when he cabled:

The Platt amendment is, of course, final and the members of the Convention who may be responsible for refusing to establish relations on that basis will injure only themselves and their country. If the convention takes such a course it will have failed to perform the duty for which it was elected and the duty must be performed by others.[51]

A committee was appointed to come to the United States for consultation. This Wood approved both as an educational experience and as a face saving procedure.[52] Further concessions were not to be secured but a definition of the provision on the troublesome right of intervention, was given by Root on April 3rd as follows:

You are authorized to state officially that in view of the President the intervention described in the third clause of the Platt amendment is not synonymous with intermeddling or interference with the affairs of the Cuban Government, but the formal action of the Government of the United

[49] Beals, *op. cit.*, p. 179.

[50] Jessup, I, 323; Tarafa to Conant, August 4, 1899; Conant to Griggs, August 5, 1899, and Hollander to Root, September 12, 1899, LC., Root MS.

[51] Root to Wood, March 20, 1901, *ibid.*

[52] Wood to Secretary of War, April 15, 1901, *ibid.*, Jessup, I, 318 ff.

States, based upon just and substantial grounds, for the preservation of Cuban independence and the maintenance of a government adequate for the protection of life, property, and individual liberty, and adequate for discharging the obligations with respect to Cuba imposed by the Treaty of Paris on the United States.[53]

With this the radicals had to be satisfied, and on June 12 Wood was able to report that the Amendment had been approved without change by a vote of 16 to 11.[54]

Before leaving this topic it would be well to repeat that it is easy indeed to over emphasize the active interest of the Cuban people in these legal technicalities. Relatively few of them had ever had any voice in government, and showed little interest now. Such affairs always had been handled outside their ken and Wood was able to write:

There is no excitement in the Island whatever as to whether the Convention accepts the Platt Amendment or goes fishing. The majority of the people are not talking nor paying attention to the present situation, and you would not know, if you were in the Island, that there was any important political matter being discussed, unless you happened to read some of the more violent newspapers. The only people who are paying any attention to the situation are bankers, merchants and people owning property, who are fighting against the Amendment, for they do not want a change in the government at present.[55]

The reasons given by General Wood for the opposition may be questioned but the statement is well worth consideration.

Slowly the talk of Cuban annexation died out though

[53] Quoted by Munro, *op. cit.*, p. 13.
[54] Wood to Root, June 12, 1901 (in code and translated), LC., Root MS.
[55] Wood to Root, June 9, 1901, *ibid.*

there were still those in both countries who thought that the move would be undertaken sooner or later. Meanwhile United States consuls continued to represent Cuba abroad until the new nation could organize its own system.[56] Whether its new status was that of a protectorate, a client state, or a ward (all terms being used by authorities to identify the new relationship)[57] there could be but little doubt that the United States policy, whatever it might be or might become, was understood to be dominant. Moon comments that the arrangement

was an interesting improvement on European methods of imperialism. It was designed to reconcile the Cuban desire for self-government with American strategic and economic interests—to accomplish the non-political objects of imperialism, without the disagreeable political methods.[58]

The President approached another major problem in his annual message of 1902 when he urged Congress to adopt a reciprocity treaty saying that " in a sense Cuba has become a part of our international political system. This makes it necessary that in return she should be given some of the benefits of becoming part of our economic system." The fight in Congress was long and bitter with able lobbying on the part of beet sugar interests as well as local cane sugar producers who feared the competition of the cheap Cuban product. After much debate the bill finally passed the House of Representatives in April, 1902, but other matters were allowed to prevent consideration in the Senate

[56] Zaldo to Hay, May 22, 1902, and Hay to Zaldo, May 24, 1902, Foreign Relations, 1902, p. 329.

[57] Fitzgibbon, op. cit., pp. 89-90.

[58] Parker Thomas Moon, Imperialism and World Politics (New York, 1926), p. 419.

[59] Foreign Relations, 1902, p. xx.

until adjournment on July 1st. A special session was
called by the President in March, 1903, to consider, among
other matters, the Cuban treaty and Panama canal treaty.
But again the Senate allowed the session to expire without
taking action. Finally, after continued executive pressure,
ratification was advised in December, 1903.

The effects could be seen at once for whereas in the
period from 1900-1903 Cuba had sent 75.3% of its exports to the United States, in the period from 1904-1907
the percentage rose to 85.5%. So far reaching was the
effect of this agreement that Cuba speedily became a one-
crop country and in 1927 an observer could write with
much justification:

> Reduced to its simplest terms, Cuba's foreign policy must
> be a matter of finding markets for her sugar, and, very
> secondarily, for her tobacco. Everything else is but the
> frills and fireworks of diplomacy—the assertion of her
> national *amour propre* as a sovereign state.[61]

With an essentially guaranteed market Cuban sugar production rose in a spectacular fashion. In 1899 with a
Cuban crop of only 345,000 gross tons the United States
imported 1,196,000 tons from other foreign countries but
by 1907 Cuba produced 1,428,000 tons and the United
States only imported 288,000 from other countries.[62]

Not surprisingly United States investors and adventurers
poured into the island so that by 1905 it was stated that
13,000 United States citizens had paid $50,000,000 for
land in Cuba and general investments had risen to approxi-

[60] Tariff Commission, *Reciprocity and Commercial Treaties,* p.
326.

[61] O., " Cuba and the United States," *Foreign Affairs,* VI, 236-7.

[62] E. F. Atkins, " Tariff Relations with Cuba—Actual and Desirable," *The Annals,* XXXII, p. 327.

mately $120,000,000.[63] Meanwhile the first Cuban President, Estrada Palma, had been duly elected under the new constitution. He was very friendly to the United States [64] though it must be admitted that the early legislation passed was " to say the least, not pro-American." [65] United States troops were withdrawn promptly but the United States Minister was the Dean of the Diplomatic Corps. In sentiment he was an annexationist and kept a careful watch on developments. When the first Cuban foreign loan was to be negotiated, the local authorities made a gesture of considering a European bid, but promptly settled down and for the next quarter of a century regularly accepted the offers of New York bankers. In considering the first loan, the State Department notified the bankers that it did not object to the proposal though Hay informed Minister Squires that there were many rumors of a reckless financial program of loans in Cuba and that these had

caused a good deal of anxiety in the mind of the President in regard to the future solvency of the Republic of Cuba. He does not wish you to assume the attitude of taking charge of the financial system of the Republic, but he desires that *you shall at all times, in a discreet and friendly manner, impress upon the mind of* President Palma and the Cuban Government the disasterous consequences of this wasteful and thoughtless policy.

In a postscript he added:

The President is very reluctant to avail himself of the provisions of the Platt Amendment in this and similar cases;

[63] Guggenheim, *U. S. and Cuba,* pp. 113-4; Jenks, *Our Cuban Colony,* p. 144.

[64] Fitzgibbon, *op. cit.,* p. 112.

[65] Quoted by Dennis, *Adventures in American Diplomacy,* p. 267.

but will understand that this will become imperative unless the present dangerous tendency is checked.[66]

Meanwhile details were slowly being worked out with regard to a naval base or bases. Surveys showed that only one of the proposed sites was fully suited to United States needs and this was acquired on nominal rental terms in Guantánamo Bay.[67] The question of ownership of the Isle of Pines was left in abeyance for the time in spite of pressure from United States speculators who wished their country to take over the region where they had invested their money. Also sanitation and educational problems of a serious nature developed, and corruption appeared in the government. Such questions were of course more irritating than surprising with a people who had never practiced self government.

At the end of the first presidential term of four years there was a more or less formal election held in which there was obviously much fraud at the polls. Palma was re-elected but a serious rebellion started at once. The United States was exceedingly reluctant to intervene for it was just then making a special effort to bring about better relations with Latin America and Root was actually on his famous good will trip to the Pan American Conference at Río de Janeiro. However, matters became increasingly critical and finally as will be seen later [68] President Palma insisted on resigning. William Howard Taft, the new Secretary of War who had made such an excellent record in installing the Philippine Government, was sent down to attempt to reconcile the factions. Failing to do this Magoon was

[66] Quoted by Guggenheim, pp. 218; 219.
[67] Munro, *U. S. and Cuba*, pp. 17-8.
[68] *Infra*, pp. 230 ff.

installed as military governor. Thus at first glance a cycle had been completed, the effort at self-government had failed and military control was again necessary. The Wood faction could feel that their urging of direct acquisition was vindicated but for the most part the public reacted almost violently against the whole idea. They were inclined to the view: keep out of the whole thing, let 'em stew in their own juice.

And now appeared the third phase of the Caribbean program at the opening of the century that dealt with the evolution of a general policy. Basic in consideration of the whole region was the fact that in 1900 both navy and army were actively engaged in considering ways and means of carrying on a war in the Caribbean and, as had happened before, in this connection both Haiti and Santo Domingo came in for careful study.[69] It will also be recalled that at the moment the whole people were gripped by a spirit of evangelism on behalf of their " little brown brothers " and were willing to justify almost any kind of program which would provide an opportunity for them to preach and practice their gospel.[70]

Then when it came to justification for the mooted word " intervention " the bankers had an argument ready to hand: the ever-satisfying plea for the protection of United States property. The revolutionary conditions of the Dominican republic had long been notorious and, after 1893 the San Domingo Improvement Company incorporated in New Jersey, was a chief holder of Dominican securities while the Clyde Steamship Company practically monopo-

[69] Long, Secretary of the Navy, to the Secretary of War, December 13, 1900, LC., Root MS.

[70] Welles, *Naboth's Vineyard*, II, 917.

lized the important sugar trade of the country.[71] After
President Heureaux was assassinated in 1899 the new government would not agree to the claims of the Improvement
Company and ousted its agents from the customs houses.
Foreign bondholders of France and Belgium in 1901 secured a mortgage on certain customs revenues to secure
their bonds, and the German, Italian and Spanish governments followed suit in 1903. The next year Italy made its
demands still more specific and heavy.[72]

Not surprisingly the United States began to be alarmed
and soon decided to act on behalf of the Improvement
Company which was about to lose its influence. The Bel-
gian Government feeling that it could not compete with
larger nations as Germany which had sent a warship to
enforce its demands, suggested that it would be glad to
undertake joint action with the United States to secure a
settlement. To add to the confusion rebel activities forced
the landing of United States, French and Italian forces
toward the end of 1903,[73] though the marines of Germany
and the United States had barely retired from a similar
landing party in April. Obviously, the Dominicans were
thoroughly demoralized but were likewise seriously alarmed.
General Desiderio Arías wrote to his chief, Jiménez:

When we obtain Puerta Plata again, special consideration
must be shown to nobody and such foreigners as . . .
should be kicked out of the country so that they never come
back, without paying any attention to the Consuls or to the

[71] Melvin H. Knight, *The Americans in Santo Domingo* (New
York, 1928), pp. 17-8.
[72] Welles, *op. cit.,* II, 602-4; Munro, *U. S. and the Caribbean,*
pp. 104-6; Jones, *Caribbean and the U. S.,* p. 103.
[73] Welles, *op. cit.*; Jones, *op. cit.*

Americans . . . Order Andres (Navarro) to use his cannons more actively against the Capital and to keep his courage up; tell him that affairs require, in fact demand, today more than ever, a very decided and firm attitude . . . Cannon shots from all sides of the City are what is needed because that terrifies the enemy and makes the Consuls and the families oblige them to give in . . . Offer Puerta Plata to be pillaged by the troops when you are going to attack it and see how contentedly and greedily they go about it. Always your friend,[74]

European powers wanted full protection of their interests but did not relish the difficulties involved and so would have been glad for the United States to be associated in the enterprise. However, the New World power had no intention of allowing such interference with its sphere of influence so all such suggestions were courteously declined or simply ignored.[75] Also the United States had no intention of allowing promiscuous naval demonstrations for the award of the tribunal in the Venezuelan debt case had just indicated that claims of those who resorted to such methods would probably receive preferential treatment. Meanwhile the diplomatic representations of the United States on behalf of the Improvement Company resulted in an arrangement by which the claims of the company were scaled down from $11,000,000 to $4,500,000 and this sum was guaranteed by monthly installments to be derived from the customs collected at certain ports. A financial agent was appointed who was also to be the financial adviser of the Dominican Government. When the first payment was not made the agent

[74] Welles, II, 610.
[75] George H. Blakeslee, *Recent Foreign Policy of the United States* (New York, 1925), p. 127.

took over the active collection of revenues at the port of Puerto Plata in October, 1904.[76]

Other governments were quite restless at the position of the United States and either wanted this country to assume more responsibility so as to care for their interests also or substantially less, for the collections being made were likely to interfere with the receipts of their nationals. In addition the old *bête noire* of Roosevelt and Hay cropped up, the idea that Germany was trying to secure a foothold in the Caribbean. Probably the Dominicans were quite willing to capitalize on this by getting Germany to assume the claims of Spain, Belgium and Italy and then present the joint claims demanding control of the customs houses in return, and then by using the situation thus developed to secure better offers from the United States by means of the competition provided.[77] On the other side of the picture it should be remembered that the Russo-Japanese War came at this time and that that contest was followed by the crisis in Morocco so there could not be very grave danger of European intervention at the moment.[78] A more logical interpretation would seem to be the simple one that on the one hand Germany was keeping as many irons as possible in the fire in the hope that some of them would get hot, while John Hay and Theodore Roosevelt had reached the conclusion that Dominican conditions provided the opportunity to take another logical step in their imperial program.

Administration contacts with the *Independent* and with

[76] Munro, *op. cit.,* pp. 105-6.

[77] Welles, II, 613; 620-1; J. F. Rippy, "Initiation of Customs Receivership in Santo Domingo," *Hisp. Amer. Hist. Rev.,* XVII, 430-2.

[78] Rippy, *ibid.,* pp. 437-8; 453-4; Perkins, p. 428.

the *Review of Reviews* are well known. In both, in March, 1904, appeared articles quite transparently inspired urging United States intervention in Santo Domingo. The next month Elihu Root at a banquet in honor of Cuban independence read the now well-known letter of Roosevelt in which the latter stated:

If a nation shows that it knows how to act with decency in industrial and political matters, if it keeps order and pays its obligations, then it need fear no interference from the United States. Brutal wrong-doing, or an impotence which results in a general loosening of the ties of civilized society, may finally require intervention by some civilized nation, and in the Western Hemisphere the United States cannot ignore this duty.[79]

All this was but the overture to the theme that was soon to be developed. December 30th Hay cabled Minister Dawson in Santo Domingo to point out the danger that foreign governments might intervene. He then continued: " You will ascertain whether the Government of Santo Domingo would be disposed to request the United States to take charge of the collection of duties and effect an equitable distribution of the assigned quotas among the Dominican Government and the several claimants." January 2, 1905, the response came that the Dominican President was " disposed to request " the United States to take charge of distributing the receipts, 60% to the Dominican Government and 40% [80] to the creditors (later negotiations changed this to 45% for Santo Domingo and 55% for creditors.) [81] In reporting the matter to the Senate Roosevelt

[79] Pringle, *Theodore Roosevelt,* p. 294.

[80] Dawson to the Secretary of State, January 2, 1905, *Foreign Relations,* 1905, p. 299.

[81] Dillingham to the Secretary of State, January 21, 1905, *ibid.,* p. 306.

frankly pointed out that the beneficiaries of the Monroe Doctrine " must accept certain responsibilities along with the rights which it confers." He repudiated the idea of territorial acquisitions in Santo Domingo but insisted that a financial protectorate was needed for the sake of the Dominicans, because of United States relations with other foreign powers, for the security of United States interests abroad, and for the sake of the commercial interests of the United States whose Gulf coast area was increasingly interested in this direction.[82] In fact, he went so far as to suggest the Platt Amendment as a solution.

But events did not await congressional debate on policies. Minister Dawson and Commander A. C. Dillingham who had been associated with him suggested sending an expert to investigate and to give financial advice. The result was the selection of President J. H. Hollander of Johns Hopkins University who had had experience in revising the tax laws of Puerto Rico.[83] He reached the island in March and in spite of considerable local excitement helped to work out the details of an agreement pretty much as outlined by the United States.[84] The one point on which the Northern Republic modified its position was in providing a guarantee that it would " respect the complete territorial integrity of the Dominican Republic." [85] The agreement really provided that the United States should act as a receiver for a

[82] Roosevelt to the Senate, February 7, 1905, *ibid.,* pp. 334 ff.

[83] Taft to the Secretary of the Navy, March 23, 1905, LC., Taft MS.

For conditions in Santo Domingo see Dawson to the Secretary of State, January 23, 1905, *Foreign Relations,* 1905, pp. 301 ff.

[84] Henry Merritt Wriston, *Executive Agents in American Foreign Relations* (Baltimore, 1929), p. 757.

[85] Hay to Dawson, February 6, 1905, *ibid.,* p. 322.

bankrupt state, the President nominating the customs receiver who would be officially appointed by the Dominican President.[86] Once the system was set up the President of the United States was to support the receiver by naval units as, and if, needed.

However, once more the reaction in public opinion asserted itself. People were not pleased at developments in Cuba, Puerto Rico was providing complications, and it was costing the United States $60,000,000 a year to conquer those Filipinoes who did not appreciate the freedom given them. It was all quite disconcerting, if not incongruous with popular conceptions of government " for the people " and " by the people," so again the cry of isolation was heard—and, as usual, Congress responded. The Senate declined to advise ratification of the treaty and adjourned March 4th without taking action.

This only made Roosevelt the more determined not to be balked. He had already put the treaty into operation as a *modus vivendi* in the shape of an Executive Agreement pending the action of the Senate. Most of the foreign creditors were quite willing for the agreement to be continued for it gave them a good chance to collect a reasonable amount of their claims.[87] Washington informed the Dominicans that the Senate action did not mean the death of the treaty and that the *modus vivendi* would continue in operation.[88] The receivership acted promptly and efficiently. United States gold became the monetary standard

[86] For letter of notification of the nomination and general instructions to first Customs Receiver see Taft to Colton, April 8, 1905, LC., Taft MS.

[87] Welles, *op. cit.,* II, 629-30.

[88] Dawson to Sanchez, March 27, 1905, *Foreign Relations,* 1905, p. 360.

of the country [89] and when revolutionary activity threatened to break out an embargo on arms shipments was promptly declared.[90] Supporters of the administration beguiled the public with praises of the wealth of the island [91] while the President bluntly notified the Secretary of the Navy, September 5, 1905:

As to the Santo Domingo matter, tell Admiral Bradford to stop any revolution. I intend to keep the island in statu quo until the Senate has had time to act on the treaty, and I shall treat any revolutionary movement as an effort to upset the modus vivendi. That this is ethically right, I am dead sure, even though there may be some technical or red tape difficulty.[92]

By this time John Hay had died and Elihu Root had taken charge of the State Department. He had a real "feel" for the susceptibilities of the Latin American nations and insisted that future good relations must be built on mutual confidence. When a revolutionary conspiracy was reported by Dawson who asked that a warship be sent, Root replied:

War ship ordered to Macoris. If Marines required to restore order, there should be first an express and clear request from the Dominican Government that they be landed for temporary protection of life of American citizens which Dominican Government declares itself for time being unable to protect. Upon such request necessary force will be landed.[93]

A different tone to that recently employed.

[89] Dawson to Secretary of State, November 23, 1905, *ibid.*, p. 412.

[90] Dawson to Secretary of State, October 14, 1905, *ibid.*, pp. 399 ff.; *British and Foreign State Papers,* CI, 638-9.

[91] H. J. Hancock, "The Situation in Santo Domingo," *The Annals,* XXVI, 49.

[92] Quoted by Hill, *Roosevelt and the Caribbean,* p. 164.

[93] Root to Dawson, November 7, 1905, *Foreign Relations,* 1905, p. 405.

Root was clearly perturbed about the position of the United States in Santo Domingo and the Senate was in an increasingly contentious frame of mind. He wrote to the Secretary of War, November 16, 1905:

If the Senate refuses to give the President the legal right to act officially in regard to Dominican finances, I do not think that we should go on as we are now. The result sooner or later would be an uprising against the existing Dominican Government to which the customs officers supposed to represent the United States, although not legally doing so, would have to yield, to the great injury of our prestige and credit, or which would be suppressed by a use of force on the part of our Government difficult to justify on constitutional grounds.[94]

Roosevelt, however, felt otherwise. He did all in his power to secure senatorial approval but when that was not forthcoming he was not to be deterred though he tried to reassure the public with the statement that the Constitution did not forbid him to proceed on this course and so the Constitution evidently did not object to his conduct.[95] Interestingly enough he was practicing the suggestion of Blaine who had proposed that the United States collect Venezuelan customs back in 1881.[96]

Beyond doubt the Dominican episode had been most suggestive for the United States was in a position to act or not to act since there could be little serious danger of European intervention with the international crises then on hand. But, was the Dominican affair an isolated, haphazard and erratic activity of Roosevelt or was it part of a studied policy such as Hay might have developed? Other

[94] Root to Secretary of War, November 16, 1905, LC., Taft MS.
[95] Roosevelt, *Autobiography*, p. 551.
[96] Hill, *op. cit.*, p. 159; note, gives references on this.

minor incidents in the Caribbean go far to answer the question.

Just west of Santo Domingo lay the far more populous but long troublesome Haiti. In 1900 the German Minister there suggested that since the local courts did not take jurisdiction of suits between foreigners, foreign governments themselves should set up an independent tribunal to handle such cases. In response to the suggestion Washington sent word that since this a tribunal " would appear to be such an essential interference with the sovereign rights of Hayti that the Government of the United States could not view with approval " [97] its establishment. However, when Haitian rebels stopped a German vessels and removed a shipment of arms and supplies destined for the regular Government of Haiti the Kaiser issued orders for a warship to search out and sink the offender. This was done in the fall of 1902 and there was little or no adverse comment in the United States, certainly no official protest.[98]

Of course rebel activity was carefully watched but in the first two or three years of the century other matters demanded prior attention and no special action was taken, though awkward claims were piling up to provide future complications.[99] In fact it would seem that the State Department contented itself with strict applications of the right of asylum,[100] the efforts to secure proper consideration for United States citizens in the island,[101] and an occasional

[97] See Alvarez, *Monroe Doctrine*, pp. 98-9.

[98] Perkins, pp. 331 ff.

[99] D. Y. Thomas, *One Hundred Years of the Monroe Doctrine* (New York, 1927), p. 241.

[100] See Pierce to Powell, June 24, 1905, *Foreign Relations*, 1905, pp. 552-3.

[101] Furniss to State Department, January 6, 1906, and February 3, 1906, *Foreign Relations*, 1906, II, 897-8; Thomas, *op. cit.*, pp. 243-4.

act of generosity such as that of Mr. Root in 1906. One Michael J. Kouri had been acquitted in Haiti on a charge of counterfeiting and he then urged the State Department to press for damages on the grounds of defamation of character. Root pointed out that the acquittal was due to the fact that his act was interrupted by the authorities before his obvious plans could be carried out hence the evidence necessary for conviction had not been available. As a result: " From this point of view, the department is unable to see any equity in the claim, as submitted, of Mr. Kouri, and must therefore, decline either to bring it to the notice of, or press it upon, the Haitian Government." [102]

In general it may be said that when Panama and Dominican issues were sufficiently settled to leave hands free for Haiti the reaction had set in. As a matter of fact Roosevelt was forced later to state reluctantly that he would have " exercised some supervision " over Haiti but his people were not then willing to endorse a " reasonable and intelligent " foreign policy.[103]

About the same time the idea of acquiring the Virgin Islands was again revived as rumors spread that the Standard Oil Company was interested in them [104] and because of the fact that the General Board urged the acquisition as a vital part of the naval defense system of the canal and the United States. Hay too was probably anxious to complete something of a rounded program to present to the Senate.[105] The negotiations carried on from 1900 to 1902

[102] Root to Furniss, May 4, 1906, *Foreign Relations,* 1906, II, 871-2.

[103] Rippy, *Caribbean Danger Zone,* p. 145.

[104] Bangs to Root, May 1, 1900, LC., Root MS.

[105] Dennett, *Hay,* pp. 271-2.

were more than a little obscure as the nebulous, romantic and a bit off-color Captain Christmas dabbled in the picture primarily for his own interest. But to simplify the story so ably examined by Professor Tansill it might be said that Hay gradually raised his price and the King of Denmark finally reluctantly agreed to the treaty providing a consideration of $5,000,000 to be paid by the United States.[106] Again the German danger was talked about [107] but by January, 1902, the document was submitted to the legislative bodies of the two countries for consideration. In the United States the treaty had been approved the preceding February 17th before the reaction against expansionism had become acute.[108] Finally, after spectacular pressure and bitter controversy the treaty was killed in October, 1902, in the Danish Rigsdag by the votes of two members of eighty-seven and ninety-seven years of age whose physical condition was such that they had to be carried to their seats. This ended the question for the time though Henry Cabot Lodge and others were still talking about the matter and urging the acquisition of both the Virgin Islands and Greenland for strategic reasons and for the sake of the fisheries interests of the United States.[109]

Relations with Mexico continued satisfactory. A gracious step was taken in 1900 by the return of over $287,000 by the United States when it was found that an award by the United States-Mexican Mixed Claims Commission had been obtained by fraud. A similar happy result came from the

---

[106] Tansill, *Purchase of Danish West Indies,* pp. 339 ff.

[107] *Ibid.,* pp. 417-8; 436-7; Nevins, *White,* p. 207.

[108] Tansill, *op. cit.,* pp. 361; 349.

[109] Lodge to Roosevelt, May 12, 1905, and June 10, 1905, Roosevelt to Lodge, May 24, 1905, in Lodge, *Roosevelt-Lodge Correspondence,* II, 119-20; 135-6; 124-5.

settlement of the long standing Pious Fund Case which was the first referred by the United States to the Hague Court. Agreements as to the submission of the case were completed in 1902.[110] United States money was pouring into all kinds of Mexican enterprises; it was starting in petroleum and well established in mines and railroads. By 1902 a consular report estimated that 117 United States companies held investments in Mexico valued at over half a billion dollars.[111]

For three months following October 22, 1901, the Second International Conference of American States met at Mexico City. Here one of the chief questions discussed was that of arbitration and delegates from ten of the states represented signed a project of a treaty for compulsory settlement of international disputes. Of these Santo Domingo, Salvador, Guatemala, Mexico and Venezuela were in the Caribbean area. In addition seventeen indicated approval of arbitration of pecuniary claims; of these Colombia, Costa Rica, the Dominican Republic, Guatemala, Haiti, Honduras, Mexico, Nicaragua, Salvador and the United States were Caribbean countries. This latter agreement was to go into effect when five ratified and so was proclaimed in 1905 when Guatemala, Salvador, Peru, Honduras and the United States had ratified.[112] It will be noted that four of these five were in the Caribbean.

However, when it came to general arbitration treaties Roosevelt was extremely cautious. The active part taken in

[110] See *Foreign Relations*, 1900, cir. p. 781; *ibid.*, 1901, p. liii; *ibid.*, 1902, cir. p. 780.

[111] Callahan, *American Policy in Mexican Relations*, pp. 510; 517-9.

[112] Moore, *Digest*, VII. 94-5.

the establishment of the Hague Court had recognized the elimination of the old fear expressed by Blaine when he blocked the settlement of the Colombia-Costa Rica Boundary dispute by an European arbitrator. In truth, this was the method employed in the Pious Fund case and others.[113] But when it came to promiscuous arbitration the President expressed his opinion while visiting in Chile at the end of his administration. He said that Mexcio had a legal right to sell Magdalena Bay to a foreign or non-American power, just as Denmark had a right to sell the Virgin Islands, and any arbitral court would uphold the right. Just the same the United States would be internationally idiotic and simple-minded to allow either proceeding to take place.

Needless to say the President, Hay, Taft and other members of the executive staff were exceedingly restless at the control exercised by the Senate over arbitration and other treaties,[114] but this is hardly a part of the present study except as the Senate reflected the growing popular reaction that was to check the imperialistic policy of the administration. In fact, Roosevelt practically ran the State Department,[115] and his actions were based on an innate feeling that the strong and capable ought to run things on general principles. When it came to smaller countries they ought to recognize their position and act accordingly. Bluntly put the idea was expressed while he was Vice-President in

[113] Thomas, *op. cit.,* pp. 186-7.

[114] Taft to Lodge, February 11, 1905, LC., Taft MS; Adams, *Education of Henry Adams,* pp. 374-5; 394; Thayer, *Hay,* II, 225-6.

[115] Jusserand to Delcassé, January 25, 1905, and Jusserand to Rouvier, June 28, 1905, *Documents Diplomatiques,* 2d Série, VI, 61-4; VII, 181; Thayer, *op. cit.,* 297.

1901: "If any South American country misbehaves toward
any European country . . . let the European country spank
it." [116] He bitterly resented domestic opposition toward
his policies and sent word to Root through his Private
Secretary Cortelyou, urging Root to make an address in
which he "would skin these wretched creatures . . . and
the rest of the minor vermin," [117] who had dared criticize
the policy of the United States in the Philippines and
implied that isolationism was advisable.

Increasingly after 1900 the opinion in the United States
had important economic repercussions in connection with
all Caribbean countries. For instance, when the President
clearly indicated that his country had a " duty " to see that
its southern neighbors paid their " obligations " the Report
of the Council of the British Foreign Bondholders noted
that the value of the bonds of Costa Rica and Honduras
more than doubled within a year. And it will be recalled that the Council was none too pleased with the
simultaneous effects of Yankee actions in Panama, Santo
Domingo and Guatemala.[118]

Probably Roosevelt was not consciously swayed by financial considerations. In fact, a carefully planned financial
program was essentially foreign to his very nature. When
necessary he would press vigorously the claims of the
United States against a Castro in Venezuela, even to the
point of breaking off diplomatic relations, but such actions
usually followed political rather than purely economic
friction.[119]

[116] Quoted by Pringle, *Roosevelt,* p. 283.

[117] Cortelyou to Root, December 29, 1902, LC., Root MS.

[118] J. F. Rippy, " British Bondholders and the Roosevelt Corollary of the Monroe Doctrine," *Pol. Sc. Quar.,* XLIX, 199-202.

[119] Hill, *op. cit.,* pp. 211-2.

With the passage of time it may be that Roosevelt became more aware of the possibilities of Dollar Diplomacy and there are evidences that this was the case. He strongly urged a larger merchant marine for New World trade,[120] and was obviously aware of the spectacular rise in profits resulting from United States control of specified regions. Reciprocal trade treaties in general were no longer seriously urged but the value of the trade which followed the flag could not be disputed. Root, connected closely with business interests was willing to consider intervention in Haiti and Honduras, but as has been seen was not at all willing to strain legality or good relations to secure this object. Roosevelt, similarly, was willing to act in Venezuela but felt the time was not ripe.[121]

Somewhat better known and certainly in character was the Big Stick element in the policy. A few such as Henry Watterson dared to defy the current and to denounce the imperialism of the moment as " wanton, senseless, hypocritical jingoism," [122] while Woodrow Wilson described the district from the Gila River to Oregon acquired after the war with Mexico as one to which we had " no conceivable right except that of conquest." [123] The public, however, preferred to hear Roosevelt say " The one unpardonable sin is to bluff," our people " have no business to uphold the Monroe Doctrine unless they are willing to fight for it," [64] or the words of Senator Albert J. Beveridge,

[120] Message to Congress, December 5, 1905, *Foreign Relations, 1905*, p. xlv.

[121] Rippy, *Caribbean Danger Zone,* p. 145.

[122] Quoted by Perkins, p. 391.

[123] See Harley Notter, *Origins of the Foreign Policy of Woodrow Wilson* (Baltimore, 1937), p. 127.

[124] Roosevelt to Root, April 30, 1900, LC., Root MS.

" none of our possessions will ever be given up until our power has begun to wane. . . . 'What we have we hold,' is the motto of our blood "; [125] or Seth Low's raptures when he said that except for the brief incident of Napoleon III in Mexico, " By the Monroe Doctrine the United States has preserved both the American continents from European complications for almost a century" and now these blessings were being extended to the Far East.[126] Concerning such statements the German Ambassador Bernstorff wrote:

The American daily papers are more important as a medium for influencing public opinion than as a mirror for reflecting it. The United States is the land of propaganda par excellence! . . . Not only the great news agencies, but also all leading newspapers of the Union maintain their permanent special correspondents in Washington, and these are received almost daily by the Secretary of State, and as a rule once a week by the President. The information that they receive at these interviews they communicate to their papers in the greatest detail, without naming the high officials from whom it has emanated, and in this way they naturally act as megaphones through which the views of the government are spread throughout the whole country.[127]

Though the conclusion of the Ambassador may be a bit overdrawn the constant statements of the President doubtless had an effect, for he followed his private opinion on bluffing with numerous statements while President to the same effect. In his annual message of December 6, 1904, he wrote: " It is not merely unwise, it is contemptible, for a nation, as for an individual, to use high-sounding lan-

---

[125] A. J. Beveridge, " Development of a Colonial Policy for the United States, *The Annals,* XXX, 4-5.

[126] Seth Low, " Position of the United States among the Nations," *The Annals,* XXVI, 9.

[127] Bernstorff, *My Three Years in America,* p. 33.

guage to proclaim its purpose, or to take positions which are ridiculous if unsupported by potential force, and then refuse to provide this force." "Generally peace tells for righteousness; but if there is conflict between the two, then our fealty is due first to the cause of righteousness." [128]

Now it should not be forgotten that the President's aims were high with regard to actual possessions and he desired to eliminate politics in appointments as much as possible. In the meanwhile a government was to be provided *for* the inhabitants while they were being trained so that their government could become one *by* them.[129] Senator Beveridge made this even more specific when he said:

Administration is the principle upon which our colonial policy should proceed for a century to come. . . . Not sudden " self-government " for peoples who have not yet learned the alphabet of liberty; not territorial independence for islands whose ignorant, suspicious and primitive inhabitants, left to themselves, would prey upon one another until they become the inevitable spoil of other powers, not the flimsy application of abstract governmental theories possible only to the most advanced races and which, applied to undeveloped peoples, work out grotesque and fatal results. . . . And common sense in the management of our dependencies means practical administration of government until our wards are trained in continuous industry, in orderly liberty and in that reserve and steadiness of character through which alone self-government is possible.[130]

The never forgotten early acts of Roosevelt's national career as Assistant Secretary of the Navy and as a Rough Rider in Cuba when he gloated over being a man among men making history, guaranteed that he would always

---

[128] *Foreign Relations,* 1904, p. xxxix.
[129] Hill, *Roosevelt and the Caribbean,* p. 206.
[130] Beveridge, *op. cit.,* p. 3.

lend an ear to the plea of the strategists for naval bases. And now he was surrounded by men who thought much as he did. Loomis, Assistant Secretary of State, wrote in 1904: "to deal with specific cases, it seems plain that no picture of our future is complete which does not contemplate and comprehend the United States as the dominant power in the Caribbean Sea. . . ."[131] On March 15, 1903, the President followed his earlier interest in mapping the Caribbean by a letter saying that he had followed up the matter further by talking to two army men and that it seemed wise to send the men in civilian dress and on board the private yacht of Mr. Armour who was a public-spirited man and would be glad to have his yacht used for the purpose.[132] Also, the War Department was naturally interested in cable connections and somewhat later one finds a three-page report from Taft direct to the President on this matter.[133] Just another straw in the wind.

Toward the end of the Administration when the reaction had set in definitely there appeared an " injured innocence " note in the President's writing. By this time he was emphasizing the benefits to both his country and the regions concerned as a result of United States intervention. He openly blamed his people for selfishness and blindness and lack of intelligent interest.[134] However, Professor Moon strips off the veneer when he says:

It is a matter of plain honesty with ourselves, moreover, to face the fact that sanitation, education, and uplift are not

[131] W. W. Pierson, " Political Influences of an Interoceanic Canal," *Hisp. Amer. Hist. Rev.*, VI, 226.

[132] Roosevelt to Root, March 14, 1903, and March 15, 1903, LC., Root MS.

[133] Taft to the President, March 21, 1907, LC., Taft MS.

[134] Roosevelt to Taft, August 21, 1907, LC., Root MS.

the original aims of our interventions in the Caribbean. Search the records! I have yet to find a case in which the State Department has selected some Caribbean country because it was particularly unsanitary and illiterate, and has decided to send the marines there for the sole purpose of uplifting the people.[135]

Professor A. B. Hart was striking close to the heart of the matter when he still used the term Monroe Doctrine but defined the United States policy as one based on "Permanent Interests" of the nation.[136] Hiram Bingham was soon to declare the sanctified, if not sanctimonious, doctrine an "obsolete shibboleth"[137] but throughout the Roosevelt administration it was constantly appealed to as a shibboleth. Regardless of what question that might arise it was defined in terms of the Monroe Doctrine until Weinberg bluntly states that the foundation of Roosevelt's ideology "has nothing to do with Monroe."[138] In fact the President was passionately devoted to the idea of national defense and justified himself in his own eyes and in those of his people by pointing out the moral and material blessings that resulted.

Probably the President himself realized the incongruity of the situation for in another connection he wrote to his British friend, Sir Cecil Spring-Rice:

It would be well nigh impossible, even if it were not highly undesirable, for this country to engage with another to carry out any policy, save one which had become a part

---

[135] Chester Lloyd Jones, H. K. Norton and Parker T. Moon, *The United States and the Caribbean* (Chicago, 1929), p. 194.

[136] A. B. Hart, "The Monroe Doctrine and the Doctrine of Permanent Interests," *Amer. Hist. Rev.*, VII, 88-91.

[137] Hiram Bingham, *The Monroe Doctrine, an Obsolete Shibboleth* (New Haven, 1913).

[138] Weinberg, *Manifest Destiny*, p. 429.

of the inherited tradition of the country, like the Monroe Doctrine. Not merely could I, for instance, only make such an engagement for four years, but I would have to reckon with a possible overthrow in Congress, with the temper of the people, with many different conditions. In consequence, my policy must of necessity be somewhat opportunist. . . . [139]

Feeling this public resistance keenly the President tried to offset criticism by disclaimers of expansionism [140] and by a genuine cooperation with Mexico to bring about the establishment of a Central American Union and the establishment of the Peace Court for these five small republics. This was unquestionably much appreciated and constituted a real advance, [141] and also fitted into the general policy. Mere police work had already caused too much trouble so if this could be obviated by fostering such a union, the scheme was certainly worth trying. The summary of the whole matter may be found in the now well known Roosevelt Corollary. This constituted a frank assumption of responsibility for the Caribbean and neighboring small countries. " Chronic wrong-doing " was subject to punishment or intervention; by outside nations if necessary, but preferably by the United States. " It is far better that this country should put through such an arrangement, rather than *allow* any foreign country to undertake it." [142]

The same attitude was expressed toward the Galapagos

[139] Roosevelt to Spring-Rice, December 27, 1904, Gwynn, *Letters and Firendships of Spring-Rice,* I, 442-3.

[140] Perkins, pp. 456 ff.

[141] George T. Weitzel, *American Policy in Nicaragua . . .* (Senate Document No. 334, 64th cong., 1st sess.) (Washington, 1916), pp. 3-4.

[142] Message to Congress, December 5, 1905, *Foreign Relations,* 1905, p. xxxv. The italics in the quotation are inserted by the author.

Islands off the coast of Ecuador and owned by that country. Talk of using them as a naval base found the Navy uninterested and the whole affair was dropped except for efforts of Ecuador to use the islands as a means of securing attempted loans from the United States. These were declined though Adee, in the State Department, doubtless expressed the view of the administration when he endorsed one report on the subject " We don't want them ourselves and won't allow any European (or extra-American) power to acquire control of them." As late as 1908 Root stated that the United States would not object to Chilean acquisition but made it certain that a suggested German or French acquisition would not be permitted.[143]

What evolves out of the fog of talk and varying acts and interpretations? Root in effect was saying: We do not want the small countries of the Caribbean for ourselves; we do not want any foreign nations to take them; we want to help them.[144]   Roosevelt was frankly practicing the theory: these are our younger brothers, when they need spanking we expect to do the job, and, incidentally when we think it advisable we shall take charge of their spending money, and, maybe of certain other choice possessions in the meantime. One man, as early as 1902, seems to have caught the real significance of what was needed and what would inevitably happen. He stated:

When an isthmian canal shall have been constructed it will be approached from Europe most conveniently by the Anegada passage, and from Atlantic ports of the United States by the Windward and Mona passages. Each passage will become the highway of a great commerce.

[143] Quoted by Rippy, *Caribbean Danger Zone,* p. 131.
[144] Elihu Root, "Development of the Foreign Trade of the United States," *The Annals,* XXIX, pp. 444-5.

No matter how strongly the isthmian canal may be forti-field it would, in war, serve us no purpose—indeed, through war, we might lost it entirely—if our fleet could not control its approaches.[145]

And here is found the central policy that was to control the real activities of the State Department for the twenty years following the turn of the century. It was not the Monroe Doctrine at all but a new and parallel policy that had come into existence to face the new needs of the new century. Because of the precedent loving people of the United States and their reluctance to admit any change in their foreign policy, all applications of the new program still had to be sanctified by the use of the old name. Thus altruism and avarice, destruction of native crafts and crops side by side with business efficiency and progress, and inter-ference and non-interference in Caribbean affairs took place in apparently hopeless confusion and with endless contra-dictions—unless the observer seizes the one essential idea of control of the canal and its approaches. Once this is realized the program of administrations, Republican or Democratic, fall into a reasonably consistent pattern. Popu-lar confusion, resulting from ignorance and political ora-tory, further confounded by the arguments for and against Dollar Diplomacy which was merely an irritating barnacle that attached itself to the main idea, brought about occa-sional notable recessions in the vigor with which the pro-gram was applied, but it is now no longer possible to doubt that the program existed in fact.

[145] W. V. Judson, "The Strategic Value of the West Indies to the United States," *The Annals,* XIX, p. 61.

At the time the above article was written the author held the rank of captain of the Corps of Engineers, U. S. Army. Later he was sent as Military Attaché to the Russian Army in the Russo-Japanese War. In 1917-9 he held the rank of Brigadier General, N. A.

CHAPTER V

REACTION: MASTERFUL COOPERATION

And now it is necessary to look more carefully at this period of reaction already mentioned several times when the people of the country expressed their disappointment with the results of imperialism. As was perfectly natural the business interests made the most of opportunities that were presented. Having ready access to administration leaders they pointed to the beneficent results of business efficiency and beyond question at times the administration appeared to be blind or certainly complacent with regard to methods employed. This gave rise to the term Dollar Diplomacy which in the last section was characterized as a barnacle that had attached itself to the foreign policy of the nation. Ignoring the pest only allowed it to batten and wax fat.

Now a new personality was more and more obvious in the affairs of the State Department after the early part of 1905. This was Elihu Root who sprang from parents of modest means but who early associated himself, thanks largely to his initiative, ability, personality and ambition, with wealthy New York interests. As attorney for these clients he became one of the best known attorneys in the city. He was asked to become Secretary of War when the affairs of the Department were found to be in serious disorder toward the close of the Spanish-American contest. This did not appeal to him at all but when he was informed that the Secretary would have the responsibility for organizing governments for the newly acquired dependencies, he felt that the opportunity was too great to be declined, so he resigned his lucrative private practice and began a public service that was to last the rest of his active career. When John Hay died, as already indicated Root succeeded him in the Department of State.

There was no violent wrench in the way of a change of policy—Root was too much of a business man for that. As an attorney, his passion was for law and order; as a practicing attorney, he firmly believed that even a crook should have advantage of the best legal talent; as an honest attorney he really believed in the law and was not willing to ride rough-shod over the rights of others. Thus his innate kindliness and respect for the rights of others, whom he was willing to meet on a footing of equality, opened a new day in the relations of the Head of the State Department with the delegates of the smaller republics of the New World.[1] In addition, due to his profound knowledge and strength of character he gradually recovered more and more responsibility from the President for the administration of the affairs of his Department which Hay's health and Roosevelt's force of character had tended to place increasingly in the hands of the executive. Roosevelt himself wrote to Andrew Carnegie, February 26, 1909:

The work on Latin American affairs was entirely Root's. . . . My part in it has been little beyond cordially backing him up. It was he who thought of making that extraordinary trip around South America which did more than has ever been done previously to bring the South American States into close touch with us. It was he who made the Pan-American Congress a matter of real and great importance for the Commonwealths of the Western Hemisphere. It was he who gave life to the Bureau of American Repub-

[1] Jessup, *Elihu Root,* I, 473-4.

lics. It was he who brought about the formation of the international court for the Central American States. It was he who finally got the Senate to accept the Santo Domingo treaty, which secured an extraordinary increase in peace and prosperity in Santo Domingo and may prove literally invaluable in pointing out the way for introducing peace and order in the Caribbean and around its borders.[2]

However it must always be remembered that Root was a practical attorney accustomed to advise business interests. He strongly believed in protecting vested interests and properties acquired. He wrote early in 1905: "The inevitable effect of our building the Canal must be to require us to police the surrounding premises. In the nature of things, trade and control, and the obligation to keep order which go with them, must come our way. . . ." This he tempered with the statement:

The South Americans now hate us, . . . largely because they think we despise them and try to bully them. I really like them and intend to show it. I think their friendship is really important to the United States, and that the best way to secure it is by treating them like gentlemen. If you want to make a man your friend, it does not pay to treat him like a yellow dog.[3]

Under Root's guidance both his practical knowledge and his personal theories were applied by the State Department. He felt that business methods practiced by business men in newly acquired dependencies were nationally advisable and internationally essential. As a result it is not surprising that the United States, partly at least as a result of his recommendations, adopted tariff assimilation for Puerto Rico, Alaska and Hawaii while it levied preferential tariffs in favor of United States trade in the Philippines, Guam, and

[2] Quoted in *ibid.*, I, 560.   [3] *Ibid.*, pp. 471; 469.

later in the Virgin Islands. Only the Canal Zone (because of its peculiar international relationships) and Guam whose trade was quite negligible, retained the open door. Thus it developed that the United States maintained "the closed door in her dependencies as compared with the open door at something like the ratio of 365:1 [on a population basis]." [4] The policy not only represented an effort to secure economic prosperity but was a conscious attack on the causes of unrest in the Caribbean. It was hoped that prosperity would eliminate revolutions. [5]

Advocates of the policy felt it amply justified by the reports of health conditions, sanitation, population growth, peace and domestic order that resulted from the injection of United States dollars and control in the regions involved. True, some Latin Americans protested that it fostered a dictatorship for it asked few questions and was satisfied when there was peace and dictatorial control that protected foreign investments. They argued that interventions came when an exasperated people took matters into their own hands and fought for liberties denied them by self-perpetuating dictatorships. [6] However, it is significant that this same policy was enthusiastically supported by Taft and Knox, and that even the altruistic and conscientious Woodrow Wilson endorsed it to a certain extent; while the administrations in the 1920's took its application as a matter of course. If a single phrase can be used to describe it probably no better one could be devised than that of "masterful cooperation," with varying degrees of emphasis on each of the two words.

[4] Williams, *Economic Foreign Policy of the U. S.*, p. 321.

[5] Welles, *Naboth's Vineyard*, II, 925.

[6] F. García Calderón, "Dictatorship and Democracy in Latin America," *Foreign Affairs*, III, 473-4.

With Root in charge system and efficiency were emphasized in the conduct of affairs. This was seen in the
reorganization of the consular and diplomatic service to
eliminate spoilsmanship and promote efficiency.[7] Similarly,
there was a definite recommendation that all colonial administration should be centralized in Washington. This was
endorsed by the President but failed to secure the approval
of Congress.[8] Educational institutions were encouraged to
make special efforts to attract students and potential colonial
leaders to the United States for training, and increasing
numbers took advantage of the offers.[9]

Also in the field of general policy was the question of
cooperation on an organized scale. To clear the air somewhat and to take up a suggestion still being urged, further
consideration was given to the proposal of the Honorable
Luis M. Drago to prevent the collection of international
debts by force. It was possible to use this to good advantage
to supplement the idea of preventing European intervention
in the New World, but it was necessary to proceed so as
not to preclude adequate protection of the rapidly increasing
investments of the United States itself. The result was the
presentation of the idea by the United States delegate,
General Horace Porter, at the Hague Conference which met
in 1907. The well-known result needs no discussion and

[7] James Brown Scott, "Root," in Bemis, *Secretaries of State*,
IX, 239-41; Jessup, *op. cit.*, II, 101-2; 108.

[8] Major General Frank McIntyre, "American Territorial Administration," *Foreign Affairs*, X, 298.

[9] Stokes to Root, January 9, 1907, and Root to Stokes, January
12, 1907, LC., Root MS; M. G. Brumbaugh, "An Educational
Policy for Spanish-American Civilization," *The Annals*, XXX,
67-8; William Spence Robertson, *Hispanic American Relations
with the United States* (New York, 1923), pp. 297-8.

it is sufficient to say that it was finally endorsed at the Conference with the proviso that the prohibition against the use of force would not apply if the debtor refused to submit the matter to arbitration by an adequate court. Since the Hague Court was already in operation the solution was considered a most happy one for thus law and orderly procedure would protect the investor of all nations while the most likely cause of European intervention in New World affairs was eliminated.[10]

Another situation awaiting a unifying force was the set of complications arising perennially in Central America. The potential value of the Nicaraguan Canal route was still an ever present item in all calculations as was noted by United States Minister George T. Weitzel, Minister to Nicaragua:

In brief, it may be said that the canal question is the principal disturbing issue in Nicaraguan affairs, whether international, interstate, or internal; and this is none the less true, even though the Panama route has long since been chosen as the world's highway of commerce. It still offers to the cupidity of the professional revolutionist a prize as valuable as the possession of the customhouses and affords as much as ever an opportunity for intrigues among the Central American republics and a basis for negotiation with foreign countries, if not a provocation for their interference in the affairs of Nicaragua.[11]

Root personally had no patience with dabblers in Central

[10] For proposals at the Hague see *Foreign Relations*, 1907, *cir.* pp. 1154; 1200. See also Drago to Root, January 2, 1907, LC., Root MS; Charles Evans Hughes, *Our Relations to the Nations of the Western Hemisphere* (Princeton, 1928), pp. 65 ff.; Drago in Alvarez, *The Monroe Doctrine,* pp. 252-3.

[11] T. A. Bailey, "Interest in Nicaraguan Canal, 1903-1931," *Hisp. Amer. Hist. Rev.*, XVI, 2-3. A general and full statement is found in Weitzel, *American Policy in Nicaragua.*

American affairs [12] but the constantly arising boundary disputes as those between Nicaragua and Honduras,[13] between Costa Rica and Colombia (claims later assumed by Panama), and between Mexico and Guatemala, to say nothing of revolutions and quarrels arising from other causes could not be ignored. The Central American republics themselves acted in 1902 by trying to prevent the mobilization of troops during mediation or conciliation efforts [14] but all too often this only provided a better opportunity for the unscrupulus to take advantage of a more law abiding adversary.

Following his convictions that cooperation and good will were essentials in securing permanent results Root associated the largest Latin American nation of the Caribbean, Mexico, with the United States in his new venture. President Díaz was asked if he would cooperate with President Roosevelt in issuing a joint invitation to the troubled republics to discuss terms of peace with the idea of a permanent arrangement. This was cordially agreed to.[15] Root himself was busily engaged in the preparations for his trip to Rio de Janeiro but he took time to write to the President in regard to the Central American situation:

I doubt if it would be wise for you to act as arbitrator [as had been suggested], for the questions are probably largely

[12] Jessup, *Elihu Root,* I, 507-9.

[13] *British and Foreign State Papers,* C, 1103-4; *Foreign Relations,* 1907, pt. 2, pp. 618; 619.

[14] J. B. Scott, " Central American Peace Conference of 1902," *American Journal of International Law,* II, 133 ff.; Max Henríquez Ureña, *La Liga de Naciones Americanas* (Nueva York, 1937), pp. 10-1.

[15] *Foreign Relations,* 1906, pt. 1, pp. 836-7; *ibid.,* 1907, pt. 2, pp. 637-8.

personal and matters of prejudice and recrimination which no arbitration could settle. I think if Mexico and the United States together undertake the role of mediation, it would be a good thing and might keep the peace. . . . We have, moreover, important railroad interests which require peace.[16]

This suggestion was followed in the main, and in conferences at San José and on board the U. S. S. *Marblehead* it was agreed to submit differences among El Salvador, Guatemala and Honduras to the arbitration of Presidents Díaz and Roosevelt while those of Costa Rica, El Salvador and Honduras were submitted to tribunals set up in Central America in 1902. True, little that was permanent resulted from these agreements of 1906 but the way was opened for the Washington Conference of the next year. For years the chief trouble maker in the region was the dictator Zelaya who aspired to dominate his four neighbors. When trouble actually broke out in 1907 Nicaragua and Honduras, the ones primarily involved, refused to abide by the agreements reached for bringing about a settlement.[17]

Again the northern neighbors acted and this time advised that a conference should meet in Washington. Root called the meeting to order and urged not only that the existing troubles be considered but that the future be safeguarded by satisfactory sanctions to prevent recurring disorders:

It would ill become me to attempt to propose or suggest the steps which you should take; but I will venture to observe that the all-important thing for you to accomplish

[16] Jessup, I, 501.

[17] For extensive correspondence consult *Foreign Relations, 1907.* See also Offutt, *Protection of Citizens Abroad,* pp. 103-4; Hill, *Roosevelt and the Caribbean,* pp. 182-3.

is that while you enter into agreements which will, I am sure, be framed in consonance with the most peaceful aspirations and the most rigid sense of justice, you shall devise also some practical methods under which it will be possible to secure the performance of those agreements. The mere declarations of general principles, the mere agreement upon lines of policy and of conduct, are of little value unless there be practical and definite methods provided by which the responsibility for failing to keep the agreement may be fixed upon some definite person, and the public sentiment of Central America brought to bear to prevent the violation.[18]

The less troublesome questions were first disposed of by the conference which then approached the more delicate problem of steps to be taken that would set up something in the way of a permanent machine to handle future problems.[19] Each of the five republics was to be represented on the Court which was to maintain peace and dispose of such international controversies as might arise, while other commissions worked out the standardization of weights and measures, moneys, tariff provisions, educational systems, legal systems, and the like.[20] The new court was installed in January, 1908, with great ceremony in Costa Rica[21] in a building for which Mr. Andrew Carnegie willingly gave $100,000.[22]

Approbation came from all quarters though at least one

[18] Elihu Root, *Latin America and the United States. Addresses* (Cambridge, 1917), p. 216.

[19] *Foreign Relations,* 1907, pt. 2, pp. 667 ff.

[20] *Ibid.,* Graham H. Stuart, *Latin America and the United States* (New York, 1922 and 1938), pp. 268.

[21] Buchanan to Root, July 21, 1908, *Foreign Relations,* 1908, pp. 217 ff.

[22] Carnegie to Root, June 9, 1908, LC., Root MS. This shows the philanthropist would gladly have given more if it had been needed.

interpretation of Mr. Root's motives might be noted. Mr. Albert Shaw wrote on December 30, 1907, applauding the creation of the Republic of Panama on such grounds that thereby the United States had the ultimate right of intervention to maintain order and preserve " sound finance." He added " I have hoped that the time would come when we could straighten out the Central American republics," [23] and presumably he considered the Washington agreements the appropriate beginning of the " straightening " process. Root responded on January 3rd:

I am immensely interested in those poor people down in Central America, and it is delightful to see how readily and gratefully they respond to a little genuine interest combined with respectful consideration. They are perfectly willing to sit at the feet of Gamaliel if Gamaliel won't kick them or bat them on the head. . . . Of course, there will be disagreeable incidents and antagonistic forces, but patience and a few years of the right kind of treatment I am sure will give us in that part of the world the only kind of hegemony we need to seek or ought to want.[24]

A still further step in the direction of securing cooperation and this on an ever broadening scale was the famous trip of Root to the Third International American Conference held at Rio de Janeiro in 1906. As noted above this was largely the idea of Root himself though the President cordially endorsed it. In his well known address to the Conference the Secretary urged cooperation to the full and pledged his word that the United States would seek no further victories except those of peace; no territory except its own; no sovereignty except over its own people.[25] The

[23] Shaw to Root, December 30, 1907, *ibid.*

[24] Quoted by Jessup, I, 513.

[25] Root, *Latin America and the U. S.*, pp. xiv-xv; Lloyd C. Griscom, *Diplomatically Speaking* (Boston, 1940), pp. 266-76.

acclaim with which the address and the man were received was truly spectacular, and nowhere with greater relief and enthusiasm than in and around the Caribbean.

Naturally enough Europe watched the developments with a certain degree of suspicion, for in the New World cooperation was making real progress.[26] In fact the Brazilian delegation seriously proposed that Latin America thank its great Sister Nation of the North for the Monroe Doctrine.[27] Differences of opinion made formal debate unwise when unanimity could not be secured, but that the proposal should have been made indicated enormous progress in view of the so recent Panama affair. Also, the activities and influence of the Bureau of the American Republics were endorsed [28] and it was given further publicity when Andrew Carnegie offered on December 15, 1907, to provide funds for a palace for its headquarters.[29]

Thus the work continued: now an effort to reduce consular fees through the work of Taft in the War Department,[30] now the calling of a Pan-American Medical conference at Panama,[31] now the forwarding of a notice to diplomatic officers that Latin American army officers would be admitted to training at the special army training schools for infantry, cavalry and medical officers,[32] and now the

[26] A. C. Wilgus, "Third International American Conference," *Hisp. Amer. Hist. Rev.*, XII, 442-3.

[27] Alvarez, *The Monroe Doctrine*, pp. 193 ff.

[28] Delegates to the Secretary of State, January 10, 1907, *Foreign Relations*, 1907, pt. 2, pp. 1578-9.

[29] For Carnegie's original proposal see Carnegie to Root, December 15, 1907, LC., Root MS.

[30] Taft to Ministers of Costa Rica, Nicaragua, Guatemala and others in South America, May 10, 1905, LC., Taft MS.

[31] Taft to Secretary of State, December 28, 1904, *ibid.*

[32] Root to diplomatic officers in Mexico, Central and South America, January 8, 1906, *Foreign Relations*, 1906, pt. 1, pp. 2-3.

proclamation of a sanitary convention between eleven New World republics, eight of which were in the Caribbean area.[33]

Possibly it was coincidence, or possibly design in part for the President was a shrewd politician indeed and could sense public opinion even when it differed with him but certainly the new cooperative note came just at the time when the public reaction had set in. Root with his firm belief in common decency kept in touch with the protestants, while his firm conviction that it was " the right of every sovereign state to protect itself " [34] kept him in harmony with the President's old faction. Actually a new program was developing and Root realized the fact,[35] though any suggestion of giving up the hallowed traditional phrases was greeted as rank heresy.[36] As James Bryce pertinently commented the people of the United States had not been seized by the lust for further conquests after 1903. They appeared to lose interest in their newly acquired possessions, while their public men entered into an active debate as to whether any of the acquired possessions should be released and if so under what conditions this should take place. However, almost all of them were agreed that the country should make no further conquests and should avoid annexations if possible.[37]

But the management of the foreign affairs of the United States is not as simple as the mere concoction of a recipe of good principles and the drawing up of logical plans.

[33] *Foreign Relations*, 1909, p. 636.

[34] Root, *Addresses on International Subjects,* p. 111.

[35] Perkins, *Monroe Doctrine, 1867-1907,* p. 465.

[36] Root, *op. cit.,* p. 109.

[37] James Bryce, *The American Commonwealth* (New York, 1910), II, 584-5.

Would the recipe provide an edible pudding when some of the awkward incidents that have a way of developing among the nations to the south were substituted for the basic ingredient of peace?

Across the Río Grande lay an increasingly restless Mexico to which Root paid the special courtesy of a visit following his South American tour. Of President Díaz he said:

Above all things, I feel impelled to say that the most interesting thing in Mexico, so far as my knowledge goes is your President. It has seemed to me that of all men now living, Porfirio Diaz, of Mexico, is best worth seeing. Whether one considers the adventurous, daring, chivalric incidents of his early career; whether one considers the vast work of government which his wisdom and courage and commanding character have accomplished; whether one considers his singularly attractive personality; no one lives today whom I would rather see than President Diaz. . . . As I am neither poet, musician, nor Mexican, but only an American who loves justice and liberty and hopes to see their reign among mankind progress and strengthen and become perpetual, I look to Porfirio Diaz, the President of Mexico, as one of the men to be held up for the hero worship of mankind.[38]

And Mexican responses were equally enthusiastic.[39] Petty incidents of border irritations,[40] and even quite important exchanges of courtesies and accommodations for the navies of the countries, such as the use of Magdalena Bay as a location for two coaling vessels of the United States navy, were satisfactorily arranged.[41]

[38] Root, *Latin America and the U. S.*, pp. 167-8.
[39] *Ibid.*, pp. 169-70; Nebuco to Root with enclosure, November 7, 1907, and Creel to Root, December 17, 1908, LC., Root MS.
[40] Moore, *Digest*, VI, 747.
[41] President Díaz to the Mexican Congress, April 1 [?], 1908, *Foreign Relations*, 1908, p. 602.

But some exceedingly significant straws were in the wind. Mexican economic progress was spectacular and the great work of the Tehuantepec railroad was completed in 1907 and opened with elaborate ceremony [42] but the octogenarian Díaz the same year gave out the Creelman interview in which he again stated that he was serving his last presidential term and that he planned to retire in 1910. Heretofore such suggestions had always been met with an overwhelming demand for reconsideration. True, this happened again, but the demand was definitely slower in developing and the promptness with which other candidates appeared for his office was more than a little disconcerting. Thus, by 1910, a three years' preparatory campaign " had pulverized the foundations of the dictatorship." [43]

Meanwhile, under the leadership of the able José Yves Limantour and his associates Mexican financiers were beginning to provide real competition to foreign capitalists doing business in the country. The plans of E. H. Harriman, the railroad king, to unify and dominate the Mexican railway system, were quietly sidetracked while Limantour organized the National Railways of Mexico on a strikingly similar basis.

In addition, the relations of United States Ambassador Clayton had been far from happy in Mexico City and he had been glad to retire in 1905 after considerable personal and family friction with Mexican officialdom.[44] At the

[42] R. H. K. Marett, *An Eye-Witness of Mexico* (London, New York and Toronto, 1939), pp. 193-5.

[43] Francisco Bulnes, *The Whole Truth about Mexico, President Wilson's Responsibility* (New York, 1916), p. 153.

[44] Callahan, *American Policy in Mexican Relations*, p. 446.

same time a definite anti-foreign feeling was rapidly rising. The railway consolidation had made possible a strike of Mexican laborers to force the discharge of United States employees, but this developed after Root had left office as Secretary of State.[45] As early as 1906 anti-foreign feeling was so acute that Ambassador Thompson telegraphed thirty-one United States consuls in the country asking if they felt there was danger of a wholesale rising by the Mexicans in their districts to slaughter United States citizens there resident. The responses were reassuring though serious dislike and hatred were reported in numerous sections.[46] Prompt reports to President Díaz secured equally prompt reassurances of precautions taken and a quieting of fears, but many felt that there was no little fire behind the smoke.[47] Evidently the masses were about to awake though Root did not have to face the problem directly and his trip had a sedative influence and left the impression that all was well.

Still further south the Panama and Colombian problem remained. With regard to Panama and the Canal Zone it appears that the chief originator of plans followed was William Howard Taft, the Secretary of War, rather than the Secretary of State.[48] Taft's service in the Philippines had been outstanding in his effective cooperation with the military so his appointment was a logical one. When suitable arrangements for the construction of the Canal could not be made with private companies the problem was placed under the direction of the War Department. Thus

[45] *Ibid.*, p. 521.   [46] *Ibid.*, pp. 524 ff.

[47] *Foreign Relations*, 1906, pt. 2, pp. 1124-5.

[48] Taft to Roosevelt, April 27, 1905 [date inserted by hand] and June 20, 1905, LC., Taft MS.

it was natural and proper that the plans should be made by Taft in direct consultation with President Roosevelt. And of course the work in the Canal Zone was intimately tied up with relations with Panama. However, there can be no doubt that Root cordially endorsed the program adopted and did all in his power to support it, even though it was of a stronger and less conciliatory variety than he would probably have initiated himself. The subject of Panama is deferred for the time since it provides the logical transfer from the program of Root as Secretary of State to that of Taft and Knox who were to adopt the sterner policy first seen here to the four years after March 1909 when they were to become President and Secretary of State respectively.

Another of the pestiferous incidents was the debt problem in Venezuela.[49] It would appear that the United States Minister to Venezuela had at times been indiscreet in his relations with business corporations but there is no evidence that he was inefficient in office.[50] However Venezuela was obviously running rough shod over the interests of foreign countries apparently thinking that the United States would protect it against retribution from European powers and would not itself intervene.[51]

In spite of repeated diplomatic protests and requests [52] for arbitration nothing was done and finally diplomatic relations were broken off and Brazil took over the legation of the United States at Caracas about the middle of 1908.[53]

---

[49] Perkins, p. 449.
[50] *Foreign Relations*, 1906, pt. 2, pp. 1432-8.
[51] Jessup, *Root*, I, 495.
[52] For correspondence see *Foreign Relations*, 1908, pp. 774 ff.
[53] *Ibid.*, pp. 820-2.

Finally the storm became too severe so Castro resigned and left the country while Juan Vicente Gómez took charge in the latter part of 1908.

About this time Mr. W. I. Buchanan was sent to Caracas as executive agent and after some skillful work was able to report early in 1909 that most of the outstanding cases were in course of solution, either by direct negotiation or by submission to the Hague.[54] To make this easier the Gómez administration was one that idealized the foreign business man and encouraged his investments but probably Roosevelt's impatience and his penchant for intervention also had an influence. Some Venezuelans frankly feared him and insisted that he considered the New World to be " the property of the United States "[55] and his ideas in favor of intervention to " show these Dagoes that they will have to behave decently "[56] must have been well known. However, the Dominican Treaty as a test case had met with serious Senate delays so this time the President contented himself with writing to Root to ask about the status of the Venezuela affair. He felt that the United States had suffered " a great deal of wrong doing " from Venezuela and asked " Has the time come when we ought to take action, or not? "[57] Thus where not committed to a program or driven by President Roosevelt's impetuosity Root was able to follow the more peaceful program.[58]

[54] Wriston, *Executive Agents in Foreign Relations*, pp. 375-6; *Foreign Relations*, 1909, pp. 609 ff.

[55] Robertson, *Hispanic American Relations with the U. S.*, pp. 126-7.

[56] Pringle, *Roosevelt*, p. 294.

[57] Roosevelt to the Secretary of State, February 29, 1908, LC., Root MS.

[58] Here there was also a slight suggestion of German intrigue on behalf of the ousted dictator Castro. The implication was that

Some consider that one of Root's outstanding accomplishments was the final approval of the Dominican treaty by the Senate. Certainly his correspondence books bear ample testimony to his activity in organizing sentiment and in presenting the right interpretations in the right quarters throughout 1906 and 1907. Meanwhile the actual terms of the arrangements between the two republics had been significantly modified in at least three respects: first, The provision to " respect the complete territorial integrity of the Dominican Republic " was omitted as unnecessary; second, the pledge of United States assistance in the internal affairs of Santo Domingo whenever the United States considered it wise was omitted on the ground that it might involve the United States needlessly; and third, the responsibility of the United States to determine the validity of claims pending against Santo Domingo was changed so that the Caribbean country would retain the responsibility,[59] though the United States Commissioner, Mr. Hollander, was later most active in bringing the claims to a satisfactory compromise.[60]

When the matter was finally brought to a vote in the Senate Root's careful preliminary work showed its effects. Satisfactory trade tendencies of the island were gleefully reported [61] and the vote of the Senate stood 43 to 19 with

---

Castro had gone to Germany to get supplies for his military activities. Doubtless the Venezuelan would have followed such a course gladly if he could have gotten the supplies but there is no evidence that the idea was considered seriously in Germany, even though some writers have liked to play with the idea. Bonsal, *The American Mediterranean*, pp. 142-3.

[59] Hill, *Roosevelt and the Caribbean*, pp. 166-7; Welles, *op. cit.*, II, 651 ff.

[60] *Ibid.*, II, 648-9.

[61] Otto Schoenrich, *Santo Domingo, a Country with a Future* (New York, 1918), p. 232.

no Republican votes against the measure while four Democrats voted for it and thus guaranteed its acceptance by the required two-thirds endorsement.[62]

Clearly the United States had taken quite a step forward in its supervision of the Caribbean. As has been noted, the Cuban and Panama treaties were notoriously weak when it came to the important question of financial relations with foreign countries and the actual supervision of local expenditures. This Dominican treaty rectified the earlier omissions substantially,[63] though a blunder was committed when Mr. Hollander, apparently through carelessness on the part of a minor State Department official, was permitted to collect a private fee (figure reported as $100,000) from Santo Domingo at the time that he was acting as United States Commissioner and receiving a salary as such. Root himself vigorously repudiated having approved any such arrangements when the matter was brought up in 1911 by the House Sub-Committee on Expenditures in the Department of State.[64] Thus another lesson was learned by the government in the handling and training of colonial supervisors.

In the neighboring country of Haiti the United States continued to watch developments carefully. Consular agents of the United States who allowed themselves to become involved with revolutionary leaders were severely warned when the consul at St. Marc was dismissed in January, 1908.[65] As the year wore on revolutionary activities continued but the State Department contented itself

---

[62] Perkins, p. 441.

[63] C. L. Jones, "Loan Controls in the Caribbean," *Hisp. Amer. Hist. Rev.*, XIV, 146-7.

[64] Jessup, *Root*, I, 551-2.

[65] *Foreign Relations*, 1908, pp. 427-35.

with sending instructions to the Minister, Mr. Furniss, stating that protection should be given to Europeans in the country when they were in distress and when no agent of their own was at hand to provide aid.[66]   The old imperialists in the United States began to lick their lips in anticipation and Albert Shaw wrote to Root, asking bluntly if he could not " invent a way to put Haiti under bonds before you leave the Department," saying that if so he would add a " black pearl " to his " crown of glory." [67] Root responded that he wished that something of the kind were possible but that the Haitians were naturally suspicious.   He added that he had been watching the situation closely for several years but had reached the conclusion that any " positive step " must await the " psychological moment." [68]   And thus he sidestepped the matter and left it.

However of all the special incidents that arose probably the most regretted by the Administration was the one that precipitated the first Cuban intervention under the Platt Amendment.   There was no question of the increasing trade and prosperity of the island in terms of money but trouble started in 1906 in spite of every wish of the United States to avoid it.   Prior to this date a careful watch had been maintained on Cuban loans [69] but apparently little or no actual interference had been practiced.   No complaints were made over the considerable numbers of pardons

[66] Secretary of State to Furniss, December 5, 1908, and Acting Secretary of State to Furniss, December 7, 1908, *ibid.*, pp. 442; 444.

[67] Shaw to Root, December 11, 1908, LC., Root MS.

[68] See Jessup, I, 554-5.

[69] Adee to Barnes with enclosure, July 25, 1905, and Hay to Sleeper with enclosure, June 9, 1904, LC., Root MS.

granted [70] by the Tomás Estrada Palma administration and Root even went so far as to ask President Eliot of Harvard to grant an honorary degree to the Cuban " not only because I have a warm regard for Mr. Palma, but because I think the effect on the Cuban people would be good." He continued:

The Cubans have done admirably in their experiment in self government; they have maintained the governmental organization and methods which we turned over to them four years ago, far better than anyone dared to hope; and everything which tends to increase their respect for their own government and make them proud of the man whom they have chosen for their leader, is good for them.[71]

In the discussion as to the ownership of the Isle of Pines Root wrote to Americans on the island that he was urging the Senate to approve a treaty pending before it to return the island to Cuba saying, " In my judgment the United States has no substantial claim to the Isle of Pines." [72] When a suit was appealed to the Supreme Court of the United States as to customs collected on imports from the island it was decided on the basis that the region was under the *de facto* control of Cuba and therefore that it was foreign territory under the Dingley tariff act.[73]

Further, it must always be borne in mind that Root was planning his good-will trip to Latin America and did not want anything to discount the impressions that he hoped to make. However, the auguries for the Cuban presidential election of 1905 were not good. Liberals were

[70] Guggenheim, *U. S. and Cuba,* p. 165.

[71] Quoted by Jessup, I, 530-1.

[72] *Ibid.,* I, 529-30.

[73] Janet D. Frost, " Cuban-American Relations concerning the Isle of Pines," *Hisp. Amer. Hist. Rev.,* XI, 344-45.

ousted from local offices and the rolls of registered voters were so heavily padded that it was estimated one-third of the names listed were fictitious.[74] In the election itself many Liberals were refused the right to vote, and others, seeing how things were going, refused to do so. Not surprisingly the Liberals protested the reelection of Estrada Palma and numbers of them urged United States intervention under the Platt Amendment for the maintenance of a democratic form of government.[75]

In Washington Taft was left in charge of the State Department while Root was in South America so he was especially anxious not to disrupt his friend's plans. To offset this there was his own somewhat sterner colonial policy as developed in the Philippines and Roosevelt's quick temper and Big Stick tendencies. However, one further element in the situation could not be ignored. The election of 1906 was at hand and the people of the United States had shown a most determined inclination to avoid overseas complications of late, so this was no time to be recklessly indulging in intervention in Cuba.[76]

In the absence of the regular minister Consul General Frank Steinhart was the United States spokesman in the island. He had been a sergeant in the first United States army of occupation and was later affiliated with wealthy interests in Cuba [77] With such a background he was easily convinced that only intervention could cope with the increasing complications that were arising. Of course some

[74] Hill, *Roosevelt and the Caribbean*, p. 89.

[75] Chapman, *History of the Cuban Republic*, pp. 189-90.

[76] Henry F. Pringle, *Life and Times of William Howard Taft* (New York and Toronto, 1939), I, 309.

[77] Chapman, pp. 199-201; Scott Nearing and Joseph Freeman, *Dollar Diplomacy* (New York, 1925), pp. 178-9.

interests hoped for permanent annexation but they hesitated to precipitate insurrection because of the property damage that was likely to ensue.[78]   Rebels took the field however and steadily advanced in spite of the moral support of the United States given to the established government.   Steinhart bombarded the State Department with requests for warships, intervention and protection for United States property interests, and with reports that Estrada Palma was going to resign.[79]   September 14, 1906, he again telegraphed:

President Palma has resolved not to continue at the head of the Government, and is ready to present his resignation, even though the present disturbances should cease at once. The vice-president has resolved not to accept the office. Cabinet ministers have declared that they will previously resign.   Under these conditions it is impossible that Congress will meet for the lack of a proper person to convoke same to designate a new president.   The consequences will be absence of legal power, and therefore the prevailing state of anarchy will continue unless the United States Government will adopt the measures necessary to avoid this danger.[80]

At his wit's end the President determined to send Taft and First Assistant Secretary of State Robert Bacon to Cuba to investigate.   Of this trip Taft wrote:

To me, this trip is a little like purchasing a pig in a poke, I know so little of the actual situation.   I do know a good deal about the character of the people I have to deal with, and we may possibly work out something, but the chances, I should think, are about even, and I beg to assure

[78] Chapman, p. 217.

[79] *Foreign Relations,* 1906, pt. i, various.

[80] Steinhart to Secretary of State, September 14, 1901, *ibid.*, 1905, pt. 1, p 479.

you that everything has been done to act promptly should it be necessary to proceed to armed intervention.[81]

The commissioners arrived in Havana on the U. S. S. *Des Moines* on the morning of September 19th during a truce which had been agreed to by the contestants at the request of the President of the United States. Forthwith began a hectic week or ten days for the commissioners. October 4th Taft wrote to Root:

This has been the greatest crisis I ever passed through and some of the sleepless nights I passed I hope I may not have to pass again. I am anxious to get away from here out of this atmosphere which is one of disappointment intrigue and discouragement.

Bacon and I have suffered much from the thought of your disappointment keen and deep, at the wretched development and I have tried in what I have done to do as I thought you would have done under the circumstances.[82]

In the same letter he wrote of the actual situation:

Old man Palma has his limitations but in point of honesty, patriotism and earnest wish for the prosperity of his country, he is head and shoulders above everyone else here. He is weak and obstinate and unable to cope with the politicans of the Cuban variety and his own friends have misled him. But withal there is something heroic about him. He knows what civil liberty is and I fear those who are about him do not.

This explains why the Commissioners had drawn up a compromise arrangement providing for Palma to remain as president with a coalition cabinet and for new congressional elections. The Liberals agreed but the Moderates

---

[81] Taft to the President, September 16, 1906, LC., Taft MS. An idea of these detailed instructions may be seen in Taft to the President, September 15, 1906, marked "Confidential," LC., *ibid.*

[82] Taft to Root, October 4, 1906, LC., Root MS.

rejected the proposal whereupon Palma called Congress in session for the 28th of September and tendered his resignation and that of his whole cabinet. Congress urged the President to remain in office but he flatly refused.[83] The Cuban baby of government was once more dumped squarely on the lap of its Uncle Sam for nursing.

The next day, September 29th, a provisional government under Taft was installed to exercise authority under the direction of the President of the United States. Insurgents were disarmed by a commission of Cuban and United States military officers while a court attempted to adjust claims arising from disorders. By the 10th of October Taft as Provisional Governor was able to announce the restoration of order through a proclamation of amnesty, and on the 13th transferred his authority to Charles E. Magoon.[84]

During this excellent piece of work by Mr. Taft every effort was made to proceed regularly and in a way that could not be challenged. However, there was already criticism and demands by those who wished to wrest power from the Executive and give Congress control of the intervention. Such a suggestion the President had hotly repudiated [85] though as a good political leader he hoped to avoid further criticism. November 22nd, Taft instructed Magoon to follow up the earlier policy of Bacon and himself in trying to conciliate the Cuban Liberals,[86] to give them the benefit of the doubt in filling vacant offices but to be sure that they understood the action was not taken

[83] Inclosure with Morgan to Secretary of State, October 13, 1906, *Foreign Relations,* 1906, pt. 1, pp. 489-90.

[84] *Ibid.*

[85] Pringle, *Life and Times of Taft,* I, 307-8.

[86] Herbert S. Duffy, *William Howard Taft* (New York, 1930), pp. 186 ff.

through fear of what they might do if dissatisfied.[87] Characteristically enough Roosevelt was more impetuous than Taft who wished to make sure of the support for each step taken.   Restless at these precautions the President wrote:

Upon my word, I do not see that with Cuba in the position it is we need bother our heads much about the exact way in which the Cubans observe or do not observe so much of their own constitution as does not concern us . . . I do not care in the least for the fact that such an agreement is not constitutional.[88]

The government set up was supported at first by 5600 troops under General James Franklin Bell,[89] but these were scattered and kept as much in the background as possible. In view of the obvious election irregularities a wholesale housecleaning of the members of congress was undertaken,[90] also the new administration installed some fifty-eight United States army officers in charge of practically all executive posts of importance in the departments of Justice, Government, Public Works and Sanitation, as well as in the Claims Commission, Election Bureau and Rural Guard.[91] In addition some civilians from the United States were employed.

In an administration of this kind in Cuba there were endless opportunities for personal peculation, and the charges against Magoon are legion.   However, Chapman comes to the conclusion that Magoon was " painstakingly,

[87] Taft to Magoon, November 22, 1906, LC., Taft MS.

[88] Chapman, p. 208.

[89] *Ibid.*, p. 227.

[90] Duffy, *op. cit.*, p. 191; Memo for Bureau of Insular Affairs signed by Carpenter, November 28, 1906, LC., Taft MS.

[91] Raymond Leslie Buell, *Cuba and the Platt Amendment* (Foreign Policy Association, Information Service, Vol. V, No. 3) (New York, 1929), pp. 50-1.

almost picayunishly " honest in the handling of his personal funds.[92]   On the other hand there seems to have developed a very extensive spoils system while the exceptionally lavish granting of pardons (on the grounds that the prisons were filled with men who had really been condemned by the courts for political reasons)[93] was unfortunate to say the least.

Likewise no special effort was made to scrutinize too carefully the contracts let by the administration.   Paving and sewerage contracts were urged from Washington [94] which later were to be severely condemned as inadequate or corrupt.[95]   Consul General Steinhart who had urged the intervention himself received concessions that made him wealthy, while the surplus of $13,000,000 at the opening of the intervention rapidly shrank (due in part to business uncertainty), to a deficit of nearly that much before the foreigners left.[96]

Thus the faithful may have been rewarded by jobs or by contracts but even critics admit that Roosevelt, Root and Taft were honest in attempting to build a new nation to the southward.[97]   When Magoon suggested that a protectorate be actually established Taft responded: " It is simply out of the question, and you must not give any encouragement

[92] Chapman, *op. cit.*, p. 233.

[93] Jenks, *Our Cuban Colony*, pp. 96-8.

[94] Taft to Magoon, December 22, 1906, LC., Taft MS; William E. Gonzales, *Concerning Dollar Diplomacy* . . .([Columbia, S. C., 1937]), pp. 2-3.

[95] *Ibid.*, Jenks, pp. 126-7.

[96] Nearing and Freeman, *Dollar Diplomacy*, p. 180; see also Taft to Magoon, June 30, 1908, and Taft to the President, June 30, 1908, LC., Taft MS.

[97] Jenks, p. 85.

to it." [98] In an eleven-page communication sent to Magoon in May 1907 there were careful instructions which showed a real desire to undertake and maintain a scrupulously honest administration. With regard to concessions Taft said:

The question is being agitated of granting a concession for the telephone franchise to the whole island. I deprecate this, it seems to me that in so far as possible, you should delay the granting of franchises until the restoration of power of the Republican government.[99]

He insisted that the fiction of independence of the island was to be maintained even to the point of sending delegates to the Hague. Taft had approved this verbally and Root urgently supported the idea in Cabinet meeting.

As the election of 1908 approached Taft was more and more involved in the campaign which he described in anticipation as a "kind of nightmare for me." [100] Naturally enough, every effort was made to forestall unpleasant rumors from Cuba and to secure an efficient administration there while every effort was made to show that Cuba was prospering under United States supervision. Many in the United States felt with Professor Coolidge:

Now, no nation will go to the trouble and expense of continually occupying and then evacuating an unruly region. As history runs, we may wonder that the Americans ever evacuated Cuba at all. If they do it a second time, they will deserve still more credit. But if the Cubans rise in insurrection before the Americans leave, and have to be repressed, perhaps at the cost of a long and arduous campaign, or if they soon force the American army to return

[98] Taft to Magoon, January 23, 1907, LC., Taft MS.
[99] Taft to Magoon, May 9, 1907, *ibid.*
[100] Taft to Magoon, July 10, 1908, *ibid.*

once more, the occupation may be a long one, and the days of Cuban independence numbered.[101]

However, preparations were made for the preliminary Cuban elections and on August 1st the presidential nominee of the Republican Party was able to cable (carefully giving the cable to the press immediately) :

Hot Springs, Va., August 1, 1908.
Magoon, Havana.
I congratulate the people of Cuba on the successful operation of the new election law.   It indicates a successful outcome in the Presidential election to follow and a desire on the part of the people to have lawful and just elections.   It insures the turning over of the government as directed by President Roosevelt and is an evidence that the people are determined to make permanent their government, dependent as it must be on peaceable and fair elections.   Please accept for yourself my personal congratulations and convey them also to the leaders of all the parties, to the legislative commission, and to the people of Cuba on the successful outcome of the day.   Viva la Cuba Libre.

William H. Taft.[102]

Good politics and good diplomacy!

In the December elections José Miguel Gómez who had been associated with wealthy sugar interests was elected president [103] and soon thereafter the last United States troops were withdrawn and again Cuba was allowed to manage its own affairs before the world with only a periodic suggestion from Washington as to what was advisable. With all the good intentions and intense desire of the

[101] Archibald Cary Coolidge, *The United States as a World Power* (New York, 1909), p. 288.

[102] LC., Taft MS.

[103] *Foreign Relations*, 1908, pp. 251-2.

United States Government to keep out in the first place, and to get out as soon as possible in the second place, the second intervention was to bring recurring recriminations. These were due largely to the fact that, in Washington, Roosevelt was impetuous and had no eye for detail, Root had little to do with the matter, and Taft was busy with the presidential campaign and did not exercise too much discrimination in selecting some of his subordinates; while in Cuba, Magoon's lordly gestures were quite far from Leonard Wood's efficiency in organization and business supervision.[104]

As has already been said, relations with Panama and the Canal Zone were the actual connecting link between the policies of Elihu Root and those of Taft and Knox, though the associated problems with Colombia were primarily in the hands of Secretary Root. In many ways this was the most difficult problem of the Secretary of State for it rested on a background that was contradictory to the whole spirit of a New World foreign policy as he conceived it. It was impossible to forget the past and start all over again for it was the old issues that were clamoring for solution.

Inevitably popular feeling in Colombia was exceedingly bitter. Early in 1904 a report from the United States legation stated: "The bitter feeling against Americans, while not so strongly manifested by outbreaks among the people or attacks through the press, has not, however, abated one particle." [105] By the end of that year Minister Russell was able to report that the administration was more willing to accept the Panama loss as a " fait accompli " and might be

---

[104] Fitzgibbon, *Cuba and the U. S.,* pp. 143-4.
[105] Snyder to Hay, January 2, 1904, *Foreign Relations,* 1904, p. 204.

brought to recognize the fact publicly if in some way Colombia could be allowed to enjoy part of the advantages it had hoped to secure from the construction of the canal.[106]

In 1905 and 1906 relations improved slightly when the United States used its good offices to bring about a settlement of the boundary dispute between Venezuela and Colombia. As a result diplomatic relations between the two were resumed and Colombia even indicated its willingness for the United States to act as arbitrator.[107] But in the background was a gnawing fear that additional provinces of Colombia might be induced to join Panama either because of their own desire to share in the expected prosperity of that country or because of active machinations of the United States. The matter received official notice in a long dispatch of Minister John Barrett to Root in May, 1906.[108] Of course the Minister gave full assurances to Colombia that his nation in no way would abet such a movement but only time could allay the fears.

And what was worse such feelings were not restricted to Colombia. The President of Ecuador saw fit to address his Congress, August 10, 1904:

What occurred in Panama a few months ago is, in my judgment, an awful lesson by which we should profit.

I have said that we owed consideration to Colombia, apart from the fact that the event of Panama, in view of the assistance given the latter and the motives which led to the event, implied a disregard of South American interests; for these reasons, I repeat, I hastened to express to the head of the Columbian nation that we citizens of Ecuador all feel a

[106] *Dip. Hist. of Pan. Canal,* p. 110.

[107] *Foreign Relations,* 1906, pt. 2, pp. 1438 ff.; P. F. Fenton, "Diplomatic Relations of the United States and Venezuela," *Hisp. Amer. Hist. Rev.,* VIII, 346.

[108] *Dip. Hist. of Pan. Canal,* pp. 112 ff.

profound regret at an occurrence so unfortunate for that Republic and for Latin America in general.[109]

Such a feeling was dangerous as viewed by Root.

All through 1905 Colombia urged the settlement of outstanding issues by arbitration but this Roosevelt was unwilling to approve since he considered the question of national honor was involved. Fortunately, the United States was ably represented in the South American capital by Minister Russell, and then by the conciliatory John Barrett who made an especially pleasing impression though at times his conduct was resented and criticized by Magoon, Cromwell and their group.[110] Colombia, meanwhile appointed a minister to resume relations with the United States. When discriminatory tariffs were levied on United States flour a statement of the facts in the case brought about an adjustment promptly and so there could be no idea that Colombia was trying to penalize United States interests.[111]

Quite naturally Bogotá watched Root's visit to South America attentively. In July the Secretary sent word to Barrett that the Minister should meet the travellers at Guayaquil and proceed with them to Cartegena.[112] During the trip details of a treaty with Colombia were to be discussed.[113] Root commented:

---

[109] *Foreign Relations*, 1904, p. 296.

[110] Barrett to Root, December 7, 1905, and January 11, 1907, LC., Root MS; Taft to the President, April 13, 1905, LC., Taft MS.

[111] *Foreign Relations*, 1906, pt. 1, pp. 450 ff.

[112] Root to Colombian Minister, February 10, 1906, *Foreign Relations*, pt. 1, pp. 419-21; James Brown Scott, " Treaty between Colombia and the U. S.," *Amer. Jour. Int. Law*, XV, 436-7.

[113] Barrett to Acting Secretary of State, July 13, 1906, *Foreign Relations*, 1906, pt. 1, p. 435.

It is evident that the negotiations will involve a very thorough knowledge of the debt of Colombia, its origin and history, and the relations of Panama to each class of debts. The preparation of this material should be begun immediately and prosecuted diligently.[114]

Meeting the party at Cartagena was General A. Vásquez Cobo, Acting Minister of Foreign Affairs of Colombia,[115] and there the problems pending were discussed at length and a confidential memorandum drawn up dealing extensively with trade relations of Panama, Colombia and the United States and with trade rights in and through the Canal Zone.[116] Thus the ground work for a treaty was completed. Much correspondence as to details may be found in the W. H. Taft and Elihu Root Papers throughout the year 1907. This was between W. N. Cromwell, Root, Taft and others and concerned payments to be made and boundaries to be drawn. To repeat the details is needless since the treaty was not put into effect, but the obvious fact is that the administration was anxious to clear up the matter before the coming election and that both Root and Taft were honestly seeking a " fair " settlement for all concerned. Root later wrote: " I spent more time personally in negotiation of the Tripartite Agreements of January 1909 than in any other single matter during my time in the State Department." [117] One of the provisions was for the free transit of Colombia warships through the

[114] Root to Barrett, July 2, 1906, *Dip. Hist. of Pan. Canal,* pp. 128-9.

[115] See *Foreign Relations,* 1907, pt. 1, p. 286.

[116] *Dip. Hist. of Pan. Canal,* pp. 131-3.

[117] Root to Lansing, April 6, 1917, LC., Robert Lansing MS. Note that these are to be distinguished from *The Lansing Papers* which have been printed and which are referred to from time to time in later parts of this study.

canal. This of course involved the Hay-Pauncefote treaty and an inquiry came from Great Britain that took the form of a mild protest.[118] After some correspondence on the subject Ambassador James Bryce notified the United States that Great Britain would not protest the treaty arrangement in view of the explanation that Colombia was in such a special position with regard to the canal and in view of the fact that this could not possibly be considered a precedent for other countries.[119] The treaties between the three countries were finally signed January 9, 1909, under such circumstances that the Colombian Minister wrote Secretary Root the next day a most cordial letter applauding his conduct as marked by the " highest degree of kindness, consideration, fairness, spirit of justice, and enlightened foresight as to the future relations of your country and ours." [120] Panama accepted the treaties early in February and the Colombian Congress was called in session to consider them on the 22nd.

At first there were numerous indications that the Congress would give its approval.[121] Beyond question Reyes, the President of Colombia, hoped for ratification for both political and private reasons, but the old story was repeated.[122] On March 1st opposition was developing but ratification was still thought to be certain; by the 10th student demonstrations against the treaty had begun; by the 14th rioting was reported to be serious. After violent debate the President recommended that the treaties be referred to the congress that was to meet the following July after the pending congressional elections were held on May 30th.[123]

[118] Dip. Hist. Pan. Canal, pp. 69 ff.
[119] Ibid., p. 81.
[120] Ibid., p. 186.   [121] Ibid., pp. 190-1.
[122] Rippy, Capitalists and Colombia, p. 104.
[123] Dip. Hist. of Pan. Canal, pp. 212-3; 220-1.

This meant the submission of the matter to the people in a general election so hope of settlement during the administration of Roosevelt was doomed and it was left for Taft and Knox to consider the matter later.

Of course anything dealing with Panama came close to the heart of Roosevelt so his influence on relations was brought directly to bear through the new Secretary of War, Taft. Root clearly felt it necessary to " explain " why the United States changed its attitude toward Panama in 1903,[124] so he probably was glad for Taft to take the initiative.

The new Republic found the helping hand of the United States useful in making available its consular service pending the installation of one of its own, and as has been seen foreign governments promptly extended recognition.[125] As President Díaz of Mexico informed his Congress: " At length popular suffrage in those regions gave to the new government a status of regularity, and on the other hand there is no danger of its being soon or easily overthrown. In view of these facts the Mexican government has recognized it . . . ." [126] February 19, 1904, Manuel Amador Guerrero was duly installed as president of the new Republic with two admirals of the United States navy, together with their staff and a colonel and twenty officers of the United States Marines to lend color and sanctity to the occasion.[127]

[124] Before Union League Club of Chicago, February 22, 1904, Root, *Addresses on International Subjects,* pp. 196-7.

[125] A very interesting sidelight on the attitude of foreign governments is to be seen in the fact that notifications of recognition of Panama were in very many cases sent first to Washington rather than to the new republic.

[126] *Foreign Relations,* 1904, p. 486.

[127] Russell to Hay, February 22, 1904, *ibid.,* 1904, p. 581.

During the year a number of details had to be worked out. These varied all the way from questions of whether to use Japanese,[128] Jamaican, local or United States labor in the construction of the canal to the far more serious one of sovereignty over the canal zone. The Panamanian position was fully asserted as early as August 11, 1904, by the Minister at Washington when he urged that the special limitations mentioned in the treaty showed that Panama retained all rights not ceded, including sovereignty.[129] On October 24th Hay rejoined:

That the United States may acquire territory and sovereignty in this way and for this purpose from its sister republics in this hemisphere is so manifest as to preclude discussion.

If it could or should be admitted that the titular sovereign of the canal zone is the Republic of Panama, such sovereign is mediatized by its own acts, solemnly declared and publicly proclaimed by treaty stipulations, induced by a desire to make possible the completion of a great work which will confer inestimable benefit upon the people of the Isthmus and the nations of the world. It is difficult to believe that a member of the family of nations seriously contemplates abandoning so high and honorable a position, in order to engage in an endeavor to secure what at best is a " barren scepter." [130]

The immediate problem was that of shipping, especially at the port of Ancón for increasing numbers of vessels were arriving and the right to collect tariffs in both the chief cities of the new nation was at stake. Similarly the use of United States stamps in the canal zone was protested by Panama.[131] In addition the numerous details connected with

---

[128] Taft to Guerrero, December 24, 1904, LC., Taft MS.

[129] Munro, *The U. S. and the Caribbean Area,* pp. 74-5.

[130] Hay to Obaldia, October 24, 1904, *Foreign Relations,* 1904, pp. 614; 615.

[131] McCain, *The U. S. and Panama,* p. 33.

the opening of construction of the canal proper demanded attention.

Moreover, there was serious dissatisfaction in the new republic and a possibility that ambitious leaders would use the army for attempts to seize the government. In view of the whole situation it was deemed wise to send the Secretary of War down in person to try to bring about a general settlement of the troubles. He set out November 17th by way of New Orleans and reached Colón on the 27th. In the meantime the United States Chargé, J. W. J. Lee, was instructed from Washington to tender assistance to President Amador to suppress mutineers. All saloons were closed for three days and ample troops were on hand for use if needed since several warships were kept available, and presumably the " four or five bands " stationed in Panama City to furnish " diverting music " were available also.[132] In addition, Major General George W. Davis, Governor of the Canal Zone, was instructed to use his police force if it were needed to assist the Marines in maintaining order as " may be requested by Amador." [133]

[132] Lee to Hay, November 14, 1904, *Foreign Relations*, 1904, pp. 647 ff. See also McCain, *op. cit.*, p. 51 ff.

[133] The following instruction found in LC., Taft MS is interesting:

Charge to War Dept.
    Government rate.

OFFICIAL BUSINESS
WAR DEPARTMENT TELEGRAM.

November 16, 1904.

To Major General George W. Davis,
    Governor of Canal Zone,
        Colon, Panama.

Lee and Goodrich have been advised to suppress any mutinous or seditious uprising in the city of Colon or Panama under the

To get rid of the standing army, the real menace to peace in Panama, was something of a problem. The chief trouble maker, an officer named Huertas, was retired on a $500 per month pension and the men were notified they were to be discharged with sixty days' pay. Half of this to be given them on demobilization and the rest one week later, depending on good conduct in the mean time. After some tense moments during which Minister John Barrett played a quite prominent part, the men took their pay and the army of Panama was no more with the exception of "about three men and twenty officers" retained to fulfill "the statutory requirements for a standing army." [134] These too were soon

---

treaty, but have been directed to act upon the request of the President. You will first of all maintain order in the Canal Zone over which you have of course absolute control. Secondly, if it be deemed necessary, although this hardly seems possible, you may use your police force to assist Goodrich and his marines in suppression of disorder as they may be requested by Amador. Keep us advised of the situation.

By direction of the Secretary of War:
[The following "confidential" insertion is hand written:]
Confidential

November 16, 1904.

My dear Admiral:

I enclose you herewith a telegram which the Secretary prepared for your signature to General Davis. Will you please sign and send this as soon as possible?

Very respectfully yours,
(Signed)   Fred W. Carpenter
Private Secretary.

Admiral John G. Walker,
    Chairman, Isthmian Canal Commission,
        Star Building,
        Washington, D. C.
1 Inclosure.

[134] Barrett to Hay, November 22, 1904, *Foreign Relations,* 1904, p. 648.

dismissed and arms and ammunition stored in the canal zone while even the cannon were dismounted from the sea wall in front of Panama City.

The disbanding of the army had just taken place when Taft arrived with a party including his wife, Rear-Admiral (retired) J. G. Walker and Charles E. Magoon of the Canal Commission, the ubiquitous W. N. Cromwell, J. Domingo de Obaldía, Panama Minister at Washington, three representatives of the press, secretaries and an interpreter. Not surprisingly this party in general felt that they were going to view " a kind of opera bouffe republic and nation," [135] but there were real problems connected with it so far as the United States Caribbean policy were concerned.

Fortunately, the Secretary on his return sent President Roosevelt a splendid 31-page confidential report that is available in the Taft Papers. With specific approval from Washington he had issued an executive order in which trade on and through the Canal Zone was defined and imports coming into the zone limited to merchandise for the actual use of the canal workers and the construction of the canal, coal and crude oil for fuel purposes and goods in transit from outside the zone to points outside the zone. All other goods were to go through the ports of Panama and to be subjected to the regular duties there collected. The duties to be charged by Panama, the monopolies let and the consular fees collected were also agreed upon. The Dingley Tariff was suspended for the Canal Zone but Panama stamps were to be used though they were to be " crossed with the words of the Canal Zone." The value of the Panama *peso* was changed from forty to fifty cents

[135] Pringle, *Life and Times of Taft*, I, 281.

and was guaranteed by stipulating that certain deposits be maintained in a New York bank.

In Taft's words:

Stated shortly, the arrangement secures to Panama, first, the payment into its treasury of all import duties upon all goods imported into the Isthmus, whether into the territory of the Republic or the Zone, which by law pay duty; second, it provides for and recognizes the existence of terminal canal ports for which any vessel at any part of the world may be cleared. I was at first inclined to think that we might give up the ports, but an examination of the situation made it perfectly clear to me that the existence of the Canal ports . . . was absolutely necessary in the construction, maintenance and protection of the Canal. . . . In the matter of posts . . . it seemed to me wise to gratify the national pride of Panama by providing for the use of Panama rather than United States stamps, and by securing to Panama as profit forty per cent of the gross receipts. . . . The acquiescence in the provisional delimitation of the Canal Zone was an important concession. . . . The execution of the currency agreement . . . I regard as of much importance. . . . The truth is that while we have all the attributes of sovereignty necessary in the construction, maintenance and protection of the Canal, the very form in which these attributes are conferred in the Treaty seems to preserve the titular sovereignty over the Canal Zone in the Republic of Panama, and as we have conceded to us complete judicial and police power and control of two ports at the end of the canal, I can see no reason for creating a resentment on the parts of the people of the Isthmus by quarreling over that which is dear to them, but which to us is of no real moment whatever.[136]

Taft then recommended that barracks for marines be built close to each of the terminal cities so as to have a sedative effect on ebullient spirits and went so far as to confer with Roman Catholic leaders with regard to hospital

---

[136] Taft to the President, December 19, 1904, LC., Taft MS.

facilities.   He further advised important official changes
as to the Minister to Panama, the Federal judge there, the
organization of the Canal Commission, etc.   He characterized the Conservatives as the old families and persons
of substance " mostly whites," while the Liberals " look for
their support largely to the negroes. . . . The only danger,
it seems to me, of any trouble will be the accession to
power of the Liberal party " for these Negroes are " less
intelligent than the colored people of the United States."
The Secretary felt it was out of the question to secure
United States laborers for the enterprise, that to import
Chinese would create adverse comment in the United States
and that the best solution was to secure Jamaicans.   To this
end his party visited the British island and discussed ways
and means with the authorities there.[137]   Thus was completed a visit far-reaching in its consequences for it had
crystallized the relations between the two countries for
years to come.

During the next few years the papers of Mr. Taft give
an excellent insight into happenings and policies in the
Canal Zone.   Though warned that Cromwell " was not
always nice in his methods " Taft was convinced then and
later that the lawyer was honest and obviously valued his
services and advice highly.   Others felt, however, that
Cromwell's fee of $800,000 which he charged Panama was
a bit excessive.[138]   But the fact is that there were many
financial questions where skilled advice was needed.   These
included bankers' loans and the maintenance of parity of
the new Panama currency,[139] as well as requests to be sent

[137] *Ibid.* See also McCain, pp. 42-5.
[138] Pringle, *op. cit.,* I, 284. It is also to be noted that many
letters from and to Cromwell are to be found in the Taft MS.
[139] Taft to Shaw, January 17, 1905, LC., *ibid.*

to Panama to secure the issuance of a million *pesos* more
of currency so as to provide properly for the growing business needs of the Republic "and for the requirements of
the Isthmian Canal Commission and the Panama Railway." [140]   In an early communication Cromwell used the
words "I consent and request" the issuance of 500,000
silver *pesos* "in accordance with the provisions of Article V
of the Currency Agreement" between the United States and
Panama dated June 20, 1904.

In such affairs Taft may have been overreached at times
but he was a shrewd individual who was perfectly willing
for a man to have his fee and a generous one at that.   However, the Secretary of War certainly had no intention of
allowing the Government to be "rooked" as may be seen
in his letter to his brother Horace on public criticism of his
rulings as to the purchase of supplies:

I had no idea of evoking such a political discussion as has
arisen.   I knew it would cause some squealing from manufacturers.   We are moderate.   All we ask is that the hogs
should take their hind feet out of the trough and let us
have the goods we need at the prices at which they furnish
their foreign customers.[141]

The maintenance of good order was naturally very important.   Would-be filibusters were watched, the training
of the Panama police force encouraged,[143] and health questions rigidly controlled especially as regards the scourge of
yellow fever.[144]   Foreign corporations interested in estab-
lishing telegraph lines in Panama were discouraged and

[140] Taft to Loomis, June 11, 1905, *ibid.*
[141] "Will" to Horace D. Taft, May 22, 1905, *ibid.*
[142] Taft to Wilkie, June 8, 1906, *ibid.*
[143] Taft to McAdoo, October 14, 1905, *ibid.*
[144] Munro, *op. cit.*, pp. 81-2.

word was sent the President of Panama in a letter marked
" confidential ": " I hope you will do nothing until you
confer with Barrett and Davis, because I think that there
are some American persons who would be glad to have an
opportunity to make you an offer." [145]   However, a commercial company was warned: " The question of rights, as
you know, between the Canal and your company is one
thing; the question of using our diplomatic influence with
the Republic of Panama to secure exclusive rights for your
company for the laying of a cable south of Panama is
quite another." [146]   To the President he wrote " I am not
prepared to say that we ought to force an exclusive American franchise on Panama." [147]   Again it was this " hind
legs in the trough " idea that was troubling him.

As to the international relations of the New Nation the
United States continued to be looked to in case of complications involving the nationals of foreign powers. Throughout the period whenever trouble arose with Chinese citizens
the United States was asked to speak for the Orientals.[148]
Of course the more troublesome questions were those arising from questions of boundaries and land ownership. The
original treaty with the United States provided that additional lands, not in the Canal Zone proper, if needed for
uses of the Canal might be acquired by the United States.
By 1908 it became obvious that stone was needed and
application for a quarry located in Portobello was made.
Panama was inclined to quibble and to urge diplomatic
consideration of the matter but the United States gave the

[145] Taft to Guerrero, March 27, 1905, LC., Taft MS.
[146] Taft to W. Emlen Roosevelt, May 31, 1905, *ibid*.
[147] Taft to Roosevelt, May 22, 1905, *ibid*.
[148] *Foreign Relations*, 1905, pp. 708-9; *ibid.*, 1907, pt. 2, p. 933.

question short shrift.   By the end of that year sand was needed from the Punta de Chamé beaches and Panama agreed without needless argument.[149]   In this, however, lay the basis of later complications and considerable hard feeling.

When the question of Panama expansion and the annexation of additional provinces from Colombia was raised Root cabled Magoon the flat statement: " The United States does not approve any such movement." [150]   Another similar question was the long standing dispute which Panama inherited from Colombia as to the boundary with Costa Rica.   The implications soon were seen to be rather far reaching for some quite valuable fruit lands were involved and United States fruit companies were claiming the lands through concessions.   In addition to the actual values involved there were some rather nice legal questions that might cause trouble if applied to questions of land ownership in the Canal Zone.[151]   After correspondence and periodic discussions Costa Rica suggested that the matter be submitted to the Chief Justice or an Associate Justice of the United States Supreme Court for settlement.   This was agreed to in principle by Panama in 1908 [152] and thereafter it was a matter of working out details.

While construction of the Canal proceeded apace [153] Panama was to hold elections in the year 1906.   The Secre-

[149] McCain, p. 146.

[150] Jessup, *Elihu Root*, I, 519; Taft to Root, August 17, 1907, LC., Taft MS.

[151] McCain, p. 124.

[152] *Foreign Relations,* 1910, pp. 772 ff.

[153] For a good account of this see Joseph Bucklin Bishop, *Goethals: Genius of the Panama Canal* (New York and London, 1930).

tary of State wrote the Secretary of War saying that the
United States would take it for granted that Panama would
assume full responsibility for conducting free elections as
an independent nation though if trouble developed the
United States would consider the provisions of the treaty
signed November 18, 1903, as constituting the " necessary
assent " for intervention and that such a step would not
therefore be considered as war.[154]

As for threatened insurrection the Secretary of War wrote
Magoon:

I have no hesitation whatever in saying that in my judgment an insurrection in any part of the Republic would
disturb the order in Panama and Colon and adjacent territory and would greatly increase the difficulties that the
United States would have in constructing the canal, and
while of course the forces of our Government ought not to
intervene until it is established that the Republic of Panama
cannot maintain order in its own territory, I think the
United States may properly, . . . and to prevent its inevitable
interference with the work of canal construction, suppress
any insurrection in any part of the Republic.[155]

Just as soon as the election of the members of the Na-
tional Assembly was held the extra marines were with-
drawn.[156] In November, President Roosevelt paid a visit to
Panama, thus becoming the first President of the United
States to leave its soil while in office. Speaking to the
President of Panama in a public address he said:

Such progress and prosperity, Mr. President, can come only
through the preservation of both order and liberty; through

[154] Root to Secretary of War, February 21, 1906; *Foreign
Relations,* 1906, pt. 2, pp. 1203-6. See also Root to Magoon,
December 4, 1905, *ibid.,* 1905, pp. 719-20.

[155] Taft to Magoon, April 26, 1906, *ibid.*

[156] Taft to Bonaparte, July 5, 1906, *ibid.*

the observance of those in power of all their rights, obligations, and duties to their fellow citizens, and through the
realization of those out of power that the insurrectionary
habit, the habit of civil war, ultimately means destruction
to the republic.[157]

Somewhat later Mr. Taft sent additional judicious advice to
a member of the Canal Commission: March 12, 1908, in a
letter headed " strictly personal and confidential ":

My information is that Arias, the Secretary of State, is
undermining as far as he can the cause of Obaldia in the
fight for the Presidency, and that he has finally enlisted
Amador in his favor, or at least made him lukewarm in his
former open support of Obaldia. I think it is of the utmost
portance that we should have Obaldia as President instead
of Arias, and I will state shortly the reasons. Arias represents that which has always been the worst element in all
South American Republics, to wit,—strong personal ability
and political skill with an utter lack of scruple or sense of
propriety in respect to the methods pursued in securing
private emolument to the chief actor and his followers. I
need not say to you how very awkward and embarrassing it
would be for us to have to deal with such a man at the
head of the Government. . . .

Now, I suggest to you confidentially, and it is not necessary for you to invite your fellow-commissioners into this
matter at all, that you stiffen brother Amador where you
get an opportunity in favor of Obaldia as he was originally,
and not allow him to be misled by Arias, because support
of Arias is support of a cause that will ultimately lead to
corruption and great friction between the United States and
Panama—*verbum sap.*[158]

The actual conduct of the presidential election of 1908,
at the request of both parties, was placed under the supervision of a special electoral commission from the United

[157] Bishop, *Roosevelt and his Time,* I, 452-3.
[158] Taft to Blackburn, March 12, 1908, LC., Taft MS.

States.   On July 14, 1908, while opening his presidential campaign, Taft wrote to the new Secretary of War:

The situation in Panama seems to have cleared up and Obaldia has doubtless been elected.   From what I know of the situation, I am very sure that had we not taken the steps which we did, Amador and Arias would have forced the election of Arias; would have bulldozed the Obaldistas, and we would have had a man in power of great shrewdness and cunning and ability, who would have thwarted as much as possible our legitimate purposes in the Zone. There is not the slightest doubt that Obaldia was the choice of two-thirds of those entitled to vote in Panama, and I think the cause of good government has been helped by securing the return of the man thus the choice of the people.[159]

And so the organization of Panama was essentially completed and in and of itself became representative of the transfer of power and policy from the Roosevelt Big Stick as softened by Root to the new firm policy, i. e., that of systematic control as recommended by Taft and applied by Knox.

[159] Taft to Wright, July 14, 1908, LC., Taft MS.

Chapter VI

DOLLAR DIPLOMACY

With the election of Taft as President of the United States in the fall of 1908 the change from the Root program to that of Philander C. Knox was rapidly completed. The President himself was promptly involved in the multitudinous distractions of his office, complicated by a rapidly widening split in his own party. He was never a precedent breaker, nor even much of a precedent maker. Like many lawyers when new steps were to be taken he preferred to follow the old forms if possible even though the results obtained were quite foreign to the original intentions of the law itself. Further, he was the typical business man's lawyer who sought to please his client without disturbing a suspicious public with novel ideas. As has been seen he was really close to Root in his actual sympathies, and generally approved when Root had slowly modified Roosevelt's and Hay's imperialism through adherence to the spirit of liberal laws as interpreted by real fellowship and a wish to cooperate with the Caribbean republics. Taft's sense of justice was keen but he lacked something of Root's feeling of fellowship. As President he reached still further to the right to appoint Knox his Secretary of State. Quickly the feeling of cordiality, as well as the feeling of cooperation, was lost and the advice of the State Department on which the new policy was to be based, was that of the cold logic and legal reasoning of the business man's attorney.

The new Secretary had served as Attorney General but resigned in 1904 to enter the Senate. Evidently Roosevelt held him in high regard,[1] and Taft had found him an able man and most capable in his office. However, if Taft through his family connections, through Cromwell [2] and others was closely associated with the business interests of the nation Knox was much more so. Of Knox it was said: " The State Department was conducted by . . . a skilled lawyer whose conception of his place was that he was employed by the United States to represent her material interests. . . . As an experienced corporation lawyer, in close association with capitalists, he felt the necessity that the State Department should push American business interests." [3] And this is not surprising when it is realized that the national wealth of the United States was estimated to have increased from eighty-eight billion dollars in 1900 to over one hundred and eighty-six billion in 1912.[4] Knox, accustomed to deal with these money makers, considered them the people worthy of consideration, and non-money makers, as folk of inferior type. That the hostility of necessity engendered by such lack of consideration would redound to the injury of his beloved business interests does not seem to have occurred to him.[5]

Knox started with Root's statement " You shall not push your remedies for wrong against these republics to the point of occupying their territory," and himself added " We are bound to say that whenever the wrong cannot otherwise be redressed we ourselves will see that it is re-

[1] Roosevelt to Knox, December 5, 1902, and June 11, 1904, LC., Philander Chase Knox MS.

[2] Taft to Bliss, July 4, 1908, and Taft to Roosevelt, August 10, 1908, LC., Taft MS.

[3] Hart, *The Monroe Doctrine*, p. 234.

[4] Nearing and Freeman, *Dollar Diplomacy*, p. 5.

[5] Welles, *Naboth's Vineyard*, II, 692.

dressed." [6]   But to him the only sensible procedure was to accompany such action by economic control so as to prevent future complications and incidentally to provide the profits expected to accrue from colonial enterprises. The general idea of reciprocity treaties was essentially given up in the Payne-Aldrich tariff of 1909 but the conditional most-favored-nation interpretation of treaties was insisted on so as to secure a *quid pro quo* in every case and to maintain the principle of tariff barriers to the full.[7]

Since actual ownership of colonies had resulted in a public reaction and had incurred heavy expenses in the Philippines and elsewhere the logical tendency was for a big business lawyer to retain the legal status quo as to government, adopt what Moon later refers to as " non-imperialistic " imperialism [8] by leaving the existing governments in charge and then financing them (on due security offered) so they could overthrow rebellions at their own expense and repay the money borrowed. This would satisfy the recently troublesome public conscience yet enable wealthy interests to enjoy good business and increasing profits from protected loans and protracted peace. Meanwhile there was continued cooperation with the Pan American Union and endorsement of the activities of the Fourth International American Conference which met in 1910, for

[6] Before the New York State Bar Association, January 19, 1912; Alvarez, *The Monroe Doctrine*, p. 467.

[7] Williams, *Economic Foreign Policy of the U. S.*, p. 298; Tariff Commission, *Reciprocity and Commercial Treaties*, p. 227.

The conditional interpretation limited the application of the most-favored-nation treaties to such nations as would offer the same benefits for identical privileges as were offered by the first nation to secure them.

[8] James, Norton and Moon, *U. S. and the Caribbean*, p. 146.

these also contributed to peace and the systematic settlement of claims and business cooperation in general.[9]

Naturally enough economic exploitation created a prompt reaction to the southward. In 1900 the brilliant José Enrique Rodó had aptly expressed one type of Latin American sentiments when he wrote in his *Ariel*: "the spirit of that titanic social organism [the United States] which has thus far been characterized by will and utility alone, may some day be that of intelligence, sentiment, and idealism,"[10] Now the feelings rapidly developed toward the opinions of Manuel Ugarte:

Oh, the land of democracy, of puritanism and liberty! . . . It was enough to see the position of the Negro in this equalitarian republic to understand the insincerity of the premises which were proclaimed. Excluded from the universities, hotels, cafes, theatres, and tramways, he only seemed to be in his right place when in the name of lynch law he was dragged through the streets by the crowd. . . . the rough, imperious masses . . . have exercised dominion throughout the centuries . . . the mentality of the country, from the point of view of general ideas, smacks of the rough and ready morality of the cow-boy . . . who civilized the Far West by exterminating simultaneously the virgin forest and the aboriginal races in the same high-handed act of pride and dominion.[11]

What more skillful appeal could have been made to the

[9] John Barrett, "South America—Our Manufacturers' Greatest Opportunity," *The Annals*, XXXIV, 524; Taft to Congress, December 6, 1910, *Foreign Relations*, 1910, p. xiii; *British and Foreign State Papers*, CVI, 829; 834; Bryce, *American Commonwealth*, II, 581-2.

[10] W. E. Dunn, "Post-War Attitude of Hispanic America toward U. S., *Hisp. Amer. Hist. Rev.*, III, 179-80.

[11] Manuel Ugarte, *The Destiny of a Continent* (J. Fred Rippy, editor) (New York, 1925), pp. 11-2.

Caribbean nations with their large proportions of Negro and Indian blood?

As early as 1910 the able international lawyer Alejandro Alvarez stated that the United States had developed a special policy in addition to the Monroe Doctrine and that this was a policy of hegemony practiced "almost exclusively on the countries that are the immediate neighbors of the United States, those bordering on the Gulf of Mexico (with the exception of Mexico [and this was soon to be included]) and those situated on the Caribbean or located near it." [12]   Others were more inclined to the Ugarte point of view and even the scholar F. García Calderón did not hesitate to warn the Latin Americans that the civilization of the United States was that of a people with no unity in their own society,[13] that the pleas for economic cooperation were purely and frankly selfish and that to save themselves the Latins might have to resort to either a Japanese or a German alliance as the lesser of two evils.[14] He added: "everywhere the Americans of the North are feared. In the Antilles and in Central America hostility against the Anglo-Saxon invaders assumes the character of a Latin crusade." [15]

On its part the administration was fully convinced of the advisability of its policy and did not hesitate. Taft steadily urged legislation to improve the trade mark situation, to provide subsidies for a merchant marine and to allow freer access of United States banks to overseas banking.[16] He

[12] Alvarez, *op. cit.,* p. 205.

[13] F. García Calderón, *Latin America: Its Rise and Progress* (London, 6th edition, 1919), pp. 608-9.

[14] *Ibid.,* pp. 305-6.   [15] *Ibid.,* p. 298.

[16] Annual Message, December 7, 1909, and December 7, 1911, *Foreign Relations,* 1909, pp. xxxiv-xxxv; *ibid.,* pp. xxvi-xxvii.

frankly boasted to Congress that the State Department had been largely responsible for securing battleship contracts, railway equipment and government ship contracts for United States business concerns. Further he commented: " The diplomacy of the present administration has sought to respond to the modern idea of commercial intercourse. This policy has been characterized as substituting dollars for bullets." [17] With regard to the Caribbean area he was equally specific:

. . . it is obvious that the Monroe Doctrine [everything still had to be attributed to that sacred term] is more vital in the neighborhood of the Panama Canal and the zone of the Caribbean than anywhere else. . . . It is therefore essential that the countries within that sphere shall be removed from the jeopardy involved by heavy foreign debt and chaotic national finances and from the ever present danger of international complications due to disorder at home. Hence the United States has been glad to encourage and support American bankers who were willing to lend a helping hand to the financial rehabilitation of such countries. . . . [18]

He continued with the statement that the interests of American investors were protected by the landing of "over 2,000 marines and blue-jackets in Nicaragua."

Both Taft and Knox were accustomed to efficiency and so they steadily hammered at the idea of reorganization of the State Department that Root had begun. The result was substantial improvements authorized by act of Congress in 1909, and among these was the creation of the Latin American Division of the State Department. Thus system and method steadily began to make their appearance, and

[17] Annual Message, December 3, 1912, *ibid.*, 1912, p. x.
[18] *Ibid.*, p. xii.

responsibility for action or delay could be the more readily determined.[19]

So far as Europe was concerned it applauded the program and extended more and more of both actual and tacit recognition of the priority of the United States in the Western Hemisphere. Sir Edward Grey speaking to the Committee of Imperial Defense May 26, 1911, commented:

As long as it is the policy of the United States as I believe it always will be not to disturb existing British possessions, she may be perfectly certain we are willing at any time to give her any amount of assurance that we shall certainly not try to disturb, not only her possessions, but the possessions of other independent countries in Central and South America. . . . [In this area] we have kept, and shall keep, carefully clear of all entanglements in the politics, which are often very complicated, of the Central and South American Republics with each other, so we shall not come across the United States as regards our policy in South America.[20]

With regard to Panama Taft naturally maintained a direct interest probably greater than in connection with any other phase of foreign relations with the possible exception of the Philippines. His attitude was still that of a somewhat condescending mentor. September 16, 1908, he had written to Root: " Obaldia [the new president of Panama] is to be inaugurated in October. He will be in a pliable condition for the first month or two of his administration." [21] There was an announced policy of refraining

[19] *Ibid.*, pp. viii-ix; John Mabry Matthews, *Conduct of American Foreign Relations* (New York, 1922), pp. 47-8; Gaillard Hunt, *The Department of State of the United States, Its History and Functions* (New Haven, 1914), pp. 244-7.

[20] Gooch and Temperley, *British Documents on the Origins of the War*, VI, 786.

[21] Letter addressed to "Athos " and signed " Porthos." This was the familiar form of address, based on Dumas, *Three Musketeers,* used by the two, Roosevelt being D'Artagnan. LC., Taft MS.

from public intervention in the elections and an insistence on freedom for all to go to the polls. However, it was agreed that the United States would again supervise the contest in 1912 as it had done in 1908. In view of Taft's earlier action while Secretary of War, possibly this note may be significant:

Introducing to the Secretary of War
                Senor Arias, the Panamanian Minister.

I would like to have you arrange a meeting between yourself, Senor Arias and Colonel·Goethals to consider exigencies of the next Panamanian election and the wise course for us to pursue.

Feb. 14, 1912   W. H. T.[22]

Of course this may have referred to nothing but the details of the supervision of the election. On the other hand the President of Panama wrote:

The position of Panama grows constantly more difficult . . . my government cannot establish any real authority. I lack means for carrying out its decisions. I meet with difficulties even in arming the police properly, and they are frequently the victims of mysterious outrages. Persons from the Canal Zone, assault my police agents, and return with impunity to North American territory, after committing breaches of the laws and municipal ordinances. If a political insurrection were to break out tomorrow on Panamanian territory, I could not suppress it unless the United States authorized me to equip troops and transport them from one division of our country to another.[23]

And in connection with such matters the attitude of the United States was definite enough. To protect properly

[22] This was written on one of the President's own cards and in his handwriting. LC., Taft MS.

[23] Ugarte, *op. cit.,* p. 146.

the Canal interests the Northern Republic insisted that no foreign power or its nationals should secure concessions to railways or lands that might affect important waters since full rights to protect the Canal interests were granted in the treaty of November 18, 1903.[24] Repeatedly railroad construction was discussed and clearly the United States retained the last word in approving or vetoing all new enterprises.[25] Similarly it was maintained that the provision giving the United States full rights to construct, maintain, operate and protect, as well as make sanitary the Canal meant the authority to operate wireless stations anywhere in Panama " and further that any interfering wireless stations owned by private parties may be treated and disposed of under the provisions of Article 6 of the treaty." [26]

As the construction of the Canal neared completion there arose the question of fortifications. Some in the United States objected but Great Britain presented no opposition to the idea,[27] and Goethals, after a visit to Europe to study the Kiel Canal and similar works presented a strong report to the House and Senate committees favoring fortification. He stated that the German Emperor advised fortification against either Great Britain or Japan. This practically ended the matter and legislation was enacted providing for batteries and the construction of quarters for a permanent garrison.[28]

[24] Acting Secretary of State Wilson to Chargé in Panama, September 20, 1911, *Foreign Relations,* 1912, pp. 1181-3.

[25] Numerous references in *Foreign Relations.* See also McCain, *U. S. and Panama,* pp. 167-8; 173.

[26] *Foreign Relations,* 1912, pp. 1132-3.

[27] Gooch and Temperley, *op. cit.,* VIII, 578-82.

[28] Bishop, *Goethals,* pp. 219-20.

When Venezuelan and Colombian rebels threatened to use Panamanian soil for their activities Washington sent word that the little Republic was to see that this stopped forthwith, since if the United States was to guarantee the independence of the country it must see that that country did not make itself liable to punitive action because of negligence.[29] A further bit of tutorial guidance appeared in connection with the submission of the Costa Rican boundary dispute to the arbitration of the Chief Justice of the United States. In this Knox, in 1910, showed little patience and insisted that Panama accept his interpretation of the terms of the submission, which incidentally apparently protected certain endangered claims of the United Fruit Company.[30]

Toward the end of the Taft administration there arose the question of the tolls that would be charged when the Canal was opened for traffic. The British insisted that under the Hay-Pauncefote treaty they had equality of rates with the shipping of the United States and Root, Choate, White and Hay (now dead) had agreed.[31] When the dispute arose White and others suggested that the question be submitted to arbitration.[32] Taft feared arbitration saying that all Europe would feel the same as Great Britain and that it would be exceedingly difficult to secure

[29] *Foreign Relations,* 1909, pp. 468-70.

[30] McCain, *op. cit.,* p. 134.

[31] Root, *Addresses on International Subjects,* pp. 238; 246; 256; *Dip. Hist. of Pan. Canal,* pp. 82-3; Mowat, *Diplomatic Relations of Great Britain and U. S.,* pp. 330-1; George Macaulay Trevelyan, *Grey of Fallodon* (Boston, 1937), p. 235.

[32] T. R. White and Charlemagne Tower, *Our Duty Concerning the Panama Canal Tolls* (Boston, 1913) (World Peace Foundation Pamphlet Series, III, No. 1, pt. 1).

impartial judges. In his uncertainty he suggested that the question be referred to the Supreme Court of the United States but Congress opposed this and passed the discrimina-tory measure. By this time recriminations were exceedingly bitter over domestic affairs between the Progressive Re-publicans and the Standpatters so Taft threw himself fully into the arms of the conservatives, changed his tentative opinion on the tolls as expressed late in 1910, and signed the measure.[33] To British protests that the bill constituted an act of bad faith there was no satisfactory response until the election was over and the Democrats took office in 1913.

With the old mother country, Colombia, the tripartite treaties were still pending when Taft and Knox took office. Panama and the United States ratified promptly as has been seen, but the opposition became increasingly serious as the debate progressed in Colombia. The Congress in Bogotá postponed action throughout 1909 and finally the Minister of Foreign Affairs had to admit that it was useless to press the treaties on Congress.[34] Thus the matter was dropped for the time. Fresh fuel was added to the flame of Colom-bian resentment in March, 1911, when ex-President Roose-velt, speaking in California used his apt but unfortunate expression to the effect that he "took" the Canal Zone. The Colombian Minister wrote to the State Department that this was an admission that his nation had been "gra-tuitously, profoundly, and unexpectedly offended and in-jured." The protest was not discussed diplomatically but Colombia continued to clamor for arbitration.[35] When

[33] Pringle, *Life and Times of Taft,* II, 648-50.

[34] Numerous references in *Foreign Relations.* See also *Dip. Hist. of Pan. Canal.*

[35] Pedro Nel Ospina to Secretary of State, November 25, 1911, *Foreign Relations,* 1913, pp. 284-7; also Latané, *U. S. and Latin Amer.,* pp. 271-2.

Knox was to make his tour of the Caribbean and it was intimated that he would be glad to visit Colombia, the response was that such a visit would be "inopportune." True, the answer came from the minister only and was disapproved by his government but it engendered ill feeling just the same.[36]

Just before the end of the administration real efforts were made to appease Colombia and bring about a settlement. The discussions revolved around the question of paying $10,000,000 to Colombia for the option of constructing a canal through the Atrato route which lies just south of the isthmus and makes use of the Atrato river valley. In return Colombia would receive some privileges in the use of the Panama canal, also certain questions of damages in connection with United States acquisition of the Panama Canal and Railroad were to be submitted to arbitration. These proposals were rejected by Bogotá and in response to a direct question as to what the South American Republic would consider satisfactory the answer was:

The arbitration of the whole Panama question or a direct proposition from the United States to compensate Colombia for all the moral, physical, and financial losses sustained by it because of the separation of Panama.[37]

The truth of the matter appears to be that as soon as the elections of 1912 showed the defeat of Taft, Colombia determined to accept no terms until the new Wilson ad-

[36] P. C. Knox, *Relations between the United States and the Republic of Colombia* (Washington, 1913) (House Document No. 1444, 62d cong., 3d sess.), pp. 6-8.

[37] *Ibid.*, p. 12; also Knox to Taft, March 1, 1913, *Foreign Relations*, 1913, p. 307.

ministration was in office.   In spite of all obstacles, however, trade between the republics was doubled from 1910 to 1913 [39] and there was a rising clamor from business interests to settle the outstanding questions so that they could more firmly establish prosperity.   As yet the clamor was not loud enough to overpower simultaneously the opposition in the two countries, so resentment, pride, and party politics were to reign for another decade.

In the meantime, two of the island republics could not wait upon the formation of new policies for they both came under the head of unfinished business and demanded a continuation of the program that had been started.   At best, or worst, in both Santo Domingo and Cuba relatively slight modifications in trends only could be expected.

The five to six thousand troops sent to Cuba were steadily reduced in numbers after the successful elections of 1908 [40] so that Taft and Knox could proceed on the basis of diplomacy rather than force.   Having learned the costs and difficulties of actual intervention special efforts were to be taken to avoid such complications if at all possible for the future. In spite of local opposition Guantánamo naval base was enlarged [41] following Taft's recommendation to Congress that it be materially strengthened.[42]   When rumors of revolts reached Washington in 1910 Secretary Knox emphatically repudiated the idea that the United States would encourage any disturbance and stated that his Government " would

[38] *Ibid.,* p. 308; Du Bois to Secretary of State, February 5, 1913, *ibid.,* pp. 287 ff.

[39] Rippy, *Capitalists and Colombia,* p. 12.

[40] Fitzgibbon, *Cuba and the U. S.,* p. 134.

[41] For extended correspondence see *Foreign Relations,* 1911, pp. 110 ff.

[42] Messages to Congress, December 6, 1910, *ibid.,* 1910, p. xlvii.

view with profound regret and disfavor any political agitation or activity involving violence and bloodshed by whomsoever undertaken " when this tended to a situation in which the United States might again have to intervene.[43]

Meanwhile oversight and coaching from the sidelines was obviously active as may be seen from an exchange between United States Minister Jackson in Cuba and President Taft through Secretary of State Knox. Jackson wired that there was a report current in Cuba that the President had " lectured Cuban Secretary of State and Government with regard to domestic political situation " and asked that this be denied and the facts of the interview be made public. The President responded to Secretary Knox:

Of course, there is no truth in the intimation of the opposition papers referred to by Jackson. I have no objection to your denying it in any way, but as you know, I do not think it would be wise to say what the subject of the conference was.[44]

Meanwhile the business man's administration in Washington was more or less complacent and did not ask too many questions about the expense accounts of Cuban officials. The result was that graft and corruption flourished and there can be little doubt that President Gómez was seriously culpable.[45]

One interesting tendency was the reaction against Yankee and in favor of the English capital after the intervention. The total foreign investment in the country was estimated at upwards of $400,000,000 in 1913, and of this United States citizens held upwards of $200,000,000. But from

[43] Knox to Jackson, June 21, 1910, *ibid.*, p. 416.
[44] Taft to Knox, November 25, 1910, LC., Taft MS.
[45] Chapman, *History of Cuban Republic*, pp. 278-9; 286-7.

1909 to 1913 new United States capital invested amounted to only $35,000,000 while new British capital totaled $60,-000,000 and French and German about $17,000,000.[46] Thus it would seem that while there were some malodorous concessions like the Zapata Swamp affair,[47] some paving concessions and probably others that deserve to be condemned the outstanding fact is that even under the era of dollar diplomacy such concessions were not the chief objective of the Caribbean policy of the nation. They were in fact an unfortunate adjunct, or again simply a barnacle that was unsightly, rough and a serious nuisance. They were to be fostered on the grounds that they were advantageous, yet it must be admitted that foreign competitors were not eliminated though probably their success was occasionally protested and even blocked by Washington. In general it appears that commercial investments received little official attention but concessions such as that to the Zapata Swamp—whose granting to foreign concerns were of strategic importance or were thought to carry possibilities of involvments that might bring about intervention— were promptly frowned on [48] and very effectively at that.

As early as January, 1912, a troublesome political controversy had developed along racial lines with the Negroes in opposition.[49] By May it was serious, especially in the district around Guantánamo Bay, and Taft and both State and Navy Departments acted. A communication was sent

[46] Jenks, *Our Cuban Colony,* pp. 164-5.

[47] *Foreign Relations,* 1912, pp. 509 ff.; Jenks, *op. cit.,* pp. 108-10.

[48] Knox to Chargé, August 15, 1912, *Foreign Relations,* 1912, pp. 314-5.

[49] *Ibid.,* pp. 240; 242 ff.; Taft to Knox, May 22, 1912 (two letters) and Taft to Gómez, May 27, 1912, LC., Taft MS.

to the Cuban Government that was immediately given to the Press in the United States:

Information reaching the Department of State has indicated a serious state of disturbance in the easternmost Province of the Island of Cuba, especially in the neighborhood of Guantánamo and Santiago, where there are important American interests, which have already made representations to the Department to the effect that their property is being seized and the lives of their employees endangered, and have requested that the Government of the United States procure for them adequate protection. The Department of State has accordingly requested the Navy Department to send vessels and marines to the United States naval station at Guantánamo, which is near the center of the disturbance. The *Prairie* is to take 500 marines and join the *Paducah* and *Nashville* there. These steps have, of course, been taken simply in order that, in case of necessity, protection may be accorded to the Americans in that vicinity.[50]

In communicating the notice to the Cuban Government the hope was expressed that this would stabilize conditions and enable local officials to secure control of the situation. However, it was added that if the conditions required additional vessels would be ordered to Guantánamo. Some troops were actually landed and additional vessels dispatched to Havana itself even though the President of Cuba protested that he could handle the situation. The United States was obviously taking no chances.[51] Thus with indirect aid and some direct assistance an extended period of military control was avoided. True enough the United States fleet was a " sword of Damocles " but was hardly an active police force. In summing up his action

[50] Knox to American Minister, May 23, 1912, *Foreign Relations*. 1912, pp. 245-6.
[51] Chapman, *op. cit.*, pp. 310-11.

the Secretary of State insisted that his policy had been a " preventive " one.[52] The term was appropriate—and the policy was effective.

By this time new elections were due in both Cuba and the United States. Knox and Taft did not want further complications and this may have tempered their action. However, in Cuba the suppression of the threatened revolt had really settled the election issues, and without serious trouble Menocal was elected. He had been Chief of Police of Havana during the active intervention, and was popular as a prosperous sugar planter and war hero. At the same time he was well liked by the laborers and so seemed to be an almost ideal candidate from both Cuban and United States viewpoints.[53]

Few comments are needed on Puerto Rico. This new possession of the United States was developing steadily. Protests that the islanders did not have the liberties and rights they expected, for the most part fell on rather deaf ears. True, a bill was introduced and passed the House of Representatives June 15, 1910, to make certain changes. Taft endorsed the provision to remove the judiciary from politics and then said:

The provision in the bill for a partially elective senate, the number of elective members being progressively increased, is of doubtful wisdom, and the composition of the senate as provided in the bill when introduced in the House, seems better to meet conditions existing in Porto Rico. This is an important measure, and I recommend its early consideration and passage.[54]

[52] Knox to American Minister, June 14, 1912, *Foreign Relations,* 1912, p. 266.

[53] Chapman, p. 321.

[54] Message to Congress, December 6, 1910, *Foreign Relations,* 1910, p. xxxiii.

But nothing happened. The administration closed while the measure slumbered, only to be awakened, revised and adopted some years later.

The other case of unfinished business was Santo Domingo. During the first year or so of the Knox incumbency in the State Department there were few changes and all seemed to be running fairly well. It is true that the total increase of trade was not very noticeable but that could be explained by the fact that early advances required consolidation. Imports into the country were rising and that could mean either success for Dollar Diplomacy in stimulating sales, a change from the raising of " small " crops for domestic consumption to crops for export, or a rising standard of living.[55]

One significant law enacted in 1911 provided for the division of communal lands. This meant that the communes were to be divided and hence were available for private purchase—and that the way was open for foreign sugar corporations to buy up the village lands for their special crop. In fact the law has been characterized as the " magna carta " of the foreign sugar industry.[56]

By the time Knox embarked on his Caribbean tour there was a good deal of discontent and a rather clear indication that a revolt might be brewing. So while in the island Knox stated publicly:

It behooves them [all the nations which are to reap the far-reaching benefits of the Panama Canal] to be cooperative, not obstructive. Each is concerned in uplifting itself; each is benefitted by the uplifting of its neighbors. No more signal obstruction could be interposed in the path of

[55] F. F. Fairchild, " Public Finance of Santo Domingo," *Pol. Sc. Quar.*, XXXIII, 465-6.

[56] Knight, *Americans in Santo Domingo*, p. 48.

general progress than for any of the affected countries to fall into disrepute through subversive disturbances or failure to discharge its international obligations.[57]

The existing government was corrupt and inefficient but the leaders of the rebels failed to inspire confidence.[58] In September, 1912, Mr. W. T. S. Doyle, Chief of the new Latin American Division of the State Department, and General McIntyre of the Bureau of Insular Affairs, went to Santo Domingo accompanied by 750 marines. President Victoria at first seemed willing to accept the demands for a revision of his cabinet and for modifications of certain objectionable laws, especially the electoral law, but later proved recalcitrant. The response of the United States was that in view of misuse of funds in the past instructions would be given to the General Receiver of Dominican Customs to cease all payments to the established government. Likewise no monies were to be paid to the rebel forces and any government set up by them would be refused recognition by the United States. Not surprisingly Victoria resigned by the end of November and on December 2nd the Archbishop of Santo Domingo, Monsignor Adolfo A. Nouel, was selected unanimously by Senate and House of Deputies for a two year provisional presidency.[59]

The Archbishop was far from desiring the office and threatened to resign forthwith. To avoid such action everything possible was done to bolster his morale and to hold him in office, even to the extent of sending a United

[57] Philander Chase Knox, *Speeches Incident to Visit of . . . to . . . the Caribbean* (Washington, 1913), p. 151.

[58] Russell to Secretary of State, September 9, 1912, *Foreign Relations, 1912*, p. 366; Welles, *Naboth's Vineyard*, II, 697 ff.

[59] *Ibid.*, II, 699; Munro, *U. S. and the Caribbean*, p. 113; *Foreign Relations, 1912*, p. 377.

States warship to Santo Domingo City.[60] Thus once more Knox and Taft skated to safety over very thin ice indeed. Here, as in Cuba, the interventions resorted to were not very expensive and were seemingly successful.[61]

In the western end of the island, Haiti, conditions were steadily becoming worse and United States warships appeared because of local disturbances in six of the seven years between 1907 and 1913.[62] But the State Department did not want to be responsible for another intervention if it could be avoided. An alternative course, and one congenial to the Knox temperament, appeared in 1910 in connection with the reorganization of the National Bank of the Republic. Heretofore, loans to Haiti had regularly been negotiated through French bankers and now a new loan was obtained from the same source. The terms provided that the Bank was to conduct the treasury service of the Government and was to be paid a commission of 1% on all deposits; $\frac{1}{2}$% on all sums paid out plus an additional $\frac{1}{2}$% if the sum was paid in a foreign country, while the Bank allowed no interest to the Government on deposits held. All disputes were to be settled by an arbitral board of three: one selected by the Government, one by the bankers, and one by the Hague Court.

[60] Correspondence found in *Foreign Relations,* 1912, pp. 376 ff.

[61] It might be noted that there had been repeated efforts by the United States to secure a settlement of the long standing boundary dispute between the Dominican Republic and Haiti, but all of these were fruitless and the quarreling continued. Correspondence on the subject is found in *Foreign Relations* at scattered points after 1906.

[62] *Inquiry into the Occupation and Administration of Haiti and Santo Domingo. Hearings before a Select Committee of the United States Senate* (Washington, 1922), I, 63. Hereafter cited as *Inquiry into Haiti and S. D.*

These terms were so onerous as to create considerable comment in banking and diplomatic circles. However, Dollar Diplomats knew a good thing when they saw it. Promptly protests went from Washington stating the " entire disapproval " of any contract that was " so prejudicial to American interests, so disastrous to the sovereignty of Haiti and so unjust in its operations in regard to the people and government of Haiti." Several New York bankers were called to discuss the situation with the Secretary of State. The result was the opening of negotiations with the French bankers so that each of four New York banks was allowed to subscribe 5% of the stock of the new bank that was to be chartered; and at the same time a German bank was allowed to take 5%. In addition, three United States citizens became directors of the bank whose headquarters remained in Paris, and one United States citizen became vice-president and another the active manager of the bank in Haiti. Thus the matter was considered satisfactorily closed. The terms of the contract remained essentially the same, so it became clear that it was not the terms of the contract that had been so bad in the first place, but the fact that they had been obtained by the wrong parties.[63] Clearly the Caribbean was considered to be the United States barnyard, and if the geese therein were to be plucked, regardless of who had raised them them to this point, the dollar diplomats were determined that a substantial part of the feathers should be acquired for Yankee feather beds.

From 1908 to 1911 there had been a period of reasonable peace in the island under the administration of President

---

[63] Raymond Leslie Buell, *American Occupation of Haiti* (Foreign Policy Association Information Service, Vol. V, Nos. 19-20) (New York, 1929), pp. 333-4; P. H. Douglas, "American Occupation of Haiti," *Pol. Sc. Quar.*, XLII, 229 ff.

Simon [64] but his power had disintegrated. On his trip Secretary Knox specifically urged peace and orderly procedures of government [65] but in spite of his advice conditions grew worse.[66] About all the Government at Washington could do was to "worry through," avoid active intervention, secure concessions for its nationals and then hope that they would not be interfered with too much.

The key to the Central American situation was of course Nicaragua where the incubus Santos Zelaya bestrode the isthmus, hated the United States, and was determined to control the region thereabouts. He apparently had antagonized certain foreign interests by attempts to adjust or cancel their contracts and it is said that one of these was "La Luz and Angeles" Company in which Philander C. Knox was reported to be a heavy stockholder, and his nephew the resident manager of the company in Bluefields. A revolution said to have been financed by this company soon threatened.[67] As early as October, 1909, United States consul Moffatt had reported that he had reason to believe that a revolution would soon break out under the leadership of the local governor in Bluefields with General Emiliano Chamorro, who had just landed secretly the night before, leading the forces in the field.[68] Five days later the offi-

[64] Buell, *op. cit.*, p. 337.

[65] Knox, *Speeches Incident to Visit to Caribbean*, pp. 169-70.

[66] *Foreign Relations,* 1911, pp. 281 ff.

[67] The account of this affair as seen by three typical Latin American critics of the United States are found in Horacio Blanco Fombona, *Crimenes del Imperialismo Norteamericano* (México, D. F., 1927), pp. 5-7; Rafael de Nogales, *The Looting of Nicaragua* (New York, 1928), pp. 7-8; Ugarte, *Destiny of a Continent,* p. 106, note.

[68] Moffatt to Secretary of State, undated but received October 7, 1909, *Foreign Relations,* 1909, p. 452.

cial paraphrase of another of the consul's reports stated the revolution was entirely successful locally and continued:

He [the Consul] says leaders will immediately strike down Managua Government; that troops will proceed to interior today; that overthrow of Zelaya appears absolutely assured, and that it is intended later to separate Republic of Nicaragua, consolidating Pacific Coast States into a separate Republic, both republics to be under the control of the conservative party. Mr. Moffatt adds that immediate reduction tariff is assured; also the annulment of all concessions not owned by foreigners. He says new Government here is friendly to American interests and is progressive; that the new President has granted him recognition; has formed new cabinet; and has sent him assurance in writing friendship American Government.[69]

Truly an interesting report!

The Department confined its instructions to non-committal orders for the consul to watch his step carefully and not to do anything that would indicate formal recognition of the rebels.[70] About the middle of November two United States citizens who were apparently regularly enlisted in the rebel forces were captured by Zelaya and soon thereafter shot. Apparently they were rather well known characters in Central American revolutions[71] but their execution was rather summary to say the least. The response of the State Department was a letter to the Nicaraguan Chargé in Washington:

Sir: I have the honor to request you . . . immediately to telegraph to that Government [of Zelaya] that the Govern-

[69] *Ibid.*

[70] Acting Secretary of State to Moffatt, October 13, 1909, *ibid.,* p. 453.

[71] Moffatt to Secretary of State, November 25, 1909, *ibid.,* p. 451; Rodriguez to Secretary of State, November 19, 1909, *ibid.,* pp. 447-8.

ment of the United States can scarcely believe the report that two Americans captured with the revolutionary army of Gen. Estrada have been summarily executed, and that if this grievous report be true the Government of the United States demands instant information of all particulars, meanwhile reserving for future decision the measures to be taken in such an eventuality.[72]

Meanwhile the executions were bitterly condemned in the United States Senate.[73] On the first of December Knox notified the Nicaraguan Chargé that his Government could not maintain diplomatic relations with the tyrant of Nicaragua who was keeping the neighboring countries of Costa Rica, El Salvador and Guatemala in disorder and fear. At the same time the rebels were encouraged by the statement that the United States was convinced that they more faithfully represented the ideals and will of the Nicaraguan people than did the Dictator.[74]

Zelaya soon realized that he could not successfully withstand United States pressure and so resigned on December 17th, the while he denounced the " immoral and shameful " revolution and the " hostile attitude " of the powerful nation which " against all right " had interfered in the internal affairs of the Republic.[75] The ex-dictator then took refuge on board a Mexican warship. Meanwhile the Mexican Minister in Washington notified the State Department that Mexico was willing to do whatever the

[72] Knox to Nicaraguan Chargé, November 18, 1909, *ibid.,* p. 447.

[73] Weitzel, *American Policy in Nicaragua,* pp. 12-3.

[74] Knox to Nicaraguan Chargé, December 1, 1909, *Foreign Relations,* 1909, pp. 455-7; Department of State, *The United States and Nicaragua* (Washington, 1932), pp. 7-8.

[75] Manifesto of Zelaya to National Assembly, December 17, 1909, *Foreign Relations,* 1909, p. 459.

United States desired in the matter.[76]   The next day Taft wrote to Knox that at an interview he had with the Mexican Minister the latter stated that President Díaz " had promised Zelaya this asylum, but that he was most anxious to preserve good relations between the United States and Mexico, and that if the United States entered an objection he would have broken the promise."   Taft added that he had told the Mexican that both Knox and he were

distressed over the Central American situation, and that I was not content until we secured some formal right to compel the peace between those Central American Governments, and used the expression ' to have the right to knock their heads together until they should maintain peace between them,' to which I understood the Ambassador to assent heartily.[77]

The Congress of Nicaragua proved stubborn and so selected Dr. José Madriz, one of Zelaya's men, as President. Thus the struggle continued for some months with the moral support of the United States behind the opposition, or Estrada, faction.   At times this support took the form of preventing blockades and of insisting that the rebels had the right to collect customs duties in and near Bluefields while the United States forbade all fighting in the city and thus prevented any attempt to recapture it.   Nicaraguan protests received little response.[78]   The pressure continued and August 20, 1910, came word that Madriz had " deposited the so-called presidency of Nicaragua in José Dolores Estrada " while the rebels steadily advanced on the capital.[79]

[76] Taft to Knox, December 21, 1909, LC., Taft MS.

[77] Taft to Knox, December 22, 1909, *ibid*.

[78] Caldera to Secretary of State, December 26, 1909, *Foreign Relations,* 1910, p. 738. See also *ibid.,* pp. 745 ff.

[79] Olivares to Secretary of State, August 20, 1910, *ibid.,* p. 759.

To secure some kind of orderly settlement of details the United States now sent its Minister to Panama, T. C. Dawson, to Nicaragua to interview the various factions and bring about a settlement. The arrangements made were:

1. For immediate elections to select Estrada as President, and Díaz as vice-president. The election to be by a constituent assembly which would proceed to adopt a constitution to abolish monopolies, guarantee the rights of foreigners and provide for a general election in two years. Estrada not to be a candidate for reelection.

2. For a mixed claims commission to settle outstanding claims. It was finally agreed this was to be constituted with one United States and one Nicaraguan citizen, and an umpire selected by the State Department at Washington.[80] (This composition was held by many to vitiate the original purpose of the commission.)

3. To punish the executioners of Cannon and Groce and to indemnify their families.

4. To solicit the good offices of the United States to secure a loan to the new Government; the loan to be guaranteed by a percentage of the customs receipts.[81]

It now remained to be seen if the opening provided for Dollar Diplomacy in the fourth provision would be utilized. Early in 1911 Estrada appointed a financial adviser at the suggestion of the State Department to make a study of the situation,[82] and as a result Mr. Clifford D. Ham was in-

[80] For material on this Mixed Claims Commission see *Foreign Relations,* 1910, pp. 625 ff.; State Department, *U. S. and Nicaragua,* p. 15; Munro, *U. S. and the Caribbean,* pp. 233-4.

[81] Williams, *Economic Foreign Policy of the U. S.,* p. 143.

It might be said that the Central American Peace Court had been trying to bring about peace in the long protracted struggle but had been ineffective in the face of powerful obstacles (*Foreign Relations,* 1910, p. 744).

[82] Dana G. Munro, *The Five Republics of Central America* (New York, 1918), pp. 233-5.

stalled as Customs Collector on December 16th. He had already served in the Philippine Customs Service and so was not without experience for his new duties.[83] There can be no doubt that the financial end was being watched most closely from Washington. In fact on October 3rd the report came in that the loan contracts were almost sure to be accepted promptly. The response was:

> The Department in reply to your September 29 and October 3 believes that attention should be steadily directed to the loan and the claims commission matters; they are of the first importance and should be disposed of before con-sideration of political subjects, which should not be discussed unnecessarily.[84]

This instruction was carried out apparently and the Knox-Castrillo Treaty was duly signed. It provided for a custom's collector and for a loan of $15,000,000 through Brown Brothers and J. & W. Seligman and Company for the settlement of claims, the construction of a much needed railway and for miscellaneous purposes.[85] Incidentally the Claims Commission which was dominated by the United States only awarded $538,750 to United States claimants out of $7,500,000 claimed by them.[86] This would indicate to many that the Department could hardly have been gullible enough to consider the original claims too seriously and that it used them primarily as an approach to the loan proposition which was the really important problem.

[83] *Ibid.*, pp. 238-9; State Department, *U. S. and Nicaragua,* p. 14.

[84] Acting Secretary of State Adee to Chargé, October 5, 1911, *Foreign Relations,* 1911, p. 668.

[85] Cox, *Nicaragua and the U. S.,* p. 712; Crowther, *Romance and Rise of the Tropics,* pp. 291-2.

[86] Jones, Norton and Moon, *U. S. and the Caribbean,* p. 199.

Meanwhile the new Constitutional Convention in Nicaragua threatened to get out of hand. It resented tutelage from Washington, and openly resisted pressure. January 12th it irregularly promulgated a new constitution in spite of the fact that the United States was not satisfied with it and further published a statement which characterized the interposition of the United States chargé as " in effect, an insult to the national autonomy and the honor of the Assembly." [87]

Things were far from going well. Opposition to the treaty was vociferous and soon culminated in active revolution in December, 1911. The United States promptly landed marines and bluejackets who stormed one rebel post at a cost of seven of their number killed.[88] The situation was brought under control by seizing communications and by aid from one or more of the eight naval vessels that were in Nicaraguan waters during 1912. During the procedure there was a " good deal of fighting and the surrender of two rebel gunboats." [89]

In spite of United States protests the President had resigned and the vice president Díaz was now in office and continued for the ensuing term from 1913 to 1917.[90] Of course such a situation was far from pleasant to Knox or Taft as their administration was coming to an end. With

[87] Nogales, *op. cit.,* p. 18; Gunther to Secretary of State, January 13, 1912, *Foreign Relations,* 1912, p. 994.

[88] State Department, *U. S. and Nicaragua,* pp. 20-2.

[89] J. R. C., *Right to Protect Citizens in Foreign Countries . . . Memorandum of the Solicitor for the Department of State* (Washington, 1929), pp. 120-1; Munro, *op. cit.,* pp. 243-4; Nearing and Freeman, *Dollar Diplomacy,* pp. 164-5; Cox, *Nicaragua and the U. S.,* pp. 717-8.

[90] Munro, *U. S. and the Caribbean,* pp. 230-1.

the reaction they were already facing they certainly did not want such an airing of public linen as this provided. The best way to hush the rampant criticism would be by securing Senate approval of the pending loan treaty.[91] This Knox urged and on July 17th Taft wrote the Senate: "I have already on three occasions endeavored to impress upon the Senate the great importance which I attach to the consummation of this convention and the like convention with Honduras." [92] In spite of the pressure however, the Senate which now had ten more Democrat members than were present to vote on the Dominican treaty in 1907, refused to advise ratification and so the matter was of necessity dropped.

So far as finances were concerned the bankers advanced $1,500,000 on the security of national customs and railroad stock pending the Senate vote on the treaty itself. This agreement also was ably supported in Nicaragua by the American minister and by the judicious appearance of United States naval vessels from time to time as occasion seemed to warrant.[93] Subsequent loans were made in relatively small sums and were protected by customs collections, a controlling interest in railway or bank stock,[94] as well as by substantial considerations with regard to handling the moneys of the government through the bank so controlled.[95]

But Nicaragua still needed money so even the new Democratic administration soon presented Congress with a treaty

[91] Address of Knox to New York State Bar Association, January 19, 1912, *Foreign Relations,* 1912, pp. 1091-2.

[92] *Ibid.,* p. 1078.

[93] Williams, *American Diplomacy,* p. 191.

[94] Weitzel, *American Pol. in Nic.,* pp. 5-6; State Department, *op. cit.,* p. 23; *Munro, U. S. and the Caribbean,* p. 240.

[95] Nogales, *op. cit.,* p. 21.

of its own in this connection. The dollar diplomats had maneuvered themselves into active intervention and through that intervention were maintaining a kind of peace in Nicaragua. Their treaty had been rejected so they were forced to proceed with hand to mouth expedients but even so there were signs of steadily rising trade between the two countries. In 1909 Nicaragua sent the United States 29% of its total exports, but in 1913 it sent 35%; while imports had risen from 39% to 56%.[96]

The program in the rest of Central America is less well known but followed a similar course though with less spectacular results. From the beginning of his administration Taft evidently hoped to exercise a dominating influence in the region. In October, 1909, he wrote to Knox agreeing with the latter that the situation was about as " good as we could expect " in view of a recent notification from Mexico declaring " her lack of interest in all the states south of Quatemala [sic]." He continued: " We are not likely to have her [Mexico's] assistance under any conditions, and this declaration relieves us from consulting her when we shall feel called upon to act." [97]

The fact that the condition of finances in Honduras was already giving concern to Washington may be seen from the following memorandum of the State Department:

Owing to the Department's keen interest, for diplomatic reasons, in the Honduran financial adjustment, whenever anyone at all likely to be interested happened to call at the Department the Honduran situation was freely discussed on the chance that some one might be willing to go into it. In this way, about the middle of June it was discussed with

[96] Cox, op. cit., p. 859.
[97] Taft to Knox, October 9, 1909, LC., Knox MS.

Mr. Albert Strauss, representing J. and W. Seligman and Company, who had called at the Department in regard to another matter.

Similarly the attention of Mr. James Speyer " was frankly drawn to the Honduran situation " on June 14th when he had called about another matter.[98] By 1910 the negotiations were proceeding apace. In May in a public address the President stated that it was highly advisable to bring stability to Honduras through a loan. He endorsed Dollar Diplomacy by name, denied evil connotations for the term and said that the annual foreign trade of the United States exceeded two billion dollars per year and that " our State Department could not vindicate its existence or justify a policy which in any way withheld a fostering, protecting and stimulating hand in the development and extension of that trade." He further claimed such loans were the direct means to the end sought.[99] The next month Knox added the Secretary's support saying: " Believing that a strong Honduras would tend enormously toward a stable and prosperous Central America, this Government is heartily supporting the plan for its financial rehabilitation." By way of proof of the success of such plans Santo Domingo was glowingly referred to.[100]

Actual negotiations and diplomatic correspondence meanwhile were running the gamut of petty troop landings in connection with local disorders,[101] filibustering expeditions

[98] Memorandum of Department of State, September, 1909, *Foreign Relations,* 1912, p. 551.

[99] Speech of Taft to Americus Club, May 2, 1910, LC., Knox MS.

[100] Speech of Knox at University of Pennsylvania, June 15, 1910, LC., Knox MS.

[101] J. R. C., *op. cit.,* pp. 77-8.

active or threatened,[102] the sending of trouble-shooter Thomas C. Dawson to attempt to straighten out complications when conditions had become sufficiently serious for both British and United States troops to be landed,[103] the selection of a proper presidential candidate,[104] and the actual drawing of terms for a loan which it was hoped would provide peace and guarantee control to the acceptable candidates. In brief it may be said that the loan agreed upon January 10, 1911 (which, it may be noted incidentally, antedated the Nicaraguan treaty), provided for the sanction of the State Department in the form of a treaty. J. P. Morgan and Company was to provide $10,000,000 for the refunding of the Honduran debt and for certain internal improvements. In return the supervision of the Honduran customs was to be under an agent appointed by the Central American country after being approved by the President of the United States. The customs duties were to remain fixed unless the United States agreed to changes.[105]

Once terms were agreed to the President and Secretary redoubled their efforts to secure the adoption of both the Honduran and the Nicaraguan loan plans. The fate of the two became linked and in spite of all the administration and the bankers could do the Senate refused to be reasoned, argued or cajoled into acquiescence; even appeals to humanitarianism now fell flat.[106] Temporarily, at least the

[102] *Foreign Relations*, 1911, pp. 291 ff.; *ibid.*, 1912, pp. 1310-11.
[103] *Ibid.*, 1911, pp. 299-300; Offutt, *Protection of Citizens Abroad*, pp. 107-9.
[104] Wriston, *Executive Agents in Foreign Relations*, p. 800.
[105] For loan convention of January 10, 1911, see *Foreign Relations*, 1912, pp. 560-2; G. H. Stuart, *Latin America and the U. S.*, pp. 356-7.
[106] Message of Taft to Congress, January 26, 1911, *Foreign Relations*, 1912, pp. 555-60.

Senate echoed American public opinion that such involvements meant trouble, expense and criticism and it would have none of them.

In Guatemala a different situation developed for President Estrada Cabrera was jockeying his finances by modifying his customs rates which were the guarantee of loans secured from the British a number of years earlier, as well as by varying the gold value of the currency in which other taxes were paid. The Department of State was not pleased with the conduct of Estrada Cabrera in the recent disturbances in Honduras [107] anyway and so did not have any extra patience to waste on the situation. By 1912 the British were assuming a rather firm tone in their protests and the United States notified Guatemala that something had better be done or else Britain might not be restrained further by Washington. The United States then tried to arrange arbitration of existing claims while a loan could be floated in New York to transfer the responsibility. Nothing came of this so in 1913 the British sent over a cruiser whose persuasive power secured the resumption of payments.[108] Clearly, in this case, the program had not worked and one is inclined to wonder if an administration which was seriously under fire did not rather " pull its punches " in this non-critical instance so as to prove to doubting Thomases that foreign nations were willing to act in the Caribbean if Washington failed to do so.

In other Central American Republics there were no important policy forming developments in their relations with

[107] *Ibid.*, pp. 1310-1.
[108] See *ibid.*, pp. 503-4; Williams, *Econ. For. Pol. of the U. S.*, pp. 54-5; Chester Lloyd Jones, *Guatemala, Past and Present* (Minneapolis, 1940), pp. 84-5.

the United States. The United Fruit Company was largely dominating the national financing and most of the active capital of Costa Rica but there were no diplomatic activities of importance as the negotiations were on a private basis through the personal activities of Mr. Minor C. Keith.[109] Negotiations over the boundary dispute with Panama [110] were proceeding slowly without major developments. Periodically there were repercussions and more or less opposition expressed to the overpowering expansion of the United States [111] but these had not yet come to a head and obvious benefits of employment at better wages did much to offset popular demonstrations led by excitable agitators. In fact it is quite probable that many applauded the agitators but still encouraged the foreigner to invest so that they could get their share of easy money. After a new foreign corporation had invested its money it was always popular to berate the foreigner, claim he was ruining the country and demand that his corporation be squeezed.

[109] Thomas, *One Hundred Years of the Monroe Doctrine*, pp. 276-7.

[110] *Foreign Relations*, 1910, cir. p. 814.

[111] For anti-United States activity and propaganda see *Foreign Relations*, 1912, p. 1046; *ibid.*, 1913, pp. 5-6; Ugarte, *op. cit.*, pp. 95 ff.; Editorial from *La Informacion*, February 24, 1912, LC., Knox MS.

The following table may be of interest:

FOREIGNERS IN CENTRAL AMERICA, 1911

	German	French	American	English	Spanish	Italian
Guatemala ...	7,500	1,100	1,850	1,200	1,100	1,300
Honduras	450	300	1,975	1,500	450	200
Nicaragua ...	250	100	525	750	200	150
Salvador	475	1,250	250	1,200	600	450
Costa Rica....	525	300	1,140	350	500	200

(E. B. Filsinger, "Immigration—A Central American Problem," *The Annals*, XXXVII, 745-6).

And now, for the first time in nearly half a century, Mexico demanded very careful consideration. Besides huge investments of United States capital in mines, railways and miscellaneous enterprises there were approximately 15,000 settlers from north of the Río Grande who had entered into the small farming and ranching life of the southern republic by 1912.[112] Also, petroleum investments were beginning to prove a bonanza. A production of about 3,000,000 barrels per year in 1909 steadily rose until in 1913 it was over 25,000,000 barrels. And that was only the beginning,[113] though the success was so spectacular that it attracted especial attention. In all, United States investments of half a billion dollars in 1900 had doubled within a decade.[114]

As seen above (*supra* pp. 224 ff.) a real fear of northern capital began to develop south of the border. This was based on the enormous growth of United States investments in Mexico, on the well known expansive tendencies of the Northern Republic, and the innate feeling of superiority on the part of the Anglo-Saxon.[115] True enough, there were tens of thousands of Mexicans in the United States but they were on an entirely different footing. They were of the *peón* or day-laborer type, hence as a group were generally

[112] J. Fred Rippy, *The U. S. and Mexico* (New York, 1931), p. 315.

[113] Guy Stevens, *Current Controversies with Mexico* (Address delivered August 6, 1927, at Institute of Politics, Williamstown, Mass.) pp. 278-9.

[114] Callahan, *American Pol. in Mex. Relations,* pp. 515 ff.; *Investigation of Mexican Affairs* (Senate Document No. 285, 66th cong., 2d sess.) (Washington), pp. 3321-2.

[115] García Calderón, *Latin America,* p. 312, note; Ernest Gruening, *Mexico and Its Heritage* (New York and London, 1928), pp. 553-4.

looked upon in the southwestern part of the country as a substitute for the Negro laborer of the southeast.

By 1910 the anti-United States feeling in Mexico was becoming acute and the diplomatic correspondence of the time carries frequent reports of riots or threatened riots against the now feared and disliked Yankee.[116] This was so serious that during the disorders from 1910 to 1912 not less than forty-seven United States citizens were killed in Mexico—and these numbers increased rather than decreased as the next few years passed.[117] Attempts to suppress the attacks failed and even though the United States ambassador demanded and secured suppression of offending newspapers and magazines [118] still the agitation continued.

As early as May 3, 1909, Taft had written to a friend that he was considering H. L. Wilson, then Minister in Belgium, as Ambassador at Mexico City.[119] In July, 1910, writing to the Governor of Massachusetts, the President stated that Wilson would go to Mexico and commented: " Our relations with Mexico are important and are of such a character that it is well for us to observe every courtesy and give the Republic and President Díaz every evidence of our friendship and deep interest in their welfare." [120]

---

[116] Wilson to Secretary of State, November 16, 1910, *Foreign Relations,* 1911, p. 361; Henry Lane Wilson, *Diplomatic Episodes in Mexico, Belgium and Chile* (New York, 1927), pp. 191-3; Callahan, *op. cit.,* p. 455.

[117] " Report of Secretary of State to the President," *Foreign Relations,* 1916, pp. 476 ff.; *Investigation of Mexican Affairs,* p. 3315.

[118] H. L. Wilson to President Díaz, November 18, 1910, and Creel to American Ambassador, November 24, 1910, *Foreign Relations,* 1911, pp. 363; 366; Gruening, *op. cit.,* p. 560.

[119] Taft to Bourne, May 3, 1909, LC., Taft MS.

[120] Taft to Guild, July 3, 1910, *ibid.*

Wilson later stated that he had let it be known that he wished the Mexican post but knew nothing for certain until October, 1909, when he understood that the man to whom the post was first offered had refused it and that he had been chosen at the suggestion of Senators Lodge and Elihu Root because they " anticipating serious developments south of the Río Grande because of the age and infirmity of President Díaz, were desirous of having a man sent to the post who was acquainted with Latin American psychology and the Spanish language." [121] This statement is true in part for Mr. Wilson had served as Minister in Chile, however, he was far from having the attitude that Mr. Root was known to advocate. He was certainly connected intimately with wealthy United States corporations doing business in Mexico and promptly surrounded himself with their agents in a most indiscreet fashion.[122]

Soon after Taft became president a rather unusual incident had taken place when he was travelling in the southwest. This was a meeting arranged between him and President Díaz on the border on October 16, 1909.[123] The day before the meeting Taft wrote:

The meeting with Diaz is to be a historical one. . . . I am glad to aid him . . . for the reason that we have two billions [of] American capital in Mexico that will be greatly endangered if Diaz were to die and his government go to pieces. It is questionable what will happen if he does die. He has designated a man to succeed him, but that is likely to lead to a revolution. I can only hope and pray that his demise does not come until I am out of office.[124]

---

[121] Wilson, *op. cit.,* p. 159.

[122] Edward I. Bell, *The Political Shame of Mexico* (New York, 1914), pp. 137-8; George Creel, *The People Next Door . . .* (New York, 1926), pp. 302-3.

[123] *Foreign Relations,* 1909, pp. 425 ff.

[124] Pringle, *Life and Times of Taft,* I, 462.

To a well-wisher the age of the Mexican administrative staff was appalling. The President was eighty, two of his eight cabinet members were older and the youngest fifty-five, while seventeen of twenty state governors were over sixty.[125] The Mexican court system under Díaz was far from efficient [126] but executive pressure had usually secured justice— or more—for foreign investors. Now this executive pressure was obviously waning, Díaz had apparently begun to fear the overpowering expansion of United States investments and was trying to offset them by a Mexican railway system and by encouraging British and other foreign investments. This was clearly a sowing of the wind when the administration simply did not have the physical energy to reap the whirlwind that would inevitably follow.[127]

With the coming of the year 1911 events followed each other with startling rapidity, but Taft was entirely sincere in saying that he hoped and prayed that Díaz would hold on until he, Taft, was out of office. Again it was a case of being torn between the sincere desire to avoid complications and the implications of Dollar Diplomacy to which his administration was committed. And in the case of Mexico these complications arose in a fashion for which the administration was not prepared, and which it had not anticipated.

The eighty-two year old Díaz did not wish to run for re-election in 1910 but allowed himself to be persuaded to do so. Other candidates dropped out of the picture except the young radical, Francisco I. Madero. He was arrested on trumped-up charges, " roughed up a bit " and allowed to escape. But he did not learn his lesson and

---

[125] Bulnes, *The Whole Truth about Mexico,* pp. 116-7.

[126] Wilson, *ip. cit.,* pp. 200-1.

[127] L. S. Rowe, " Scope and Limits of our Obligations toward Mexico," *The Annals,* LIV, 222-3.

after making his way to the United States, issued a call for
a revolt saying that the wishes and rights of the Mexican
people were being violated. Besides denouncing dictatorship and continuism in office he made two demands which
were destined to become slogans of the Revolution: " Lands
for the landless," and " Mexico for the Mexicans." The
first appealed to the masses in a nation of villages whose
people were passionately devoted to the land which had
been taken recently from the village communes and absorbed
by the wealthy landlords. The second appealed to the rising
antagonism toward foreigners. The old régime in Mexico
once so efficient was now corrupt, and like the well known
egg proved to have a hard outer shell but once this was
cracked, no resistance remained.

As the Mexican administration felt its grip weakening
it actively protested propaganda in the United States that
criticized it. Washington did not feel that there was very
serious danger apparently and under any circumstances
found that there would be difficulty in suppressing such
material unless it could be proved to be libelous before the
courts.[128] Certainly the United States Ambassador and
Washington wished to do everything possible to bolster the
Mexican administration, and when Díaz was forced to flee
his capital Taft sent him a personal message of sympathy
and of appreciation for his work.[129] Madero, the head of
the Revolution, was a wealthy man through his family connections and may have had some aid from United States
financiers,[130] but there is no doubt that any such was

[128] Mexican Ambassador to Secretary of State, December 16,
1910, and Secretary of State to Mexican Chargé, February 15, 1911,
Foreign Relations, 1911, pp. 377; 406-7.
[129] Taft to Díaz, June 7, 1911, LC., Taft MS.
[130] Nearing and Freeman, *Dollar Diplomacy,* pp. 88-9.

advanced without the connivance or encouragement of Washington.

Early in 1911 conditions were obviously becoming serious and Mexico urged the arrest of the fugitive Madero, then in San Antonio, Texas. Knox responded that his Government would investigate carefully.[131] With the surprising overthrow and flight of Díaz the situation became critical and there is a note resembling irritated surprise in the President's letter books when he realized that this problem had been dumped into the lap of his administration at this inconvenient time. A long letter to the Secretary of State, dated March 11th, stated that naval and military maneuvers had been ordered for the Gulf of Mexico and the Mexican border. These were to be advertised as regular maneuvers only but the military exercises, at least, were ordered especially because of the recent developments south of the Río Grande. The Mexican Ambassador had been reassured that the purpose was primarily to strengthen Díaz by curtailing insurgent activities on the border and incidentally to provide a deterrent if and when property of United States citizens might be threatened.[132] The next day careful instructions of the same kind were sent to General Leonard Wood, the Chief of Staff of the Army.[133]

Knox clearly did not appreciate the gravity of the situation though he realized its complicated nature. In a draft of a letter in his own hand to the President, March 15, 1911, he wrote:

---

[131] *Foreign Relations,* 1911, numerous references cir. p. 400.

[132] Taft to Knox, March 11, 1911, in both Taft MS and Knox MS in LC.; Taft to Acting Secretary of State, March 12, 1911, LC., Taft MS; Taft to Secretary of the Navy, March 14, 1911, LC., Knox MS.

[133] Taft to Wood, March 12, 1911, LC., in both Taft MS and Knox MS.

I suppose we may look for a shindy in Congress about the Mexican situation.

What with De La Barra howling for a strict enforcement of neutrality and some pronounced expression of disapproval of American aid to their insurrectos; with Wilson throwing fits about the iminence [sic] of Diaz going up in an explosion; with Americans with interests in Mexico demanding protection against real and fancied dangers and Americans with no interests in Mexico but large newspaper investments at home wanting to see the worst happen; with the Monroe Doctrine constantly requiring a measure of benevolent supervision over Latin American countries to meet its logical requirements; with the delicate entente with the Latins which has been nourished and maintained largely in the past upon champaign and other alcoholic preservatives; what in view of all these and many other factors bearing on the situation is one to do upon whom responsibility rests, except his duty as he sees it upon the facts presented to him? [134]

The President had recently had a personal conference with Ambassador Wilson and had received an ominous warning of impending disaster [135] so his action was reasonably prompt. March 20th he asked the Secretary of State to have all consuls report fully and frequently on conditions.[136] When Wilson returned to Mexico he sent word that conditions had steadily become worse and that United States citizens in Mexico and President Díaz greatly appreciated the steps taken by Washington.[137]

In May Díaz was overthrown and Madero was duly installed as President after a brief interregnum while De La

[134] LC., Knox MS.

[135] Message to Congress, December 7, 1911, *Foreign Relations,* 1911, pp. xi-xii.

[136] Letter marked " Confidential," Taft to Secretary of State, March 20, 1911, LC., Taft MS.

[137] Wilson to Secretary of State, March 20, 1911, and March 21, 1911, *Foreign Relations,* 1911, pp. 430-1.

Barra officiated and ordered the holding of an election. From the beginning H. L. Wilson was convinced that Madero was antagonistic to the United States and its interests.[138] As the year passed and unsatisfactory reports of the new administration continued to come from Wilson it is not surprising that Knox assumed much the same attitude as his ambassador. On the request of Knox the guard on the border was increased [139] early in February, 1912, and a month later an embargo was placed on arms shipments across the Río Grande.[140]

The frequent complaints and protests and even statements to the press of the United States denouncing conditions were interpreted by Madero as hostility and this is not surprising when the direct medium of intercourse was Ambassador Wilson.[141] In fact there were some who insisted that this very hostility of the United States strengthened the Mexican President in the eyes of his own people.[142] One means of showing the Mexican resentment was the new order which required the exclusive use of Spanish on all Mexican railroads and which by other pressure forced out

---

[138] Wilson, *Diplomatic Episodes,* pp. 219-20; H. L. Wilson, "Errors with Reference to Mexico and Events that have Occurred There," *The Annals,* LIV, 150-1. See also Bell, *Pol. Shame of Mexico,* p. 142, and M. Márquez Sterling, *Los Ultimos Días del Presidente Madero* (Habana, 1917), pp. 336-9. The Mexican point of view is well presented in Luis Manuel Rojas, *La Culpa de Henry Lane Wilson en el gran desastre de Mexico* (Mexico, 1928).

[139] Knox to the President, February 3, 1912, and Knox to American Ambassador, February 12, 1912, *Foreign Relations,* 1912, pp. 716; 720; Taft to Secretary of War, February 4, 1912, LC., Taft MS.

[140] *Foreign Relations,* 1912, pp. 745-6, and various.

[141] For such a statement see *ibid.,* p. 733.

[142] Rippy, *The U. S. and Mexico,* pp. 336-7.

considerable numbers of United States citizens who had been in positions of importance.[143]

Throughout 1912 the Administration was harrassed by Senate disapproval of its Caribbean program and had to keep one eye on the fall elections. Thus the Mexican question was soft-pedaled to the utmost. Arms were shipped to United States citizens in the Southern Republic, the navy was urged to be ready for emergencies, and United States properties when damaged were lamented and claims for damages promptly presented. Wilson was clamoring for an ultimatum or intervention but this was the last thing the authorities at Washington wanted. The result was a period of bickering and uncertainty with mutual recriminations. Meanwhile the Madero administration was attempting to secure its grip on home conditions and became increasingly resentful and suspicious of Wilson and the whole United States program. Officially, it contented itself with efforts to forestall formal presentations of United States claims [144] and with generalizations on the subject of international good will.[145]

The truth was that Madero was far from being the executive type. He had excellent ideals but did not stick to one of them long enough to put it into effect. A spiritualist and a vegetarian he was looked upon as " peculiar " by many of his own people and as plain crazy by others. Naturally enough, the old Mexican conservatives resented him and the foreign investors feared him. His mottoes of " Mexico for the Mexicans " and " Lands for the Landless " if applied would mean injury, if not ruin, to both groups.

[143] *Ibid.*, pp. 312-3; Blakeslee, *Mexico and the Caribbean*, p. 84.
[144] *Foreign Relations*, 1912, p. 708.
[145] Ugarte, *Destiny of a Continent*, p. 66.

Murmurs and fears begot unrest and plots for his overthrow which by the end of 1912 were serious indeed.
Unfortunately for the consistency of the foreign policy of
the United States Taft had been defeated and the Democrats
returned to power after an absence of sixteen years.

Woodrow Wilson was known to be a scholar and student
of domestic government and there were many who considered him efficient as an administrator in view of his
success as Governor of New Jersey. He pretended to know
little or nothing of foreign affairs so in the interim between
election in November and inauguration in March the United
States representative in Mexico did not know what future
policy he was to lead up to. In Washington there was
a tendency to stall off decisions and to let the new Administration formulate its own program while caution was
suggested to Ambassador Wilson.[146] In the meanwhile a
stiff " front " was maintained so as to preserve appearances.

In Mexico, H. L. Wilson was in a most difficult position.
He doubtless suspected the new program would be a conciliatory one and so he seems to have determined to use
the time left to him to crystallize relations in such fashion
that the Democrats would be committed in spite of
themselves.

Early in 1913 the lid blew off and a number of revolts
broke out in Mexico. Concerning the planning of these
there can be little doubt that the United States Ambassador
knew far more than was wise. He obviously associated
himself with the rebel leaders and gave them substantial
advice at the same time that his conduct was injuring, if
not undermining, the president whom his government had

[146] Knox to Wilson, February 12, 1913, and February 15, 1913,
Foreign Relations, 1913, pp. 706; 710.

recognized. The month of February was a hectic one in which Mexico City was subjected to a promiscuous bombardment for ten days while Victoriano Huerta, the leader of Madero's troops, secretly conducted a revolt against the troops which he commanded; the while he was scheming for more complete control of the rebels among whom there were other ambitious leaders. H. L. Wilson strove to eliminate rivalries among the rebels and boasted of his success. Next he urged the immediate recognition of the new leader who had secured his position by treason to his own chief, and later by assassination of that chief. Wilson further urged United States consuls in Mexico to endorse the new dictator, Huerta, as the man who would lead the nation back to the good old conservative days of Díaz when property rights were secure, the classes were supreme and only the people were suffering.

Knox fully believed that " What Huerta may have done since his election is a matter of local criminal law and not of international law," and also that the Monroe Doctrine was not involved since no foreign power was threatening intervention.[147] It was plainly, in his eyes, a matter of United States interests at stake so he was willing to support his ambassador and to accord recognition to Huerta promptly if the Dictator would agree to the settlement of United States claims against Mexico.[148] On this Huerta hesitated—fatally many think. But until United States interests and claims were fully cared for Knox was unwilling to act, especially since there were reports reaching the State Department that a revolt of serious proportions was

[147] See carefully corrected and interlined " Suggestive Points on the Mexican Situation," initialled by " J. R. C.," LC., Knox MS.
[148] Wilson, *Diplomatic Episodes,* p. 296.

developing in North Mexico.[149] Thus matters stood on March 4, 1913.[150]

One other incident arose in connection with Mexico. Among the numerous foreign corporations and individuals obtaining important conscessions and land grants in Mexico was a Japanese syndicate whose holdings were in Lower California, adjacent to Magdalena Bay. There is no doubt that some Japanese were actively interested in the New World but there is no acceptable evidence that they were seriously attempting to challenge the United States position of priority in Mexico even though rumors were rife in diplomatic circles.[151] Among the rumors current was one to the effect that the Magdalena Bay concession was likely to be turned over to the Japanese government to be developed as a naval base.

Knox later characterized Lodge, who promptly urged a Senate resolution condemning such a step, as a " mare's nester " [152] but the public became excited about the whole affair. It has been suggested that a chief purpose of the resolution was to secure support for a naval building program but regardless of its causes its passage indicated really sensitive susceptibilities concerning anything that might menace control of the approaches to the new United States

[149] Callahan, *American Pol. in Mexican Relations,* pp. 536-7.

[150] For a more effective bibliography and a more complete account of events in Mexico see Wilfrid Hardy Callcott, *Liberalism in Mexico, 1857-1929* (Stanford, 1931).

[151] An interesting account showing the active British interest in this situation is found in Sir Claude M. MacDonald to Sir Edward Grey, from Tokio, March 17, 1911. This is marked "Very Confidential," Gooch and Temperley, *British Documents on Origins of the War,* VIII, 508-9.

[152] Knox to Taft, April 28, 1914, LC., Knox MS.

canal.[153] The resolution was reported unanimously from the Senate committee and on August 2nd was passed by a vote of 51 to 4. It provided:

Resolved, that when any harbor or other place in the American continents is so situated that the occupation thereof for naval or military purposes might threaten the communications or the safety of the United States, the Government of the United States could not see without grave concern the possession of such harbor or other place by any corporation or association which has such a relation to another Government, not American, as to give that Government practical power of control for naval or military purposes.[154]

Taft like Knox was not at all enthusiastic about this.[155] They both felt it was not necessary at this time for there was no real danger and they did not wish to give offense to Japan. For another thing the resolution came perilously near to announcing a general restriction on the sale of properties in Latin America to any foreign national without the approval of the United States.[156] To lawyers of the Knox and Taft type this was a statement with serious implications indeed and was sure to result in adverse and needless repercussions to the southward. The matter was officially closed by a report of the Department of State, dated April 30, 1912, saying that reports from Mexico and Japan and thorough investigation showed that there was " no evidence whatever adequate to show any acquisition of land or any intention or desire to acquire land, whether

---

[153] T. A. Bailey, " Lodge Corollary of the Monroe Doctrine," *Pol. Sc. Quar.*, XLVII, 233.

[154] *Ibid.*, pp. 223-4.

[155] H. F. Wright, " Knox " in Bemis, *Secretaries of State*, IX, 341.

[156] Editorial, *American Journal of International Law*, VI, 939.

directly or indirectly, in Mexico by or on the part of the Imperial Japanese Government." [157]

In taking leave of the Taft administration it should be noted that at the Fourth Pan-American Conference meeting at Buenos Aires the emphasis had been kept steadily on economic questions and that some real progress had been made. Efforts by Brazil to bring about an endorsement of the Monroe Doctrine had resulted in failure but that was not at all surprising and the mere introduction of the proposal was a tribute to the earlier efforts of Root to stimulate cooperation.

European nations were especially interested in the opening of the Canal so it was not surprising that there was a demand for Britain to strengthen its naval program in the Caribbean.[158] At the same time there was talk of limiting United States influence,[159] of organizing the British colonies in the Caribbean into a confederation and of closer cooperation between them and Canada in both trade and government.[160] Further it was suggested that both France and Denmark dispose of their existing colonies in the Caribbean by sale or otherwise, presumably to the United States.[161] Of course these proposals were primarily talk but the fact that they were relatively widespread is circumstantial evidence of the recognized priority and tacitly feared supremacy of the United States in the area and

[157] Bailey, *op. cit.*, p. 222.

[158] Chester Lloyd Jones, *Caribbean Interests of the United States* (New York, 1916), pp. 307; 317-22.

[159] W. R. Shepherd, "Common Sense in Foreign Policy," *Pol. Sc. Quar.*, pp. 128 ff.

[160] Bonsal, *The American Mediterranean*, pp. 16-7; 384-5; 448.

[161] *Ibid.*, pp. 287-8; Tansill, *Purchase of Danish West Indies*, pp. 459-63.

indicates that they cannot be completely ignored in a study of this kind.

As time passed Taft was anxious to offset the recently developed hatred and fear of the United States to the southward. And having in mind the splendid response to the Root trip a few years earlier he now proposed that Knox make a similar trip, this one to be to the Caribbean, West Indies and Mexico.[162] But the approach of the two men was utterly different. Root who professed real liking for Knox said " it was a delight to have anything to do with him in any matter that came within the training and experience of an American lawyer. He was, however, absolutely antipathetic to all Spanish-American modes of thought and feeling and action, and pretty much everything he did with them was like mixing a Seidlitz powder." [163]

Also, the Knox tour did not have the background of that of Root for Knox was too well known for having used such comments as that the Monroe Doctrine " does not depend upon technical legal right, but upon policy and power." [164] True, Latin Americans had often stated just that but it was hardly a popular statement on the lips of a man who was later to make a good will tour. Likewise Knox's endorsement of Dollar Diplomacy in connection with Caribbean treaties had not made for popularity.[165] And lastly, all too often his remarks carried the aggravating implication that the United

[162] Taft to Knox, February 10, 1912, LC., copies in both Taft MS and Knox MS; Taft's annual message, December 3, 1912, *Foreign Relations,* 1912, pp. xiii-xiv; Editorial, *Amer. Jour. Int. Law,* VI, 493-4.

[163] Jessup, *Elihu Root,* II, 251.

[164] Quoted by Clark, *Memorandum on the Monroe Doctrine,* p. 176.

[165] For instance, see *Foreign Relations,* 1912, p. 581.

States people and society was superior in quality—and this was flatly resented. In Panama City he said:

In my judgment the Monroe Doctrine will reach the acme of its beneficence when it is regarded by the people of the United States as a reason why we should constantly respond to the needs of those of our Latin-American neighbors who may find necessity for our assistance in their progress toward better government. . . . [166]

So they needed better government and the United States was the country to provide it! Such was the interpretation only too likely to be made. In Nicaragua he complimented the nation on the man at the head of the government who had been " quick to realize the necessities of the country " in making financial arrangements with the United States [167]— and these were the very financial arrangements that were so severely criticized at the moment.

One speaker frankly confessed in addressing Knox that his visit had aroused "fears and misgivings in timid minds." [168] Thus the Secretary returned to Washington and no particular mile stones had been passed except those placed by Father Time whose sand in the administration hour glass had left the upper crystal almost clear.

All too pertinently that shrewd Latin American observer, García Calderón expressed the view of increasing numbers of thinking observers to the south when, in discussing Cuba, he said:

The loss of her independence would be a painful lesson to the republics of Central America, and to Mexico even, where anarchy is paving the way for servitude. The United

[166] Knox, *Speeches Incident to Visit to Caribbean,* pp. 15-6.
[167] *Ibid.,* p. 40.
[168] *Ibid.,* p. 47.

States offer peace at the cost of liberty. The alternatives are independence or wealth, material progress or tradition. The choice between dignity and a future is a painful one.[169]

Beyond doubt Knox had done his best to apply the principles he held and those principles were not as sordid as often pictured. He firmly believed in the innate rightness and success of prosperity and defined his terms accordingly. The elimination of foreign danger by assuming control of the finances of Haiti, Nicaragua, Honduras and Guatemala was real to him,[170] as was the advisability of acquiring strategic bases where needed; be they in the Galapagos,[171] the Pacific or the Caribbean. His program was not popular and his treaties were rejected by the Senate because of a popular reaction. But that reaction it must be admitted, was a mixture of disappointment at costs versus profits of empire, and of plain politics as well as of principles.[172]

The German, Count von Bernstorff, then Ambassador at Washington, wrote in June, 1911:

I don't think the Pan-American business will come to much. Since the Mexican Revolution the atmosphere in the whole of Latin America seems very bitter against the United States, and the Senate here much dislikes Knox's policy. The latter has not proved very fortunate of late.[173]

Would the new Democratic broom sweep clean after March 4, 1913?

[169] García Calderón, *Latin America*, p. 322.

[170] Williams, *Econ. For. Policy of the U. S.*, pp. 52-3.

[171] G. H. Blakeslee, "Future of American Samoa," *Foreign Affairs*, VII, 143.

[172] W. Stull Holt, *Treaties Defeated by the Senate . . .* (Baltimore, 1933), pp. 240-2.

[173] *Memoirs of Count Von Bernstorff* (Eric Sutton, translator) (New York, 1936), p. 114.

CHAPTER VII

PATERNAL DESPOTISM: PRINCIPLES AND
THEORIES

When Woodrow Wilson became president in March, 1913, the established machinery of the State Department was that set up by the Dollar Diplomats. Of these probably the chief remaining spokesman still in office was the Assistant Secretary of State, Mr. Huntington Wilson. He had frankly stated his position in May, 1911, when he said that Dollar Diplomacy:

means the substitution of dollars for bullets. It means the creation of a prosperity which will be preferred to predatory strife. It means availing of capital's self interest in peace. It means taking advantage of the interest in peace of those who benefit by the investment of capital. It recognizes that financial soundness is a potent factor in political stability; that prosperity means contentment and that contentment means repose.

This thought is at the basis of the policy of the United States in Central America and the zone of the Caribbean.[1]

Associated with Mr. Wilson were other members of the Department staff, some of them in quite significant positions, who had secured their positions as kindred spirits or as a result of the old connections of the Department with business enterprises. It can be said that these men as a group honestly believed in the old principles and naturally continued to apply them insofar as their discretion or opportunities extended. In many instances the President and

[1] Address at Baltimore, May 4, 1911, LC., Knox MS.

Secretary probably did not know what was happening but there can be little doubt that well meaning diplomats of the new order had their problems complicated by the lack of sympathy of these men of the old régime.[2] Recognizing this situation in the Foreign Service Wilson himself wrote September 17, 1913, that many representatives " have had the material interests of individuals in the United States very much more in mind than the moral and public considerations which . . . ought to control." [3]

The new President was a man who had carefully studied the principles and working of a democratic form of government as it applied to domestic issues. In fact he professed to be an expert along these lines. As a result it is interesting to compare his masterly handling of his Congress in having a liberal and Democratic tariff presented by the conservative Democrat Underwood; his use of the Republican plan for the Federal Reserve System and his other skillful maneuvers in mixing conservatism with liberalism in his domestic program with his handling of foreign relations in which he did not pretend to be an expert. On the domestic scene his theories had been tempered by careful research and practical experience as governor of the industrialized state of New Jersey; on the foreign scene his theories had had no restraining influence from either special study or experience. By the fortune of politics William Jennings Bryan, the " king maker," had inevitably been appointed as Secretary of State simply because that position was arbitrarily denominated as head of the Cabinet. And though Bryan was an outstanding practical politician and splendidly sincere in his personal life he was entirely unfitted for his new

[2] Gonzales, *Concerning Dollar Diplomacy*, pp. 1-2.
[3] Notter, *Origins of Foreign Policy of Wilson*, p. 234.

position either by disposition or training. The two men sincerely respected each other but there is little reason to think that the President ever changed his opinion very much as to the soundness of Bryan's thinking processes from that more youthful occasion when he had so fervently wished to knock Bryan theories into a " cocked hat." As a result it is not surprising that Wilson decided to handle the most important foreign problems himself.

This was seen quite clearly within a week of the inauguration. Houston, the new Secretary of Agriculture recorded that on March 11th the President read the Cabinet a prepared statement on Latin American affairs while Bryan listened with a " smile on his face " and nodded approval. Houston summed up his impressions with the statement " This interested me at this time particularly because it clearly indicated that the President was going to be his own Secretary of State." [4]

How would the theorist, unrestrained by experience or research, approach the complications of the Caribbean? In the first place, " His conception of America was that of a nation whose purity in ideals and spirit and action must be impeccable, and whose shortcomings were a source of personal pain to him." [5] Dignity and honor were absolute values with him. But side by side with this theory that would not be suppressed came a scholar's tendency to give the devil his due. It is significant that the new banking and anti-monopoly legislation provided for overseas branches for large banks and for the establishment of overseas sales agencies on a cooperative basis of a type which had been prescribed by the existing anti-monopoly laws.

[4] David F. Houston, *Eight Years with Wilson's Cabinet* (Garden City, 1926), I, 44.
[5] Notter, *op. cit.*, p. 295.

Thus it developed that the longer he dealt with the New World program the more " practical" became his applications, especially in view of early disillusionments and of ever more serious European complications. In 1913 for the nations of the Caribbean area United States investments and trade were already nearly as large as those of the British but this was just the beginning for investments in 1920 were to be over two and a half times the 1912 figures.[6] The outbreak of the European War in 1914 upset the most carefully laid plans, as this forced a 400% increase in trade values by 1920.[7] At the same time there was a somewhat slower but very definite increase in investments.[8]

Latin American securities offered in the United States in 1914 were less than fifteen millions of dollars and increased slowly for the next six years but it was quite obvious that the tendency was in this direction so a Pan-American Financial Conference was called in Washington in May, 1915. In addressing this conference to which all Latin American countries except Mexico were invited Wilson urged the improvement of means of communication between the Americas,[9] a proposal which he likewise made to Con-

[6] Max Winkler, *Investments of United States Capital in Latin America* (Boston, 1929), pp. 284-5; Chester Lloyd Jones, *Caribbean Backgrounds and Prospects* (New York, 1931), p. 293.

[7] Stuart, *Latin America and the U. S.*, p. 13; James A. Farrell, " Central and South American Trade as Affected by European War," *The Annals*, LX, 64-5. See also Charles M. Pepper, " South American Markets," *ibid.*, LIX, 312 ff.

[8] Lewis, *America's Stake*, pp. 347; 355; W. S. Kies, " Latin American Securities," *The Annals*, LXXXVIII, 145.

[9] James Brown Scott, *President Wilson's Foreign Policy. Messages, Addresses, Papers, edited with introduction and notes* (New York, 1918), p. 105.

gress in his message of December 8, 1914.[10] In regard to his general policy the President said of the Conference:

Its purpose is to draw the American Republics together by bonds of common interest and of mutual understanding; and we comprehend, I hope, just what the meaning of that is. There can be no sort of union of interest if there is a purpose of exploitation by any one of the parties to a great conference of this sort. The basis of successful commercial intercourse is common interest, not selfish interest. It is an actual interchange of services and of values: it is based upon reciprocal relations and not selfish relations. It is based upon those things upon which all successful economic intercourse must be based, because selfishness breeds suspicion; suspicion, hostility; and hostility, failure. We are not, therefore, trying to make use of each other, but we are trying to be of use to one another.[11]

The Conference recommended the setting up of the International High Commission to consider especially the establishment of a gold standard for the Americas, standardization of commercial forms, customs regulations, consular forms, and regulation of commercial travellers. It likewise advised improvement of parcel post regulations and rates, and improvement of the procedure for the arbitration of commercial disputes. The program was launched promptly and a general meeting of the Commission was held in Buenos Aires the next year.[12] Meanwhile there was active discussion of monetary unity with the United States as the motivating center of the process.[13]

[10] *Foreign Relations,* 1914, p. xii.

[11] Scott, *op. cit.,* pp. 102-3.

[12] W. G. McAdoo, "The International High Commission and Pan-American Cooperation," *Amer. Jour. of Int. Law,* XI, 772-3.

[13] E. W. Kemmermer, "Pan-American Monteary Unity," *Pol. Sc. Quar.,* XXXI, 68 ff.

Other similar group meetings were actively fostered. In 1915 two international expositions, the Panama-Pacific at San Francisco, and the Panama-California at San Diego were held. In addition there was the First Pan-American Financial Conference already referred to, the International Conference on Education at Oakland, California, the Second Pan-American Scientific Congress at Washington,[14] and the Christian Conference at Panama early in 1916.[15]

Meanwhile the President was rapidly committing himself to a specific program. The Monroe Doctrine was clearly not popular in Europe but he had no intention of giving it up,[16] even though he was anxious that it should not be understood to be a cloak for aggression. In his March 12, 1913, statement, given to the press the day before, and sent to the United States Diplomatic officers in Latin America he gave the first sign of the Paternal Despotism that was to develop to the point that it was as much a fact as Taft's Dollar Diplomacy, though it is true the term was not employed. He said:

cooperation is possible only when supported . . . by the orderly processes of just government based upon law, not upon arbitrary or irregular force. . . . We can have no sympathy with those who seek to seize the power of government to advance their own personal interests or ambition. We are the friends of peace, but we know that there can be no lasting or stable peace in such circumstances. As friends, therefore, we shall prefer those who act in the interests of peace and honor, who protect private rights and respect the restraints of constitutional provision. . . .

[14] *Foreign Relations,* 1915, p. 1310.

[15] Robertson, *Hisp. Amer. Relations with the U. S.,* pp. 321; 403-4.

[16] Herbert Kraus, " What European Countries think of the Monroe Doctrine," *The Annals,* LIV, 107-8; A. M. Low, " Monroe Doctrine," *ibid.,* pp. 101-5.

The United States has nothing to seek in Central and South America except the lasting interests of the peoples of the two continents, and the security of governments intended for the people and for no special group or interest, and the development of personal and trade relationships between the two continents which shall redound to the profit and advantage of both and interfere with the rights and liberties of neither.[17]

That keen analyst of international relations, J. B. Moore, has pointed out that this was a radical departure from earlier United States policies since it declared that cooperation with other governments was dependent upon their observance of orderly processes, and that the United States intended to make such observance the basis of mutual intercourse and respect. The promise to " lend the influence " of this government to secure such principles in practice and the declaration that there could be no lasting or stable peace between it and those who seized power to " advance their own personal interests or ambitions " and that the United States would " prefer " those who acted in the interests of peace and honor and constitutional provisions were also quite surprising.[15] As Baker has commented, there were notes of bitterness in the responses from Mexico and Latin America and " amused astonishment " from Europe. " It was amateur diplomacy with a vengeance, but there was somehow mastery in it." [19]

But this opening gun was to be followed by another especially disconcerting. In October the President made his

[17] *Foreign Relations,* 1915, p. 7. See also Robinson and West, *The Foreign Policy of Woodrow Wilson* (New York, 1918), pp. 179-80.

[18] Moore, *Candor and Common Sense,* p. 24.

[19] Ray Stannard Baker, *Woodrow Wilson, Life and Letters* (Garden City, 1931-7, Vols. iv-vi), IV, 69.

historic address to the Southern Commercial Congress at Mobile, Alabama. He stated that the United States must prove itself " friend and champion upon terms of equality and honor " of Latin America. He further stated that " I want to take this occasion to say that the United States will never again seek one additional foot of territory by conquest." So far as principles were concerned he insisted that morality, not expediency, must be the guide. And all of this followed hard upon expressions of sympathy for the neighbors to the South for the hard bargains they had had driven with them in connection with loans and investments made there.[20]

Six weeks later in his message to Congress the President elaborated his ideas a little further so that the general outlines thus appeared to one commentator:

As the Monroe Doctrine was aimed at the Holy Alliance, so the Wilson doctrine is aimed at the professional revolutionists, the corrupting concessionaires and the corrupt dictators in Latin America. . . .

It is a bold doctrine and a radical doctrine.[21]

All of this was something of a contradiction to the conditions existing as a result of recent activities in Haiti, Panama, Nicaragua and Santo Domingo—and there were not a few sardonic grins and comments as this was realized. However, in the mind of the President these were merely unfortunate rough spots that were to be smoothed out and brought into the main current of his policy as soon as possible. Mexico he considered as the " test " of his determination not to acquire " political suzerainty or selfish control." [22] He

[20] Robinson and West, *op. cit.*, pp. 200; 201. See also Notter, *op. cit.*, p. 272; Houston, *op. cit.*, I, 76-7.

[21] Frank I. Cobb quoted by Baker, IV, 294.

[22] Notter, *Origins of the Foreign Policy of Wilson*, p. 459.

continued to insist on his general program in January, 1916, when he again laid down the basic requirement that the republics of the New World should guarantee each other absolute " political independence and territorial integrity." [23]

It soon appeared that this was meant as the objective to be striven toward—not necessarily as an arbitrary principle to be applied forthwith. For instance, the determination not to mix in any way in the internal affairs of Ecuador when the question of a policy toward a revolution there arose, was not to be applied later as a precedent with regard to similar revolutionary activities in the Caribbean. In other words, as time passed and experience accumulated more and more the " practical " man applied common sense and the theorist was held to have good principles that were not yet suitable for application to every case in hand.[24] By August, 1916, the President publicly recognized the necessity for a special Caribbean policy when he said:

The Caribbean is within the peculiar sphere of influence of the United States, especially since the completion of the Panama Canal, and the possibility of a change of sovereignty of any of the islands now under foreign jurisdiction is of grave concern to the United States.[25]

Truly this would have provided ample elbow room for either a Roosevelt of a Taft, at least so far as the Caribbean was concerned!

But the same month he reasserted his original thesis thus:

So long as the power of recognition rests with me the Government of the United States will refuse to extend the hand of welcome to any one who obtains power in a sister republic by treachery and violence. No permanency can be given the affairs of any republic by a title based upon

[23] Scott, *op. cit.,* p. 160.
[24] Notter, pp. 364-5.   [25] *Ibid.,* p. 537.

intrigue and assasination. I declared that to be the policy of this Administration within three weeks after I assumed the presidency. I here again vow it. I am more interested in the fortunes of oppressed men and pitiful women and children than in any property rights whatever. Mistakes I have no doubt made in this perplexing business, but not in purpose or object.[26]

Even at the time when intervention was most active in Mexico he could plead for " genuine equality and unquestioned independence " for all New World republics, saying " We will aid and befriend Mexico, but we will not coerce her." To many this was mere legal hair-splitting and a smoke screen but to Woodrow Wilson it was very real. To him:

The moral is, that the states of America are not hostile rivals but coöperating friends, and that their growing sense of community of interest, alike in matters political and in matters economic, is likely to give them a new significance as factors in international affairs and in the political history of the world. It presents them as in a very deep and true sense a unit in world affairs, spiritual partners, standing together because thinking together, quick with common sympathies and common ideals. Separated they are subject to all the cross currents of the confused politics of a world of hostile rivalries; united in spirit and purpose they cannot be disappointed of their peaceful destiny.

This is Pan-Americanism. It has none of the spirit of empire in it. It is the embodiment, the effectual embodiment, of the spirit of law and independence and liberty and mutual service.[27]

Of course such statements brought on a veritable fever of debate on the foreign policies of the United States.

[26] Robinson and West, p. 346.

[27] Message to Congress, December 7, 1915, *Foreign Relations, 1915*, p. xi.

Root, long an ardent cooperationist, sounded what he felt to be a needed warning note when he urged that the Monroe Doctrine was a United States policy strictly and that " it cannot be transmuted into a joint or common declaration by American states or any number of them." [28] Taft discounted the effectiveness of Latin American cooperation in bringing about results and urged that Washington pursue its own policies with due emphasis on the financial ends involved.[29] Ex-Secretary of State Olney, in spite of his belligerent attitude of earlier days urged that the United States should proceed " not by making itself an international ' boss ' but . . . by initiating, cultivating, and working through an American concert." [30] John Barrett urged an enlarged Pan-American policy to take the place of the Monroe Doctrine,[31] and S. G. Inman bluntly agreed that the Monroe Doctrine was obsolete.[32] J. H. Latané followed the President, wished to internationalize the Monroe Doctrine and use the new program as a model for world peace,[33] while Albert Bushnell Hart stuck to his idea of a doctrine of " permanent interest " as being that which the United States was going to follow in the future just as it

[28] Address to American Society of International Law, April 22, 1914, Root, *Addresses on International Subjects*, p. 120.

[29] William H. Taft, *The United States and Peace* (New York, 1918), pp. 20-1; 31-4.

[30] Blakeslee, *Recent Foreign Policy of the U. S.*, p. 83.

[31] "A Pan-American Policy: The Monroe Doctrine Modernized," *The Annals*, LIV, 2.

[32] S. G. Inman, " The Monroe Doctrine and Hispanic America," *Hisp. Amer. Hist. Rev.*, IV, *cir.* p. 651.

[33] J. H. Latané, " The Monroe Doctrine and the Amer. Policy of Isolation in Relation to a Just and Durable Peace," *The Annals.* LXXII, 101.

had pursued it in the past. In his opinion " three administrators, Roosevelt, Taft, and Wilson, have for ten years
been pushing the influence of the United States into Latin
America, by their combined policy of gold and steel." This
he felt was leading toward the acquisition of the whole
island of Haiti and Santo Domingo as well as the five
republics of Central America, which would mean 12,000,000
new citizens (or inhabitants under the flag), not 2% of
whom could speak English, and not 5% of whom had
shown any capacity for self-government. So the best thing
to do was to think what we were going to do about the
whole matter.[34]

As for the Latin Americans their response to the Wilson
program varied considerably. The first response to Wilson's
idealism was restrained in view of the possible implications
of the paternal attitude expressed. However, the Administration persistently tried to cultivate good feelings as may
be seen from House's letter to Bryan concerning the possible appointment of Hugh Wallace to a position in the
Embassy in London saying: " He should make it a point to
cultivate the representatives from Central and South America
and let the American Embassy be the rallying ground in
London for the Americas." [35] A United States citizen felt
that the idealism of Wilson in the World War brought a
surprising response from Latin America and carried Pan-
Americanism to its greatest height,[36] while Luis F. Corea

---

[34] Hart, *Monroe Doctrine, an Interpretation,* pp. 335-6; 368-70.
[35] House to Secretary of State, December 18, 1916, Sterling
Memorial Library, Yale University (hereafter cited as " SL "),
Edward M. House MS.·
[36] Blakeslee, *Recent Foreign Policy,* pp. 136-8.

stated that "the spirit of solidarity and good will among the Latin American nations is markedly stronger and a growing intimacy between these countries and the United States is now apparent." [37] Regardless of backgrounds or viewpoints it was generally acknowledged that the United States was the spokesman of the New World.[38] Increasingly the new note appeared and was expressed by the Minister of Venezuela in Portugal to the effect that the Monroe Doctrine was not discredited by its distortions any more than civilization was discredited by the outrages committed in its name, and that the underlying principle was one that all New World Nations should endorse. Of course, some denied this outright and insisted that Wilson's program of non-recognition of those who secured power by "treachery and violence" constituted "pure and simple intervention" and that the Wilson program in practice was as interventionist as any of its predecessors.[39] Policarpo Bonilla of Honduras insisted that the new treaty with Nicaragua undid the good work for Pan-Americanism that had been initiated by Blaine and Root.[40]

Out of these contradictory impressions arises a fairly clear-cut picture. The idealism of Wilson was much appreciated by all but the practical side of his nature was as yet unknown. When this came to the front and resulted in some stand of paternalistic intervention which in the

[37] L. F. Corea, "Relations of Central and South America with the U. S. as affected by the European War," *The Annals*, LXI, 66.

[38] Alvarez, *The Monroe Doctrine* (quoting Argentine and Brazilian spokesmen), pp. 367; 365; Baker, V, 300, note.

[39] Alvarez, pp. 333-9; for opposition opinions see *ibid.*, 312; 321-3, and Nerval, *Autopsy of the Monroe Doctrine*, 281-4.

[40] Alvarez, p. 243.

President's mind was not for imperialistic purposes at all but for necessary discipline and as an aid to self-government, the outraged victims and their fearful neighbors suddenly plunged to the other extreme and denounced his statements as hypocritical mouthings. Inevitably it was the Caribbean nations that felt the sterner methods and that were the most skeptical as a result of frequent appearances of United States troops. Interestingly enough, at a somewhat greater distance there was increasing recognition of the fact that " The United States has the right to exercise its influence within certain American zones affecting its interests in a more or less immediate manner," and these zones were mentioned as " those republics bathed by the waters of the Gulf of Mexico, the Caribbean Sea and on the Pacific Coast north of Colombia." [41]

Soon after Wilson took office incidents arose that forced the new administration to apply its principles. The Secretary of State was engrossed in his ideas of bilateral peace treaties but Wilson had in mind something broader and more inclusive. It soon developed that Bryan was not the man to handle the matter and the President turned to his " other self," E. M. House, and asked him to look into the matter. Possibly the first concrete suggestion came from House who on November 15, 1914, urged the President to turn from domestic affairs and take up the problem of " welding together of the two western continents." A month later House went further and urged that such an arrangement would also serve as a model for the European

[41] Address of Estanislao S. Zeballos, former Argentine Minister of Foreign Affairs, at Buenos Aires on conferring honorary degree on Theodore Roosevelt, Alvarez, pp. 380-1.

peace. With obvious enthusiasm the President took a pencil and wrote:

1st. Mutal guarantees of political independence under republican form of government and mutual guarantees of territorial integrity.

2nd. Mutual agreement that the Government of each of the contracting parties acquire complete control within its jurisdiction of the manufacture and sale of munitions of war.

This, taken with the Bryan treaties, House thought to be sufficient for the problems in hand.[42] And it must always be remembered that the immediate and sinister testing ground for this and for all New World programs at the moment would be the handling of such complications as had arisen in Mexico.

House next proceeded to sound out Argentina, Brazil and Chile (familiarly known as the ABC powers). One question pending was the Fifth Pan-American Conference scheduled to meet in Chile. Though outbreak of the War in 1914 created serious complications, Chile sent out the invitations [44] and Wilson was inclined to think the Conference should assemble.[45] As complications thickened the idea was dropped and the meeting postponed so attention was more directly focused on the proposed Pan-American Pact as the most important inter-American program pending.

H. P. Fletcher was named as the first United States

---

[42] Charles Seymour, *The Intimate Papers of Colonel House* (Boston and New York, 1926-8), I, 209-10.

[43] Fletcher to House, July 28, 1914 [copy], SL., House Mc; Bryan to Suarez, August 21, 1914, LC., William Jennings Bryan MS.

[44] Welles, *Naboth's Vineyard*, II, 933.

[45] For Fletcher's comments on this see Fletcher to House, October 3, 1914, SL., House MS.

ambassador to Chile [46] just as that position proved to be one of considerable significance. Argentina and Brazil approved the idea of a pact promptly but Chile proved hesitant and even recalcitrant,[47] due in part to boundary disputes with Bolivia and Peru. House assured the Chilean Ambassador that this, as well as the Costa Rica-Panama dispute would be provided for. Chile was only partly reassured. On December 26th House wrote of the Pact negotiations:

This is a matter of such far reaching consequence that I feel we should pay more attention to it just now than even the European affair for the reason that if brought to a successful conclusion, the one must have a decided influence upon the other.

It is true he modified this statement slightly by adding that he did not think the European situation ready for action yet but he certainly did not minimize the importance of the matter in hand.

Bryan was chiefly interested in a scheme to keep the New World nations out of the European conflict and approved of the House plans rather casually hoping that the two programs would be connected in some way.[48] Unfortunately, House was sent to Europe the latter part of January, 1915, and so the Pact proposals had no active protagonist with sufficient power or influence to eliminate the complications arising during the ensuing six months. When Chile suggested that House had agreed to the requirement of

[46] Fletcher to House, letters headed " April 12 [1915] " and " Tuesday," SL., House MS; Argentine Ambassador Naon to House, December 26, 1914, SL., House MS; and Morgan to Lansing, July 26, 1915, LC., Lansing MS.

[47] House to the President, December 26, 1914, SL., House MS.

[48] Anonymous [J. V. Fuller], " Bryan " in Bemis, *Secretaries of State*, X, 20.

unanimous approval of the ABC powers for any action a cable from Wilson to House brought back a prompt negative but stated that he had suggested that the ABC powers might "prefer to approach the smaller republics themselves rather than to have you do so direct." [49] But problems involving delicate New World technicalities could not be solved with the chief mediator in an unofficial position at best and now absent in Europe for half a year. The negotiations languished except for the President's address to the Pan-American Financial Congress in which he stated that he hoped the Americas would be able to show the world "the way to peace, to permanent peace." [50]

In July, 1915, Bryan resigned as Secretary of State and Robert Lansing took over the direction of foreign affairs. On the 24th House, who had returned, talked matters over with him and confided to his Diary:

The South American proposal was one. I was surprised to find that Lansing was ignorant of what had been done. He said, as far as he knew there was nothing on file in the Department. I was surprised, too, that the President had

[49] House to the President, April 23, 1915; SL., House MS; Wilson to Secretary of State, April 26, 1915, LC., Bryan MS.

House to the Secretary of State, October 12, 1915, gives a summary of the negotiations. The last paragraph of the copy found in the House MS reads:

"Of course you understand that (one of)* the President's purpose(s) is to broaden the Monroe Doctrine so that it may be upheld by all the American Republics instead of by the United States as now."

* Two marginal notes comment: the words "one of" are not in the copy sent to Lansing (see *The Lansing Papers, 1914-25*, II, 486); and "I asked L. to eliminate this entire paragraph."

For other pertinent letters see *The Lansing Papers*, II, 475-6; 479.

[50] Notter, *Origins of the Foreign Policy of Wilson*, p. 410.

not talked with him more freely and given him fuller information concerning pending matters. . . .

We took up the Mexican situation and he is getting under way the arrangement to have the A.B.C. Powers join us in composing the difficulties there. He did not know the suggestion was mine and was made as far back as January and lying dormant until now. I do not think the President can altogether relieve himself of blame in this delay, for, while he would have probably gone ahead with it if . . . he had had as Secretary of State a better executive, yet it might have been done even under the unfavorable circumstances with which he had to contend. . . . [51]

The President's point of view may be best seen from the following letter:

Washington, *11 September, 1915.*

My Dear Mr. Secretary: I am so exceedingly anxious to push this matter to an early settlement that I hope that you will authorize Fletcher to go ahead by all means, if you think we can do this without discourtesy to Suárez, through whom we have been able to do virtually nothing in this affair.

I regard it as of the utmost importance that these negotiations be completed and carried to a successful outcome at this particular time.

Am I right in understanding that Brazil has assented in all essential particulars?

Faithfully Yours,

W. W.[52]

By November negotiations had again been resumed and Lansing submitted a proposal of four articles to the ABC representatives.[53] The Argentine and Brazilian Ambassadors

[51] Seymour, *Intimate Papers,* I, 222-3.

[52] Wilson to Secretary of State, September 11, 1915, *The Lansing Papers,* II, 486.

[53] Lansing to the President, November 3, 1915, *ibid.,* II, 490-1; Lansing to House, November 18, 1915, LC., Lansing MS.

approved cordially and the Chilean gave his personal endorsement.[54] Article 1 of the proposed pact provided a " mutual guarantee of territorial integrity and of political independence under republican forms of government." Article 2 stated the contracting parties were to " endeavor forthwith to reach a settlement of all disputes as to boundaries or territories now pending " by means of amicable agreement or international arbitration.   Article 3 provided a one-year cooling off period to ensue after the arising of a question not capable of settlement by diplomacy before beginning of hostilities.   During this time investigation was to be made by a permanent international commission.   If the matter was not thus settled it was to be submitted to arbitration " provided the question in dispute does not affect the honour, independence, or vital interests " of these or other nations.   Article 4 prevented the departure of military or naval expeditions from one country hostile to the established government of another, also the export of " arms, ammunition or other munitions of war " for the use of insurrections against established governments.[55]

In writing to the President Lansing submitted these proposals in a communication marked " Personal and Private " on November 11th and observed:

You will observe that I have added a new article (Article IV) in place of the one which covered the control of the manufacture and sale of arms and ammunition. In order to prevent hostile action between neighbors it is necessary, I think, to bind the parties not to assist insurgents or revolutionists in the country.   Such aid is a source of constant irritation in Central American countries and

[54] Lansing to the President, November 18, 1915, *ibid*.
[55] Copy marked " Handed to Chilean Amb. Thurs. Nov. 18/5 " and " Mailed copy to Brazilian Amb. Thurs. Nov. 18/15," *ibid*.

as you know it is one of the causes of disorder in Haiti
and the Dominican Republic.[56]

The President concurred saying that he thought this " on
the whole, the most satisfactory " statement they could hope
to have adopted.[57]

But House still exerted an influence. In July, 1915, he
had written the President that he thought Fletcher, the
ambassador to Chile, " is the best man that we could get
to button up the South American matter." [58] Eight months
later he sent the following interesting letter:

Dear Governor:

Fletcher is here. I have taken up the Pan American
Peace Pact with him and now have the Chilian sentiment in
regard to it.

I would suggest that you tell Lansing that now Fletcher
is here, you would like the matter closed before he leaves
for Mexico, and you would appreciate it if he would write
me a letter asking me to work with Fletcher and give him
what knowledge I have concerning it.

I asked Fletcher if there was any reason it could not be
closed within ten days. He said there was none. He is to
forget that I have said anything to him and the first he is
to know of it will come from Lansing.

If you will let Lansing send for Fletcher and have him in
Washington Monday I believe the matter can soon be
closed. I have told him exactly what I think should be
done and he is willing to devote his entire time to it, referring everything to Lansing as it progresses. He will
also keep me advised so I can really direct it.

This, I think, is the wisest course and if you agree with
me we will work it that way.[59]

[56] *Ibid.*
[57] Wilson to Secretary of State, November 17, 1915, *ibid.*
[58] House to the President, July 19, 1915, SL., House MS.
[59] House to the President, March 31, 1916, *ibid.*

While House was in Europe he had constantly borne in mind the Pact idea. In fact he had discussed it in February with Sir Edward Grey and Lord Lansdowne and secured their hearty endorsement provided it was not considered to be directed at the Japanese. Sir Edward went so far as to ask House to dictate a question to be put to him in Parliament as to " whether the Government was taking cognizance of the Pan-American Pact recently announced, guaranteeing the political and territorial integrity of the American republics, and what effect it would have upon the British Dominions in America." [60]

But complications developed especially in connection with Chile and the ten days—and many more—passed [61] and Fletcher was still worrying with conflicting proposals,[62] though the ministers of the smaller countries at Washington indicated hearty approval of the project.[63] Wilson and House more and more envisioned this as a basis for a worldwide program, but the New World nations were more interested in private objectives than world principles. June 16, 1916, House wrote Fletcher saying that he had asked the President " to see you and to tell you directly that he wishes to have as many of the smaller republics as possible

[60] Seymour, *Intimate Papers*, I, 228.

[61] Fletcher to Lansing, November 1, 1915, and Lansing to House, November 23, 1915, LC., Lansing MS; Lansing to Wilson, January 6, 1916, January 24, 1916, and March 9, 1916, *The Lansing Papers*, II, 493-4.

[62] Fletcher to House, " Thursday " [May 11, 1916]; " Saturday " [May 20, 1916]; " Saturday " [May 27, 1916], and June 15, 1916, SL., House MS.

[63] Lansing to Wilson, December 30, 1915, *The Lansing Papers*, III, 492.

sign the pact simultaneously with the A.B.C. governments." [64] Two days later he wrote Wilson:

I remember your having called attention to the fact that
if we left the wording in Article One of the Pan American
Peace Pact as it now is, (guaranteeing territorial and political integrity under republican forms of government) British
America could not come in.

In talking it over with Gregory today he suggested
having it read " existing forms of Government." This
would cover our desires and would leave Great Britain free
to come in if she wished. If you think this a good suggestion, will you not communicate it to Secretary Lansing so
he may instruct Mr. Fletcher.

It need not be necessary for Fletcher or the South American governments to know just why the change was made.

But few people realize the tremendous import of this
great pact but I believe you will find as soon as it is closed,
it will create world-wide interest. It is epoch making and
the outside nations will soon begin to give it a proper
place. [65]

By July 10th Fletcher pointed out that the Mexican
situation was causing complications, [66] and a month later he
was frankly pessimistic, for Chile had become " definitely
and decidedly opposed to the treaty " and the Argentine
Minister had informed Fletcher that he was unwilling to
sign without special instructions from his government because of " the tense United States-Mexican situation." [67]
With these countries hesitant it was useless to carry the
matter further with the smaller republics.

---

[64] House to Fletcher, June 16, 1916, SL., House MS. See also
House to Fletcher, June 19, 1916, and confidential memorandum
of " H. P. F.," June 16, 1916, *ibid*.

[65] House to Wilson, June 18, 1916, *ibid*.

[66] Fletcher to House, July 10, 1916, *ibid*.

[67] Memorandum of H. P. Fletcher, August 9, 1916, *ibid*.

Another major complication arose when the United States entered the World War. Wilson faced this in a letter of April 19th to Lansing in which he stated that if a New World power became an ally of Germany under the Pact the United States would have to protect the New World power " against any loss of territory or any curtailment of her political independence," but that the United States would be forced to do that under the Monroe Doctrine anyway. If any New World power allowed the use of its territory as a base of hostile action against the United States it would have violated the Pact already and the Northern Republic would be free to act as if the Pact did not exist. He did not think that any of the signatories would be expected to declare war on Germany simply because of having signed the Pact unless " our political independence or territorial integrity were evidently and immediately threatened." [68] However, the complications had now become so involved that it was not surprising that the whole matter was shelved as the Administration turned its full attention to the War, and then projected its league or pact idea directly onto the world scene instead of merely on the hemisphere basis.[69]

The collapse of the proposal may have been due, in part at least, to the fact that there was too much of the left hand not knowing what the right hand was doing. The layman comes to the conclusion that either House should have been Secretary of State, or the conduct of the negotiations should have been kept either in the hands of the President or actual Secretary. With so many reservations in the

[68] Baker, VII, 28; *The Lansing Papers,* II, 499.
[69] Lansing to Morgan, May 24, 1917, *ibid.,* II, 500.

mind of one man as is shown in House's letters of March 31st and June 18th, and that man not in an official position in the first place, it stands to reason that there was not much chance of wholehearted cooperation on the part of others.

Meanwhile Secretary of State Bryan was not to be overlooked for he was launching his program of world peace to be secured by bilateral treaties. The fact would seem to be that Wilson personally directed whatever negotiations appeared to be of most serious import while the Department handled routine affairs. In the Caribbean this meant that Wilson made himself personally responsible for Mexico and the Panama tolls question and left miscellaneous Caribbean problems for Bryan.[70] Unfortunately, the iron of political defeat had been so sunk into the very being of Bryan that he had become convinced that party organization was a prerequisite to success and must first be considered. His personal papers and the correspondence of his associates bear testimony to his constant interest in patronage[71] as a means to this end. Then, to add to the disconcerting features of the situation, was the new Secretary's disregard of conventionalities and form.[72] In his own papers and the Wilson Papers there are numerous bits of paper carrying manuscript notes of Bryan, frequently on very important matters, that are undated and unclassified. Obviously no duplicates were ever filed in the Department of State so that they could be referred to

[70] Baker, IV, 439.

[71] For a sweeping seven-page criticism of Bryan's appointments in the New World country by country see SL., House MS. See also Bryan to the President, May 24, 1913, LC., Bryan MS; Baker, IV, 40, and numerous letters in the Bryan MS.

[72] Anon., " Bryan " in Bemis, *Secretaries of State,* X, 9.

or even their existence be known by those who were trying to develop a consecutive and consistent policy. The Secretary was unfamiliar with such work and was too often befuddled by what went on and so became the dupe of scheming underlings.[73] But through it all it should be remembered that here was a man of tremendous sincerity and a crusader for what he considered to be the right.

His one great desire as Secretary was the successful negotiation of his set of peace treaties which he hoped would save the world from impending catastrophe. Wilson's communications to the Secretary show his real respect for the sincerity of the man from the time of the campaign of 1912 to the resignation of the Secretary in 1915.[74] The amazing contrast between Bryan and Knox as Secretaries of State is amply shown in their attitude to Andrew Carnegie. Knox could enjoy writing to Taft of the " ignorance, mendacity and impudence" of Carnegie for meddling in foreign affairs [75] while Bryan could write the gentleman and ask him to endow chairs of American history and government in the Latin American countries.[76] Could the transfer to sweetness and light be made effectively?

Before the Mobile speech, which Bryan probably thought was all too moderate,[77] the Secretary of State submitted his

[73] Gonzales, *Concerning Dollar Diplomacy*, pp. 2 ff.

[74] For early samples of this see Wilson to Bryan, September 4, 1912, November 5, 1912 (telegram) and February 23, 1913, LC., Bryan MS.

[75] Knox to Taft, March 3, 1913, LC., Knox MS.

[76] Bryan to Carnegie, January 7, 1915, LC., Bryan MS.

[77] Selig Adler, " Bryan and Wilsonian Caribbean Penetration,' *Hisp. Amer. Hist. Rev.*, XX, 210 ff.

proposal for a set of peace treaties to the cabinet.[78] This obligated signatories to await an investigation and report by an international commission before the opening of hostilities which might arise from " disputes . . . of every nature whatsoever " and so inevitably included any that might derive from the Monroe Doctrine and its applications.[79] The proposals were hailed as the hand of a de-

[78] The following is a copy of the plan discussed and changed by the Cabinet:

" MEMORANDUM BY MR. BRYAN.

The parties hereto agree that all questions of every character and nature whatever, in dispute between them, shall, when diplomatic efforts fail, be submitted for investigation and report to an international commission composed (of five persons, one member from each nation, two other members, one chosen by each nation, and a fifth member chosen by the four) (the composition to be agreed upon) ; and the contracting parties agree not to declare war or begin hostilities until such investigation is made and report submitted.

The investigation will be conducted as a matter of course, without the formality of a request from either party; the report shall be submitted within (six months [or one year]) (time to be agreed upon) from the date of the submission of the dispute, and neither party shall utilize the period of investigation to (improve) (change) its military or naval (status) (program), but the parties hereto reserve the right to act independently on the subject matter in dispute after the report is submitted."

This is headed in handwriting " Typewritten proposition submitted the President to the Cabinet early in April 1913," and at the bottom are the words, " Changes made in pen were made after and as a result of consideration by Cabinet." These " changes made in pen appear above as the second set of words in each pair of parentheses.

Also for a copy of this as submitted to all nations on April 24, 1913, with a memorandum by the Secretary of State, see Bryan MS.

[79] W. E. Linglebach, " The Monroe Doctrine and American Participation in European Affairs," The Annals, XCVI, 39-40; Blakeslee, Recent Caribbean Policy, p. 126.

liverer, or certainly as a guarantee against tyranny, in the Caribbean area. El Salvador was the first to sign, quickly followed by Guatemala, Panama, Honduras and Nicaragua. Later Costa Rica, the Dominican Republic and Venezuela were to sign.[80] What is of decided interest is the fact that the treaties with Panama and Santo Domingo remained unratified because the Senate failed to advise it. One commentator states that there was neither politics nor a contest between the President and the Senate to account for this— instead only indifference. " Apparently the Senate believed that the relations of the United States with those two countries were of such a nature that it would be unwise to agree not to resort to force until a commission should report on the facts of a dispute." [81] Certainly not a very reassuring prospect for the Caribbean, but in harmony with the recognition by the President and the Senate of the fact that the Caribbean was a region demanding distinctive treatment.

For the omnipresent financial difficulties, admittedly one of the most serious features of Caribbean international existence, Bryan also had a remedy. This was nothing less than to have the United States underwrite bond issues of the weak New World republics so as to extend them United States credit and cheap money. The proposals were first made in 1913,[82] and received a somewhat non-committal

[80] William Jennings Bryan and Mary B. Bryan, *Memoirs of William Jennings Bryan* (Philadelphia, 1925), pp. 386-7.

In all some thirty such treaties were negotiated but with these as a whole this paper is not concerned. In general, the small powers were the first to take advantage of such protection as the treaties provided.

[81] Holt, *Treaties Defeated by the Senate*, p. 244.

[82] Bryan to the President, August 6, 1913, LC., Bryan MS.

postponement from the President. Not satisfied to let the matter drop the Secretary returned to the charge in 1914 apparently not realizing that the approval of wealthy business interests which he had cited earlier might well be interpreted as the chucklings of those who hoped the Government would thus rake their chestnuts out of the fire by allowing them to " get out from under " difficult financial obligations. In 1914 Bryan wrote:

> Pardon me for bringing the matter to your attention again, but it occurs to me that this might be a good place to try out the proposal which I laid before you in regard to Nicaragua and Ecuador, viz., that the government should offer an issue of its own bonds at three per cent and accept bonds at four and a half per cent, the one and a half being used as a sinking fund.
>
> Our intimate relations with Panama might justify us in making this proposal to her, and I have no doubt it would be accepted gladly. I feel quite sure then that other countries in Central America would ask us to extend to them the same favor, and that we would soon be in a position to exert a controlling influence through the benefit we would thus be able to bring to them without any risk of loss.[83]

Is it possible the Secretary realized the significance of his last sentence? How could there be no risk of loss unless the United States stood ready to intervene by force to guarantee the bond payments when due? And this being the case what about the guarantees of territorial integrity that House and Wilson were trying to secure and what about the Byran peace treaties themselves? Of course the President stopped the whole affair though he avoided hurting his Secretary's feelings by the explanation that there

---

[83] Bryan to the President, February 21, 1914, *ibid.*

were "enough difficult questions on the carpet" at the moment and so he did not feel justified in taking up this one.[84]

In truth there were two sides to this Dollar Diplomacy in the naive brain of Bryan. He wrote to the United States Minister in Haiti:

Capital will not flow into Haiti except upon exorbitant terms and for speculative profits unless there is an assurance of peace and orderly government. . . . Our obligation to the American people requires that we shall give all legitimate assistance to America investors in Haiti, but we are under obligations just as binding to protect Haiti . . . from injustice and exploitation at the hands of Americans.[85]

Is this a direct contradiction or does it mean he has become enamored of the capitalist's point of view and is now merely rendering lip service to old ideals? Shades of Knox and Taft! But it was all very real to Bryan; he still was convinced he was consistent. Once he had reached the point in his thinking that American investors actually had rights in the Caribbean it was inevitable that those interests would bulk ever larger in his thinking until he would find his course deflected practically into the beaten path of his predecessors.

With the resignation of Bryan, Robert Lansing, a thoroughly trained international lawyer, took his place and this uncertain type of thinking largely disappeared. However, the overwhelming European complications monopolized most of the new Secretary's attention. He was anxious to strengthen New World solidarity and revived the Peace Pact proposals, as already seen. Also, he wished to culti-

---

[84] Wilson to Bryan, March 20, 1914, *ibid*.
[85] Anon., " Bryan " in Bemis, *Secretaries of State*, X, 13.

vate friendly relations with Mexico—in other words to carry on the Wilson program there—and to secure the safety of the Caribbean by the acquisition of the Virgin Islands and the exclusion of German influence wherever found.[86]

Primarily a realist, while Counselor for the State Department in 1914, Lansing had submitted a memorandum to the President in which he stated:

In its advocacy of the Monroe Doctrine the United States considers its own interests. The integrity of other American nations is an incident, not an end. While this may seem based on selfishness alone, the author of the Doctrine had no higher or more generous motive in its declaration. To assert for it a nobler purpose is to proclaim a new Doctrine.[87]

He specifically warned against European investments that might lead to political dominance, and finally concluded that it was time to consider whether the United States should abandon " purely selfish " principles in favor of " the sense of fraternal responsibility, which is increasingly dominant in all our international relations." Later he urged the idea of Pan-Americanism as an " international policy of the Americas " to accomplish the same ends as the Monroe Doctrine from the standpoint of the United States alone.[88] For the American family of nations he coveted the old Dumas motto " One for all; all for one." [89] This

[86] Julius W. Pratt, " Lansing " in Bemis, *ibid.,* X, 111.

[87] John McCormac, *Canada: America's Problem* (New York, 1940), p. 37; for the whole memorandum see *The Lansing Papers,* II, 459 ff.

[88] Address of Welcome to Second Pan-American Scientific Congress, December 27, 1915, Alvarez, *op. cit.,* p. 472.

[89] *Ibid.*

was as far as Lansing would go in the direction of abstract idealism and he kept his eyes open to developing realities. On November 24, 1915, he wrote the President concerning the " possible extension" of the Monroe Doctrine " to constitute a policy which may be termed a ' Caribbean Policy.' " This was based on the strategic importance and revolutionary conditions existing in the region. Brushing aside humanitarian grounds " because too many international crimes have been committed in the name of Humanity " he urged national safety and the conservation of national interests to justify United States conduct in Cuba, Panama, Nicaragua, the Dominican Republic and Haiti and what might need to be done elsewhere. Then he added that existing European colonies in the Caribbean ought also to be remembered because " through a change in their sovereignty they might become a serious menace " to the United States. Wilson answered: "The argument of this paper seems to be unanswerable." [90]

But it is time to turn from personalities and general policies to the actual problems faced. Beyond question about as severe a test as has ever been visited on altruistic international principles was that endured by the ideals and theories of Woodrow Wilson under the driving force of the Mexican problem. For months Taft had been doing his best to " sit on the lid " and avoid any drastic commitment, at first because of the imminence of the election and then because he did not wish to start a program that a man of another party would have to complete. As has been seen he had applied an arms embargo on shipments going to Mexico

[90] Lansing to the President and Wilson to Lansing, November 24, 1915, and November 29, 1915, *The Lansing Papers*, II, 466-7; 470.

but had attempted to modify the drastic stand which Ambassador H. L. Wilson recommended. The Ambassador himself meanwhile tried to aid the new dictator to secure control of his own country. He wrote to the United States consul at Hermosillo: " You should exert yourself without ceasing to bring about the general submission to the provisional government . . . Move actively in this matter . . ." [91] He followed this by sending word to the new Secretary of State on March 5th admitting that a few rebel bands were operating in the State of Nuevo León, that the position of Sonora was uncertain but that only Coahuila refused submission to the Provisional Government, adding: " The States which have submitted represent 90 per cent of the people of Mexico and order has been re-established over three-fourths of the territory they represent." [92]

In view of other reports pouring in it is not surprising that the new administration was skeptical. Washington was not pleased with the disconcerting news that the ex-President, Madero, was killed on February 22nd under circumstances that pointed to assassination at the hands of the dictatorship. The Ambassador calmly admitted the deplorable features of the affair but recommended the acceptance of the official version issued by the dictatorship and added that he had publicly accepted it.[93] He frankly said that Huerta was a man " who knows what he wants and how to get it " and added, he " believes in the cultivation of the closest and most friendly relations with the

[91] Baker, IV, 240.

[92] Wilson to Secretary of State, March 5, 1913, *Foreign Relations,* 1913, pp. 756-7.

[93] *Ibid.,* 1913, 772. This is taken from a long report by the Ambassador to Bryan, March 12, 1913, which was calculated to " bring the Secretary up-to-date."

United States." [94]   Also the Ambassador urged formal recognition of the Dictator.

At first foreign governments hesitated to act but first the British and later others changed their minds and did so.[95] This may have been the result of pressure from commercial interests as Washington apparently thought,[96] or it may have been this in part plus the British conviction that Wilson was simply taking time to make up his mind and that he would surely follow the policy which Taft was thought to endorse.[97] And indeed, before long Taft was convinced that *de facto* recognition was advisable. He wrote: " Huerta may be a murderer in fact as Diaz doubtless was before he became president. . . . They are not Sunday-school superintendents down there, and we cannot make the qualifications of Sunday-school superintendents square with the necessities of the situation where anarchy prevails." Realistically, he added that he hoped there would be no war but if one came he hoped advantage could be taken of it to secure a new and more specific border which would include part of northern Mexico and Lower California.[98]

Of course many business concerns in the United States with Mexican holdings clamored for recognition of the Provisional Government which was professedly favorable to capital and above all they wanted peace. Their arguments did not appeal to Wilson in the least. He rejected the Six Power

[94] *Ibid.,* pp. 774-5.

[95] Burton J. Hendrick, *Life and Letters of Walter Hines Page* (New York, 1922 and 1925), I, 180.

[96] *Ibid.,* I, 180-1; Nearing and Freeman, *Dollar Diplomacy,* pp. 92-3.

[97] John Hays Hammond, *Autobiography of,* (Murray Hill, N. Y., 1935), II, 573-4.

[98] Pringle, *Life and Times of Taft,* II, 865.

Loan proposals for China and took the position that investments in any country were placed there under the risks of
the locality and that interest rates and profits were charged
accordingly. Hence, it did not comport with proper respect
for national sovereignty to bring pressure to bear, and
it did not comport with honesty for a government to
guarantee investments that were originally made and charged
for as risky undertakings. If further proof of the wisdom
of suspending action in recognition of the new dictatorship
were needed, it came from the constant report of gambling,
social scandals, financial rascality and terrorism that were
rampant under Huerta.[99] But reasoning from such premises
was new for a large country and the cause was not grasped
in Mexico. Politial leaders there knew that the United States
had long exercised an influence on them and felt that it
was likely to continue to do so.[100] For a country to cease
to protect its citizens abroad from dangers partly incident to
their business activities was for Wilson more or less of a
corollary of his own principles, but in much of the New
World it must be confessed that it was looked upon as a
quixotic step at best, and a tacit admission of weakness.[101]

To H. L. Wilson's clamor the Department turned a deaf
ear even though conditions were becoming critical for
Huerta as a result.[102] Bryan was convinced that business
men who urged recognition of Huerta as a follower of
Díaz were answered by the following:

If, after thirty years of experiment with his policy, Diaz,
with world-wide prestige and splendid credit, could not

---

[99] For conditions in Mexico under Huerta see Callcott, *Liberal-ism in Mexico,* pp. 228-41.

[100] Bulnes, *Whole Truth about Mexico,* p. 247.

[101] *Ibid.,* pp. 193; 196-7.

[102] Wilson, *Diplomatic Episodes,* p. 300.

maintain himself against Madero, but saw his government crushed like an eggshell, what reason have you to believe that Huerta, not only without prestige and credit, but guilty of high treason and blamed for the death of Madero, will be able to succeed where Diaz failed? [103]

Sir Edward Grey summarized his impression of the Wilson policy:

The policy was altruistic; it was not being pushed for material interests; it was a policy of using the influence of the United States to lift a backward neighbor to a higher plane. . . . It appealed to him [Ambassador Page of the United States] as a policy with an ideal.

Grey stated that he " could not be enthusiastic about the prospect," especially since the first step was to get rid of Huerta and the cut-throat Villa was likely to be used as the " sword of the Revolution." However, the region was in the United States backyard and Britain " should look passively on with acquiescence in whatever policy the United States saw fit to pursue about Mexico." [104]

[103] Bryan and Bryan, *Memoirs,* p. 358.

[104] Viscount Grey of Fallodon, *Twenty-Five Years* (New York, 1925), p. 99. See also Gwynn, *Letters and Friendships of Spring-Rice,* II, 191-2.

Page's spicy account of his contacts with Sir Edward Grey on this same matter is worth quoting:

" They [the English] have a mania for order, sheer order, order for the sake of order. They can't see how anything can come in anyone's thought before order or how anything need come afterward. Even Sir Edward Grey jocularly ran me across our history with questions like this:

' Suppose you have to intervene, what then? '

' Make 'em vote and live by their decisions.'

' But suppose they will not so live?'

' We'll go in again and make 'em vote again.'

' And keep this up 200 years? ' asked he.

' Yes,' said I. ' The United States will be here two hundred

By the end of May, 1913, the ABC powers asked what the policy of the United States was to be with regard to recognition of Huerta. The same day the answer was sent: " This Government is not ready to consider recognizing Mexico. It is hoped the countries mentioned . . . may see their way clear to withhold action until our course has been determined." [105] Meanwhile warnings were sent to the English and French to the effect that loans to Huerta based on the customs houses of the country could not be enforced and hence such loans would be inadvisable.[106] By the middle of June something of a policy was agreed on after a conference between Secretary of War Garrison, Bryan and the President and a confidential message was sent to H. L. Wilson for his guidance. It stated that the administration was convinced that there was little confidence in the Huerta Government in Mexico itself and continued that if the Dictator would give the United States " satisfactory assurances " of an early election in which he would not be a candidate, and of an " absolute amnesty " to follow, this country would be glad to use its good offices to secure an armistice among the struggling factions and to bring about a conference among the leaders of the various parties.

The Ambassador, however, was hopelessly out of step with Washington and knew it. He wrote Taft and asked

---

years and it can continue to shoot men for that little space till they learn to vote and to rule themselves.'

I have never seen him laugh so heartily. Shooting men into self-government! Shooting men into orderliness—he comprehends that; and that's all right. But that's as far as his habit of mind goes " (Hendrick, *op. cit.*, I, 188.)

[105] Bryan to Ambassador Morgan, May 31, 1913, *Foreign Relations*, 1913, p. 806.

[106] Houston, *Eight Years*, I, 69.

for a public endorsement of his course. This Taft referred to Knox who cautiously pointed out that all the facts were not known to the ex-President and hence he should be very careful but suggested that a " general expression of appreciation of Mr. Wilson's zeal, courage and effective effort in the [sic] protection of American and other foreign interests would be no more than just." [107]

The Ambassador continued to press his course on Washington as to recognition of Huerta and even invited the Dictator to dine at the Embassy. At news of this the President in Washington was very indignant.[108] He had lost confidence in his Ambassador and started sending a succession of agents to Mexico to make personal reports. On April 19th he wrote Mr. William Bayard Hale, a well known journalist:

I think that the situation of affairs in Central America and South America is very much more difficult to get the threads of than the situation in California, and, with the full acquiescence of Mr. Bryan I am writing to ask if you would be willing to undertake a tour of the Central and South American states, ostensibly on your own hook, in order that officially and through the eyes of an independent observer we might find out just what is going on down there.[109]

Inevitably the Ambassador resented Hale's coming to Mexico and later insisted that the journalist had formed his opinion from a most unfortunate group.[110] Whether this was true or not, the reports were seriously considered as is evident from Wilson's note to Bryan, dated July 3rd,

---

[107] Wilson to Taft, June 3, 1914; Taft to Knox, June 19, 1913, and interlined and corrected draft of Knox to Taft, no date, LC., Knox MS.

[108] Baker, IV, 255.   [109] *Ibid.*, IV, 243-4.

[110] Wilson, *Diplomatic Episodes,* pp. 306-7.

in which the President said that in the light of the Ambassador's telegrams and the report of Hale, he asked the Secretary seriosuly to consider recalling the Ambassador.[111] Soon the Ambassador was asked to return to Washington and two weeks later left Nelson O'Shaughnessy as Chargé d'affaires at Mexico City.[112] On August 4th the Ambassador's resignation was publicly accepted with the statement that " The part which he felt it his duty to take in the earlier stages of the recent revolution in Mexico would make it difficult for him to represent the views of the present administration in view of the situation which now exists." At the same time the Chargé in Mexico was notified that ex-Governor John Lind, of Minnesota, was being sent down as " adviser to the Embassy " " as. the personal representative of the President." [113]

By this time the revolution lead by Venustiano Carranza and other Mexican rebels was becoming serious as could be seen from the fact that gross earnings of Mexican railroads in 1913-1914 dropped 40% from the figures for the preceding year,[114] even though heavy executive pressure was apparently maintaining Government revenues reasonably well.[115]

[111] Wilson to Bryan, July 3, 1913, LC., Bryan MS.

[112] Callahan, *American Policy in Mexican Relations,* p. 539.

[113] Bryan to Chargé, August 4, 1913, *Foreign Relations,* 1913, pp. 817-8.

It may be noted here that from time to time other special investigators were sent by Bryan, such as Mr. Del Valle, or by the President, as Leon J. Canova, John P. Silliman, John W. Belt, and a number of others. Wilson, *op. cit.,* 307-8; Wriston, *Executive Agents,* pp. 492 ff.

[114] A. W. Donly in Blakeslee, *Mexico and the Caribbean,* p. 88.

[115] H. L. Wilson, " Errors with Reference to Mexico," *The Annals,* XLIV, 160.

In his paternalistic attitude the President now determined to use all pressure short of war to accomplish his purposes. He had withheld recognition and influenced others to do the same; he had cut off the supply of arms to Mexico by using both the embargo and a blockade of Mexican ports; and finally he had discouraged loans to the Dictator. Embassy adviser John Lind, who was instructed to act " in the spirit of the most earnest and disinterested friendship " outlined what was considered as a satisfactory settlement:

1. An immediate cessation of fighting and the establishment of an armistice.
2. A guarantee of an early and free election.
3. Huerta to bind himself not to be a candidate.
4. All factions to agree to abide by the results of the election.[116]

Foreign representatives at Washington were asked to support the United States program by notifying Mexico that they advised the acceptance of the Lind mission. Grey sent word unofficially to Huerta that failure to receive Lind would " in our opinion be a grave mistake and put Mexico in the wrong." The French were a little slow but agreed to do about the same; the Germans quite reluctantly followed suit.[117] All in all Europe was at a loss how to define the United States policy, and apparently House added to, rather than clarified, the confusion when he told Grey in July, 1913, that it made little difference which Mexican faction was in power, just so long as order was maintained—for that was quite at variance with the Page-Wilson

[116] Address of Wilson to Congress, August 27, 1913, *Foreign Relations,* 1913, p. 822.

[117] Baker, IV, 269.

pronouncements which had been understood to have classi-
fied these factions as good and bad, right and wrong.[118]
Sir Edward's Secretary, Sir William Tyrrell, came to Washington and talked to Wilson and got the definite impression
that Wilson's obsession was "I propose to teach the South
American Republics to elect good men." [119] Sir Cecil
Spring-Rice likewise felt the whole program an anomaly.
But Europe had its own serious problems and so long as
the United States acted as intermediary for them while
trying to protect their citizens in Mexico those nations
remained inclined to keep hands off.[120]

Lind sent back ample reports stating that he felt the
influence of the Ambassador had been "baneful and
malevolent," and added that the Mexicans politically
seemed "more like children than like men" with the only
political motives he could discern as "appetite and vanity."
He severely criticized both local and foreign landlords for
ruthless exploitation and bluntly said "Intervention at this
time unless forced upon us, is not to be thought of, *1st,*
because our own work at this time makes it inexpedient to
divert the public mind from . . . domestic questions. . . .
2nd, The time is not [*sic*] opportune. The Mexicans have
not yet demonstrated to the world the utter helplessness that
I charge them with. *3d,* The estimate of their capacity
which I have ventured to make may be erroneous." He felt
that the rebels might not rate very high but that as a whole
they were better than the *Huertistas.* Finally, he suggested
it might not be a bad idea to let the Mexicans use up a
bit more of their ammunition and energies before the

[118] *Ibid.,* IV, 259-60.
[119] Hendrick, *Life and Letters of Page,* I, 205.
[120] Callahan, *op. cit.,* pp. 543-4.

United States took a hand.[121] Wilson expressed much interest in the ideas expressed by his agent.[122]

Meanwhile Mr. Lind's proposals to Huerta had been summarily rejected.[123] Could anything else have been seriously anticipated when the third demand was that Huerta would not be a candidate for the presidency when he had recently jostled himself into that position through treason to his chief if not actual assassination?

Mr. Lind had permitted himself to state that if the demands presented to Mexico were accepted promptly Washington would look with favor upon an immediate loan to Mexico. The Mexican Secretary of State Gamboa took full advantage of the opening thus presented and retorted: "When the dignity of the nation is at stake, I believe that there are not loans enough to induce those charged by the law to maintain it to permit it to be lessened." [124] As the pressure continued Huerta dissolved his Congress and called for new elections. Wilson responded to this October 13th:

General Huerta's course in dissolving Congress and arresting deputies the President finds it impossible to regard otherwise than as an act of bad faith toward the United States. It is not only a violation of constitutional guarantees but it destroys all possibility of a free and fair election. . . . The President would not feel justified in accepting the result of such an election or in recognizing a president so chosen.[125]

[121] Lind to Bryan, September 19 [1913], LC., Bryan MS. This is a detailed fifteen-page report.

[122] Wilson to Bryan, October 6, 1913, *ibid.*

[123] Mexican Secretary of Foreign Affairs Gamboa to Lind, August 26, 1913, *Foreign Affairs,* 1913, pp. 832-5.

[124] *Ibid.,* p. 835.

[125] Bryan to Chargé, October 13, 1913, *ibid.,* pp. 838.

To Congress Wilson reported that Huerta's rejection was because the spirit of friendliness of the American people was not realized south of the Río Grande. He stated that impatience on the part of the United States would be childish and called for the " self-restraint of a really great nation." [126] Steady pressure was brought on Great Britain to support the United States program and this was rather hesitantly agreed to. The British Minister in Mexico, who had been in sympathy with the Lord Cowdray interests on which Huerta had learned heavily, notified the Dictator of the change in policy which practically sealed his doom.[127]

October 27th Wilson delivered his Mobile speech which Bryan elaborated further in November when he said:

The present policy of the Government of the United States is to isolate General Huerta entirely; to cut him off from foreign sympathy and aid and from domestic credit, whether moral or material, and to force him out. . . . If General Huerta does not retire by force of circumstances it will become the duty of the United States to use less peaceful means to put him out.[128]

This notice was sent directly to Huerta and meant that the issue was squarely joined. The problem for Washington evidently was to continue its strangle hold on all means of aid for the Dictator until he fell. In December Wilson notified Congress:

There can be no certain prospect of peace in America until Gen. Huerta has surrendered his usurped authority in

[126] Robinson and West, *Foreign Policy of Wilson,* p. 193.

[127] Lind to Bryan, November 1, 1913, LC., Bryan MS.; *Foreign Relations,* 1913, pp. 852-61; Hendrick, *op. cit.,* I, 209-10. See also Seymour, *Intimate Papers of House,* I, 199-200; Baker, IV, 279-80.

[128] Bryan to O'Shaughnessy, November 24, 1913, *Foreign Relations,* 1914, pp. 444-5.

Mexico; until it is understood on all hands, indeed, that such pretended governments will not be countenanced or dealt with by the Government of the United States. We are the friends of constitutional government in America; we are more than its friends, we are its champions; because in no other way can our neighbors, to whom we would wish in every way to make proof of our friendship, work out their own development in peace and liberty.

We shall not, I believe, be obliged to alter our policy of watchful waiting. And then, when the ends comes, we shall hope to see constitutional order restored in distressed Mexico by the concert and energy of such of her leaders as prefer the liberty of their people to their own ambitions.[129]

Watchful waiting, but with a punch added!

Clearly, in Wilson's mind the Mexican had become a symbol and the slogan was "Huerta must go." The program seemed to be working and again Great Britain cooperated, this time by withdrawing its Minister, the erstwhile friend of Huerta, and substituting one more in sympathy with United States desires.[131] This of course was in spite of financial circles in Great Britain which released their choice sarcasm on Wilson's fiddling while Mexico burned.[132] This was especially the case when one William H. Benton, an Englishman, was executed—or murdered—by order of General Francisco Villa.[133]

With indications of slowly rising support the President was of course greatly pleased and all the more determined to proceed with his theory even though a bombardment of

[129] Annual Message, December 2, 1913, *Foreign Relations*, 1913, pp. x-xi.

[130] Hendrick, *op. cit.*, I, 182-3.

[131] *Ibid.*, I, 196-224; Seymour, *op. cit.*, I, 202.

[132] Editorial in *London Financial News*, February 5, 1914, copy in LC., Bryan MS.; Page to House, February 28, 1914, LC., *ibid.*

[133] Hendrick, III, 106-7; Baker, IV, 309.

criticism was coming from some quarters to which he was accustomed to lend ear. Also, it is probable that he had some serious qualms from his own thinking. He had once written that " Self-government is not a thing that can be ' given ' to any people, because it is a form of character and not a form of constitution." [134] Also it was notable that Lind was urging positive and prompt action in Mexico in his extensive and almost daily reports. The constant pressure was having its effect and in January, 1914, came a recommendation to the effect that Carranza badly needed ammunition; that his faction had contracted for 10,000 Krag-Jorgensen rifles as well as ammunition. These could be put on board a tramp steamer in San Francisco which would secure clearance papers for a Chinese port but which would put in at Topolobampo, Sinaloa, if the San Francisco authorities could show " a little lenience." Also " carloads " of ammunition could be gotten through at Douglas, Arizona, with a little " indulgence " shown there.[135] On the 15th Wilson wrote to McAdoo, Secretary of the Treasury:

My dear McAdoo:

Here are memoranda from Hale upon which I based what I said to you last night. May I not suggest that in some confidential way the arrangements be made at San Francisco and Douglas, Arizona, which Hale suggests?

In haste

Faithfully yours,[136]

It should not be implied from this that Wilson approved such " beating the devil around the stump " for he followed

[134] Quoted by L. S. Rowe, " Scope and Limits of our Obligations toward Mexico," *The Annals*, LIV, 225.

[135] Copy of memorandum in LC., Woodrow Wilson MS.

[136] *Ibid.*

up this irregular suggestion by raising the embargo on arms shipments on the 3rd of the next month [137] even though Bryan urged its retention.[138] If " Huerta must go " was the slogan it was only sensible to arm those who would do the dirty work of ousting him. This was all the more the case since the long continued friction was resulting in a rising number of casualties among United States citizens who remained in Mexico in spite of the continued warnings of the State Department.[139] True, Wilson felt that they had remained at their own risk and were not entitled to much in the way of special protests on their behalf when trouble did arise, but just the same much feeling and a demand for action was arising in the country.

The diplomatic correspondence of 1914 and 1915 is full of letters in which the United States presents the interests of various foreign nationals in Mexico. These included Chinese, Englishmen, Frenchmen, Germans, Italians, Turks and Spaniards, as well as others probably. Steadily the tone of the State Department stiffened and the " soft " answer largely disappeared, as may be seen from the communication of January 29th, which read: " Bring to the attention of the appropriate authorities with renewed demand for release of Cantu and intimate that unless this demand is immediately complied with, this Government will find it necessary to consider drastic measures in the premises." Two days later the reply came from the consul:

[137] *Foreign Relations,* 1914, pp. 447-8.

[138] Bryan to the President, undated, but in opposition to the idea and apparently written on this occasion, LC., Bryan MS.

[139] Data from War Department, *Foreign Relations,* 1915, p. 786; Secretary of State to the President, *Foreign Relations,* 1916, pp. 469 ff.

" Samuel Cantu released and brought to Laredo, Texas, by myself at eleven o'clock today." [140]

By this time the irregular reports from personal agents were probably causing some trouble and much uncertainty. Page was wittily sarcastic on the negligence and incompetence of Bryan in notifying him of what was happening.[141] But this was probably the case in part at least because of the fact that Bryan did not know too much of what was happening. The President's private agents, House and the President himself were the policy makers so Bryan naturally found himself at a loss, and this added to his careless habits and his lack of diplomatic training and knowledge of what was customary, aggravated the difficulties under which Page in London and Chargé O'Shaughnessy in Mexico City were operating.

But the obvious fact that the President's policy was crystallizing and stiffening was apparent to all with the opening of the month of April, 1914. On the 9th sailors from the U. S. S. *Dolphin* in port at Tampico went to shore in a small boat and started to land in a forbidden district.

[140] *Ibid.*, 1914, pp. 901; 903.

[141] Page to House, February 28, 1914.

In writing to Sir Edward Grey, Spring-Rice commented:

" Mr. Bryan is I should think unlike any other Secretary of State or Minister of Foreign Affairs that has ever been known. He regards the matter simply from the politician's point of view; that is, if Huerta wins it is bad for Bryan's record, and if Huerta falls it is good for Bryan's record. As Villa is the only man on the Constitutional side who can win victories, Villa is the man to whom all his hopes are attached. Any aspersion on Villa is a personal attack on Bryan . . . he [Bryan] told me that he [Benton] was dead without one word of regret. He merely remarked that he had attacked Villa (as if he had laid hands on the Lord's anointed). . . ." (Gwynn, *op. cit.*, II, 203-4.)

While two of them were still in their whaleboat flying United States flags at stem and stern they were arrested by local police. After considerable protest they were released but not before sharp exchanges had taken place between the local authorities and Admiral Mayo of the United States fleet.[142] Mayo's demands for a formal apology were endorsed, possibly with reluctance, by Wilson. These Huerta declined as unreasonable.[143] A despatch from O'Shaughnessy had also been delayed and a mail orderly of the U. S. S. *Minnesota* had been arrested at Vera Cruz on April 11th so Wilson was convinced that this was a deliberate series of insults and on April 14th ordered the flag officer at Hampton Roads, with " all available ships " (ten being named) and a regiment of marines to Tampico.[144] The President was seriously perturbed and openly contemplated the possibility of war saying: " I have no enthusiasm for war; but I have an enthusiasm for the dignity of the United States." [145]

On the 20th Wilson went before Congress and asked its approval of his use of the armed forces of the country to obtain " the fullest recognition of the rights and dignity of the United States." Senator Root pointed out that this was war but felt that only " through respect for the American flag, the American uniform, the American Government "

---

[142] *Foreign Relations,* 1914, numerous; Daniels, *Life of Woodrow Wilson, 1856-1924* (Chicago, Philadelphia and Toronto, 1924), pp. 180-1.

[143] O'Shaughnessy to Secretary of State, April 12, 1914, *Foreign Relations,* 1914, pp. 453-5.

[144] Offut, *Protection of Citizens Abroad,* pp. 118 ff.; Notter, *Origins of Foreign Policy of Wilson,* pp. 288-9.

[145] Quoted by Baker, IV, 324.

was it possible to proceed in the Mexican issue.[146] Approval
was expressed in the House by a vote of 323 to 29 on the
20th. The Senate then passed a somewhat different resolution 72 to 13 and the House concurred 337 to 37.[147] Actual
intervention was not planned but events were breaking
rapidly and about 2.30 the next morning word reached
Washington that the *Ypiranga*, a merchant vessel, was
headed for Vera Cruz with 200 machine guns and 15,000,-
000 rounds of ammunition from Germany for Huerta.
Daniels, Bryan, Tumulty and Wilson immediately got busy.
Bryan urged the occupation of Vera Cruz, the President
demurred but gave the order.[149]

Wilson had been assured that the occupation would not
involve anything more than a demonstration and that there
would be no resistence. When word came that a score of
United States sailors and probably ten times that number of
Mexicans had been killed the situation took on a decidedly
serious aspect. Diplomatic relations were forthwith ruptured
and Brazil took over the United States Embassy in Mexico.[150]

There was a general outburst of approval of the President's stand. Taft was outspoken, saying "All that those of

---

[146] Jessup, *Elihu Root*, II, 258-9.

[147] Bryan to some twenty-five embassies and legations of the
United States, *Foreign Relations*, 1914, pp. 482-3. Cf. Bryan to
O'Shaughnessy, April 20, 1914, *ibid.*, p. 476.

[148] House to Page, April 20, 1914, SL., House MS.

[149] Canada to Secretary of State, April 20, 1914, *Foreign Relations*, 1914, p. 477. See also Houston, I, 114-6; Daniels, pp.
182-3; Baker, IV, 329-30.

These munitions finally did reach Huerta due, it is claimed, to
the fact that false assurances from German officials were believed
by Secretary Bryan. (Lind to House, November 15, 1915, SL.,
House MS.)

[150] *Foreign Relations*, 1914, numerous.

us who are not in the government can do is to support the hands of the President and Secretary of State. . . ." [151] The radicals urged that Mexico was in chaos, that all its progress was due to foreign blood, that it was an integral part of our industrial system, that the country should be " broken up " and reformed on the basis of United States control.[152] A. B. Hart was more cautious. He felt it was far easier to get an army into Mexico than to get it out again, that there was no rush for the United States to recognize any government in Mexico, and that he could find no sense in trying to foist on Mexico a man who " if he tried his policy within the bounds of the United States, would be stoned out of civilized society." [153]

But the temporary approval did not change the President's mind as to his intentions. On the 27th he stated his position once more in saying that " when properly directed, there is no people not fitted for self-government." He pled for the submerged 85 per cent of the people of Mexico " who are now struggling toward liberty." [154] He knew that the job was not a simple one and commented:

The function of being a policeman in Mexico has not appealed to me, nor does it appeal to our people. . . . Our duty is higher than that. If we are to go in there, restore order, and immediately get out, and invite a repetition of conflict similar to that which is in progress now, we had better have remained out.[155]

[151] Taft, *The U. S. and Peace*, p. 34.

[152] Wilson, " Errors with Reference to Mexico," *The Annals*, LIV, 153; Rear-Admiral F. E. Chadwick, "A Study of Iberic-America," *ibid.*, pp. 13-4; S. N. Patten, "A Revision of American Policies," *ibid.*, pp. 196-200.

[153] Postulates of the Mexican Situation," *ibid.*, pp. 143-7.

[154] Scott, *Wilson's Foreign Policy*, pp. 389; 383.

[155] *Ibid.*, p. 388.

After due preliminary soundings the ABC powers offered the mediation of their governments in attempting to solve the situation. The suggestion was approved promptly and became a step of the greatest importance in the general improvement of the tone of relations with Latin America as a whole.[156] Naturally the Caribbean countries felt that this was of exceedingly great importance for them also. Without going into detail it can be said that the result was the calling of the Niagara Falls conference with a prerequisite in the form of an understanding that " Huerta must go." Of course the Dictator did all he could to kick against the pricks but he was fast becoming powerless now that the effects of the blockade were becoming felt. The ABC powers endorsed the United States prerequisite so the chief remaining problem was a decision as to the successor in power and the specific procedure to be followed.

Many felt that there was danger that Mexico would

[156] Baker, IV, 336-7; Hendrick, III, 119-20.

An interesting comment on this is the letter of Von Bernstorff to Bussche, German Minister in the Argentine, dated Washington, December 6, 1914:

" Apart from the commercial losses and the mistake we made over the ' Ypiranga,' the Mexican question is a godsend to us, as ' Frisco ' is now quite forgotten. I assume that the celebrations over the opening of the Panama Canal will be severely cut down under the existing circumstances. I shall be extremely surprised if Mexico has been pacified by that date. I am quite of your opinion that the acceptance of mediation by the A. B. C. has greatly diminished American prestige. I have always reported to Berlin in this sense. But Bryan is a peace at any price ' man, and has much involved the President in many matters. For us it is always advantageous if South America plucks up courage and obtains greater freedom of action, though we can pretty well write off the countries to the North of the Panama Canal." Bernstorff, *Memoirs,* pp. 122-3.

degenerate into anarchy.[157] There were numerous factions to be considered: the Zapata brothers in south Mexico with their Indian program were demanding Wilson's attention; [158] Villa had increasingly shown relapses toward his earlier career as a bandit (also his personal conduct was not above reproach) ; and finally, there was the fatherly appearing Venustiano Carranza, with his " respectable side-whiskers " who was a most persistent factor.[159] Wilson finally determined that the Constitutionalists should be placed in charge (that meant Carranza and Villa) and that the United States would assist them after they took charge. At the same time the United States declined to accept an " indemnity or other international satisfaction " " in any form whatsoever." In Mexico the various factions somewhat reluctantly agreed to a provisional government, which was to be recognized at once by the United States.

Through Huerta was not specifically ousted it was so obviously impossible for him to remain in power that he resigned on July 15th and left the country within the week.[160] In many ways the old statement was correct here: this shut off the tap that was flooding the cellar floor, but the mopping up still had to be done. Could Carranza mop up and satisfy such men as Villa, Zapata and others, nameless here? None of these men were of the Sunday-school superintendent type truly, and many a " diplomatic " suggestion had to be made by their paternal " friend " of the North. Of course this involved dealing with the internal

[157] Gwynn, *op. cit.,* II, 207-8.

[158] Wilson to Bryan, May 19, 1914, LC., Bryan MS.

[159] Malone to the President, with inclosures, April 24 [?] 1914, and Carranza to Tupper, April 3, 1914, LC., Bryan MS.

[160] Baker, IV, 345-51.

affairs of another country [161] but it had to be done. Carranza was admittedly "a very difficult person" to deal with,[162] while Villa seemed anxious for United States approval.[163] But even so the First Chief, as Carranza became known, was more and more the chosen man,[164] probably as Villa's personality, domestic relations and inclinations became better known.[165] Active coaching from the Washington side-lines was accepted with poor grace by Carranza but accepted both with regard to general treatment of the diplomatic corps and with regard to handling other Mexican leaders and issues.[166]

Thus another weary year closed with Carranza at last formally installed as head of the new government in September. At once came a break between him and Villa that soon developed into open rebellion as the ex-bandit tried to popularize himself with the masses and seize power if possible. In spite of the disquieting features of the situation, however, Wilson ordered United States troops to retire from Vera Cruz the middle of September, and this was accomplished in the next two months.

In the early months of 1915 the gnawing pain of the Mexican toothache continued. Familiarity had bred contempt though occasional new jabs of pain aroused periodic

[161] Notter, *op. cit.,* p. 362.

[162] Wilson to Bryan, August 25, 1914, LC., Bryan MS.

[163] Garfield to House, September 10, 1914, SL., House MS.

[164] Incidentally, Carranza apparently received quite substantial aid from certain oil magnates of the United States. For instance of this see Nearing and Freeman, *Dollar Diplomacy,* pp. 111-3.

[165] Bryan to the President, August 2, 1914, LC., Bryan MS.

[166] For examples see *Foreign Relations,* 1914, pp. 589-91; *ibid.,* 1915, p. 651, and Callahan, *Amer. Policy in Mexican Relations,* pp. 551-2.

attention. Carranza had secured control of the ports of Yucatán and interfered rather seriously with the export of sisal that was of primary importance to the International Harvester Company and affiliated interests.[167] Also the more and more pronounced anti-Roman Catholic conduct of the *Carranzistas* aroused serious criticism in the United States, and concern on the part of Washington. Wilson even took note of it and cautioned Bryan that in a proposed answer to a prominent cleric he express the highest appreciation for religion and religious motives, but that he refrain from making a positive statement that the United States would refuse to " recognize any government in Mexico which does not give us satisfactory guarantees of a fair treatment of the Church," remarking that too much Mexican History " lies back of and complicates that matter." [168] Also there were uncomfortable rumors of Japanese intrigue in Mexico [169] but they probably represented mere hopes on the part of some intense but shortsighted Mexican nationalists and were to be dismissed promptly though they were later discussed by a Senate Committee.[170]

Even though diplomatic relations were conducted through the Brazilian Minister in Mexico the United States continued to speak in behalf of foreigners resident there. The persistent interest displayed brought a request from Car-

[167] Ranney to Bryan, February 22, 1915; draft of wire to Canada, February 24, 1915, and Bryan to Silliman, March 13, 1915, LC., Bryan MS. See also *Foreign Relations*, 1915, and Callcott, *Liberalism in Mexico*, pp. 242 ff.

[168] Wilson to Bryan, March 17, 1915, with draft of letter, undated, inclosed, LC., Bryan MS.

[169] Carothers to Bryan, February 5, 1915, *ibid.*

[170] *Investigation of Mexican Affairs*, pp. 1777-8.

ranza asking why the United States whose relations were conducted through the embassy of a third country constantly inquired about other nationals when those countries had representatives on the ground to plead their cases. Wilson suggested that the First Chief be informed that it was because other governments looked to the United States as Mexico's "nearest and most sincere" friend and expected it to act for them.[171]

Early in March the Argentine Ambassador at Washington proposed personally to Bryan that all the Latin American nations join in an appeal to all factions in Mexico to end their differences.[172] Wilson replied the same day saying that he feared this would lead to irritation, that he had just noted a statement from the Archbishop of Mexico indicating that joint action would be resented. The President personally thought that "they would stand more from us" than from a group from whom they were unaccustomed "to expect admonition." However, when the Cuban President offered to try to exert some influence on Carranza and Zapata, Wilson felt that the offer was "very friendly" and appreciated it "very much indeed," even though it did not seem practical at the moment.[173]

On the henequen situation Wilson finally informed Bryan he felt the United States should notify Carranza that the trade would be opened with Yucatán even if it had to be done with the protection of the United States navy,[174] but

[171] Wilson to Secretary of State, March 11, 1915, LC., Bryan MS.

[172] Bryan to Wilson, March 11, 1915, and Wilson to Secretary of State, March 11, 1915, *ibid.*

[173] Bryan to Wilson, March 19, 1915, and Wilson to Secretary of State, March 21, 1915, *ibid.*

[174] Wilson to Secretary of State, March 12, 1915, *ibid.*

he declined to be tricked into even semi-recognition of any faction in the country by personally receiving its agents. These were all required to interview the Secretary of State.[175] Further, when a report came through Bryan that a group of United States citizens in Mexico were planning to arise, seize Mexico City and force intervention, the President informed the Secretary that he might state that such conduct would have just the reverse effect from that desired for it would " absolutely outlaw " the participants and place them outside the pale of either domestic or international law.[176]

By this time Lind had submitted a long report favoring re-cognition of Carranza even though the disorders continued.[177] Wealthy companies having a great deal at stake often sup-ported their favorite leaders and either hired local armed bands for defense or were forced to bribe them by paying " protection " money.[178] House, from Europe, continued to urge the idea of using the ABC powers in some way.[179] By June 1st Wilson had received enough advice and determined to take another definite step which he discussed with his Cabinet. Bryan opposed the idea fearing that it would mean intervention for under it the United States might select some other " promising bandit " than Carranza and give him the " active moral support " necessary to enable him to secure control of the country.[180] But Wilson was ready to act and the next day published a statement which he had sent to

[175] Wilson to Secretary of State, April 21, 1915, *ibid.*

[176] Bryan to Wilson, April 5, 1915, and Wilson to Bryan, April 5, 1915, *ibid.*

[177] Lind to Bryan, April 16, 1915, *ibid.*

[178] Nearing and Freeman, *op. cit.*, pp. 118-9.

[179] House to the President, March 15, 1915, SL., House MS.

[180] Houston, *Eight Years,* I, 132-5; Anon. [Fuller], " Bryan " in Bemis, *Secretaries of State,* X, 19.

Mexico. In this he reviewed the tragic conditions existing south of the Río Grande and concluded:

I feel it to be my duty to tell them [the Mexican leaders] that, if they cannot accommodate their differences and unite for this great purpose within a very short time, this Government will be constrained to decide what means should be employed by the United States in order to help Mexico save herself and serve her people.[181]

The ABC powers promptly suggested that they would be glad to act simultaneously in the recognition of any one man whom this country might select.[182]

To the great peace lover, Bryan, the new course of action both with regard to the *Lusitania* affair and with regard to Mexico was highly distasteful so his resignation was the logical result. Lansing came in as Secretary and the new program proceeded. The army on the border had long been restless so repeated warnings were sent the troops to get them to realize the " necessity of exercising the greatest moderation and caution," and of insuring the fact that they must not cross the border.[183] Just at this point an additional complication threatened when the ex-dictator, Huerta, arrived in the United States from Spain and proceeded to the Mexican border. At the end of June he was " invited " to visit the Federal building in El Paso. There he was detained without bond and transferred to Fort Bliss while all requests for extradition from Mexico were declined

[181] *Foreign Relations,* 1915, p. 695.
[182] Wilson to Secretary of State ad interim, June 22, 1915, and Lansing to Wilson, June 25, 1915, *The Lansing Papers,* II, 536-7.
[183] General Funston to Secretary of War, August 30, 1915, *Foreign Relations,* 1915, 806; Breckinridge to Funston, July 24, 1915, and August 16, 1915, *ibid.,* 1915, pp. 800; 803-4.

" owing to the absence of a recognized Federal Government in Mexico." [184]

On June 22nd Wilson took up a suggestion of the ABC countries for joint action and developed it so that their representatives would be joined by the three ranking New World ministers at Washington, namely, those from Bolivia, Guatemala and Uruguay. Lind, Lincoln Steffens and others continued to urge that Carranza was the only man able to control the situation, but that individual was showing his obstinate characteristics and refused to attend the conference which the representatives of Latin America and the other factional leaders of the troubled republic had agreed upon.[185] The anti-clerical attitude of the Constitutionalists also continued to give trouble, and because of utterly contradictory reports [186] sincere men were at a loss how to proceed. House summarized the situation when he said:

The President and Secretary Lansing I know are sorely perplexed as to what action to take. They have in mind to do what is best for the general good of that unhappy people, but scarcely two suggestions agree.[187]

Also there was the intensely practical question of how to finance the new government once it was established. House raised the question in letters to Wilson early in August, 1915. Lansing pointed out the enormous amount of claims

[184] Extensive correspondence in *ibid.*, pp. 827 ff.; Callahan, *op. cit.*, 559.

[185] Lind to House, July 30, 1915, and August 4, 1915; Lind to Lansing, July 23, 1915, and Steffens to House, August 7, 1915, SL., House MS.

[186] Garfield to House, August 2, 1915, and August 11, 1915, *ibid.*

[187] House to Lind, August 2, 1915, *ibid.*

outstanding as a result of the disorders and the fact that under Díaz the interest on the National debt had absorbed half the Mexican revenues.[188] Toward the end of the month Lansing received word that F. A. Vanderlip of the National City Bank was interested in financing Carranza in return for an exclusive concession to mine anthracite coal in the State of Coahuila (the only anthracite coal incidentally that had then been found in Mexico).[189] Wilson asked that this be investigated saying it is "extremely important" to prevent such enterprises "from guiding and determining affairs in Mexico."[190] Lansing promptly wrote a "personal and private" letter to F. A. Vanderlip asking if the National City Bank had under consideration the financing of Carranza.[191] What facts, if any, were back of the rumor is unknown for Mr. Vanderlip's Confidential Clerk at once denied the statement by telephone and Mr. Vanderlip did the same by letter saying "under no circumstances" would his bank take such a step without informing the Secretary of State.[192]

The combined New World powers brought to bear all the influence they could [193] while the menace of the European war made the United States more than ever anxious to

[188] House to the President, August 3, 1915, ibid.; House to Lansing, August 4, 1915, in LC., Lansing MS. and SL., House MS; Lansing to House, August 7, 1915, LC., Lansing MS; Lansing to House, August 16, 1915, SL., House MS.

[189] Report of Arthur M. Allen (Department of Justice), August 23, 1915, LC., Lansing MS.

[190] Wilson to Lansing, August 31, 1915, ibid.

[191] Lansing to Vanderlip, September 1, 1915, ibid.

[192] Memorandum of September 2, 1915, signed " F. M. R.," and Vanderlip to Lansing, September 2, 1915, ibid.

[193] Appeal to Mexican factions, August 11, 1915, Foreign Relations, 1915, pp. 735-6.

avoid hostilities if possible. Slowly the fact developed that the sheer stubbornness of Carranza showed real strength, especially since he was refusing to endorse the conference on the ground that it was a case of outside nations interfering with Mexican sovereignty. In fact Lincoln Steffens made the pertinent, or impertinent, remark in a letter to House:

You quote in your letter the opinions of those that tell you it is impossible to reason with Carranza. It is impossible for anybody to reason with Carranza who does not accept the purposes of his policy and of the revolution. He is a little like President Wilson himself in this.[194]

At last the Villa faction which had broken with Carranza was pretty well dispersed and the conference finally concluded that the best thing to do was to recognize the First Chief and let it go at that even though Lansing had recently felt it wise to keep Villa in the field as a counterweight.[195] On October 11th it was announced that the conferees had " found that the Carrancista party is the only party possessing the essentials for recognition as the *de facto* government of Mexico, and they have so reported to their respective governments." [196] Formal recognition was extended by Lansing on the 19th and the same day the President raised the embargo on arms shipments to the Constitutionalists though it was still to apply to enemies of the *de facto* Government.[197]

[194] Steffens to House, September 13, 1915, SL., House MS.

[195] Lansing to the President, August 9, 1915, *The Lansing Papers*, II, 548.

[196] Lansing to principal American missions in Europe, October 11, 1915, *Foreign Relations*, 1915, p. 767.

[197] Lansing to Arredondo, October 19, 1915, and Wilson to Secretary of the Treasury, October 19, 1915, *ibid.*, pp. 771, 781-2.

Wilson felt that his policy had stood the test, having taken no advantage of Mexico during the long and complicated affair but having adhered to its principles. Villa continued to defy the United States but this was not immediately serious.[198] All possible aid was extended to Carranza to enable him to seat himself firmly in power even when that individual persistently maintained an aloof and almost hostile attitude to his outstanding benefactor.[199]

As the new year of 1916 opened Villa started his last bid for local popularity by pulling the eagle's tail feathers. This time his followers murdered sixteen United States miners at Santa Ysabel on January 10th.[200] Just six days before this Wilson had publicly urged acceptance of his Pan-American Pact.[201] At once and on all sides there was a rising clamor for action. Albert Fall of New Mexico introduced a Senate Resolution asking the President for letters and papers on ten points dealing with Mexico: whether there was a government existing in Mexico, whether such government was recognized by the United States, how this had happened and why, whether such government had given assurances United States lives and property would be respected, what orders had been issued to the border army to protect lives and propery, etc., etc.[202] An answer was declined as " incompatible with the public interest " and a simple statement issued that the existing government of Mexico was a *de facto* government, recognized by the

---

[198] Baker, VI, 65; Notter, 452-3.

[199] Bulnes, *Whole Truth,* pp. 377-8; Gruening, *Mexico and its Heritage,* pp. 594-5.

[200] Extensive correspondence in *Foreign Relations,* 1916.

[201] Notter, p. 484.

[202] *Foreign Relations,* 1916, pp. 463-4.

United States as such, that it had originated as a revolutionary government but that plans were on foot to merge it "within a reasonable time" with a new one to be organized under the laws of Mexico.[203] To make matters worse Villa next crossed the international border and attacked Columbus, New Mexico. Such an insult could not be tolerated for it trespassed on national dignity—and this it will be remembered was a fighting point with Woodrow Wilson.

Forthwith steps were taken to set out after the bandit. Carranza, appalled at the prospect, hastily agreed to a bilateral bandit-chasing agreement which would allow mutual privileges to the armed forces of both countries when following a hot trail. This was agreed to by Wilson on March 13th,[204] yet General Funston was warned by the War Department that the expedition he was to outfit was "limited to the purposes originally stated, namely the pursuit and dispersion of the band or bands that attacked Columbus, New Mexico, and it is of the utmost importance that no color of any other possibility or intention be given." The Senate by concurrent resolution expressed the same idea four days later.[205] Many honest and able men, including Elihu Root, were now disapproving Wilson's Mexican policy [206] and "demands for intervention now swelled into a roar" with Lodge, Roosevelt and Fall leading the chorus while increasing numbers urged the annexation of North

[203] Lansing to the President, February 12, 1916 (forwarded to the Senate by Wilson, February 17, 1916), *ibid.*, pp. 469-73.

[204] Baker, VI, 69; Bulnes, pp. 387-9.

[205] McCain to Funston, March 13, 1916, *Foreign Relations,* 1916, pp. 489; 491-2.

[206] Root to Republican Convention in New York, February 15, 1916, Root, *Addresses on International Subjects,* pp. 428 ff.

Mexico.[207] But the administration pursued its course. An expeditionary force of some 12,000 men continued to chase Villa disguising its limited and temporary use of Mexican railroads by making military shipments to civilian agents.[208] A careful check was made of United States citizens still resident in Mexico and the ports from which they could leave, and at the same time a request was made of the public for calm and critical judgment on affairs.[209] In Mexico, not surprisingly, the idea spread that this was the long expected intervention and as Villa had hoped he rapidly began to take on the proportions of a hero in the eyes of his people.[210] Carranza, never cordial to the United States was inclined to take the attitude that since the Expeditionary Force did not at once capture Villa, it ought to leave the country for he could do as well as it at bandit chasing, i. e., pursue the bandit and cause him to retreat. Washington advised a conference between General Scott and Alvaro Obregón of the Carranza forces. When this was agreed to the Mexicans categorically demanded that United States troops withdraw but Scott diplomatically forced an adjournment on May 1st rather than allow the ultimatum to be formally presented.[211] Negotiations on the next two days brought an agreement for a gradual with-

[207] Murray to Burleson, June 28, 1916, LC., Lansing MS.; Baker, VI, 71.

[208] Foreign Relations, 1916, cir. p. 504.

This was discontinued when unwise publicity caused Carranza to repudiate the plan (Rodgers to Secretary of State, April 6, 1916, ibid., 1916, pp. 508-9).

[209] Lansing to Secretary of the Navy, March 30, 1916, ibid., p. 687; Robinson and West, pp. 313-4.

[210] Telegrams from Funston, Foreign Relations, 1916, pp. 525-30.

[211] Scott and Funston to Secretary of War, April 30, 1916, and May 1, 1916, ibid., pp. 533-6.

drawal to the north of the Río Grande, but still grave danger of actual war continued largely because of Carranza's suspicions of the United States.[212]

Even at this time Wilson informed his later biographer on May 11 that his Mexican policy was founded on two of the most firmly seated convictions of his life.

First, his shame as an American over the first Mexican war, and his resolution that there should never be another such predatory enterprise. Second, upon his belief in the principle laid down in the Virginia bill of rights, that a people has the right " to do what they damn please with their own affairs." (He used the word " damn "). . . .

[He] declared with shut jaw that he would not be forced into war with Mexico if it could possibly be avoided. He does not want one hand tied behind him at the very moment that the nation may need all of its forces to meet the European situation. He emphasized the enormous undertaking it would be to pacify Mexico: " Five hundred thousand men at least! " [213]

In Mexico resentment continued to rise. More or less friction was inevitable with United States troops still on Mexican soil. There was trouble at Carrizal, and further south at Mazatlán shots were fired at a boat belonging to the U. S. S. *Annapolis* and there was every evidence that they had come from uniformed Mexican troops. Sailors returned the fire.[214] Wilson sadly wrote House on June 22nd: " The break seems to have come in Mexico; and all my patience to have gone for nothing. I am infinitely

---

[212] Scott and Funston to Secretary of War, May 3, 1916, *ibid.*, pp. 537-9; Notter, pp. 506-7.

[213] Conversation with Baker, *Baker,* VI, 14-5. See also Wilson to Salesmanship Congress at Detroit, July 10, 1916, Scott, *Wilson's Foreign Policy*, pp. 221-2.

[214] *Foreign Relations,* 1916, pp. 595-602.

sad about it." [215] But this was a temporary despondency and when Carranza released the men who had been captured at Carrizal Wilson again determined to wait it out. New World powers were informed that if hostilities developed there would still be no intervention in the regular sense of the word,[216] though United States consuls in Mexico were notified to inform all fellow citizens remaining there that " This Government feels that it cannot be responsible for safety such Americans unless they leave immediately." [217] Naval officers were to urge foreigners to leave Mexico but to start no trouble and see that Mexicans had no chance to start any.[218]

And once more the storm was ridden out in spite of the fact that a national election was pending with a reunited Republican party dealing sledge-hammer blows at " spineless incompetence," and " meddling and muddling " in Mexico.[219] In his acceptance of the renomination of his party on September 2nd, the President strongly reaffirmed his policy and reasserted his principles, as he did throughout the campaign.[220]

Once the election was over there again developed wearisome haggling with Carranza over final details of the withdrawal of United States troops.[221] By this time there

[215] Notter, p. 533; Baker, VI, 76.

[216] Lansing to the Argentine Ambassador, June 21, 1916, *Foreign Relations,* 1916, p. 592.

[217] Lansing to Dawson, June 28, 1916, *ibid.,* p. 700.

[218] *Investigation of Mexican Affairs,* p. 3205.

[219] House to Wilson, July 15, 1916, SL., House MS; Roosevelt, *Fear God and Take Your Own Part,* pp. 280-1.

[220] Scott, *op. cit.,* pp. 229-32; Daniels, *Life of Wilson,* pp. 186-7.

[221] Fletcher to House, December 31 [1916], SL., House MS.

was more than a little suspicion that German propaganda and activities in Mexico and Central America were influencing the attitudes of those countries materially. Evidence of this was sufficiently definite for a sharp warning to be transmitted by the State Department to Carranza on behalf of Great Britain to the effect that aid to German submarines, or other unneutral conduct, in fact, " the slightest breach of Mexican neutrality " might lead to the " most unfortunate consequences." [222] The year closed, and the new one opened with the people of the United States inclined to let the matter rock along a bit longer. By February, 1917, troops were at last out of the Southern Republic and some queried rather crossly as to what had been gained by the expenditure of $130,000,000 on the punitive expedition, but most of the people were now excited about European developments and were relieved that their country was not involved to the southward.[223] If they thought more in detail of the Villa affair they were inclined to wonder if it had not been rather shrewdly taken advantage of so as to give the United States army an excellent try-out for contingencies that now seemed at hand. For the most part, there was a rising impression that Wilson had been vindicated.[224] As for the Administration itself the Mexican problem was no longer to be considered strictly on its own merits for it was merged into the larger issue of general world rela-

[222] P. A. Martin, *Latin America and the War* (Baltimore, 1925), pp. 530-1; Carl W. Ackerman, *Mexico's Dilemma* (New York, 1918), pp. 106-8; *Investigation of Mexican Affairs,* pp. 2898-9; 3212-6.

[223] Moon, *Imperialism in World Politics,* p. 445.

[224] Robinson and West, pp. 113-5; Callahan, *American Policy in Mexican Relations,* p. 571.

tions—but that phase of the story must be left for the last chapter.

If Wilson started out with theories as his guide in the Mexican affair—and this seems to have been the case largely—he had certainly stuck to those theories in an almost unbelievable fashion.   Now he was firmly convinced that the end had vindicated the principles announced and that his stubbornness in the face of fire had been gloriously justified—and he felt that the " plain people " of his nation applauded.[225]

[225] Wilson on accepting renomination, September 2, 1916, Scott, *op. cit.*, p. 230.

CHAPTER VIII

PATERNAL DESPOTISM: PRACTICAL DIPLOMACY

The distinction, if not contrast, implied between this chapter heading and the last one may appear somewhat far-fetched at first glance but the author believes that it is nevertheless real enough to warrant careful thought. To understand the contradictions, as they have been called, which developed between Wilsonian principles and practice it is necessary to realize certain basic factors in each situation that arose. To the President, his principles were tremendously important. He had made a lifelong study of government and the influence of business on government and had reached the firm conclusion that unrestricted big business was often vicious. Another basic factor in his thinking was the fact that he came of fighting Scotch Presbyterian ancestry. As a result his flag and his nation must maintain dignity and command respect, and proper precautions must be taken on behalf of both. These facts provide the direct approach to the Panama Tolls Question, the Colombian Treaty and the treatment of the Central American countries. The same factors finally controlled the policy adopted with regard to the Caribbean island countries but they were beclouded and seriously complicated by the fact that Wilson personally directed the Mexican, Panama Tolls and Colombian Treaty questions, and maintained a moderate contact with Central American affairs, but allowed Bryan practically a free hand in the Caribbean until the complications there became so serious as to demand more direct attention. By this time policies were often so crystallized by events and under different leadership that they did not harmonize at the time and could not always be reconciled later.

It will be remembered that among the last acts of Taft as President was the signature of the Panama Tolls act which granted tolls exemption to coastwise traffic of the United States. It is obvious that Wilson had paid little attention to the early stages of the discussion. In fact during the campaign of 1912, coached by Perry Belmont, a New York lawyer and ex-Chairman of the Committee of Foreign Affairs of the House of Representatives, he endorsed the bill as passed for the sake of maintaining competition between the railroads and the water-borne freight of the country.[1] Obviously he was thinking only of domestic effects and not of the international situation at all. It soon became obvious, however, that the British were pressing the issue on moral grounds as a treaty obligation. This opened up an entirely new question.

In the eyes of Senator William E. Borah and other ardent nationalists the British contention for the repeal of the tolls act demanded a surrender of sovereignty by the United States and amounted to a " nearer consequence " of treason.[2] Wilson meanwhile had reached the conclusion that the original Hay-Pauncefote treaty substantiated the British contention and within six weeks of his inauguration was suggesting to his cabinet that the matter be considered. Bryan feared the effects of action on other domestic issues so the matter remained in abeyance for a time while Wilson

[1] Baker, IV, 396-7; Notter, pp. 193-4.
[2] Borah to Knox, May 11, 1914, LC., Knox MS.

ordered the collection of fuller economic details as to the effects of the proposal.[3] Lodge had become convinced that repeal was advisable and so wrote Sir Cecil Spring-Rice,[4] while even Roosevelt suggested arbitration of the matter.[5] Ambassador W. H. Page reassured the British and asked them to give the Administration time, and this they did though they were clearly mystified by the idealist pedagogue-politician. Early in 1914 Spring-Rice wrote to Tyrrell:

The President has maintained and rather increased his influence in Congress and in the Country, but he is as mysterious as ever. When he summons newspaper men, he talks to them at length in excellent language, but when they leave his presence they say to each other, What on earth did he say? When he sees the members of Congress he reads to them a lecture and tells them what he thinks is good for them to know, which appears to them to be very little. He asks the advice of no one.

As to changing his policy of talking, this is quite out of the question. There is nothing to do with this hardened saint.[6]

Wilson had talked the matter over with Sir William Tyrrell, the Secretary of Sir Edward Grey, and assured him that he hoped to have the matter settled as the British desired it.[7] This very frank conversation probably reassured the British leaders and after the passage of a few more months Wilson reported to the Senate on March 5, 1914, saying:

We consented to the treaty; its language we accepted, if we did not originate; and we are too big, too powerful,

[3] Notter, p. 244.
[4] Gwynn, *Letters and Friendships of Spring-Rice*, II, 188-9.
[5] Roosevelt, *Autobiography*, p. 582.
[6] Gwynn, II, 199; 202.
[7] *Ibid.*, II, 196; Seymour, *Intimate Papers of House*, I, 200-1.

too self-respecting a Nation to interpret with too strained or refined a reading the words of our own promises just because we have power enough to give us leave to read them as we please. The large thing to do is the only thing that we can afford to do, a voluntary withdrawal from a position everywhere questioned and misunderstood. We ought to reverse our action without raising the question whether we were right or wrong. . . . [8]

Elihu Root ably supported the President's position saying it was a logical request based on the obvious intent of the original treaty. He repeatedly insisted that the question at issue was not whether the United States had the right to exempt its own ships (for that was admitted) but whether the United States had the right to charge British ships discriminatory rates when such rates were prevented by a treaty honorably entered into.[9] Also, Root could and did add the powerful argument that he was associated with Hay at the time of the negotiation and knew the original intent of the negotiators.[10] Thus by the middle of June the repeal was secured, not necessarily as a right but as a matter on which there was excellent ground for argument and because the United States enjoyed the feeling that it was too big to quibble, as Wilson had suggested. Sir Edward Grey summarized the situation when he said: " President Wilson's decision in this matter of the Panama tolls was an independent and unqualified example of putting the sanctity of a treaty above immediate self-interest. As such it was noted at the time and ought still to be remembered." [11]

[8] Robinson and West, *Foreign Policy of Wilson*, pp. 208-9.
[9] Root, *Addresses on International Subjects*, pp. 231; 269-77; 299-302.
[10] Jessup, *Elihu Root*, II, 262-3.
[11] Grey of Fallodon, *Twenty-Five Years*, II, 97.

But this does not end the matter for there were other important implications for the Caribbean area. In his message to Congress of March 5, 1914, Wilson said: " I ask this of you in support of the foreign policy of the administration. I shall not know how to deal with other matters of even greater delicacy and nearer consequence if you do not grant it to me in ungrudging measure." [12] This, of course, was the well-known " pig in a poke " request of the President. Was it a mere vague reference suggesting deep and dark secrets too important to be referred to the Congress?

A few days later, in an interview with newspaper correspondents Wilson indicated that the expression referred to the very important good will that he was trying to build up with the Latin American nations and to the fact that he wanted their absolute confidence in United States observance of treaty obligations.[13] But this does not fully explain the matter for it is known that there were other matters involved. The British capitalist Weetman Pearson, first Lord Cowdray, had been very active in the Tehuantepec Railway and other important capitalistic enterprises in Mexico.[14] Also he had secured extensive concessions from Costa Rica, directly south of the San Juan River through which it was proposed that a Nicaraguan Canal be constructed. And it should be remembered that there was a suggestion that British capital might undertake a Nicaraguan Canal if the tolls issue was decided adversely to British interests.[15] In addition this same company was

[12] Robinson and West, p. 209.   [13] Baker, IV, 410, note.
[14] J. A. Spender, *Weetman Pearson, First Viscount Cowdray, 1856-1927* (London, etc., 1930).
[15] Notter, p. 252.

negotiating for the right to locate 10,000 square kilometers of oil lands wherever it wished on the national lands of the Republic of Colombia. This meant the Pearson syndicate could exploit oil fields in Colombia but perhaps even more significantly " would have received the necessary rights for building railways, docks, quays, and canals, installing telegraph and telephone systems, and everything necessary for the exploitation of the oil deposits." [16] And in Colombia there was still the Atrato canal route just south of the Isthmus of Panama. Was this a contract which would permit the construction of a rival canal, while the Costa Rican contract forestalled the United States in the Nicaraguan field, and while the same syndicate caused still more trouble by actively supporting Huerta in Mexico because of its financial interest in that country? [17]

This was the very kind of thing Wilson hated and which called forth what is meant by his " practical " diplomacy. Pearson's biographer does not hesitate to say that the State Department brought heavy pressure to bear on Colombia, using the arguments of the advantages of a proposed concession to the General Asphalt Company of New York instead of to the Pearson interests and also of the need for harmony so as to complete the negotiation of a new treaty to bury the Panama issue. Pearson's comment was:

the American Government did not scruple to bring diplomatic pressure to bear upon Colombia to such an extent as to prevent the Colombian Government ratifying the contract it had made with us for the exploration of oil in that country.

[16] J. Fred Rippy, *The United States and Colombian Oil* (Foreign Policy Association Information Service, Vol. V, No. 2) (New York, 1929), p. 23.

[17] Gwynn, II, 192-3; also Spender, *op. cit.*, pp. 189-90.

They have brought similar pressure to bear on two other American countries in which we were prospectively interested.[18]

In Britain, Page was convinced that the Dollar Diplomacy of the British had been overreaching Taft [19] and that Wilson was coming to the rescue of the New World.[20] Be that as it may, simultaneously with the repeal of the tolls act Mr. Pearson was notified that the British Government felt it would be advisable for him to withdraw his extensive New World plans. Page gleefully wrote: " they pulled Cowdray out of Colombia and Costa Rica—granting the application of the Monroe Doctrine to concessions that might imperil a country's autonomy." [21] Probably the British retained their misgivings as to the advisability of changing the rules of the good old game of concession hunting and doubted if the idealism of the Washington Government would work but just the same Wilson's stand was obviously honest and his facing of unpopularity on behalf of the tolls issue was really appreciated.[22] As a plain and simple bargain it meant profits to British ship-

[18] Spender, p. 210.

The two other countries referred to were apparently Costa Rica and Ecuador where Pearson also had contracts pending. The latter, it was felt in the United States, was likely to be used as a base of operations for the construction of a proposed canal through the northern part of Colombia so that its western terminus would be just to the north of the Ecuadorian concession. It is interesting to note further that Richard Lloyd George, son of the British Chancellor of the Exchequer was in Costa Rica with a group trying to secure what purported to be a petroleum concession. (*Foreign Relations*, 1919, I, 865.)

[19] Hendrick, *Life and Letters of Page*, III, 112.

[20] Page to House, November 26, 1913, SL., House MS.

[21] Hendrick, I, 251.

[22] Trevelyan, *Grey of Fallodon*, pp. 236-7.

owners in return for surrender of the last serious challenge from financial interests to United States dominance of the trans-isthmian traffic.[23]

Relations of the United States with Colombia have been the subject of so much debate and of so many monographs that the subject can be quickly disposed of. In July, 1913, the Department of State informed Bogotá that it preferred direct negotiations to the Colombian proposal of arbitration as a means to end the pending complications.[24] It soon developed that Colombia desired a direct apology, the payment of $50,000,000 as damages and the right of its vessels to use the canal toll free. After numerous exchanges of opinion the treaty was completed by April 6, 1914, and a couple of months later was approved by the Colombian Congress.[25] This provided that the Government of the United States in its own name and in the name of the people of the country expressed its " sincere regret that anything should have occurred to interrupt or to mar the relations of cordial friendship that had so long subsisted between the two nations." It further provided that Colombian government vessels might use the canal toll free and that the United States would pay the Southern Republic $25,000,000.

Theodore Roosevelt raged:

Either there is or there is not warrant for paying this enormous sum and for making the apology. If there is no

[23] The Hamburg-Colombian Banana Company may have had similar ambitions for it apparently had wealthy backing and a generous concession but the plans were less developed and were dropped with the German collapse during the First World War (Thompson, U. S. Minister in Colombia, to Wilson, February 2, 1916, *The Lansing Papers*, II, 514-5).

[24] Bryan to Minister of Colombia, July 18, 1913, *Foreign Relations*, 1913, p. 316.

[25] *Ibid.*, 1913 and 1914, numerous; Baker, IV, 427-8.

warrant for it—and of course not the slightest vestige of warrant exists—then the payment is simply the payment of belated blackmail.[26]

Bryan appeared before the Senate Committee on Foreign Relations and urged the acceptance of the Treaty explaining that even from the standpoint of those who denounced the conduct of Colombia as being entirely wrong the payment was a simple matter of a fair adjustment of values after due consideration when the United States had exercised the right of international eminent domain on behalf of the World's commerce. In other words, that Colombia had refused to sell its property at a reasonable valuation, the United States had taken the property and was now making this payment to settle the matter after proper investigation.[27] But all efforts to secure prompt approval were in vain: it was one thing to be noble and reverse an act of Congress on canal tolls at the desire of the proud British Empire; it was quite another matter to " eat crow " and apologize to Colombia. Also, too much nobility was becoming monotonous. As the complications of the European War developed it became more and more easy to ignore the pleadings of the administration for action and the matter lapsed until the post-war period when that mechanical and international lubricant—and abrasive—, petroleum, could bring its influence to bear on senatorial mental processes.

The sincere efforts of the administration on behalf of the treaty had a good influence on the relations of the two countries but popular opinion in Colombia continued bitter and criticism of the United States was frequent throughout

[26] Roosevelt, *Fear God and Take Your Own Part,* p. 340. See also Baker, IV, 428.

[27] Latané, *The United States and Latin America,* pp. 275-6.

the war period, especially when it was realized that the Senate had indefinitely postponed the treaty. However, the attitude of the Government of Colombia was characterized by "tact, circumspection and dignity." [28] As early as November, 1914, the United States Chargé d'affaires reported that the Minister of Foreign Relations at Bogotá had taken very kindly the protest of the British and French Governments at lack of Colombian neutrality when conveyed through himself, and continued:

. . . Dr. Suarez expressed his own and his Government's endorsement of the principle that the United States, as leader among the republics of America, was called upon to use her moral influence with her sister republics in just such cases as this, an attitude which I regret to say is not often reflected in the expressions of public men or encountered in the press of Colombia.[29]

Trade likewise benefitted as may be seen from the fact that total investments of the United States in Colombia in 1913 were probably about $3,000,000 but by 1920 they were ten times that amount.[30] This was almost as substantial an increase as was to be noted in the neighboring country of Venezuela where investments of $3,000,000 in 1912 had risen to $40,000,000 by 1920.[31]

In Central America there was another outstanding demonstration of the "practical" side of the Wilson-Bryan administration, in the negotiation of the Bryan-Chamorro Treaty. It will be remembered that Knox had tried through-

[28] Martin, *Latin America and the War*, pp. 428 ff.; 431.

[29] Harrison to Secretary of State, November 27, 1914, *Foreign Relations*, 1914, supplement, p. 700.

[30] Rippy, *Capitalists and Colombia*, p. 152.

[31] James C. Malin, *The U. S. after the World War* (Boston, etc., 1930), p. 406.

out his term as Secretary of State to get something done but his negotiated treaty had failed to secure senatorial approval. When Bryan assumed office Nicaraguan finances had reached crisis conditions. Quite naturally the bankers were refusing to advance more money until they knew the attitude of the new Administration.[32]

Negotiations were opened promptly, or it would be more accurate to say were continued, for Nicaragua had proposed the preceding December that it sell the United States the right to construct a canal across the country and to establish a naval base with a 99 year lease on a site in the Gulf of Fonseca and on the Corn Islands. This was taken as the basis of consideration and to it was added the Platt Amendment idea providing the right of intervention to guarantee independence and property rights. On June 16th Bryan sent the President a copy of a treaty recently drawn by Judge Douglas as attorney for Nicaragua saying: " He [Douglas] has embodied in this treaty the Platt Amendment. Extracts from the Platt Amendment are in red." Bryan also stated that Senator Bacon thought the Senate might be willing to accept the Platt Amendment idea but that he had not had time to make a poll of the Senate.[33] On the 19th the President responded " The proposed Nicaraguan treaty has my entire approval and I sincerely hope that the Senate may approve it, as well as our friends, the Nicaraguan Government. I have read it very carefully." [34]

By the end of July Bryan confessed to the President that " We have struck a snag " in the opposition of a determined

[32] Baker, IV, 435.
[33] Bryan to the President, June 16, 1913, LC., Wilson MS.
[34] Wilson to Bryan, June 19, 1913, *ibid.*

minority of the Committee on Foreign Relations to the Platt Amendment proposal. The Secretary suggested two treaties, one to provide for the leases and the other to provide the protectorate feature with a guarantee of the finances of the country through the extension of the credit of the United States.[35] This was his old pet scheme. The New York *Times*, knowing only of the actual treaty as proposed remarked that it made the earlier Dollar Diplomacy " more nearly resemble ten-cent diplomacy." [36] What would have been that paper's reaction had it actually known of the other proposals of the Secretary?

After the Senate Committee rejected the treaty early in August, and Wilson disapproved the idea of advancing United States credit as " novel and radical " when " so many matters of difficulty and delicacy are pending," Bryan followed the Knox policy and lent the aid of the State Department in securing private funds from prominent bankers for the unfortunate republic to the south.[37] He further suggested an active liaison officer (who had been a good Wilson Democrat in Ohio) between the Department and the bankers.[38] Wilson acquiesced. It was obvious that Bryan was largely responsible for the Nicaraguan program and Wilson simply exercised general guidance and an occasional veto over Bryan's frolicking in financial puddles.

Thus the Nicaraguan President was willing for a United

[35] Bryan to the President, July 31, 1913, and Bryan to the President, May 24, 1913, LC., Bryan MS.

[36] T. A. Bailey, " Interest in a Nicaraguan Canal," *Hisp. Amer. Hist. Rev.*, XVI, 4.

[37] Correspondence of the State Department and bankers in *Foreign Relations*, 1914, pp. 944 ff.; Notter, p. 256.

[38] Bryan to the President, November 11, 1913, LC., Bryan MS.

States protectorate,[39] Bryan favored it thinking it of advantage to both countries,[40] and Wilson agreed [41] so by August 5th the Bryan-Chamorro Treaty was negotiated. The Senate opened hearings on the question and possibly some little influence was exercised by the fact that General Emiliano Chamorro testified that Germany was willing to pay more than the $3,000,000 offered in the treaty for the monopoly on the canal route.[42] The full protectorate idea was dropped but the other provisions remained essentially unchanged. Still the Senate was not too pleased and good Republicans were now inclined to question rather sharply whether the existing government of Nicaragua actually represented the people of that country. Root raised the question but supported the treaty; Borah was vigorous in his opposition and protests from Central American countries who felt their interests endangered were presented both directly and indirectly.[43] Wilson used his personal influence to try to secure a prompt approval [44] but failed to do so and in February, 1915, Bryan even suggested calling a special session of Congress to secure endorsement of the Colombian and Nicaraguan treaties.[45] Finally, a year later, February 18,

[39] Minister of Nicaragua to the Secretary of State, February 12, 1914, *Foreign Relations*, 1914, pp. 953-4.

[40] Bryan to the President, June 12, 1914, LC., Bryan MS.

[41] Baker, IV, 94-5.

[42] T. A. Bailey, *op. cit.*, pp. 4-5.

[43] Bryan to the President, January 12, 1915, LC., Bryan MS; Aro Sanso, *Policarpo Bonilla; algunos apuntes biográficos* (México, 1936), pp. 397-8; *The U. S. and the Nicaraguan Canal* (F. P. A. Information Service, Vol. IV, No. 6) (New York, 1926), p. 123; Anna I. Powell, " Relations between the U. S. and Nicaragua," *Hisp. Amer. Hist. Rev.*, VIII, 58-60.

[44] Bryan to the President, September 31, 1914, and Wilson to Bryan, October 1, 1914, LC., Bryan MS.

[45] Bryan to the President, February 23, 1915, *ibid.*

1916, Senate approval was granted with the proviso that it was "to be expressed as a part of the instrument of ratification, that nothing in said Convention is intended to affect any existing right of any of the said named States " of Costa Rica, El Salvador and Honduras which had presented protests.[46] Early in April the Nicaraguan Congress signified its approval with only one protestant in the Senate and eight out of thirty-seven in the House.[47]

It had long since become clear that the treaty in spite of the exception made by the United States Senate was greatly feared by the neighbors of Nicaragua. Costa Rica, the country immediately to the South, felt that the use of the boundary stream, the San Juan River, for a part of its course for canal purposes was an infringement of its rights since Nicaragua was securing the cash consideration when some of Costa Rica's joint rights were involved. The establishment of a protectorate, and all three neighboring states felt that was the fact in spite of the changed wording of the agreement, was considered a grave menace. Also, the grant of the right to the United States to construct a naval base in Fonseca Bay was vigorously protested by the two northern countries since both felt that they had interests in a bay on which they had outlets. A naval station placed on a Nicaraguan island in the bay would command the only transcontinental railroad of Honduras and would likewise control lesser ports and territories of El Salvador.[48]

[46] For treaty terms and proviso see *Foreign Relations,* 1916, pp. 849-52.

[47] *Ibid.,* pp. 832; 834.

[48] It must have been slightly confusing to Central Americans, to say the least, to hear of the ratification of this treaty simultaneously with the support of the Bryan Peace Treaties then being urged. (*Foreign Relations,* 1916, pp. 955-6.)

Efforts to reassure these countries had little effect, even when it was proposed to purchase an option on the Costa Rican interest in the canal route, and on a proposed naval base in its waters.[49] When they suggested $2,000,000 as a fair consideration for the option Bryan talked of $1,250,-000 [50] and then tried to reassure El Salvador by proving his " impartiality " and proposing to lease naval bases from them also.[51] When the small child is afraid of a dog just surround him with a quantity of bounding puppies: he may laugh and be pleased with their antics—or he may go into hysterics. As early as September, 1913, Washington was aware of the danger of Central American fears of a United States protectorate and tried to reassure the small republics. All efforts to prevent protest meetings of their representatives, however, had little effect,[52] and the neighboring countries insisted on presenting their case to the Central American Peace Court.

In arguing its case Nicaragua pointed out that it was acting entirely within its rights as a sovereign nation; that Costa Rican interests were protected by a special provision in the treaty, and that the Fonseca Bay lease was legal because of the sovereign rights of Nicaragua in that Bay and by the precedent of international usage as to open seas (El Salvador and Honduras protested that the Bay was a closed sea). Finally it pointed to the damaging fact that every one of the other four Central American states had

[49] Extensive correspondence found in *Foreign Relations,* 1914-16.

[50] Bryan to the President, March 11, 1915, LC., Bryan MS.

[51] *Foreign Relations,* 1915, pp. 1105; 1115-7.

[52] Bryan to the President, September 23, 1913, and Wilson to Bryan, September 25, 1913, LC., Bryan MS; Bryan to American Minister to El Salvador, September 26, 1913, *Foreign Relations,* 1913, p. 1026.

offered naval bases to the United States or had asked for direct annexation.[53]

Wilson took no part in the controversy though Secretary of State Lansing insisted that the Peace Court had no jurisdiction over a question involving the United States.[54] Unfortunately for the Court some of its earlier decisions had been open to the charge that it was subject to political influence. In this case its action was prompt and on September 30, 1916, it declared that the treaty violated Costa Rican rights as guaranteed by an early boundary treaty of 1858, by the Central American Treaty of Peace and Friendship of 1907, and by the Cleveland Award of 1888 which provided: " The Republic of Nicaragua is obligated not to make concessions for purposes of a canal across its territory without first asking the opinion of the Republic of Costa Rica." The Court declined to declare formally that the Treaty was void but by implication it clearly did so.[55]

Thus matters remained, for all attention was soon focused on the European catastrophe. At such a time it was out of the question for the United States to give up any potential naval bases so the treaty was considered to be in effect and applied between the two countries most concerned. The original ten year term of the Peace Court was drawing to a close so the once great hope for Central American union was allowed to expire quietly now that it had offended its chief sponsor to the point where that sponsor refused to advise its continuance.

As for general relations between the United States and

[53] Weitzel, *American Policy in Nicaragua,* p. 25.

[54] Notter, p. 497.

[55] For the award of the Court see *Foreign Relations,* 1916, p. 886.

Nicaragua they proceeded along familiar lines. Careful supervision was exercised over the expenditure of the $3,000,000 paid in accordance with the treaty, even though the Nicaraguans felt that undue consideration was given to foreign claims in the process.[56] When the election of 1916 approached the Liberals asked that Washington supervise the elections. This was not done for a free election would in all probability have resulted in the choice of a man who would have opposed the financial program of the United States bankers. Emiliano Chamorro was one of the Conservative candidates and he quite frankly asked Bryan for his public support in the election.[57] The United States Minister used his influence and the less well known Conservative Dr. Carlos Cuadra Pasos opportunely withdrew in favor of Chamorro while the Liberal Dr. Julian Irías was not allowed to enter the country to conduct his campaign since he had been a former associate of the dictator Zelaya of evil fame. With the Conservative factions consolidated and the Liberals without a candidate the result was the election of Chamorro.[58]

The actual supervision exercised by the State Department was beyond question. On July 26th President Díaz of Nicaragua vigorously protested Minister Jefferson's active support of Chamorro.[59] One week later J. B. Wright of the Division of Latin American Affairs wrote that Jefferson

[56] State Department, *The U. S. and Nicaragua,* pp. 33 ff.; *Foreign Relations,* 1916, p. 909; *ibid.,* 1917, pp. 1116-7; 1134.

[57] Chamorro to Bryan, April 12, 1916, LC., Bryan MS.

[58] State Department, *op. cit.,* pp. 32-3; Munro, *Five Republics of Central America,* pp. 251-2; Cox, *Nicaragua and the U. S.,* pp. 721-2.

[59] Translation found in Polk to Lansing, August 3, 1916, LC., Lansing MS.

had been instructed: 1st, that no recurrence of Zelayaism could expect to receive the approval of the United States [this spelled the doom of Irías' candidacy]; and, that " With this exception, this Government remains neutral as between parties "; and 3rd, that it seemed desirable for all branches of the Conservative party to unite on one candidate [Cuadra Pasos to be persuaded to resign].[60] On the 28th of July J. B. W. [right] had made a memorandum of the fact that Jefferson's choice of Chamorro evidently was the result of his careful appraisal of the situation and that Chamorro was the most popular candidate of the party. The final sentence of the memo stated " In his [Minister Jefferson's] recommendations this Department will concur " [61]—and this statement was textually telegraphed to Jefferson the same day. Wright's last recommendation on August 2nd was:

Unless we are going to throw " finesse " to the winds and dictate a candidate (which I heartily wish we might do), I see no more correct or efficacious way of uniting the Conservative Party which, under Mr. Jefferson's tactful guidance in which I have great confidence, ought to result in the selection of Chamorro.[62]

The finances of the country steadily improved and a measure of peace and prosperity was enjoyed by the people.[63] True, the financial agreements insisted on by United States bankers were somewhat severe but it cannot be forgotten that the financial background of the country was of the worst possible type, and investments there had

[60] Wright to Polk, August 2, 1916, inclosed with Polk to Lansing, *ibid.*

[61] Inclosed with Polk to Lansing, *ibid.*

[62] Wright to Polk, August 2, 1916, inclosed with Polk to Lansing, *ibid.*

[63] Weitzel, p. 32; Cox, p. 738.

long since been considered little better than a gambling proposition. Some might protest that the high ideals expressed in the Mobile Address had gone astray and that the administration had contradicted itself. But there still remains the uncomfortable question as to what could have been done as an alternative. The United States refused to intervene actively (both Democrats and Republicans agreed on this). European nations after 1914 were not in a position to intervene and the United States would not have permitted it if one of those countries had showed an inclination to do so. Yet if Washington did not see that money was advanced European creditors were ready to take a hand as was shown in the case of Guatemala in 1913 [64] and that was not to be considered in view of the Lord Cowdray complications already on hand from just such investments. So what? Secure the best treaty possible and see that the money was provided. Clearly, this was no longer abstract theories and principles but old-fashioned practical diplomacy.

So far as Panama was concerned there were no significant changes as the United States maintained steady supervision. Friction over conduct of Panama police in arresting residents of the Canal Zone brought about a long correspondence and the final disarming of the force of its rifles.[65] This meant that banditry or any serious disorders at any point of the sovereign state would have to be suppressed by troops from the Canal Zone. Control over wireless stations was still insisted on by the United States [66] as well as active super-

[64] Notter, p. 246.

[65] Extensive correspondence found in *Foreign Relations*, 1915 and 1916; Munro, *U. S. and Caribbean Area*, pp. 97-8; McCain, *U. S. and Panama*, pp. 84-5.

[66] *Foreign Relations*, 1914, pp. 1036-52; *British and Foreign State Papers*, CVIII, pt. 2, pp. 834-5.

vision of railway construction.[67]   At last the long standing
boundary dispute with Costa Rica was submitted to Chief
Justice White of the United States Supreme Court for an
arbitral decision which was rendered September 12, 1914,
but was immediately protested by Panama as unfair.[68]   Wilson favored United States insistence on Panama accepting
the award [69] and Bryan urged this but the matter hung
fire until Hughes and Harding took a similar stand and
virtually forced acceptance.

In foreign affairs the United States still continued to
represent the interests of the Canal Republic when it had no
consular agents accredited in any given place.[70]   Likewise
when the interests of any foreign country were threatened
in Panama the natural thing was to protest to Washington.
Thus when a specially stringent restrictive act on Chinese
migration was proposed, China asked United States inter-
cession. The law was not enacted.[71]

With Costa Rica other irritations arose in addition to
those over the right of way for a canal. In December, 1914,
a " formal emphatic request " was sent from Washington
that trouble makers feared in Nicaragua, including Irías
and one of the Zelayas, should be forced to leave the
country. The response was a " very respectful " but emphatic statement that the " Government is not able to accede

[67] Foreign Relations, 1914, pp. 1028-36; ibid., 1917, pp. 1179-
1204; McCain, p. 162.

[68] Price to Secretary of State, October 1, 1914, Foreign Relations, 1914, p. 994; also McCain, pp. 135-6.

[69] Wilson to Bryan, March 24, 1915, LC., Bryan MS; Bryan
to Price, April 28, 1915, Foreign Relations, 1915, pp. 1147.

[70] Notice to consular offices and agents, January 21, 1916, Foreign Relations, 1916, p. 1.

[71] Ibid., 1915, pp. 1262-74.

to your demand." Bryan wisely side-stepped the issue by denying that a demand had been sent and saying the statement was " merely . . . information . . . transmitted by us in a spirit of friendship and amity in the interest of peace and order in Central America. Having done this our responsibility ends." [72] Meanwhile the " cooling off " treaty had been signed in February, 1914, and proclaimed the following November,[73] but a feeling of coolness and suspicion was to be distinctly noted.

The feeling was echoed by El Salvador and was displayed at the Second Pan-American Scientific Congress held in Washington in 1915 when its delegate Dr. Alfonso Reyes Guerra stated that the four prerequisites of any real Pan-Americanism were: 1st, a declaration that the United States as well as Europe was prohibited the right of conquest under the Monroe Doctrine; 2nd, the adoption of the Drago principle that the collection of debts was an internal question within each nation; 3rd, the elimination of all exceptions to the doctrine of non-intervention, and 4th, the acceptance of obligatory arbitration as the method of settling all international disputes.[74]

All in all the first four years of the Wilson paternal despotism had left much confusion in the thinking of Central Americans. They heard the idealism of the Mobile Address but felt the application of the " practical " diplomacy. Not surprisingly disappointed hope resorted to such terms as hypocritical bunk to describe their conception of announcements from Washington.

[72] Hale to Secretary of State, December 24, 1914, and Bryan to Hale, December 29, 1914, *ibid.*, 1914, pp. 182; 184.

[73] *Ibid.*, 1914, pp. 171-3.

[74] S. G. Inman in Blakeslee, *Mexico and the Caribbean,* pp. 267-8.

As for the island republics Wilson does not seem to have had too clear an idea of a policy when he first entered the White House—and no more did Bryan. It was just the misfortune of those small republics that conditions were not especially critical so that major attention was focused on Mexico and other points while the unpredictable Secretary of State was left to evolve a program. Unfortunately he was expected to launch it through agents selected from a party with no colonial experience and whose recent proud boast was that they were anti-imperialists. Now the administrators who had grown up with the new empire were displaced and Bryan with his obsession of party organization based on patronage was to confound the existing confusion by securing places for existing party leaders wanting jobs rather than administrators for existing colonial vacancies.

The first island republic to require attention was Santo Domingo. There the Knox administration had barely been able to finish out its term with the maintenance of a semblance of peace. As late as the fall of 1912 a revolt required the landing of 750 marines and things were barely quieted down by the following February. In any sense of the word Santo Domingo was unfinished business in March, 1913.[75] That the new Secretary of State was far from realizing the seriousness of the situation is evidenced by his much publicised letter asking what positions were available there for " deserving " Democrats.[76] Welles comments:

Secretary Bryan, while emotionally responsive to the idealism of the theories enunciated by President Wilson, was incapable of grasping intellectually the manner in which those theories might be transmuted into the daily

[75] Pringle, *Life and Times of Taft*, II, 696-7.
[76] Knight, *Americans in Santo Domingo*, p. 53.

routine of his Department. It was notorious that the great majority of the diplomatic appointees sent by the Wilson Administration to Latin America possessed no qualification for their task other than that of loyalty to the Democratic party. But nowhere . . . was this ineptitude in the selection of agents to carry out the Wilson policy more lamentably demonstrated than in the appointments made to the Dominican Republic.[77]

The two most important appointees were the Minister, James M. Sullivan, a New York politician with a somewhat shady background but with strong political supporters including banking interests with Dominican connections; and Mr. Walter W. Vick as Receiver General of Customs, who had been manager of the New York headquarters of the Democratic Party in the 1912 campaign.[78] Unfortunate conditions forthwith developed and the men lost the respect of the Dominicans and their availability for use even in the eyes of their own party leaders. They were replaced months later when the world was in turmoil and inestimable damage had been done.[79]

Vick's early impressions of his job were quite pleasing though he naively confessed his complete ignorance of the

[77] Welles, *Naboth's Vineyard,* II, 717.

[78] *Ibid.,* II, 718; Baker, II, 450.

[79] Quantities of correspondence in connection with these two men are to be found in the Wilson, Bryan and House manuscripts. The amount is large and the personalities so bitter that no effort is made here to summarize the matter for it would lead the story astray from its real purpose. Incompetence was apparently present as well as unwise personal conduct in some cases. As usual, more serious charges were bruited about by Dame Rumor and all too gladly believed by some. Apparently, the charges against Vick were of a more personal nature and many felt that an essentially innocent man had been unduly maligned; but those against Sullivan related to his official connections also.

people with whom he was to deal in the statement that
" Latin-American character seems entirely unable to grasp
the meaning of the word ' economy ' and resents—rather
than appreciates—honest, business administration." [80]   By
April 14th of the next year the two men were at cross purposes and Vick was writing Bryan, at the suggestion of
the latter, professing the " kindest and most friendly feeling for the American Minister " but listing eight charges or
incidents indicating irregular financial connections or dealings of the Minister.[81]   Vick also reported to the Secretary
of War, the Bureau of Insular Affairs, and the Private
Secretary of the President,[82] so it is not surprising that his
own record was searched and soon the pressure was so
great that a man without experience and in a strange position was to resign feeling greatly aggrieved.[83]   In truth,
the fault would seem to have been in his ever having been
sent to the place.

As to what the policy for Santo Domingo was to be, no
one seemed to know.   The agents sent there were just
supposed to " handle " things.   Being poorly chosen in the
first place and inexperienced in the second, they usually
played the opportunist, met the issues that arose and hoped
that later ones would not involve them in hopeless contra-
dictions.   The result was chaos and final military intervention that contradicted the principles of the administration

[80] Vick to House, August 25, 1913, SL., House MS.
[81] Vick to Bryan, April 14, 1914, LC., Bryan MS. A copy is also
in the House MS.
[82] Vick to House, May 7, 1914, SL., House MS.
[83] Vick to House, July 5, 1914, and April 22, 1915, and other
dates, SL., House MS; Vick to Leaders of Democratic Party,
February 22, 1915, autographed copy in LC., Bryan MS.

and left a train of bitterness in the island republic and of fear throughout the Caribbean.[84]

As the local elections approached in the fall of 1913 there was a threat of a revolution, whereupon United States warships arrived and a stern warning was sent to the effect that any activities leading to a forcible change of administrations would not be recognized by Washington.[85] In spite of the protest of the Dominican Minister at Washington thirty-three agents were dispatched from the United States and Puerto Rico to supervise the elections.[86]

But even so matters did not go well. There was constant pressure on the State Department to authorize the use of moneys for other purposes than those for which they were designated. Bryan querulously wrote that he was unable to decide if the trouble was ignorance, inability to resist importunities, or plain graft.[87] At its wits' end over political complications which steadily became worse, the Department ordered increasing management of local affairs. These included interference with court procedure in handling and punishing political prisoners, increasing supervision of the collection and disbursement of daily revenues [88] (including both internal revenues and customs collections on imports), as well as approval of appointments and dismissals of employees of the department of Public Works. Further, the State Department suggested that the Dominican police force or constabulary might well be organized with the assistance of the United States.

[84] Welles, *op. cit.*, II, 921-2.

[85] *Foreign Relations,* 1913, pp. 420 ff.

[86] *Ibid.,* 1913, cir. 446; Wriston, *Executive Agents in Foreign Relations,* pp. 801-2; Notter, p. 279.

[87] Baker, IV, 446.   [88] Welles, II, 725 ff.

By the end of March, 1914, rebellion started in spite of repeated warnings that such conduct would be disapproved. The contestants were then notified that a bombardment of Puerto Plata would be answered by United States naval vessels present.   After some days a " careful " bombardment was begun by the Dominican forces but twelve four-inch shells from the U. S. S. *Machias* resulted in a resumption of silence as the Dominican Government gave up the effort to wrest one of its own ports from rebel control.[90] By the end of July the United States determined that all hostilities should cease, the President resign, and a fair and free election be held under the supervision of a United States commission.[91]

Clearly, this intervention was far more specific than the Mexican program.   South of the Río Grande, the United States was to supervise while they " shot themselves into Democracy," to change Page's expression slightly, but in Santo Domingo it appeared that if any shooting was to be done it was more than likely that Uncle Sam would be found holding the gun.   However it should be noted that still the objective was ultimate democracy and not permanent Yankee control.

By this time the Democrats were firmly stuck to the Dominican tar-baby.   In March, 1915, the Sullivan question had reached a critical stage and demanded action,[92]   so

[69] *Foreign Relations,* 1914, pp. 193 ff.; Welles, II, 748-52.

[90] Offutt, *Protection of Citizens Abroad,* pp. 123-4; J. R. C., *Right to Protect Citizens,* p. 109.

[91] Munro, *U. S. and the Caribbean Area,* pp. 117-8; Notter, 310-1.

[92] Bryan to the President, March 10, 1915, and April 2, 1915, and Wilson to Bryan, March 10, 1915, and April 3, 1915, LC., Bryan MS.

Minister William D. Russell was soon appointed to fill the place. Difficulties continued especially over the financial supervision of the United States and the local President found himself in the impossible position of trying to reconcile the demands of Washington and the position of his own Congress which effectively rejected practically all United States demands.[93] No rebellion was tolerated but the President, the power behind the throne, and the Congress representing the people were involved in hopeless confusion.[94]

Whether true or not, many Dominicans felt that Lansing took a sterner position than did Bryan.[95] This would be in keeping with his background and training for his friends would frankly admit that he probably felt the whole situation was hopeless and the best thing to do was to intervene promptly, clean up the mess and get it over with. Thus on November 19, 1915, Minister Russell presented a set of demands to Santo Domingo which included the immediate appointment of a financial adviser to the Republic with ample powers over customs and internal revenues; the elimination of the old army and police force and the substitution of a constabulary under a commanding officer to be selected by the President of the United States and assisted by such other United States officers as he might desire. These demands the Dominican Government refused on the grounds that they were unnecessary and constituted " an abdication of the national sovereignty." [96] Russell reported:

---

[93] *Foreign Relations,* 1915, pp. 306 ff.

[94] Bryan to Sullivan, January 12, 1915, and February 2, 1915; Sullivan to State Department, February 8, 1915, *ibid.,* pp. 279-82.

[95] *Hearings on Senate Resolution 112,* II, 1095.

[96] Welles, II, 762.

The whole country had been flooded with exaggerated reports as to our demand and anti-American feeling ran high. . . . Patriotic meetings were held in the North and societies formed for the purpose of exciting the people to prepare themselves against the foreign invader.
. . . " down with the Yankees " was the slogan of the hour.[97]

The President honestly desired to reach an agreement with the United States but the ex-Secretary of War, Desiderio Arías, headed the opposition to foreign influence and became anathema to Washington as the Zelaya of Santo Domingo.[98] At all costs he was to be prevented from seizing the government. When he captured Santo Domingo City in May, 1916, marines were landed on the 14th and he was forced to retire.[99] Then to the chagrin of Washington, the Dominican Congress proceeded to select a friend of Arías as the head of a provisional government to be established. Instructions were promptly sent to the island that no selection of a candidate would be recognized even if sanctified by a general election unless the United States Minister had been assured by that candidate in advance that he would enact the measures demanded by Washington, and further that United States forces would remain in the country until the desired " reforms " were secured.[100] Additional marines were landed until some 1,800 were on shore where they undertook a systematic penetration into the interior to eliminate rebels. In this some seven marines

[97] Russell to Secretary of State, December 9, 1915, *Foreign Relations*, 1915, p. 332.
[98] Pratt, " Lansing " in Bemis, *Secretaries of State*, X, 119-21.
[99] *Foreign Relations*, 1916, cir. p. 222; Welles, II, 771-2.
[100] Lansing to Russell, August 26, 1916, *Foreign Relations*, 1916, p. 235; Welles, II, 786-7.

were killed, and sixteen wounded to an estimated one hundred killed and three hundred wounded for the rebels before Arías surrendered and his movement collapsed.[101]

By November all hope of securing acquiescence in the demands was abandoned and instructions were sent for full-fledged military occupation of the country and the proclamation of martial law. This was done by Captain H. S. Knapp on the 20th.[102] Beyond question President Wilson authorized the step with keen regret for it clearly violated his announced principles and would inevitably hamper his New World program. In a letter to Lansing he commented:

It is with the deepest reluctance that I approve and authorize the course here proposed, but I am convinced that it is the least of the evils in sight in this very perplexing situation. . . .
I have stricken out the sentences in the proposed proclamation which authorizes the commanding officer to remove judges and others in certain circumstances. It may be necessary to resort to such extreme measures, but I do not deem it wise to put so arbitrary an announcement in the proclamation itself.[103]

Welles comments that the President had probably not fully realized the seriousness of the Dominican situation up to this time since he had been absorbed in European complications.[104] In closing the discussion of the unhappy island, however, it might well be noted that it was just possible that the European situation had no little to do with

[101] Schoenrich, *Santo Domingo,* pp. 92-3.
[102] Proclamation of Occupation, November 29, 1916, *Foreign Relations,* 1916, pp. 246-7.
[103] Wilson to Secretary of State, November 26, 1916, *ibid.,* p. 242.
[104] Welles, II, 792.

the President's willingness to consent to the final drastic step that was taken. With the ever more widely ranging complications emanating from the European conflict the defense of the Canal and the control of all approaches thereto was of increasing importance—and certainly complete military dominance of the Dominican Republic, plus ownership of Puerto Rico, gave reasonably complete control over the waterway between the two islands.

In the country at large there was comparatively little interest in Dominican developments because of the impending crisis with Germany but so far as the people realized the contradiction between announced policies and practices they were inclined to agree with the idea that the situation was anomalous but justifiable and was based on plain common sense.[105] Opposition politicians could knowingly wink their eyes at each other in gleeful recognition of good or bad campaign material for the future, but unfortunately for them the national election was just over.

Another difficult problem developed in the eastern half of the same island, in the Negro republic of Haiti. By good or bad fortune the little nation of about 2,500,000 people [106] was directly to the East of Cuba and so was in a position to be of vital importance in the control of another important trade route leading to and from the Canal. The background of the history of the country included the incredible as the ordinary, the romantic and sordid as the usual, and a child-like confidence, simplicity and ignorance of world affairs as the stuff out of which a primitive people

[105] Philip Marshall Brown, "Armed Occupation of Santo Domingo," *Amer. Jour. of Int. Law*, II, 397 ff.

[106] For a good descriptive statement see Arthur C. Millspaugh, *Haiti under American Control*, 1915-1930 (Boston, 1931), cir. p. 13.

were weaving a local history in a region that was one of strategic importance to major world powers. Now in wonder, surprise and indignation they found they were no longer to be allowed to play at king-making for themselves but were suddenly expected to settle down to work as individuals and to a systematic role in world affairs as a nation. Buell comments:

The case of Haiti seems to be the only one in modern history in which a Negro population, previously subjected to a slave system marked by terrorism and brutality, has suddenly been obliged to organize a government and an economic system of its own. In view of this historic background, it is perhaps remarkable not only that the Haitian peasant should possess the qualities of gentleness, charm and hospitality so frequently attributed to him, but also that the Haitian people should have been able to maintain an independent existence for a hundred years—i. e., until 1915.[107]

After a century of independence from seventy-five to ninety-eight per cent of the people were illiterate. In the twenty years following the election of 1886 no president had served out a full term. One did serve nearly seven years and died in office but of the rest four were killed in office and five were overthrown.[108] Such government as existed was dictatorial in fact while the finances of the republic were a gambling proposition and speculation and graft were expected as a matter of course.[109] Most of the financing had been carried on through French banks, though, as already seen,[110] United States interests had

[107] Buell, *American Occupation of Haiti*, p. 328.

[108] Davis to Secretary of State, January 12, 1916, *Foreign Relations*, 1916, p. 311.

[109] Buell, p. 328; Millspaugh, *op. cit.*, pp. 17-8.

[110] *Supra* pp. 277 ff.

secured a share while Mr. Knox was Secretary of State. Incidentally, it should be noted that up to the time of the United States intervention, in spite of graft and irregularity the interest on foreign loans had been kept up faithfully though payments on several of the sinking funds were in arrears.[111]

Again Washington had no particular program in mind but world conditions forced action. Wilson really wanted all peoples to work out their own destiny but he was never blind to the strategic location of the island with regard to United States interests. As early as June 23, 1913, he wrote to Bryan concerning details of a lease to the Môle St. Nicholas.[112] The objectives were two-fold: to forestall Germany and other European powers by taking this choice naval base " out of the market," and to strengthen the Haitian Government so as to discourage and suppress revolution.[113] An agreement ensued by which it was agreed that " no power other than the United States should gain a foothold in that section of the Republic." However, the president who made the agreement was overthrown in January, 1914, so Bryan telegraphed the next month to his minister in Haiti stating that the United States wished the understanding to " remain undisturbed " though he was to assure the authorities that " this Government has, for the present, no intention of entering into negotiations regarding Môle Saint Nicholas." [114]

---

[111] Buell, pp. 332-3; see also Carl Kelsey, "American Intervention in Haiti and the Dominican Republic," *The Annals,* C, 155-6 (This is a report of exceptional value.)

[112] LC., Bryan MS.

[113] Baker, VI, 87.

[114] Bryan to Smith, February 26, 1914, *Foreign Relations,* 1914, p. 340.

Again the clamor of the expansionists was loud. Rear-Admiral Colby N. Chester referred to Haiti as " practically part of the shore line of our republic," insisted that it controlled one of the " avenues of our greatest routes of commerce " and complained that it was " in control of a government continuously engaged in internecine war, revolution and insurrection and sunk in religious and governmental degeneracy." Germany and other European governments were just awaiting an opportunity to take action and had only been deterred thus far by the Monroe Doctrine.[115] The implications of his summary were clear enough. And indeed there were those in high position who felt that only the outbreak of the European war prevented serious German action in 1914.[116] However, once the European contest had been joined further immediate danger was minimized.

Unfortunately the minister in Haiti had been sent on a temporary basis only so he felt unable to adopt a program of his own. To make matters worse " inactivity and lack of tact " still further reduced his usefulness.[117] In January, 1914, a revolution swept the country and the United States as well as Germany, Great Britain and France landed marines.[118] General Oreste Zamor quickly secured an unexpected quorum in the National Assembly and had himself elected president on February 8th. The United States Minister reported: " Zamor's elevation to the Presidency undoubtedly accomplished by revolutionary means." For-

[115] C. N. Chester, " Present Status of the Monroe Doctrine," *The Annals,* LIV, 36-7; 41.
[116] See Harold Palmer Davis, *Black Democracy* (New York, 1928), p. 312.
[117] Bryan to the President, January 21, 1914, LC., Bryan MS.
[118] Notter, p. 281; J. R. C., *op. cit.,* pp. 111-2.

eign governments as usual expressed a willingness to follow the lead of Washington and on March 1st Bryan telegraphed: " The Government formed by General Oreste Zamor, as constitutional President duly elected by the Haitian Congress, being now fully established in power with the assent of the people, you are instructed to recognize it." [119]

At first relations continued satisfactory. Bryan did not press the issue of the Môle St. Nicholas,[120] but when Haiti was suspected of aiding Dominican rebels in their activities a quite stern " cease and desist " notice was sent.[121] By July the matter of finances had to be considered for the national Bank of Haiti was anxious to have a customs' receivership established by the United States and was even reported as disposed to refuse to advance necessary funds for the running expenses of the government so as to force action on the question.[122] Incidentally, when the German Chargé d'Affaires at Washington suggested a joint foreign control of the customs he was informed this would be undesirable, " the United States having a policy not to permit even partial foreign control of the administration of any independent American state," though he was assured that any action taken would be disinterested and impartial.

[119] Smith to Bryan, February 8, 1914, and Bryan to Smith, March 1, 1914, *Foreign Relations,* 1914, pp. 337-8; 341.

[120] Bryan to the President, June 14, 1914, LC., Bryan MS.

[121] Bryan to Smith, June 18, 1914, *Foreign Relations,* 1914, pp. 238-9.

[122] Davis, *Black Democracy,* pp. 152-4; Millspaugh, pp. 27-8; Emily Greene Balch, editor, *Occupied Haiti, Being the report of . . . Americans, who . . . favor the restoration of the independence of the Negro Republic* (New York, 1927), pp. 15-7.

The French, to repeated inquiries,[123] received a similar answer, and thus a few more months passed.

By October the United States was anxious for a more permanent basis for its relations with the Black Republic and so urged a treaty to define the situation. But the Zamor government was already toppling. Some say that the pressure of the United States for a treaty leaked out and the reaction hastened the overthrow.[124] On the other hand it might be argued that such a treaty would have bolstered the administration. Regardless of theories, the fact was that the revolution made rapid headway and the President fled on the 29th. The same day the transport *Hancock* with 800 marines and the U. S. S. *Kansas* were ordered to Haitian waters.[125] The new leader was General Davilmar Theodore who went through the farce of being elected president.

This time Washington did not extend recognition as it had a few months previously but sent word that the new executive would be recognized as provisional president only when he agreed to send a commission to negotiate a treaty to deal with customs' control, the National Bank, the National Railway (a substantial part of whose stock was owned by the National City Bank, on which interest payments were in arrears because of disputes as to construction),[126] and the Môle Saint Nicholas, as well as a general

[123] Notter, p. 361; Bryan to Wilson, February 25, 1915, and Wilson to Secretary of State, February 26, 1915, *The Lansing Papers,* II, 465-6. See also Perkins, *Hands Off,* p. 263.

[124] Davis, p. 152.

[125] Lansing to Blanchard, October 29, 1914, *Foreign Relations,* 1914, p. 355.

[126] P. H. Douglas, "American Occupation of Haiti," *Pol. Sc. Quar.,* XLII, 382-5; Williams, *Economic Foreign Policy of U. S.,* pp. 30-1.

agreement by Haiti " to give full protection to all foreign interests." [127] This was supplemented on November 16th by a sixth provision to provide for settlement by arbitration of pending claims of United States citizens against Haiti. On December 4th Theodore was informed he would be granted " provisional " recognition on appointment of the commission with full powers, and " formal and complete recognition " only " after commission has signed satisfactory protocols." In the same communication Bryan added: " Report whether you consider additional United States naval forces desirable in Haitian waters at the present time." [128]

A discussion of these proposals brought violent denunciation of the United States in the Haitian Senate so the new executive stalled for time and tried to secure a modification of the terms.[129] Meanwhile the National Bank of Haiti was in touch with the State Department asking that $110,000 of its gold reserves be transferred to New York for safe-keeping. Three days later this was agreed to and orders issued for the shipment to be made on the *Machias*. However, word came from the Haitian bank that it could ship $500,000 gold so the larger sum was transferred by United States marines on board the vessel and dispatched to New York.[130] The Haitian Government pro-

[127] Bryan to Blanchard, November 12, 1914, *Foreign Relations,* 1914, p. 359.

It is interesting to note that the new Minister was Mr. Bailly-Blanchard, ex-Secretary of the United States Legation at Paris and a thorough French linguist. Kelsey, *op. cit.*, p. 135.

[128] Bryan to Blanchard, December 4, 1914, *Foreign Relations,* 1914, p. 364.

[129] Buell, *cir.* p. 338 gives a good chronological summary of events.

[130] For correspondence see *Foreign Relations,* 1914, pp. 365 ff.

tested this removal of about half of the Bank's reserves claiming that they were trust funds of the Government and could not be legally exported without that Government's consent. Bryan insisted that this was for the protection of the funds from revolutionary leaders and denied that this constituted " an arbitrary and offensive intervention which carries a flagrant invasion of the sovereignty and independence of the Republic of Haiti " as that Government had claimed.[131]

Meanwhile the United States demands were rejected and in January, 1915, a revolt against Theodore developed, with the President badly handicapped through a lack of the funds tied up by the Bank. By the end of the month it appeared that he would be overthrown partly because of the discontent of his one-time followers over his failure to distribute spoils. The leader of the new movement was one Vilbrun Gillaume Sam who entered Port au Prince the end of February and was " regularly and constitutionally " elected President on March 4th.[132] Bryan had already reached the conclusion that " there will be no peace and progress in Hayti until we have some such arrangement as we have in Santo Domingo." [133] Sam apparently was looked upon by Washington as the hope of his country for he is said to have received substantial encouragement in his advance to power.[134] However, his hold was precarious in the extreme and the opposition forthwith demanded spoils or his scalp. The Bank, financial interests and many of

[131] Bryan to Minister of Haiti, December 31, 1914, *ibid.*, p. 381.
[132] Blanchard to Secretary of State, March 4, 1915, *ibid.*, 1915, p. 467.
[133] Bryan to the President, January 7, 1915, LC., Bryan MS.
[134] Davis, p. 156.

the upper classes openly advocated intervention [135] as the best way to peace. By the end of March a French firm (suspected by Wilson at least of being backed by the French Government) [136] was suggesting a loan to Haiti and French and German interests were apparently acting together to force consideration and action by Washington, otherwise they wanted to act themselves.[137] Indeed the French landed marines and insisted that fighting should be prohibited in certain areas.[138] Yet all of this must be mentioned with the reservation in mind that France would have been exceedingly slow to antagonize the United States at such a time as this, even though it was doubtless glad to hasted action if it could.

United States financial interests put on more pressure by indicating that they were thinking of retiring from the island unless Washington gave them active support. In a long letter to the President on April 2nd Bryan stated that because foreign capitalists were controlling the Government of Haiti and because the Haitian officials were disturbing the peace of Santo Domingo by encouraging revolution he rather thought that action should be taken and that " this would be a better time than later." [139] But matters rocked along another month or so, for Wilson was apparently most unwilling further to violate his principles so long as he felt there was any possible chance of some other solution of the matter.

[135] *Ibid.*, p. 191; P. H. Douglas, *op. cit.*, pp. 236-8.

[136] Bryan to Wilson, March 25, 1915, and Wilson to Bryan, March 25, 1915, LC., Bryan MS.

[137] Bryan to Wilson, March 27, 1915, *ibid.*

[138] Davis, p. 158.

[139] LC., Bryan MS.

By the end of July the threatened revolution broke with unexpected fury. President Sam had given orders that a number of political prisoners, estimated at 170, be shot by their guards if fighting broke out. These orders were executed with appalling completeness so that only some five of the prospective victims escaped.[140] With his government in collapse the President took refuge in the French Legation. There he was seized by the mob and his body literally torn to pieces. Admiral Caperton notified Washington that the British, French and United States diplomatic agents urged intervention so he had landed troops at about 4 o'clock on the afternoon of the 28th. The French and British were assured that all foreign interests would be protected but they were asked not to land marines.[141] There was no serious local opposition to Caperton's step and it was agreed that the better class of Haitians were glad of what had been done.[142]

Lansing frankly recognized that the course of the United States was "high-handed" and an "invasion of Haytian independence" but he was clearly appalled at the developments reported.[143] He later said the two reasons for the intervention were the wish to terminate the terrible conditions of "anarchy, savagery, and oppression" in the land, and to forestall foreign efforts to establish customs control or a

[140] Hearings on Sen. Res. 112, I, 306.
[141] Lansing to Davis, July 28, 1915, Foreign Relations, 1915, p. 476.
The French actually landed a legation guard of twenty-five to fifty men but they remained inactive politically (Hearings on Sen. Res. 112, I, 357-8).
[142] Ibid., I, 308.
[143] Lansing to Wilson, August 13, 1915, The Lansing Papers, II, 526.

coaling station.[144]   He might also have added two others: the protection of United States investments in the bank, railroad and other interests, and the very important need to complete the land screen in front of the Canal.[145]

There was still a desire to maintain constitutional forms so the Haitian congress was to continue to function.   On August 2nd Caperton notified the Secretary of the Navy that bands of rebels popularly known as " Cacos," who were little better than professional bandits, were a standing menace to the country.   They had terrorized all factions to the point where they were demanding the election of a President, and the Congress could hardly be restrained from acceding to the pressure.   He urged that more marines land and undertake an active campaign to dissipate the Cacos.[146]   This was promptly authorized and troops poured into the country while the Caco bands were disarmed and in some cases were hunted down in the field during the ensuing three months.   This proceeded with drastic efficiency until the chief stronghold of the rebels was captured and until public opinion in the island reacted against the intervention as the latent fear of the Negro that he was about to be reinslaved by the White man revived.[147]

Reports needing no further comment came in as follows from Admiral Caperton; no November 17th (?) and 22nd:

On 17 November Fort Rivière was captured by forces under the command of Major Butler.   All avenues of

---

[144] Lansing to McCormick, May 4, 1922, Medill McCormick and others, *Inquiry into Occupation and Administration of Haiti* . . . (Senate Report No. 794, 67th cong., 2d sess.) (Washington), p. 37.

[145] Buell, pp. 341-2; Balch, *Occupied Haiti,* pp. 43-6.

[146] Davis, pp. 169 ff.

[147] *Hearings on Sen. Res. 112,* I, 114.

escape had been previously closed so that no Cacos escaped. Fifty-one Cacos were killed, including General Joseph and 3 division chiefs, and all others were captured. There were no casualties to our forces.

Later reports from North Haiti indicate that when fort Rivière was rushed by the 5th Company of Marines, 29 Cacos were killed in the mêlée. Many jumped over the parapet and attempted to escape. These were attacked by the remaining companies and 22 were killed. It is not known how many escaped or how many were in the fort when the attack was made. My radiogram 12018 was in error relative to the captures made at Fort Rivière. There were none captured there. 42 prisoners were captured that day, but elsewhere.[148]

Washington was becoming uneasy at developments and on the 20th Secretary of the Navy Daniels telegraphed:

Department strongly impressed with number of Haitians killed. Department feels that a severe lesson has been taught Cacos and believes that a proper patrol can be maintained to preserve order and protect innocent persons without further offensive operations. Should these measures prove inadequate inform Department before taking steps that would lead to loss of life on either side except in cases of urgent necessity. Acknowledge.[149]

But what of political developments? For the week following the intervention Admiral Caperton was busy considering possibilities for the president's office. Cooperation with the United States was essential but a number of good men would not commit themselves fully in advance and so had to be passed over.[150] The President of the Senate, Sudre Dartiguenave, " stated that Congressmen are agreed that Haiti must and will accede gladly to any terms proposed by the United States. Now, they say they will cede out-

[148] *Foreign Relations*, 1915, pp. 493-4; 496.
[149] Daniels to Caperton, November 20, 1915, *ibid.*, 1915, p. 493.
[150] Davis, pp. 173-9.

right without any restriction St. Nicholas Môle, granting us the right to intervene when necessary, custom house control, and any other terms. Only they beg us to avoid as far as possible humiliation." Caperton continued: " Next Thursday, August 12, unless otherwise directed, I will permit Congress to elect a President." [151]

On the 10th the Navy Department sent word to allow the election whenever the Haitians wished and reassure them that their welfare was the primary interest of the United States. However Haiti was not to cede territory to foreign governments and other details of relations with Washington would be taken up with the new government.[152] The State Department was more specific and wired its agent to confer with the Admiral and to make " perfectly clear ": 1st, that the United States would support the Haitian Congress but that it could not recognize action which might put in charge of affairs those whose abilities and dispositions failed to give assurance of ending factional disturbances; 2nd, that candidates should be notified " in advance of their election, that the United States expects to be entrusted with the practical control of the customs, and such financial control over the affairs of the Republic of Haiti as the United States may deem necessary for efficient administration." [153] On August 12th Dartiguenave was elected by 94 out of 116 votes cast, in an election " held under protection of marines." [154] Two days

---

[151] Caperton to the Secretary of the Navy, August 7, 1915, *Foreign Relations,* 1915, p. 431.

[152] *Hearings on Sen. Res. 112,* I, 315.

[153] Lansing to Davis, August 10, 1915, *Foreign Relations,* 1915, p. 479.

[154] Davis to Secretary of State, August 12, 1915, *ibid.,* 1915, p. 480; *Hearings on Sen. Res. 112,* I, 320-1; 362.

later the new President was informed that he would be
recognized when the Haitian Congress had authorized him
to sign a treaty allowing United States control of customs
houses and the gendarmerie.

On August 17th a draft of the required treaty was submitted to the President [155] but Congress was obviously reluctant to act, in spite of notice to the effect that the Department expected "prompt ratification." Two days later
the Secretary of the Navy ordered the assumption of control
by the Navy of the customs houses of ten of the leading
ports.[156] This evidently had the wrong effect and on the
25th further seizure of customs houses was discontinued
"for better supporting treaty negotiations." [157] The President protested the seizure and the United States Chargé reported that if there was continued insistence on the authori-
zation from the Congress for the signature of the treaty the
President and his cabinet would have to resign. Pending
developments, however, severe restrictions on financial dis-
bursements were applied so that the President, who was
really friendly to the United States, found himself practically powerless for lack of funds.[158]

The Chamber of Deputies had approved the treaty but
the Senate balked so conditions remained deadlocked until
November 10th when the Secretary of the Navy notified
Admiral Caperton that he was to have President Dartiguenave call a cabinet session with the Admiral present. He

[155] Buell, pp. 345-6; Davis, pp. 180-2.
[156] Daniels to Caperton, August 19, 1915, *Foreign Relations,*
1915, pp. 518-9.
[157] Caperton to Secretary of the Navy, August 25, 1915, *Hear-*
ings on Sen. Res. 112, I, 338; also I, 334-6.
[158] Millspaugh, pp. 42-6; Davis, pp. 184-7.

was then to state that he was glad to note that the sentiment favorable to the treaty continued so strong and that
if the treaty failed of ratification his government would find
itself forced to retain control and would proceed actively
with the pacification of the country while it supported the
present administration. The United States, the Admiral
was to state, was particularly anxious for the immediate
ratification of the treaty. Rumors of bribery to defeat the
treaty were not believed but if they proved true they would
be vigorously prosecuted. The instructions closed with this
sentence: " It is expected that you will be able to make
this sufficiently clear to remove all opposition and to secure
immediate ratification." [159] The cabinet meeting was held
the next morning and so persuasive was the Admiral's
presentation that the vote was taken in the Senate the same
day and stood 25 in favor and 9 against the ratification of
the treaty.[160]

This document provided for debt control and organization of a constabulary, but details were not fully worked
out. Haiti retained control of its foreign affairs and a
form of government by which it could and did frequently
handicap the policies, many of which had been adopted for
purely disinterested reasons, of the self-appointed guardian
whose ministrations were far from popular.[161] In the

[159] Daniels to Caperton, Nivember 10, 1915, *Foreign Relations*,
1915, p. 458.

[160] Blanchard to Secretary of State, November 12, 1915, *ibid.*

[161] For terms of the treaty see *Foreign Relations*, 1916, pp.
328-32.

For various interpretations of the treaty see: Kelsey, *op. cit.*, pp.
144-5; Jones, *Caribbean and the U. S.*, p. 157; Munro, *U. S. and
the Caribbean*, pp. 159-60; J. R. C., *Right to Protect Citizens*,
pp. 112-3.

United States very little attention was paid to the whole matter and the Senate was expected to endorse the treaty readily for it was generally taken for granted that this was another of the inevitable developments in the Caribbean while John Doe found himself far more interested in the news from Europe.

Unfortunately the United States had no central organization to direct the development of its program. The State and Navy Departments were both involved but the representatives of the two in Haiti had no recognized relation to each other. In addition there were the new officials provided for by the treaty in theory independent of both but actually in confused relation to both and to the Haitian Government. The result was lack of systematic handling of reports and even instructions so that one set of officials worked at cross purposes with and contradicted the others. To make matters worse there was a rapid turnover in personnel due to the exigencies of the European War.[163] Confusion and misunderstanding were inevitable.

Disagreements came thick and fast and the Haitian Congress seemed determined to do all in its power to block the treaty it had been forced into accepting. The immediate question on hand was the formation of a new constitution for the Republic and the opposition was determined to defeat the will of its guardian on this if at all possible.

It soon developed that a major controversy would arise over the question of foreign or absentee landlordism. This had been prohibited for over a hundred years but now

[162] Lansing to Bryan, February 28, 1916, LC., Bryan MS.
[163] Millspaugh, pp. 64-70; Davis, pp. 236-9.

United States corporations were anxious to secure holdings for the development of tropical products. An even more serious objection to the old constitution (for after all United States holdings in the island were small) lay in the veto of the popularly elected legislature over the acts of the president.[164] When it came to approving a new document eliminating these two items the Haitian Congress balked, and instead the Senate hastened to rush through a new constitution of its own. President Dartiguenave was then warned that if he did not dissolve the obstreperous Congress the forces of the United States would do so and establish military law. Under this pressure he signed the decree and the Congress was dissolved June 19, 1916.[165]

By March, 1916, the United States had 1,700 marines in the country who were under instructions to " Relinquish no part of military control which you are now exercising in Haiti, nor without receipt of further instructions put end to martial law as now in force." [166] Rigid control of finances was exercised and the details of the life of the people were supervised to a surprising degree.

The Occupation forces desired the development of roads and other public works both for military and peace time purposes and to this end invoked the old corvée system of enforced labor of the natives. At times, however, they required the men to work for longer periods of time and at greater distances from their homes than the law allowed. In the eyes of the Haitians this was slavery once more.[167]

[164] Millspaugh, p. 93; Davis, pp. 211-2; 282; Buell, pp. 347-8.
[165] Waller to Larraque, April 27, 1916, *Hearings on Sen. Res. 112*, I, 24; Douglas, *op. cit.*, pp. 249-50; Buell, p. 348.
[166] *Hearings on Sen. Res. 112*, I, 75.
[167] Davis, pp. 216-8.

True, those in authority did not order the violation of the laws but were not inclined to question methods if desired results were obtained. Further misunderstandings came in connection with court decisions affecting the Occupation. These, the United States officials were convinced, were seriously unjust and discriminatory so they retaliated with financial pressure that created more trouble and misunderstanding.[168]

On the other hand there was evidently real fear if not actual suffering if one judges from the rising number of emigrants who left their homes to go to Cuba. In 1916 they had reached nearly five thousand, they doubled the next year and reached their peak in 1920 when over thirty thousand migrated.[169] Since these were young adult males for the most part the numbers were not a little significant. But these very figures indicate that the serious development took place while the United States was involved in the European War, hence further discussion is reserved as a part of the War program. The essential fact developed thus far is that for all military purposes when war was imminent another country occupying a strategic position with regard to the land screen of the Panama Canal had been occupied and placed under effective control—at least for the duration.

In Puerto Rico a much happier condition obtained with an appreciation of the kindly feelings and intentions of the new administration. The old efforts to secure a reorganization of their governmental machinery now culminated in the Jones Bill by which the islanders were given full citi-

[168] Balch, pp. 139-40.
[169] Buell, pp. 373-4.

zenship in the United States unless the individual specifically stated that he did not desire it. The Governor's Council was changed so that only the Attorney General and the Commissioner of Education out of the six members were now appointed by the President of the United States; the remaining members were appointed by the Governor with the advice and consent of the island Senate, which in turn became an elective body subject to the Puerto Rican electorate. If bills were passed by the local legislature but vetoed by the governor, the legislature could repass the bill by a two-thirds vote and the governor could veto a second time, in which case the President of the United States had the right of final approval or veto. Also the Congress of the United States retained the right to review or annul island legislation. The court system was little changed.[170] Other details could be mentioned but it was obvious that the above details coupled with essential manhood suffrage which was now approved meant an extensive liberalizing of the machinery of government and it was generally felt that this was a direct step in the final entry of Puerto Rico into the Union as one of the states. Full ownership of this Caribbean island at least seemed to meet with popular approval therein.

In Cuba there was quite a different situation for there control was much more tenuous and the enormous sugar trade and the rapidly expanding finances of the country involved surprising amounts of United States investments. The new United States Minister to Cuba was W. E. Gonzales of Columbia, South Carolina, who was descended

---

[170] Stuart, *Latin America and the U. S.*, pp. 193-5, gives a good summary of the bill.

from Cuban patriot stock that had migrated to the United States. A sincere and honorable gentleman he was much concerned about the Dollar Diplomacy program that had been applied in the island during the preceding administration. He found that his protests in connection with the McGivney and Rokeby paving and sewerage contracts ("The name . . . yet smells to Heaven in my memory" he later commented) were systematically sidetracked in the office of a minor official of the State Department who in turn was a henchman of the attorney of the company who, Mr. Gonzales asserted, "actually drew instructions for him to send to me in Habana—in the name of the Secretary of State." [171]

Apparently the Secretary simply did not know what was going on in his Department. Beyond doubt he wished to curb vicious and discriminatory contracts forced on Cuba as is shown by his letter to Wilson, and Wilson's full endorsement, suggesting that the Cuban Government be notified that the administration would not endorse for the future the type of contracts secured by two New York banks in which they had unfair advantages in connection with future bond issues of Cuba.[172]

A vigorous protest of the Minister was pigeonholed—and then "lost" for ten months until the Minister forced the matter by cablegram, personal protests and a threat to resign. Finally by the end of 1915, under the influence of Messrs. Lansing as Secretary of State and Frank Polk as Counsellor of the Department, this malodorous connection

[171] Gonzales, *Concerning Dollar Diplomacy,* pp. 2-4.
[172] Bryan to the President, November 17, 1913, and Wilson to Bryan, November 20, 1913, LC., Wilson MS; Bryan to Gonzales, November 21, 1913, LC., Bryan MS.

of the large contracting company with the State Department was ended and the company " made terms with the Cuban Government " on long standing disputes for unsatisfactory work done by them in the island.[173]

When it came to matters that were likely to affect the defense of the land Bryan and also Wilson usually followed the advice of the War and Navy Departments, even to the disadvantage of United States contractors.[174] In general it is safe to say that their attitude was greatly appreciated in Cuba and friendly suggestion by the United States Minister more and more took the place of active direction. But occasionally the whip was still cracked as when the Cuban Congress was warned against granting a railroad concession to British capitalists without the " fullest investigation and consideration." In doing this the Minister was to emphasize " the burden it would impose on the Cuban Treasury in favor of capital which is neither American nor Cuban." [175] A little later when the Cuban President secured from his Congress the authority to make a new loan without first obtaining the approval of Washington he was promptly advised of the existing treaty provisions dealing with the matter and of the custom of " submitting full data " on such proposals to Washington.[176] Similarly informal suggestion obviously demanded and secured a presidential veto of what Washington considered an unwise amnesty bill though it was to be stated that this suggestion arose " from the friendly interest taken by the United States

[173] Gonzales, op. cit., pp. 4-7.
[174] Malin, U. S. After the War, p. 415; Lewis, America's Stake November 21, 1913, LC., Bryan MS.
[175] Quoted by Nearing and Freeman, Dollar Diplomacy, p. 267.
[176] Guggenheim, United States and Cuba, p. 224.

in matters affecting Cuba's standing before the world." [177]

And certainly Cuba lent itself readily to suggestions for the most part. When the *Lusitania* was sunk a Cuban consul-general was on board. He was saved but his baggage lost. Great Britain suggested that Cuba appoint a representative to join in the investigation of the disaster. Bryan and Wilson agreed that this would be unwise for the Cuban could hardly dissent from the findings of the British without making his position awkward and yet he might well hesitate to sign a statement that the British would desire in the heat of war.[178] In other words Cuban war policy was generally outlined in Washington even as early as 1915.

Meanwhile, because of the feeling of safety and the war prices the sugar corporations put their savings back into their business in increasing volume and others poured new money into the island. In the decade from 1911 to 1920 the percentage of the sugar production controlled by United States capital increased from 35% to 48% while the total output increased over 50%.[179] Under this "friendly but assertive guidance" the Cuban monetary system was established on a parity with that of the United States and the whole economy of the island frankly dominated.[180]

The more a person examines the record the more he is convinced that the old fear of Germany was still a real

[177] Numerous despatches on subject in *Foreign Relations,* 1913, pp. 354-65. Also see Munro, pp. 35-6.

[178] Bryan to Wilson, May 26, 1915, and Wilson to Secretary of State, May 27, 1915, LC., Bryan MS.

[179] Malin, *U. S. After the War*, p. 415; Lewis, *America's Stake in International Investments,* pp. 270-1.

[180] Jenks, *Our Cuban Colony,* p. 177; Chapman, *History of the Cuban Republic,* p. 330.

factor in determining the Caribbean policy of the State Department. Roosevelt, Lodge and others had harped on it for a long time and the generally opportunist attitude of Berlin had fostered the suspicions. The constant propaganda of ardent German expansionists had had its effects in the Caribbean too as is seen by the inquiry from Cuba if there was an agreement between Washington and Berlin to divide the Central and South American banking business between them.[181] Further, Germany had shown much interest in Mexico and had rather insisted on knowing what the United States intended to do there.[182] During the ensuing disturbances German propaganda was undoubtedly used adversely to United States interests and it was generally agreed had as a primary objective the embroiling of the Northern Republic in Central American complications when and if possible.[183]

Under these circumstances it is not surprising that attention was soon attracted to the Virgin Islands once more. Negotiations were reopened with Denmark with reference to a proposed sale. Mr. Tansill's careful study of the acquisition of these islands is well known so a further lengthy study of procedure is out of place. The motives back of the renewed negotiations, however, are of interest. The Secretary of the Navy asked the General Board about the strategic value of the islands. The answer was that the acquisition of a new base of operations in the Caribbean in view of the existing holdings in Puerto Rico and other

[181] Manuel de la Vega, Cuban Chargé, to Bryan, June 13, 1914, and Bryan to de la Vega, June 13, 1914, LC., Bryan MS.

[182] Wilson to Bryan, November 23, 1913, *ibid.*

[183] Carl W. Ackerman, *Mexico's Dilemma* (New York, 1918), pp. 106-8; *Investigation of Mexican Affairs*, pp. 3212-6.

islands was inadvisable. However the possession of the Danish West Indies by another foreign power, a potential enemy, would be a serious matter. Since Denmark probably could not resist an offer to purchase when made by a strong power it was advisable for the United States to forestall such a situation by the immediate purchase of the islands since " for military reasons the United States should not tolerate any change other than to the United States itself." [184]

In March, 1915, M. F. Egan, United States Minister to Denmark, took the initiative. Three months later Wilson and Lansing discussed the matter and the go-ahead signal was given though it was suggested that this be done " very discreetly." [185] By December the parties fully understood each other as the following letters show. On the 4th Lansing wrote the President that on November 15th the Danish Minister had told him that he was embarrassed to ask a question he had been instructed by his government to put to the Secretary of State. It was:

Whether he thought in case the Danish Government did not agree to a sale of the Islands the United States would feel it necessary to take possession of them.
In reply I told the Minister that while it had not been in my mind that action of this sort would be necessary, as I had hoped some formal negotiation would result in the transfer of the sovereignty, that I could conceive of circumstances which would compel such an act on our part.

In answer to what these circumstances were Lansing responded: " the possible consequence of absorption of Den-

[184] Tansill, *Purchase of Danish West Indies*, p. 482; Daniels, *Life of Wilson*, pp. 192-3.
[185] Notter, p. 422.

mark by one of the great powers of Europe. Such a loss of sovereignty . . . would be difficult to meet other than by occupation of the Islands." Wilson wrote the next day saying: "I am glad the Danish Minister gave you an opportunity to be so frank with him, and I hope he realizes how entirely friendly to Denmark the frankness was." [186]

Thus knowing the situation the Danish Minister of Foreign Affairs sent the following cablegram (paraphrase) on December 1st to the Secretary of State:

As I have already advised you in an earlier cablegram, the cession of the Danish West Indies would in Denmark be felt as a great national loss, and only under pressure of necessity would our country consider consenting to such a step.

When however the United States, in spite of their friendly feelings towards us and notwithstanding their respect for our sovereign rights, consider it possible that, in the situations which have been suggested, circumstances could compel them to occupy the islands, and as Denmark for this reason must count on being in the future so situated with regard to the islands, that is, if it declines to enter into negotiations, will constantly have to fear being drawn into an international conflict in the situations which have been suggested, then our country is placed in such a position that it will not be able to refuse to consider a proposition from the United States, if such a proposition should be made.[187]

Denmark suggested a price of 100,000,000 *kroner* (about $27,000,000). Wilson did not wish to quibble and was willing to pay the sum asked but Lansing shaded the offer to $25,000,000 and this Denmark accepted [188] and the treaty was pushed through and signed in New York by Lansing

---

[186] *The Lansing Papers,* II, 503.

[187] *Ibid.,* II, 502. See also *ibid.,* II, 501-5; Tansill, pp. 477-9.

[188] Wilson to Secretary of State, January 7, 1916, *The Lansing Papers,* II, 507.

and Minister Constantine Brun. August 8th the treaty was sent to the Senate with the request that the details be kept secret but two days later they had reached the press. Lansing appeared before the Foreign Relations Committee and urged approval on the basis of strategy, withdrawing the islands from the market, and preventing foreign complications. A favorable Committee report was followed by a vote of the Senate on September 7th in executive session in which the vote was about six to one in favor of the purchase. In Denmark a plebiscite had upheld the Government policy almost two to one. December 20th the Folkething voted for ratification 90 to 16, while the Landsthing endorsed it the next day by 40 to 19. The King ratified it the 22nd, and Wilson on January 16, 1917, with ratifications exchanged on the 17th.[189]

Theorists continued to urge their policies and to debate pro and con as is seen from the articles appearing in a single learned journal in the period of a few months. Naval men like Rear-Admirals F. E. Chadwick and Colby N. Chester were long agreed that the United States must dominate the Caribbean willy-nilly.[190] Publicists like Oswald Garrison Villard confessed bewilderment and asked for an announced program.[191] Some still pointed out the steadily rising menace of Dollar Diplomacy as the United States had more and more money available for foreign investment,[192] but even

[189] Tansill, pp. 484-515, has an excellent account of the negotiations.

[190] F. E. Chadwick, "A Study of Iberic America," *The Annals*, LIV, 16-7; C. N. Chester, "Present Status of the Monroe Doctrine," *ibid.*, pp. 25-6.

[191] "Rights of Small Nations in America," *ibid.*, LXXII, 165-9.

[192] F. C. Howe, "Dollar Diplomacy and Financial Imperialism under Wilson . . . ," *ibid.*, LXVIII, 319-20.

the cooperationist L. S. Rowe commented: " It is evident that, irrespective of any question of European interference, we cannot remain indifferent to a condition of disorder or instability in any part of Central America, in Mexico or in the West Indies." [193]

The logic of events which were themselves the result of expanding United States economic life and political influence as well as of the World War had driven the administration of the idealist Wilson into the adoption of a realistic policy. Unwilling to follow the old models and precedents and adhering to objectives of democracy and self-government for all peoples he had resorted to a paternal despotism to " shoot peoples into democracy " in the first place, the while he insisted on maintaining the dignity and respect that he felt should be accorded the major power of the New World in the second place. The result was active interference in the internal affairs of Mexico, Nicaragua, Haiti and Santo Domingo, and the giving of generous portions of advice, which it was advisable to accept, to Panama, Cuba and miscellaneous Central American countries from time to time. In addition, the Virgin Islands were purchased. In the eyes of the idealist this paternal despotism was no less than a great and holy cause adopted on behalf of unfortunate humanity; in the eyes of cynical critics it was the hypocritical disguise assumed by the wolf of imperialism when he disposed of Little Red Riding-hood's grandmother and took her place in bed to deceive the next trusting and hoped-for victim.

To the impartial narrator of events it is obvious that certain early hopes had gone astray; that many unfortunate

[193] " Scope and Limits of our Obligations," *ibid.*, LIV, 220-1.

appointments had been made; that Bryan had gotten lost in the maze of complications of his office and frequently talked principles while blind to the actual practices that he was condoning; that Lansing adopted a procedure much nearer to the old " practical " program but which still gave credence and considerable heed to the idealism of his chief, and that Wilson himself still held his ultimate objectives in mind but in the pressure of events could not supervise all acts of the State Department. In the familiar language of the barnyard, he had a rampant bull by the tail. He certainly could not turn loose, he definitely could not stop the animal, so from time to time as opportunity offered he gave a vigorous yank that caused the animal to pause, change his direction a bit, and even at times to turn an undesired corner.

CHAPTER IX

THE CARIBBEAN IN THE WORLD WAR—NEEDS MUST WHEN THE DEVIL DRIVES

With the entrance of the United States into the holocaust of the First World War European affairs took priority over all other details in international planning at Washington, and Caribbean issues had to be interpreted in the light of the new relationships. However, for the purposes of this study the new situation causes the last years of the Wilson Administration to assume especial importance as indicating the results of world crisis and war on the New World Mediterranean area.

Just south of the Río Grande the problem remained complicated due to the heritage of bitterness from the preceding years and to the new war needs of the United States for Mexican products, notably henequin and petroleum. Also, the United States reacted from its own recent and moderate sociological experiments to a capitalistic conservatism for its gigantic war efforts while Mexico crystallized its Revolution in an ultra liberal if not radical new constitution frankly based on socialism.

Carranza still had the problem of domestic pacification before him [1] and was convinced that the episodes on the border, where the last of the United States punitive expeditionary forces retired on February 6, 1917,[2] had weakened

---

[1] Ackerman, *Mexico's Dilemma*, pp. 54-5.
[2] Funston to Adjutant General, February 6, 1917, *Foreign Relations*, 1917, p. 908.

his prestige. That bitter critic of the United States, Manuel Ugarte, reported that Carranza said to him in April, 1917: " be sure that nothing you can ever say against imperialism will go beyond what I think." [3] At the same time Carranza was stirring public opinion against the United States by official reports to his Congress as when he reminded that body of the irregular conduct of H. L. Wilson in 1913 and clearly left it to be implied that this was typical Washington diplomacy [4]—and all of this when only six weeks before the new United States Ambassador, Henry P. Fletcher, had presented his credentials. On March 11th Carranza had been duly elected president of Mexico but at the ensuing inauguration it was noticeable that the German Ambassador Von Eckhardt was greeted by applause when he entered the Chamber of Deputies for the ceremonies but Fletcher's appearance was greeted with hisses.[5]

The new Mexican Ambassador at Washington, Ygnacio Bonillas, was received by Wilson on April 17th [6] and shortly thereafter the Mexican Government received approval of the State Department to import 2,733,000 rounds of ammunition which had been detained at the border for some months.[7] But there still remained a none-too-thinly veiled antagonism to the United States in official circles. In January the famous Zimmermann notes propos-

[3] Ugarte, *Destiny of a Continent,* p. 263.
[4] Report at opening of Mexican Congress, April 15, 1917, *Foreign Relations,* 1917, pp. 984-5.
[5] Callahan, *American Policy in Mexican Relations,* pp. 571-2.
[6] Fletcher to Secretary of State, March 13, 1917, and Lansing to Fletcher, April 21, 1917, *Foreign Relations,* 1917, pp. 910-2; 915; Baker, VII, 23.
[7] Lansing to de Negri, February 10, 1917, and Polk to Summerlin, July 19, 1917, *Foreign Relations,* 1917, pp. 1079; 1085.

ing a Mexican-German-Japanese alliance against the United States had been sent. On February 24th the contents of these were made known to the State Department through the United States Ambassador at London who forwarded them on information received from the British.[8] The plan briefly proposed that the two new German allies should receive territorial spoils at the expense of the United States. Just how far Japan was involved is uncertain but there seems to have been some fire back of the smoke.[9] To requests from the United States for a statement of Mexican aims and purposes in the War, Carranza was evasive [10] and talked about a conference of neutrals which he professed to hope his Northern Neighbor would sponsor.

The three or four thousand Germans in Mexico were a splendid entering wedge for the propaganda that now flooded the Southern Republic. This was bitterly anti-United States and was pro-Latin at least, if it did not urge active cooperation with the Central Powers.[11] It developed further through the efforts of the German Ambassador in Mexico and took the direction of organizing revolutionists in Honduras, Nicaragua and Guatemala who would handicap the United States with the direct or indirect aid of supplies drawn from Mexico.[12] The seriousness of this can

[8] For discussion of this see Hendrick, *Life and Letters of Page,* III, 332 ff.; Martin, *Latin America and the War,* pp. 533-6; Notter, *Origins of Foreign Policy of Wilson,* pp. 627-8.

[9] Rippy, *Latin America in World Politics,* pp. 232-3.

[10] Fletcher to Secretary of State, March 10, 1917, *Foreign Relations,* 1917, supplement 1, pp. 238-9. Copy also in LC., House MS.

[11] Martin, *op. cit.,* pp. 524-5; Ackerman, pp. 57-9; Clarence H. Haring, *South America Looks at the United States* (New York, 1929), pp. 140-2.

[12] *Investigation of Mexican Affairs,* pp. 2898-9.

be seen by the vote in secret session in the Mexican Senate
on a resolution to declare a "benevolent neutrality toward
the Entente nations" as "indispensable for the maintenance
of the Government and for the restoration of the peace,
progress, and life of the nation." This was defeated by
a vote of 35 to 13.[18]

As early as April 18th Lansing wrote the President that
Mexico would likely allege an effort to enforce strict neutrality in the War and demand the withdrawal of United
States naval vessels from Tampico. He continued: "Technically they will have right on their side, but from a practical point of view we cannot respect Mexican neutrality so
far as Tampico is concerned." He frankly admitted that
refusal to withdraw protection from the oil fields might
result in war.

To the present day observer Wilson's response con-
tained a trace of humor though he was deadly serious.
He said he could not be sure which was the anti-United
States party, Carranza or his opponents, and then added:

The United States cannot afford to be too "practical."
She is the leading champion of the right of self-government and of political independence everywhere. Only the
most extraordinary circumstances of arbitrary injustice on
the part of the Mexican government would make me feel
that we had the right to take control at Tampico. . . .

He felt the same about the Tehuantepec railroad which was
considered another danger point. Then the President made a
notable suggestion that probably British influences could

[18] Fletcher to Secretary of State, October 20, 1917, and Decem-
ber 19, 1917, *Foreign Relations,* 1917, supplement i, pp. 349; 392;
Eckhardt to Zimmermann, April 14, 1917, and April 16, 1917,
Hendrick, III, 354; 355.

control affairs at Tampico and asked his Secretary to confer with the British Ambassador saying: "There is absolutely no breach of the Monroe Doctrine in allowing the British to exercise an influence there which anti-American sentiment in Mexico for the time being prevents our exercising." [14]

It was at this time that the interesting development took place at Tampico where Manuel Pelaez, a rebel against Carranza, was able to dominate the oil region. As an efficient gangster he had first terrorized the oil companies and then sold them protection from miscellaneous brigandage so long as they paid him. Under the arrangement petroleum production was mounting steadily.[15] The companies were satisfied and wanted the situation to continue, and foreign countries including the United States who desperately wanted the oil, acquiesced. Only the Mexican Government was likely to protest.[16] The Washington position is revealed in the Chandler P. Anderson Diary. On March 10, 1917, Anderson recorded:

. . . he [Lansing] said that our government was entirely willing that General Peleyas [Pelaez] should be supplied with arms and ammunition from this country so long as the matter was not brought to the attention of the government, and that I might rest assured that the Administration would not prosecute any one who was assisting Peleyas so long as he remained friendly to the foreign interests in that region.[17]

[14] Letter in Baker, VII, 26-7.
[15] Ackerman, pp. 71-9.
[16] *Foreign Relations,* 1917, cir. p. 1062.
[17] LC., Chandler Parsons Anderson MS.

Mr. Anderson was a prominent Washington attorney who had acted as agent in many international complications for New World countries and who had, on occasion, served in various capacities in the State Department. A Republican, he had a personal contact

On April 13th Mr. Thomas Braniff called on Anderson and the Diary records:

> I asked him just what he had in mind. After considerable discussion of the situation it developed that what he wants is to send into the Peleyas forces a considerable amount of military supplies. I told him that it would be impossible for me to be connected with any such plan, if it was displeasing to our own government. . . . I said, however, that in view of the dangerous situation in the oil fields, and the importance of protecting those fields, it was possible that my Government would not be displeased if military supplies could be sent to Peleyas, provided that it was not done in such a way as to embarrass its relations with Carranza . . .

How much of this was done by the Secretary of State on his own responsibility and how much with the approval of the President the present writer does not know.

The Mexican Government continued its efforts for a conference of neutrals after the United States entered the War. At first proposed by Carranza in February, 1917, the Congress was to invite all belligerents to attend a conference "with absolutely perfect equality on either side to bring this war to an end" by their own efforts or through the use of the good offices of the neutrals. "If within a reasonable term peace could not be restored by this means, the neutral countries would then take the necessary measures to reduce the conflagration to its narrowest limits by refusing any kind of implements to the belligerents and suspending commercial relations with the warring nations until

---

with Secretary Lansing and in many ways served as a contact man between the State Department and the United States corporations with petroleum and mining interests in Mexico. His diary is especially valuable and is here cited as *Anderson Diary* with dates of entries.

the said conflagration shall have been smothered." [18] The potential injury to Allied and United States interests involved was obvious once the United States had entered the contest in April, 1917.

By July Colombia was reported to be supporting the proposal,[19] though for various reasons this endorsement was later withdrawn. At one time it looked as though most of the New World nations would join in but the State Department became exceedingly busy and various complications began to develop.[20] Argentina had agreed to invite the conference to meet at Buenos Aires but time was consumed with extended correspondence. By November Colombia sent word it would not attend and Peru and Brazil were cooperating on a counter proposal with the approval of Washington.[21] To make a complicated story short, the matter was dropped.

The other problem with Mexico was that concerned with the new Constitution of 1917. This document was based on the idea that the rights of man were obsolete and that the rights of society were preeminent; rugged individualism was to give place to socialism. In addition to social legislation and drastic restrictions on religious organizations of the country, there were provisions with regard to the nationalization of subsoil rights in minerals, the distribution of lands to the landless under the right of eminent domain, and the establishment of zones fifty and one hundred kilometers wide along the coast and borders of Mexico

[18] Martin, p. 532.

[19] Stimson to Secretary of State, July 19, 1917, *Foreign Relations,* 1917, supplement i, p. 308.

[20] Martin, pp. 255-7.

[21] *Foreign Relations,* 1917, supplement i, numerous.

in which no foreigner was allowed to own real estate. In the case of properties owned or inherited in such zones they were to be sold within a given period of time.

It is true that so far as subsoil rights were concerned the constitution provided against retroactive enforcement of constitutional provisions but this was felt to be an exceedingly flimsy protection in view of the obvious intent of the new documents as a whole. A further respite might obtain from the fact that the mere adoption of the Constitution did not *ipso facto* provide for the enforcement of its provisions. These were to be applied by special enactment or decrees specifically applying the provisions. A somewhat analogous situation was found in the 18th amendment to the United States Constitution which provided for prohibition, though it had no effect until the Volstead Act defined and applied the law. Hence, the new constitution became for the time being a measure to be invoked at the desire of the executive. Now Carranza was far from being as radical as his Constituent Assembly and so refrained from applying the whole document immediately but its mere existence was a thorn in the side of all foreign landlords and promised to be much more than that eventually.

The United States had on occasion protested what it considered unwise financial enactments of the Mexican Government, as well as confiscatory procedure that affected its citizens.[22] But these protests were far from satisfying the oil men whose immense holdings were endangered. They constantly presented their protests to the State Department

[22] For correspondence see *Foreign Relations,* 1917, pp. 998 ff.,; Williams, *Econ. For. Pol. of U. S.,* pp. 112-3; 128-9.

through all avenues available. They were convinced that Ambassador Fletcher was not getting at the heart of the matter in his negotiations,[23] and furthermore that " The President seems to be wholly lacking in interest in the protection of property and material interests, and is chiefly concerned with the establishment of a stable government in Mexico, on the theory of serving humanity." [24] The State Department meanwhile made periodic protests to Carranza and on August 2, 1917, Fletcher reported that he had had an interview with the Mexican President that morning and had asked the attitude of the Mexican Government as to the nationalization of United States oil and mining interests south of the Río Grande. " In reply he assured me that they need not be [concerned]; that it was not the intention of the Mexican Government to take over properties now in exploitation and distinctly stated that there would be no confiscation of these properties." [25]

Lansing and Fletcher were not reassured and were much perturbed about the matter [26] but since Carranza did not move actively to apply the constitution and the oil was coming out of Mexico in increasing volume officialdom let sleeping dogs lie though the oil men still were uneasy.[27] Both nations were sparring for openings. Such oil decrees

[23] LC., *Anderson Diary*, entries for May 31, 1917, and July 17, 1917.

[24] *Ibid.*, March 8, 1917. In the Diary the word "chiefly" is inserted by hand, after crossing out the word "wholly."

[25] Fletcher to Secretary of State, August 2, 1917, *Foreign Relations, 1917*, p. 1072.

[26] Williams, *American Diplomacy*, pp. 216-8; Fletcher to House, July 17, 1918, SL., House MS.

[27] *Investigation of Mexican Affairs*, pp. 189-90; 333; Blakeslee *Mexico and the Caribbean*, pp. 60-1.

as were issued in contravention of United States interests were ably protested [28]—and then the matter dropped. When Mexico saw a good chance, it issued new decrees, at least one of which appeared under circumstances that smacked strongly of trying to create propaganda against its Northern Neighbor. By November, 1918, things had again simmered down [29] with only occasional instances of banditry to provide grounds for interest, the United States was more and more inclined to insist that it would protest diplomatically on behalf of commercial holdings but would not resort to armed intervention on their behalf.[30]

British interests were guided by the action of United States capitalists as to their own attitude [31] while the State Department was doing everything in its power to court Carranza and maintain the *status quo*.[32] Export licenses for all types of goods to go southward were freely issued and the State Department repeatedly urged the War Department to take every possible precaution to suppress firing across the international boundary or any other type of friction.[33]

Washington courted Mexico further by taking up the

[28] Lansing to Thurston, January 19, 1917, *Foreign Relations*, 1917, p. 1059.

[29] Correspondence in *ibid.*, 1917 and 1918.

[30] Carranza to Mexican Congress, September 1, 1919, *ibid.*, 1919, II, 532. See also Callahan, pp. 576-7, and *Anderson Diary*, entry for April 23, 1918.

[31] *Ibid.*, entry for November 7, 1918; *Foreign Relations*, 1918, p. 792-ff.

[32] House to Fletcher, July 1, 1918, SL., House MS; and memorandum of G. A[uchincloss] to Secretary of State, June 4, 1918, *ibid.*

[33] For export licenses issued see *Foreign Relations*, 1918, pp. 631-2. For military orders see *ibid.*, pp. 565-72.

question of money for a loan. Financial experts from the United States lent their aid [34] and a request from Fletcher to know if the Department would stand in the way of Mexico securing a loan from United States bankers was answered in the negative on August 8th.[35] A week earlier Polk, the Counselor of the State Department, wrote the President saying that Carranza had been urged frequently to apply to Washington for a loan but had not done so, probably through pride and the hope of securing ample aid from Germany once the war was over. At last he was willing to ask for a loan through United States bankers but the latter were skeptical and would not move unless reassured by the Government. Polk suggested that Wilson authorize him to confer with the bankers and induce them to open negotiations so as:

1. To prove the earnest desire of the United States to aid Mexico.
2. To offset German influence based on German promises of financial aid once the war was over.
3. To direct attention from oil revenues by relieving immediate needs of Mexico.[36]

Wilson replied the next day:

I answered orally this morning your note of yesterday about getting the bankers interested in a loan to Mexico. I am merely writing this line to confirm our conversation and to say that I hope you will make the effort.[37]

With the close of the World War the United States policy began to stiffen while the Mexican Government was

[34] Ackerman, pp. 127-8.
[35] Lansing to Fletcher, August 8, 1917, *Foreign Relations,* 1917, p. 1014.
[36] Polk to the President, August 1, 1918, LC., Wilson MS.
[37] Wilson to Polk, August 2, 1918, *ibid.*

showing its resentment by steadily increasing oil taxation.[38] Soon the resentment became more outspoken as was shown in the interview granted the Mexico City correspondent of the New York *World* by Carranza in May, 1919. The despatch covering this stated:

President Carranza this afternoon received me in national palace and explained exclusive interview why his Government is opposed to Monroe Doctrine in principle and practice. In his statements regarding Mexico's position with respect to Doctrine Carranza was most unequivocal and explicit "Recent declaration of Mexican Foreign Office" said he "to effect that in reply to interrogations from various friendly governments as to Mexico's attitude toward Monroe Doctrine never has recognized or never will recognize this or any other doctrine which attacks sovereignty or independence Mexico exactly defined our position. It may be taken as official proclamation of fixed and inalterable policy of this government." "Why" I asked "Principally for reason that Monroe doctrine is an arbitrary measure which seeks to impose and does impose upon independent nations a protectorate which they do not ask for and which they do not require" replied President.[39]

To emphasize this same idea the President repeated it in his message to the Mexican Congress on September 1, 1919.[40] There was nothing startlingly new in the report except the fact that it was publicly stated and obviously made with the intent to prod an awkward situation abroad or to make political capital at home. When this was taken in connection with a recent Mexican decree that applied taxes to owners of oil lands on the basis of an annual rental it was serious. The result was a tacit reduction of the owners to

[38] Stevens, *Current Controversies with Mexico*, p. 280; *Investigation of Mexican Affairs*, p. 248.

[39] *Foreign Relations*, 1919, II, 546.

[40] *Ibid.*, II, 542-3.

the position of lessees and was a direct step toward a retroactive application of the subsoil provisions of the Constitution.[41] To this British, French and United States governments protested, but Carranza emphasized his position by seizing Mexican railroads quite indiscriminately.[42]

Meanwhile revolutionists were active in the northwest where the *Villistas* were again operating with disconcerting freedom. The response of Washington was again to proclaim an embargo on arms shipments across the border. This was to be applied by the War Department and special exemptions on shipments were to be approved by the State Department under the realistic Lansing, instead of the President as had been the case under the embargo of 1915. The decree was issued July 12th ostensibly to restrict the shipment and smuggling of arms to *Villistas*.[43] Significantly enough, however, on January 7, 1920, the Mexican Ambassador at Washington addressed the Secretary of State listing eleven applications by him dated between July 7, 1919, and November 22, 1919, asking for permission to ship war material from the United States to his Government and stating that no replies had been received. On January 23rd Lansing replied " I have the honor to inform Your Excellency that, after mature deliberation, it appears to me inexpedient to permit the issuance of licenses to ship arms and munitions of war to Mexico at the present time." [44]

[41] Frederick Sherwood Dunn, *Diplomatic Protection of Americans in Mexico* (New York, 1933), pp. 340-1.

[42] A. W. Donly in Blakeslee, *op. cit.,* pp. 86-7.

[43] Polk to the President, July 9, 1919, *Foreign Relations,* 1919, II, 551.

[44] Bonillas to Secretary of State, January 7, 1920, and Lansing to Bonillas, January 23, 1920, *ibid.,* 1919, II, 554-5.

The President himself was becoming restless and notified Congress on August 1, 1919, that 217 United States citizens had been killed in the disturbances in Mexico since 1911 and that property claims amounted to $26,000,000, while the Carranza government was attempting to give retroactive applications to the property clauses of the new constitution. This was followed by a stern warning to Mexico by the State Department as to continued danger to United States citizens. To add insult to injury a United States consular agent was captured by bandits and held for ransom in November though the sum was paid by a Mexican and so the matter was smoothed over.[45] Because of his illness the President was largely out of touch with the situation and the sterner policy of the State Department was probably a reflection of the attitude of Lansing and Fletcher. The Senate appointed a committee of Senators Hitchcock and Fall to interview the President on the Mexican situation, and in connection with a proposed resolution asking that recognition of Carranza be withdrawn. The President replied on December 8th that he would be " gravely concerned to see any such resolution pass the Congress," and pointed out that the initiative in handling foreign affairs rested with the executive and not with Congress.[46] To relieve the pressure the State Department used the Jenkins' Case as a " red herring " to side-track public indignation

[45] Pratt, " Lansing " in Bemis, *Secretaries of State,* X, 169.

Summerlin to Secretary of State, August 31, 1919, states that after Fletcher reached Mexico in 1917, eight hundred and eleven notes had been sent to the Mexican Foreign Office dealing with injuries to persons or rights of United States citizens. These were distributed as follows:

1917...... 221   1918...... 275   1919...... 315

(*Foreign Relations,* 1919, II, 575.)

[46] Callahan, p. 579.

to an issue that would then be solved diplomatically while feelings cooled.[47]

Thus to the very end Wilson adhered to his idea of allowing Mexico to work out its own destiny without military intervention. Much of his old idealism was expressed in his address to a group of visiting Mexican editors in June, 1918.[48] While the State Department was still carefully watching such points as Magdalena Bay to see that no foreign country secured a foothold [49] and while Senator Ashurst was introducing a resolution asking the President to negotiate for Lower California because " if it remains in Mexican possession, it will be the same one hundred years from today as it is today, a dreary, barren waste; whereas American money, American spirit, American enterprise can make it into gardens and farms, and a blessing to civilization," [50] still the President remained unmoved and refused to give the word for action that was now demanded by increasing numbers of his official family.[51]

Whether the sick man Wilson could have withstood the pressure from many of his own advisers, and the demands of the Fall Committee of the Senate, the oil men, and banking and business interests [52] may be a question, but a

[47] Lansing to the President, December 5, 1919, *The Lansing Papers,* II, 567-8.

[48] Copy of address in *Foreign Relations,* 1918, pp. 577 ff.

[49] T. A. Bailey, " Lodge Corollary of the Monroe Doctrine," *Pol. Sc. Quar.,* XLVII, 234-5; *Anderson Diary,* entry for May 10, 1921.

[50] Weinberg, *Manifest Destiny,* p. 185; Bailey, *op. cit.,* pp. 236-7.

[51] Rippy, *U. S. and Mexico,* pp. 360-1.

[52] For recommendations of the Fall Committee see *Investigation of Mexican Affairs,* pp. 3369 ff. For other pressure see: Davis to Wilson, November 2, 1920, *Foreign Relations,* 1920, III, 234-5, and articles by John Vavasour Noel and Henry Lane Wilson in Blakeslee, *Mexico and the Caribbean.*

breathing spell was offered by the fact that the Carranza régime was about to distintegrate. As the end of his four-year elective term approached the Mexican wished to perpetuate his program by having a friend installed in his place as a kind of puppet, or so the general impression went. A forceful and important opposition developed and the able General Alvaro Obregón started a revolution on the ground that a fair and free election had been prevented. The First Chief's house of cards forthwith collapsed and he fled the capital. When the railway line to Vera Cruz was cut he took to the country and while stopping for the night at a small cabin was assassinated.

Obregón immediately repudiated the crime, placed a temporary president in charge of the executive office pending a regular election, and reassured foreign nations as to his intentions and desires. The plea of his group was: "We Mexicans of today, through our progressive young men, do not ask more of the world than a little patience and a little faith in our ability to solve our problems and to arrange our affairs." [53] Warships were sent to Mexican waters; the United States Chargé at Mexico City was urged to maintain the strictest neutrality in the disturbances so that he could not be accused of aiding the revolution; and a strict embargo was maintained on arms shipments to both parties.[54] The new crisis was tided over and slowly men rallied to the President's program once more. Roger Babson pointed out that intervention in Mexico would seriously handicap United States prestige and trade with Latin America at the very time that it was having to face the renewed competition of Europe,[55] and such men as James

[53] Quoted by Noel, Blakeslee, p. 137.
[54] *Foreign Relations,* 1920, III, 139-60.
[55] Blakeslee, pp. 158-9.

G. McDonald, Chairman of the Executive Committee of the Foreign Policy Association pled for a continuance of " our policy of forbearance " toward Mexico.[56]

When the newly elected President Obregón was to be inaugurated at midnight, November 30, 1920, the United States Chargé was instructed to appear in his private capacity but not to attend the formal reception to the diplomatic corps. Thus, though all other members of the diplomatic corps in Mexico City apparently attended and most of them extended the recognition of their respective governments the Washington administration did not wish to embarrass the incoming Republicans who had just been elected in the recent general election.[57] In fact Bainbridge Colby, who served the last months of the Wilson Administration as Secretary of State, inaugurated a new effort to settle the outstanding issues between the two countries through a special series of conferences in which Mr. Norman H. Davis, under-Secretary of State, played an important part. However discussion of these out of place here beyond the mere statement that they provided the groundwork on which Mr. Hughes built his program for the recognition of the government of Obregón.

The weary eight years had passed and the sick man and idealist in the White House could boast that he " had kept the faith " in spite of probably the heaviest imperialistic pressures and certainly about the fullest justification for it that this country has ever seen. He had so firmly established the principle of non-intervention and non-expansion at the expense of Mexico that even those who frankly repudiated his policy as a failure, and his principles

[56] *The Annals,* XCVI, 94.
[57] *Foreign Relations,* 1920, III, 194-8; Callahan, p. 582.

as bunk, did not dare reverse them when once more political control at Washington changed hands.

In war time the position and action of Panama could be open to little debate. On February 5, 1917, Lansing wrote the President that Panama had asked instructions as to what it should do about cancelling consular exequaturs and breaking off relations with Germany.[58] On March 26th he wrote that the Panama situation was not as easy to handle as that of Cuba for the Government " is less amenable " but " I think that I can influence the Panama Government to do whatever we wish in the matter." Wilson responded " It is clear to me that the only thing we can prudently do is to urge Cuba and Panama to do just what we do." [59] On April 7th Panama made the cause of the United States its own in a declaration of alliance and cooperation saying though no formal declaration of war against Germany was issued it was disposed to follow the lead of the Northern Republic.[60] This was followed by arrests of German suspects, establishment of censorships, and other war acts calculated to effect the protection of the Canal through such agencies of either Panama or the United States as seemed most likely to provide the greatest efficiency.[61] In line with this policy Panama, at the suggestion of Washington, curtly declined to have anything to do with the proposal for the

[58] Lansing to the President, February 5, 1917, *The Lansing Papers*, I, 593.

[59] Lansing to the President, March 26, 1917, and Wilson to Lansing, March 27, 1917, *ibid.*, I, 631-2.

[60] Price to Secretary of State, April 7, 1917, April 9, 1917, and November 7, 1917, *Foreign Relations,* 1917, supplement i, pp. 245; 248; 363. See also Martin, *Latin America and the War*, pp. 487-9; McCain, *U. S. and Panama*, pp. 193-4.

[61] McCain, pp. 194-202.

Conference of Neutrals.[62] Inevitably, highway construction and all such activities were carefully supervised in the light of the defense needs of the Canal and disturbances in the Chiriqui section in connection with an election were promptly suppressed by United States troops.[63]

By October, 1918, a request reached Washington to ascertain whether proposed legislation for the reorganization of the national police of Panama and for the appointment of a financial adviser to the Republic met with the approval of the State Department. The response was favorable and a new feature was introduced into the machinery of control of the little Republic.[64] It was agreed that the financial adviser should be either a native or a foreigner who was to be selected on the recommendation of Washington and was to advise the Panama Secretary of the Treasury on fiscal legislation, to supervise the accounting system and to have the power to disapprove expenditures when irregular or not in accordance with law. Washington suggested a salary of $10,000 per year, which Panama approved, and then submitted the name of Addison T. Ruan as a man who had had similar experience in Haiti.[65] Mr. Ruan is credited with doing an excellent piece of work until his resignation in 1923.[66]

---

[62] For guidance of Washington and correspondence see *Foreign Relations*, 1917, supplement 1, pp. 277-86.

[63] Jones, *Caribbean since 1900*, p. 343; J. R. C., *Right to Protect Citizens*, pp. 127-8.

[64] Price to Secretary of State, October 3, 1918, and Lansing to Price, November 19, 1918, *Foreign Relations,*, 1919, II, 682-3; 685.

[65] Lansing to Price, November 5, 1918, and November 19, 1918, *ibid.*, 1919, II, 684; 685.

[66] Munro, *U. S. and the Caribbean Area,* pp. 99-100.

Just at the end of the Wilson administration trouble threatened for a short time because of Panama's resentment over the White

In the other Central American country more or less controlled by the United States, Nicaragua, there is little to be noted. Moneys to be paid on the Bryan-Chamorro agreement provided a convenient check over Nicaragua to guarantee that that Government would follow a satisfactory financial policy,[67] part of which was the approval of a high commission of two members. One was appointed by the Secretary of State of the United States and the other by Nicaragua, with all disagreements to be appealed to the Secretary of State. These men, in effect, controlled the income and expenditures of Nicaragua while the United States appointee became a financial adviser on a similar footing to that of Mr. Ruan in Panama. At the same time foreign claims against Nicaragua were presented for the most part through Washington as spokesman and mediator.[68] So successful was the whole arrangement that the last of the deferred payments on the old debts was made in 1920 and throughout the War period the *córdoba* was the only Central American currency to remain at par.[69]

On May 18, 1917, Nicaragua suspended diplomatic relations with Germany while the Minister of Foreign Affaires stated that this, together with the placing of all necessary Nicaraguan facilities at the disposal of the United States for war purposes, was in line with the treaty of

---

award. However, troops were called from the Canal Zone and restored order. In a couple of weeks the trouble had blown over and the troops were withdrawn.

[67] Enríquez to Secretary of State, October 22, 1917, and Lansing to Chargé, October 27, 1917, *Foreign Relations,* 1917, pp. 1144-6.

[68] *Ibid.,* 1919, II, 659-71, deals with British claims alone.

[69] State Department, *U. S. and Nicaragua,* p. 97; Jones, *Caribbean since 1900,* pp. 400-1.

1916. The ensuing March a formal declaration of war against Germany and Austria was issued.[70]

As the elections of 1920 approached President Emiliano Chamorro let it be known that he again planned to be a candidate. This Washington protested as a direct violation of the Nicaraguan constitution so Chamorro reluctantly gave up the idea, but refused to reform the electoral procedure as desired by the United States.[71] An official observer of the election, sent from Washington, reported that he observed no violence or intimidation but that there was fraud on both sides in the registration of voters and the counting of ballots. Not surprisingly Diego Chamorro, an uncle of the President, was elected by a vote of some 62,000 to 32,000. The United States did not repudiate the election but did insist that there should be an immediate reform of the electoral procedure. This demand was agreed to by the incoming administration so that Mr. Harold W. Dodds went down in 1922 and drew up a plan which was accepted in March, 1923.[72]

Meanwhile United States marines were regularly stationed in the country. Considerable friction resulted with the native population for this " seems to have been a particularly rough company " and finally had to be sent out of the country.[73] However, when the Republicans took office in Washington in March, 1921, the Conservatives insisted that the presence of marines made it possible for them to balance

[70] Martin, pp. 500-1.

[71] Foreign Relations, 1920, III, 292 ff.

[72] Ibid., 1920, III, cir. p. 306-9; State Department, U. S. and Nicaragua, pp. 40-3.

[73] Thomas, One Hundred Years of the Monroe Doctrine, pp. 298-9.

their budget by avoiding heavy local military expenditures. They stated that Nicaraguans " did not object to the presence of marines, but rather enjoyed the peace and prosperity " which they brought. And, further, the chief worry of the Nicaraguan administration was not the presence of marines but the fact that Washington had disapproved the electoral procedure by which the Conservatives had remained in power with the result that there was local fear in Nicaragua that the Liberals, " the old party of Zelaya " " still tainted with his corruption and viciousness " would regain power.[74] This fear, the Conservatives felt, the United States, and especially " the Republican party " would understand " after Mr. Knox's vigorous policy." Thus skillfully did the Nicaraguans in power attempt to appeal to party prejudice in the United States in spite of the fact that they had been professing to cooperate with the Democrats these many years. It was clearly a case of lauding Wilsonian idealism as to self government so long as the Conservatives were the beneficiaries but of repudiating it in practice when the results were not favorable to their own selfish party program.

When the United States entered the World War, Guatemala, having already been assured of United States support, broke off relations on April 27th [75] and formally entered the contest a year later. In the country were quite extensive German investments including public service companies which were promptly sequestered, and a United States resident Daniel B. Hodgsdon was appointed Alien

[74] *Anderson Diary*, entry for March 12, 1921.
[75] Lansing to Leavell, April 21, 1917, and Mendez to Secretary of State, April 27, 1917, *Foreign Relations*, 1917, supplement 1, pp. 261; 271-2.

Property Custodian with the approval of Washington.[76] Honduras acted more slowly: it broke off relations with Germany May 17, 1917, but apparently did not feel it necessary to go further.[77]

Between Honduras and Guatemala there had long existed an awkward boundary dispute that had engendered suspicion and rivalry. Also, Guatemala had long feared its more powerful northern neighbor, Mexico. As early as 1917 the United States had actively urged the settlement of the boundary dispute and after various suggestions and negotiations agreed to act as mediator. In January, 1918, it invited the two countries to send special plenipotentiaries to Washington to meet each other in formal conference.[78] For this Honduras sent its eminent statesman Policarpo Bonilla who declared that he found Guatemala had a distinct advantage because it had entered the war while his country had not. He said that at a dinner given by Secretary of State Lansing the Secretary asked him point blank when his country was to declare war. To his reply that he supposed his country had not done so for fear of appearing ridiculous as a small country entering such a gigantic contest, Lansing replied: " We need moral support to demonstrate that all America is united with us in this war." Lansing

[76] See *ibid.*, 1918, supplement 2, pp. 365 ff., and *ibid.*, 1919, II, 287 ff.; Martin, pp. 498-9.

When the war was over it was obvious that as a result of the control of the German holdings many of them had been transferred to United States citizens as new owners when they had been available for sale. Others had been returned to their original owners. (McMillin to Secretary of State, October 4, 1920, *ibid.*, 1920, II, 758.)

[77] For offer of cooperation see Lansing to Vasquez, June 20, 1917, *ibid.*, 1917, supplement 1, pp. 302-3.

[78] Correspondence in *ibid.*, 1919, I, 85 ff.

then asked about business conditions in Honduras. Bonilla replied that business was bad. The Secretary responded that this was natural especially when bananas, the chief export of the country, were entirely dependent on shipping. Bonilla hastened to express the hope that no tariff would be placed on them by the United States to which came the answer: "No tariff will be imposed; but I fear that the Shipping Board will not consent to leave ships in service for this trade, except with countries allied with the United States in the war. But this last . . . is confidential. It is a secret." "I suppose you mean so far as the press is concerned; and not as regards my Government," remarked Bonilla. "Naturally" was the answer.[79]

Honduras declared war on Germany in July, 1918.[80]

The boundary dispute dragged on for some time and efforts to secure a solution failed while Wilson was in the White House for the mediators failed to agree and their home countries up to the end of 1920 declined the suggestion for an arbitral award by the United States.[81] The good Honduranian may have read too much into his account of the conversation with Lansing but it is certain that he retained a very vivid impression of danger to his region. This he carried to Versailles where, on April 22, 1919, he proposed that the reference to the Monroe Doctrine in Article XXI of the Covenant of the League of Nations be defined as "signifying that all the American republics have a right to their independent existence, without any

[79] Quoted by Sanso, *Policarpo Bonilla,* pp. 409-11.

This, it may be noted, is somewhat similar to the protests and pressure brought to bear in connection with the henequen situation and shipments from Yucatán to the United States.

[80] Martin, pp. 502-3.

[81] *Foreign Relations,* 1920, I, 311 ff.

other nation having the right to acquire, by conquest, any portion whatsoever of their territory, or the right to intervene in their Government or interior administration, nor in any way to injure their autonomy or national dignity." It was further declared that " The Monroe Doctrine does not oppose the efforts of Latin America to seek confederation or combination for the better accomplishment of their destinies." [82] As is well known the recommendation was tabled at Versailles but the fears of the Caribbean nations were all too apparent.

In both countries there was an absence of revolution (shall it be said because of United States disapproval?) during the war, in spite of the fact that Guatemala was dominated by an outright dictator. After the war revolution was still discouraged but neutrality was maintained as between contesting factions so long as they followed constitutional forms.[83] This was done in both countries to the satisfaction of Washington and to the satisfaction of successful rebels in Central America.

In both countries similar steps were taken in securing financial experts to effect fiscal reforms. This was agreed to in June, 1919, for Guatemala,[84] and was suggested for Honduras six months later, though the details were not worked out for another six months.[85] Obviously financial tutelage had evolved from the practical diplomacy of the day though it should be clearly distinguished from the connota-

[82] Sanso, p. 522.

[83] For United States position on disorders see *Foreign Relations,* 1920, II, 725 ff.; S. G. Inman in Blakeslee, *op. cit.,* pp. 272-3; Munro, p. 212.

[84] Thurston to Acting Secretary of State, May 14, 1919, and June 11, 1919, *Foreign Relations,* 1919, II, 276-7; 278.

[85] *Ibid.,* 1920, II, 872 ff.

tion of official support of private investments implied in the old term, Dollar Diplomacy. The one was a means of supervising official expenditures; the other was primarily support of private investments.

The smallest of the Central American family of nations, El Salvador, had long been a prosperous, self-sufficient little state. It had opposed the Bryan-Chamorro Treaty as infringing its rights and now found no reason to enter the World War just because the United States did so. True, it announced its sympathy and a benevolent neutrality by which United States vessels had " the same rights and privileges as the ships of El Salvador," but went no further than that.[86] Its financial condition was good so there was no way to apply the pattern of financial advice adopted for the four other Central American republics thus far considered. When hostilities threatened between El Sanvador and Honduras in the spring of 1920 there went out from Washington two communications that constituted a " Be good, both of you " warning.[87]

The latent fear of the United States was shown in December, 1919, when the Minister of Foreign Affairs addressed the Secretary of State and revived the question of the definition of the Monroe Doctrine. He stated that varying interpretations had been held in the past but that in view of the fact that the action at Versailles had transferred the Doctrine from that of an individual country " into a principle of universal law *juris et de jure*" he requested the Secretary " to be kind enough, if you think fit, to set

[86] Zaldivar to Secretary of State, April 12, 1917, *Foreign Relations,* 1917, supplement 1, p. 251; Martin, pp. 512-3.

[87] See Colby to Arnold, May 15, 1920, and Davis to Arnold, July 12, 1920, *Foreign Relations,* 1920, III, 733-4; 744-5.

forth the authentic idea of the Monroe Doctrine, as the illustrious Government of the White House understands it in the present historic moment and in its intentions for the future." [88] No reply was vouchsafed for two months when the answer was given that Wilson's views were those expressed before the Second Pan-American Financial Conference, in January, 1916.[89] And El Salvador was forced to profess itself satisfied with the evasion.

In many ways the most interesting incident occurring in Central America in the war period was the revolution led by the Tinoco brothers in Costa Rica who overthrew the established Government and took charge in January, 1917. It was probably financed or very substantially assisted by the United Fruit Company whose president was reported to be trying to secure valuable water, light and power concessions.[90] Following his principles Wilson refused to recognize the *de facto* president even though he was probably the most popular man in the Republic.[91] Efforts of the new dictator to secure a loan in the United States were stopped when the State Department warned the bank considering the matter that it would act " at its own risk." [92] In fact Washington insisted on a new election in which Federico Tinoco would not be a candidate.[93] Meanwhile, other Central American republics were urged not to recognize the Dictator.[94] On his part Tinoco declared war against Germany

[88] Paredes to Secretary of State, December 14, 1919, *ibid.*, I, 223-5.

[89] Polk to Sol, February 26, 1920, *ibid.*, I, 226.

[90] *Anderson Diary,* entry for February 15, 1917.

[91] Nerval, *Autopsy of the Monroe Doctrine,* p. 272; Jones, *op. cit.,* pp. 362-4; Munro, pp. 206-7; Martin, pp. 507-8.

[92] *Anderson Diary,* entry for April 9, 1917.

[93] *Ibid.,* entry for April 6, 1917.

[94] Lansing to Central American Legations, September 21, 1917, *Foreign Relations,* 1917, p. 343.

and offered his ports and harbors to the United States in the prosecution of the war. This was met by the statement that Tinoco was not recognized and so no response would be made.[95] It seems that the old legitimist faction was supported by pro-German influence if not money, so the United States certainly did not want it in power. It would not recognize Tinoco but did not wish him overthrown if that meant a return to power of the pro-Germans. Hence Washington adopted a consistent policy and announced that it would not countenance revolution to overthrow the Tinocos. In other words, it would starve out the existing government because it was not legal and insist on the following of democratic forms in setting up a new legal administration which would not be the old legitimist faction.[96]

From London and Paris came an unofficial request that the United States recognize the Ticonos as a war measure and this Lansing rather endorsed,[97] but Wilson was adamant, and in November the legation of the United States was closed as a protest when a pro-United States demonstration was broken up by Tinoco police.[98] The pressure on the dictator was severe by the spring of 1918 and steadily increased. Wilson insisted that his course was absolutely consistent and the only one " honorably open to us," [99] so

[95] Polk to Secretary of the Navy, May 2, 1917, *ibid.,* supplement 1, p. 274.

[96] Lansing to Price, December 29, 1917, *ibid.,* 1918, p. 349; Lansing to Jones, November 4, 1918, *ibid.,* 1918, p. 270.

[97] Lansing to the President, May 23, 1917, *The Lansing Papers,* II, 519-20.

[98] Lansing to Johnson, November 26, 1918, *Foreign Relations,* 1918, p. 275.

[99] Wilson to Ransdell, March 5, 1918, LC., Wilson MS; Lansing to Wilson, December 31, 1917, and Wilson to Lansing, January 1, 1918, *The Lansing Papers,* II, 521-2.

there was no more to be said until Tinoco was out. One of the brothers was assassinated August 11, 1919, and the Dictator resigned and fled the country the next day.[100] Certainly Moon is within the realm of reason when he states that the attitude of the United States had "encouraged" the new and successful revolution.

But the end was not quite yet, for the new administration, too, was unconstitutional and so was beyond the pale. The State Department sent word that the executive power should be placed in the hands of the alternate who would have constitutionally succeeded to power in case of death or displacement of the administration preceding Tinoco. This was done, elections were held and by December, 1919, the new government, *constitutionally elected*, was on its way.[101] Probably due to the illness of Wilson recognition was still held up but was finally extended August 2, 1920. Another country "shot into democracy"—or constitutional forms.[102]

In standing back and viewing the Central American area as a whole at the end of Wilson's eight years in the White House it is evident that Central America was far from agreed on its views of Washington policies. Nicaragua

[100] *Foreign Relations*, 1919, I, 850.   [101] *Ibid.*, 1919, I, 857 ff.

[102] An interesting question later developed when the now recognized Costa Rican government cancelled an oil concession originally made to a United States corporation by Tinoco but later transferred to a British concern. The British firm protested the cancellation but the United States upheld Costa Rica. The matter was finally referred to Chief Justice Taft of the United States Supreme Court as arbitrator. In October, 1923, his decision maintained that recognition or non-recognition of a government did not affect the validity of the acts of that government and that his decision was "controlled by the principles of international law." (A. C. Veach, "Oil, Great Britain and the United States," *Foreign Affairs*, IX, 671-2.)

and Panama were obviously dominated in their international thinking and acting by the United States and were no longer free agents even though it is logical to suppose that large numbers of the people in each country were pleased at the relationships that existed and the prosperity and peace that resulted. Guatemala, Honduras and Costa Rica under more or less pressure from Washington declared war from a year to fifteen months after the United States did,[103] but El Salvador did not.

United States investments in Central America were increased steadily from $40,000,000 in 1912 to $67,000,000 in 1916 and to $93,000,000 in 1920.[104] The State Department fostered this as is seen by Lansing's confidential instructions for the Alien Property Custodian of Guatemala saying:

that the Government of the United States deems it of the first importance that American interests be given every opportunity to offer their bids upon any German properties which might under Guatemala's Alien Property Custodian's ruling be sold. It is the duty of the United States diplomatic and consular officers to use the best efforts in every proper manner to assure to American citizens every possible advantage. There are at present important American groups anxious to enter the Guatemalan field. Request the delay of sale of any German properties until representatives of these United States groups arrive. Wire the moment legislation is passed permitting the sale of German properties.[105]

Similarly a " strictly confidential " instruction sent by Acting Secretary of State Frank Polk to the Acting Minister in Honduras expressed real apprehension in connection with

---

[103] *Foreign Relations,* 1918, supplement i, Vol. I, pp. 685 ff.

[104] Jones, Norton and Moon, *U. S. and the Caribbean,* p. 73

[105] Lansing to Leavell, September 27, 1918, *Foreign Relations,* 1918, supplement 2, p. 371.

the possible return to German owners of holdings on Fonseca Bay. Liquidation of this property was to be done preferably by the Honduran Government or by a United States concern if one capable of handling the proposition could be found in Honduras.[106]

By October, 1917, the question of saving the Central American Peace Court or of allowing it to expire was a pressing one. Chandler P. Anderson and Elihu Root were especially anxious to save the Court and went to considerable effort to do so. However, while they thought they had made some impression on the State Department they admitted that Lansing was convinced the Court " was not worth saving " since it was organized " on a political basis." [107] When El Salvador, Costa Rica and Honduras proposed to go ahead with a conference to discuss the situation and the continuance of the Court Washington sent word that it could not recognize such a step so long as Tinoco was the spokesman for Costa Rica. Nicaragua hesitated, proposed that Panama be added to the Union, and finally decided that it could not participate.[108] This ended the matter and another inherently antagonistic step toward the policy of the United States came to nothing.[109]

After the Democratic administration had been repudiated in the fall of 1920 another proposal was made for a conference to discuss union of the five little republics. Toward

[106] Polk to Jones, July 17, 1919, *ibid.*, 1919, II, 405-6.

[107] *Anderson Diary*, entries for October 15, 1917, and October 30, 1917.

[108] Cox, *Nicaragua and the U. S.*, p. 740; Leavell to Secretary of State, September 22, 1917, and December 11, 1917, *Foreign Relations*, 1917, pp. 44-5.

[109] Colby to Goold, November 18, 1920, *Foreign Relations*, 1920, I, 177.

this Secretary Colby simply expressed a disposition to regard "with friendly favor" decisions reached through the "free choice and unforced judgment of the people of Central America." At once a difference of opinion developed with regard to the Bryan-Chamorro treaty [110] and Nicaragua resigned from the conference rather than allow the treaty to be interpreted by the group. Costa Rica soon retired also leaving the three northern republics to proceed on a modified basis. But this weakened infant, in which Mr. Hughes, the New Secretary of State, expressed a prompt interest was only to be nursed for a time and was to expire in the arms of its sponsors at a later date.[111]

By and large it must be admitted that the influences of the Wilson idealism had been too little felt in Central America in the last four years. Probably the President knew little of what was happening. When he did become aware of any fact or development he tried to bring the program into line, but for the most part matters were regularly handled by the State Department. There is no doubt that revolutions were consistently frowned upon.[112] Some Central Americans like Bonilla frankly looked forward to the day when the United States program would develop so much jealousy that it would be undone [113] but more and more there was a feeling of resignation and of the uselessness of "kicking against the pricks." [114] A shrewd South American observer

[110] Martin to Secretary of State, December 23, 1920, *ibid.*, I, 178.

[111] P. M. Brown, "Federation of Central America," *Amer. Jour. of Int. Law*, XV, pp. 255 ff.; Cox, *op. cit.*, pp. 754-9; Munro, *op. cit.*, pp. 208-9.

[112] *Foreign Relations*, 1920, I, 319-23.

[113] Sanso, *Policarpo Bonilla*, pp. 528-9.

[114] S. G. Inman in Blakeslee, *Mexico and the Caribbean*, pp. 259-60; 265-7.

commented that it was not the *caudillos* " but the strong arm of the United States " which watched over the destinies of Central America.[115] That there had been variations in methods and applications was all too obvious. In general, peace had been steadily fostered (with the exception of the Tinoco situation which was unfortunate in flagrantly violating an announced principle) ; in general, economic welfare of the people had resulted (though United States interests had secured departmental if not presidential support in a fashion that would not have been expected in 1913) ; and above all, the strategic interests of the United States had been cared for and foreign interests steadily eliminated as potential or actual points of military and naval value were brought under the control of the United States.

Because of the volume of trade involved the countries entered into trade treaties and facilitated the work of travelling salesmen [116] and the like but they were by no means convinced that the program of the United States was as disinterested as the Mobile Address had led them to expect. Possibly Lansing's and Polk's " practical " instructions already quoted were sent without the knowledge of the preoccupied and later sick man in the White House, but Wilson's fetish of constitutionality sounded strained to peoples whose constitutions had long been little more than party platforms. They applauded the theory if their constitution was " in," while the opposition deplored it—and both listened for and half dreaded the " practical " notes received from time to time.

[115] F. García Calderón, " Dictatorship and Democracy in Latin America, *Foreign Affairs*,. III, 469.

[116] For a list of treaties to facilitate work of commercial agents see *Foreign Relations*, 1919, I, 45.

On the mainland south of the Canal matters remained pretty much *in statu quo*. Colombia was presented with some protests as to the conduct of radio stations in war time but these gave no serious complications. On the whole its attitude was rather well expressed by the phrase " benevolent neutrality." It listened to, but rejected, the proposal to endorse the Conference of Neutrals and like its neighbor Venezuela gave full merchandising privileges to armed United States merchantmen engaged in commerce, though it maintained diplomatic relations with Germany.[117]

In December, 1917, Wilson urged approval of the long-pending treaty because of its effects on other American States at that time [118] but the matter was not acted on. By 1919 Colombia had probably lost hope of salvation through Wilson and decided to seek results by other means than mere waiting. A tool lay ready to its hand in the fact that United States oil corporations were actively seeking concessions in Colombia.[119] That country seized its advantage and threatened to nationalize subsoil rights following the lead of Mexico. The two questions of the treaty and mineral rights were being merged in the correspondence of the State Department to the professed disappointment (possibly to the secret delight because of the appearance of the new weapon ready to hand) of the Bogotá diplomats.[120] Just as negotiations were opening to secure a more liberal law from the Colombian Congress toward oil concessionaires public feeling was inflamed by the United States Depart-

[117] *Ibid.*, 1917, supplement 2, Vol. II, pp. 1288-9; Martin, *Latin America and the War,* pp. 417-8; 424; 432-3; Robertson, *Hisp. Amer. Relations with the U. S.*, pp. 184-5.

[118] Baker, VIII, 413-4.

[119] *Foreign Relations*, 1919, I, 763 ff.

[120] Philip to Secretary of State, August 15, 1919, *ibid.*, 1919, I, 739-40.

ment of Commerce placing lighthouses on the cays of Roncador, Quita Sueño and Serranillo off the Colombian coast. These were placed in operation in June, 1919, in the belief that the said cays " appertain to the United States under the Guano Act." To a vigorous protest at an infringement of Colombian sovereignty and the information that this had injured the chances of the proposed legislation Lansing sent a " soft answer " saying the Department would be glad to discuss the matter.[121]

On the question of the petroleum legislation the Colombian Congress listened to reason and enacted a law which granted most of the desires of private companies.[122] However, Bogotá shrewdly refused to promise favorable treatment of United States concessionaires in case the treaty was approved by the Washington Senate though it could well point out that the ratification of the treaty would " open the door to many friendly acts." [123] Even Senator Lodge began to see the light but these developments came too late to be of advantage to the Wilson Administration which retired from office with the treaty still pending. A kind of poetic vengeance was accorded something like a year later when the Republican leaders called the treaty " good " and approved it.[124]

[121] *Ibid.*, 1919, I, *cir.* pp. 753 and 795 ff.

[122] *Ibid.*, 1919, I, 783 ff.; 1920, I, 823 ff.; Rippy, *U. S. and Colombian Oil*, pp. 27-8.

[123] Williams, *Economic Foreign Policy*, pp. 75-6.

[124] To keep the record clear it might be mentioned that when Colombia joined the League of Nations on July 20, 1920, its representatives recorded the fact that their acceptance of Article X of the Pact did not imply recognition of the independence of the Republic of Panama, for this was a question involving a treaty with the United States still held up by the United States Senate. Philip to Secretary of State, July 24, 1920, *Foreign Relations*, 1920, I, 825.

Of course Venezuela was under the dictatorship of the efficient General Juan Vicente Gómez who was a pronounced friend of the foreign investor, even though it was generally understood that his careful neutrality program was a cover for a real pro-German sympathy on the part of his Government throughout the contest. In fact, ratifications of a general arbitration treaty between the two New World countries signed in 1914 were not exchanged, on account of various delays, until February 12, 1921, or shortly before the Wilson administration passed into history. Also, it might be noted in passing that Venezuela was the native country of that bitter critic of United States foreign policy, Blanco Fombona, whose diatribes were "permeated with insult that reveals more heat than reason." [125] Wilson was exceedingly restless at the conditions that existed when they were drawn to his attention but his hands were so full of other affairs that he merely expressed his annoyance in a note to Lansing showing what he would have liked to do:

I have read this Memorandum with the greatest concern, as I have also the many recent communications from our Minister in Venezuela. This scoundrel [Gómez] ought to be put out. Can you think of any way in which we can do it that would not upset the peace of Latin America more than letting him alone will? [126]

The crusader's spirit still existed but there was just no way in war time that the United States could undertake to oust another Huerta at such a distance.

As has already been seen the control of the military resources of the island republics by the United States was

[125] Lewis, *America's Stake,* pp. 223 ff.; Martin, pp. 462-3; *British and Foreign State Papers,* LXIII, 1199-1201; Haring, *South America Looks at the U. S.,* pp. 156 ff.
[126] Quoted by Baker, VII, 550.

considered a prerequisite to any effective protection of the Canal in war time. Quite naturally Cuba, the nearest, largest, and most influential in economic life was the country to require the most careful handling. Fortunately the *simpático* Mr. Gonzales continued as liaison officer. As early as February 4, 1917, he telegraphed the Secretary of State:

Cuban Government will follow United States, taking action officially whenever you deem it advisable. Secretary of State Desvernine was visiting President at his country place this morning. . . . He brought a message of cordial sympathy from President Menocal.

At the suggestion of Secretary of State I accompanied him to the President's country place this afternoon. The President, with great cordiality, said that whatever Cuba had in moral and material support was at the service of the United States and he would sever relations with Germany at whatever time you deemed advisable. . . .

At my suggestion President will, from to-morrow, have a close watch kept on certain Germans here and all suspicious arrivals and will have secret-service men work at all likely places for supply bases along coast. . . .[127]

Two days later Wilson, in answering a letter of Lansing, noted the fact that Cuba might be especially vulnerable if it acted against Germany too quickly because of the danger of a prompt German attack and the seizure of bases for submarines. Lansing at once saw the Cuban Minister and advised him that his Government should proceed slowly.[128] Later, however, it was agreed that the moral effect of Cuba and Panama acting simultaneously with the United States in a declaration of war would be worth while. Thus, at 10

[127] Gonzales to Secretary of State, February 4, 1917, *Foreign Relations,* 1917, supplement 1, pp. 221-2.

[128] Wilson to Secretary of State, February 6, 1917, and memorandum of Lansing, February 7, 1917, *The Lansing Papers,* I, 594; 596.

P. M., April 7th, Gonzales reported that the Cuban Congress convened at 4.00 o'clock and that in thirty minutes the Senate had unanimously passed the measure authorizing the President to declare war on Germany, and that at " Fifteen minutes after six, House unanimously passed the act, members standing and cheering." [129]

Unanimity of this kind meant real enthusiasm for as has been seen repeatedly the United States on occasion could force legislation in these countries but it certainly had not been able to secure unanimous action when there was serious local opposition. The Cuban enthusiasm for cooperation was also seen in the actions of all from the President down. When the United States was slow to take advantage of the offer of Menocal to turn over four or five German steamships seized in Cuba he finally surrendered them personally to the United States Minister until the latter could transfer them to the Government of his country. When the Minister asked the terms of the transfer Menocal responded: " We are allies. Cuba will not accept a dollar." [130]

Though Cuba's eagerness to aid in all ways possible and to handicap the work of spies in Mexico, Spanish mails in transit were censored and at times Spanish ships were refused coal in Cuba with which to proceed to Mexico. This meant the return voyage was of necessity by way of the United States. In fact the pressure was so great that relations between Mexico and Cuba became strained and

[129] Gonzales to Secretary of State, April 7, 1917, *Foreign Relations,* 1917, supplement 1, p. 246; Fitzgibbon, *Cuba and the U. S.,* pp. 161-2; Martin, *op. cit.,* pp. 110-3.

[130] Gonzales, *Concerning Dollar Diplomacy,* p. 34; Gonzales to Secretary of State, August 21, 1917, *Foreign Relations,* 1917, supplement 1, pp. 318-9.

were broken off.[131] Gonzales recounts the following incident that had considerable influence: One morning the Sub-Chief of the Cuban secret service reported to the Minister that a Mexican minister on his way to Uruguay was going to his post via Cuba and Europe. This was strange but his baggage was covered by diplomatic immunity. Later the Sub-Chief reported that all the baggage was evidently harmless with the possible exception of a small locked trunk which was kept under the representative's bed during his short stay in Cuba.

It would be too bad if enemy secrets were therein. The Mexican Minister was leaving. In the dusk of the evening a truck bore the baggage toward the dock. Distressing calamity! Baggage truck was rammed by another truck driven by a fellow evidently drunk. Trunks scattered on street. However, all recovered. No, not all. A little trunk was missing. But the next morning it was found by efficient police in a nearby gully, and returned to a red-hot Minister whose sailing had been postponed. The Mexican Government jumped to conclusions. It demanded an apology from the Cuban Government.

" Mr. Minister," said General Menocal, " these people must be crazy. What am I to apologize for? Do they expect me to say my people committed an outrage? "

Upon apology being refused, Mexico recalled her Minister from Cuba and broke off diplomatic relations. . . .

As a final delightful touch to the story Gonzales laconically adds: " According to my information and belief there was really nothing in that precious trunk of interest to the Allies." [132]

After considerable discussion arrangements were made for

---

[131] For correspondence see *ibid.,* 1918, supplement i, Vol. II, pp. 1729 ff.; Martin, pp. 117; 126-8.

[132] Gonzales, *op. cit.,* p. 26.

a war loan to Cuba [133] to help with its military expenses. Also, Cuba arranged a price control of its major crop, sugar, that was wholly to the advantge of the United States.[134] Espionage acts, alien property management, food control and the activities of the War Trade Board of the United States were extended to Cuba as well as numerous other activities that contributed to the winning of the war. In addition upwards of $17,500,000 was subscribed in Cuba toward the second, third and fourth Liberty Loans of the United States (no bonds were placed on sale in Cuba for the first loan) and this ignores the large amounts bought through United States banks by Cuban firms and the other large sums contributed for miscellaneous war drives.[135]

In considering actual events of the war probably the most significant incident for this study was the threatened revolt in 1917. At such a time it was out of the question to permit a revolution, so while constitutional and professional critics complained at the invasion of the sacred right of revolution [136] the expected happened. Wilson was innately opposed to armed disturbances of domestic peace on general principles and his early disapproval of the revolutionary movement was automatic. When both countries had entered the war it was natural that the rebels should have been denounced as German agents, though there is no reason to consider the charge at all seriously.[137] About the middle of February the United States took a decisive stand and informed its agents throughout Cuba, with instructions to make the fact public, that:

---

[133] *Foreign Relations,* 1918, pp. 298-324.
[134] Martin, pp. 166-8.   [135] *Ibid.,* pp. 168-9.
[136] Beals, *Crime of Cuba,* pp. 221-3.
[137] Chapman, *History of Cuban Republic,* pp. 380-1.

1. The Government of the United States supports and
    sustains the Constitutional Government of the
    Republic of Cuba.
2. The armed revolt against the Constitutional Govern-
    ment of Cuba is considered by the Government of
    the United States as a lawless and unconstitutional
    act and will not be countenanced.
3. The leaders of the revolt will be held responsible for
    injury to foreign nationals and for destruction of
    foreign property.
4. The Government of the United States will give care-
    ful consideration to its future attitude towards
    those persons connected with and concerned in the
    present ·disturbance of peace in the Republic of
    Cuba.[138]

Few denied that there had been fraud in the recent
election but at such a time the question was simply not to
be agitated by any other than peaceful means, and since
Menocal had control of the government that meant that he
must remain in power. To prevent property destruction it
was urged that a strong detachment of United States marines
be landed, which would allow Cuban troops to devote all
their attention to elimination of the rebels. True, certain
United States interests encouraged the rebels to think their
action would bring United States intervention and control
but President Wilson and Gonzales would have none of
it.[140] Small detachments of marines were repeatedly landed
in February and March. In April there was considerable
destruction of property and it was obvious that more definite

[138] Lansing to Gonzales, February 18, 1917, also Lansing to Gonzales, February 13, 1917, and March 23, 1917, *Foreign Relations,*
1917, pp. 387-8; 356; 363.
[139] L. J. Meyer, "The U. S. and the Cuban Revolt of 1917,"
Hisp. Amer. Hist. Rev., X, 141-3.
[140] Gonzales, *op. cit.,* p. 27.

steps were needed. By May there was some discussion of sending United States regulars to take the place of the marines. This Menocal disapproved though he agreed to a proclamation declaring that since Cuba had entered the war " the United States will be forced to consider as its own enemies those persons in revolt against the Constitutional Government, unless they immediately return to their allegiance." [141]

Thus matters continued until July 12 when Acting Secretary of State Polk telegraphed Gonzales that he should inform Menocal that United States marines had been withdrawn from Cuba for service at other places and that Washington

now contemplates sending of forces of the United States Army to replace these marines, but in view of relations now existing between the two countries, on account of their cooperation in the war against the Imperial German Government, it desires to take this action with his full understanding.

You will add that it is also considered to be of great importance to have these troops in Cuba at this time in case the United States forces in Haiti or Santo Domingo, or in any of the Caribbean possessions of the United States might need reinforcement, as well as for the purpose of taking over the guarding of interests important for the prosecution of the war, upon which duty the marine forces are now engaged.

Two days later Gonzales responded with the happy suggestion:

Your July 12, 7 P. M. received midnight July 13. Saw President at his country place today and presented matter. He gives his cordial approval.

[141] Lansing to Gonzales, May 11, 1917, and Gonzales to Secretary of State, May 11, 1917, and May 13, 1917, *Foreign Relations,* 1917, pp. 404-5.

The President also authorizes me to offer United States sites for training camps in other parts of Cuba if it should be considered desirable to send troops to train in mild winter climate.[142]

After some delays due to conditions in the United States, upwards of 2,500 troops were despatched in August.[143] In the weeks that followed the few rebel leaders who were captured were treated with much leniency, apparently on instructions of Washington,[144] but the significant feature of the whole affair lay in the fact that not only was Cuban sugar production maintained but that Cuban military facilities were frankly integrated as a part of the whole Caribbean program at a time of crisis. What amounted to a mild form of military occupation of Cuba had taken place.

During the war Cuba enjoyed fantastic prosperity as the price of sugar skyrocketed. In 1920 the orgy of speculation reached its height with prices on sugar delivered in New York reaching the unheard of figure of twenty-two and one-half cents per pound.[145] The 3,000,000 Cubans " rolled in wealth " and reached the conclusion that happy days had come to stay. But the bubble was pricked when it became known that there was not a shortage but an actual over-supply of sugar waiting for the peace time market. The inevitable result was financial disaster for those who had recently geared their expenses to now impossible income levels and for those who had invested their money in the speculative market. To make matters worse the post-war

[142] Polk to Gonzales, July 12, 1917, and Gonzales to Secretary of State, July 14, 1917, *ibid.*, 412.

[143] Jenks, *Our Cuban Colony,* p. 195.

[144] Chapman, pp. 383-4.

[145] For a detailed list of price fluctuations see the exchange quotations, or Jenks, pp. 218-9.

reaction had gripped the United States. Now all evils that had developed during the war were recalled and aggravated and Cuba was faced with the serious possibility of political as well as economic disaster.

Mutterings over renewed frauds in the election of 1918 became more ominous but Washington certainly did not want to intervene so General E. H. Crowder was sent back to Cuba as adviser as the presidential term approached a close.[146] The electoral machinery bogged down and it was Crowder's job to attempt to iron out the troubles to the satisfaction of all concerned.[147] He was thoroughly acquainted with the island for he had been there repeatedly in the preceding twenty years and had helped to revise the electoral code in 1919. He was genuinely popular with all factions and had a unique opportunity. Troops were still in the country but there was no desire or intention to use them for police purposes. They had simply been left there " conveniently " from the training days of the World War and had not yet been recalled, though Wilson declined to allow additional warships to visit Cuban waters during the election.[148] By way of warning the Secretary of State pointed out that the United States was " by treaty pledged " to maintain a government in Cuba " adequate for the protection of life, property, and individual liberty " and that it was therefore " unalterably opposed to substitute violence and revolution for the processes of government," and that it was " no less opposed to intimidation and fraud in the

[146] *Foreign Relations,* 1919, II, 1-29. Crowder's able report is found in *ibid.,* II, 29-77.

[147] For instructions see Davis to Crowder, December 31, 1920, *ibid.,* 1920, II, 41-3.

[148] *Ibid.,* 1920, II, p. 23.

conduct of elections." [149] The total result was what has been termed " Preventative Intervention."

In a situation where business was at a standstill, finances in the grip of a moratorium, and political feelings at fever heat, Crowder started his program of rehabilitation. This had barely been initiated when the Wilson administration passed from the scene so there is no place here to discuss details. Certainly careful supervision continued to the very end as may be seen by the protest of February 11, 1921, at what Washington considered an excessive budget submitted to Congress and by the instructions to Crowder to see that it was not enacted into law.[150] However, the significant fact of the four years seems to be that a sympathetic handling of the relations of the two countries had made for little less than complete harmony in a time of crisis. The local opposition to the Cuban administration seems to have arisen primarily from local questions and not because of the pro-United States attitude of Menocal. The two alternatives facing the Caribbean countries in the World War seem to have been cooperation or military occupation—but in Cuba at least it was fundamental cooperation that developed to the mutual advantage of both parties.

Across the narrow Windward Channel to the east of Cuba lay the tortured so-called republic of Haiti. As has been seen United States forces were in essential control of the country before the entry into the World War. Now ensued one of the most debated incidents in recent United States foreign policy, and one of which the man in the street was to hear more than of almost any other with the exception of the Mexican situation.

[149] Guggenheim, *U. S. and Cuba,* p. 213.
[150] *Ibid.,* pp. 224-5.

So far as the War was concerned the President of Haiti was rather reluctant to act unless the United States would guarantee him full support against domestic opposition. Even when this was assured he still hesitated [151] and sharp prodding from Washington on May 11, 1917, secured a mere endorsement of benevolent neutrality toward the United States from his National Assembly.[152] The question of declaring war was held in abeyance pending the adoption of the new constitution but was raised once more in May, 1918. Finally, on July 15th war was formally declared on Germany.[153]

The opposition to the constitution desired by Washington continued unabated in the Assembly so it was decided to draft the document and submit it directly to the voters of the nation. The Assembly was dissolved by force and a plebiscite on the adoption of the constitution was set for June 12, 1918. Occupation officers and the representatives of the titular president of the Republic urged the adoption of the document. Marine officers called for the attendance of the people at the election, and in cases themselves distributed the " correct " ballots for illiterate voters to cast. Wholesale pressure if not actual intimidation secured the desired result.[154] Though opposition in the Assembly under-

[151] Memoranda of Chief of Division of Latin-American Affairs, April 21, 1917 and April 24, 1917, *Foreign Relations,* 1917, supplement 1, pp. 266-7.

[152] Polk to Blanchard, May 5, 1917, and Blanchard to Secretary of State, May 11, 1917, *ibid.* 1917, supplement i, pp. 276; 279.

[153] Lansing to Blanchard, May 10, 1918, Menos to Secretary of State, July 15, 1918, *ibid.,* 1918, supplement 1, Vol. I, pp. 688-9; 708-9.

[154] *Hearings on Sen. Res. 112,* I, 191-2; Millspaugh, *Haiti under Amer. Control,* pp. 74-7; Davis, *Black Democracy,* p. 209.

stood to have popular approval had been so serious as to force the dissolution of the Assembly, the vote in this election stood 69,337 to 335! As Buell summarizes the new document it was different from the one previously in force in that it: 1. Gave foreigners the right to own land; 2. Ratified the acts of the occupation, and 3. Authorized the suspension of the legislature.[155] As a result, drafted extra-constitutionally, if not unconstitutionally; and adopted by force, if not fraud; there was no further unconstitutionality in the absence of a legislative body.

Dissatisfaction, already widespread, became more and more serious as the United States entered the World War and relaxed its supervision of the details of the Occupation. In extenuation of the unfortunate developments it should be remembered that these men had not been trained for colonial administration or service. If given their preference the great majority of them would have elected to serve in Europe. Here, in a trying situation, in some cases they lost their grip on their own finer natures and the disastrous results so well known ensued.

One continuing source of trouble was the corvée, or enforced labor system by which the natives were required to build roads in their own districts. Marines supervised most of the work though the actual management of the natives was usually in the hands of Haitian gendarmes.[156] Feelings mounted steadily until they reached a climax with serious Caco uprisings in 1919. In these the commandant in charge of Marines in a report of casualties by years gave a total of 2,250 Haitians killed to thirteen Marines killed

[155] Buell, *Amer. Occupation of Haiti,* pp. 348-9.
[156] *Hearings on Sen. Res. 112,* I, 163-4; Kelsey, *The Annals,* C, 137-8.

and twenty-eight wounded.[157] In a vicious little campaign there were apparently cases where needless terrorization was resorted to in the killing of natives, destruction of their property, torture and abuse of prisoners and the like.[158] Entirely too many non-commissioned officers were given gendarme commissions or were placed in positions of authority for which they did not have proper education, restraints, or civilization when it came to dealing with an essentially primitive people.

In a country of notoriously loose public and private morals [159] numbers of the officers and men of the Marine Corps did not prove above reproach. Inevitably under such circumstances there was a storm of protest throughout Haiti—and this storm was promptly duplicated in the United States where a peculiarly bitter national election was pending. Conflicts in authority, lack of supervision and restraint due to the European War which had almost monopolized attention, and thoroughly demoralized and demoralizing local conditions in Haiti had resulted in conditions that were shameful in the eyes of a self-respecting civilized people. On the other hand there were prompt efforts to get at the facts and Secretary of the Navy Daniels ordered a prompt and full investigation together with numerous reports from the commanding officers.[160]

Reports of these investigations did not blink the fact that abuses had developed but did insist that they had been

[157] Davis, p. 318.

[158] *Hearings on Sen. Res. 112,* I, 246-7; 427; 465-76; 580-2; 759-71; II, 894-5. For conservative estimates see Munro, pp. 166-8; Buell, pp. 350-2.

[159] Kelsey, *op. cit.,* pp. 124-8.

[160] Inman in Blakeslee, *Mexico and the Caribbean,* pp. 257-8; G.H. Stuart, *Lat. Amer. and the U. S.,* pp. 235-6.

grossly exaggerated as to both geographical extent and existence in duration of time. They also insisted that the abuses were not countenanced by higher officers or by the men of the occupation in general.[161] Mr. Carl Kelsey who made a careful independent investigation insisted that prisons were far better than in the old days and came to the conclusion that the whole matter can be summed up in " Rumor is common; evidence is rare." He said that drunkenness and accompanying disorders had been relatively common; that sexual crimes had existed but that gross instances had been severely punished; that the third degree had been resorted to in order to secure evidence, and that deliberate striking, shooting, etc. of escaping prisoners had occurred in some cases. Also there had been social friction between the two races as was almost inevitable.[162] On the other hand, while it is no excuse for such misconduct it might well be remembered that these very crimes had been common in the disorders which had long cursed the country and that now they were accompanied by many features of economic improvement not then present.

So far as the finances of the Republic were concerned a simple statement can be made: they were controlled by United States officers with only occasionally successful local resistance. During the war when exorbitant profits were being made in the United States some excessive interest rates and advantages for United States bankers were also secured in Haiti.[163] Naturally the bankers dealing with

[161] McCormick, *Inquiry into Occupation* . . . . , pp. 12; 21-5.
[162] Kelsey, *The Annals*, C, 140; 142-3.
[163] Thomas, *One Hundred Years of the Monroe Doctrine*, p. 236. See also *Foreign Relations,* 1917, pp. 807-8; *ibid.,* 1919, II, 371-3, and *British and Foreign State Papers,* CXII, 1131-2.

such a country had serious difficulties and it would seem that the first two financial advisers were not as efficient as they should have been.[164] In general though, abuses were now recognized as such and talked about whereas before they had existed more or less as a matter of course. Now the basic purpose of the financial department of the Government was to see that the revenues were secured and applied to officially recognized objectives while before all possible was collected from the people and only the minimum necessary turned over to the Government after each person or institution had retained the maximum possible either through legal or illegal methods depending on opportunities and positions.

In the earlier days of the war petty financial pressure such as the suspension of salaries of cabinet officers and other public officials in order to secure desired legislative enactments or decrees was occasionally resorted to by local representatives of the United States in Haiti. This was not approved toward the end of the Wilson Administration when time made possible proper consideration of Caribbean affairs, and orders of this type were cancelled.[165] Washington had once more waked up, thanks either to renewed opportunity for consideration or because of the protests that had arrived.

Technically, the Haitians could claim that the first default on the foreign debt came after the Occupation but this was largely due to the World War and the general financial program that marked a real advance over previous conditions. (Chapman, " Development of Intervention in Haiti," *Hisp. Amer. Hist. Rev.*, VII, 308-9; Millspaugh, *op. cit.*, pp. 132-3; Davis, pp. 199-200.)

[164] Kelsey, pp. 160-1; also Balch, pp. 53-4.

[165] Ample correspondence in *Foreign Relations*, 1920, II, 770-811.

Further friction was caused by the agreement reached in August, 1918, that all proposed Haitian laws and decrees should be submitted to the Legation before being promulgated,[166] and by the installation of a new educational system. With the sums available for education pitifully small at best the situation was complicated by the fact that the Haitians liked the classical type of education based on French models, but the officers of the Occupation were convinced that a more practical education to emphasize agriculture, domestic science, manual training and the like was what was good for the native and what he ought to like. The whole question was somewhat academic and theoretical because of the exceedingly small number of children affected in any case but it was the subject of violent debate and high feelings among the best people of the country.[167]

A kindred source of friction was the rigid censorship of the press that was established. The fact that there had never been liberty of the press in the Republic, hence no adequate system of control of an intelligent opposition press—which had never been allowed to develop—is something that is frequently overlooked. However, it must be admitted, undemocratic restraints were applied and there were widely advertised and often misrepresented protests.[168]

And so in summary it appears that in a period of war the United States had assumed relatively complete control

[166] *Ibid.*, 1919, II, *cir.* p. 336; *ibid.*, 1920, II, 760 ff.; Buell, p. 354; Millspaugh, pp. 78-81.

[167] Kelsey, pp. 130-1; Buell, *op. cit.*, pp. 361-2; P. H. Douglas, "Amer. Occupation of Haiti," *Pol. Sc. Quar.*, XLII, p. 371; Balch, pp. 98-104.

[168] Kelsey, pp. 140-1; Balch, pp. 73-5.

of Haiti yet had imposed on itself a queer self-restraint in supporting the farce of a local government which had often been obstructive in its conduct. Though enjoying financial and political control and insisting on the right of foreigners to acquire lands few land acquisitions had ensued; [169] most of the foreign officers and workmen had done good work [170] under most trying conditions; efforts were made by Washington to respect Haitian courts and over-zealous officials were reprimanded for interfering in local affairs,[171] especially after 1919; a public works and an educational program were launched and a financial program adopted that eliminated old evils and provided a foundation on which future progress was possible.

Probably the most significant weakness lay in failure to establish a system for the proper training of Haitians in the art of self-government. Through a feeling of racial antagonism or self-superiority the treaty official all too often ignored his Haitian associate instead of training him. In brief, an airplane and radio system of government was installed but there was grave question if an illiterate man accustomed to walking or driving a burro or ox would be able to manage the system when, and if, he took charge of it. Mr. Kelsey came to the conclusion in 1920 that if the marines were removed there would be a revolution and that intelligent Haitians wanted them to remain but wanted them out of sight just as much as possible. " My guess is that a free and honest expression of Haitian opinion would show 90 per cent in favor of the continued maintenance of order by the United States; but opinions differ as to the

[169] Millspaugh, p. 153; Balch, pp. 73-5.
[170] Kelsey, pp. 139-40.
[171] *Foreign Relations,* 1920, II, 780-2; 796-7; 815-6.

best scheme." [172]   Much of Latin America definitely looked upon this situation as a horrible example of crass imperialism and the Republican orators in the campaign of 1920 denounced it, Mr. Harding himself stating:

If I should be elected President . . . I will not empower an Assistant Secretary of the Navy to draft a constitution for helpless neighbors in the West Indies and jam it down their throats at the points of bayonets borne by United States marines, nor will I misuse the power of the Executive to cover with a veil of secrecy repeated acts of unwarranted interference in the domestic affairs of the little republics of the Western Hemisphere, such as in the last few years have not only made enemies of those who should be our friends but have rightly discredited our country as a trusted neighbor.[173]

But this was in the heat of a campaign, and shortly the new administration when in office reached the conclusion expressed in another connection but applied here too that the United States should not allow itself to be found in a position of responsibility without commensurate authority— and again Haiti remained a problem in which the United States had about agreed that it was " muddling " and could only hope that it was " muddling through."

Just to the east lay Santo Domingo which it will be remembered had been entirely placed under the control of

[172] Kelsey, p. 163. See also *ibid.*, pp. 149-50; *Hearings on Sen. Res. 112,* II, 902.

Cardinal Gibbons wrote Lansing, September 8, 1918: " I have talked with him [Monsignor Kersuzan, bishop of Cape [*sic*] Haitien] at great length about these affairs. He and his fellow bishops, and the clergy of Haiti are all very friendly to the American occupation, and appreciate the great benefits that result from it." (LC., Lansing MS.)

[173] Quoted by Davis, p. 320. See also *Hearings on Sen. Res. 112,* I, 263.

the United States so that its very national existence was at best in a condition of suspended animation.[174] The Navy assumed complete control with Rear-Admiral Harry S. Knapp in charge. He decided to interfere in local affairs as little as possible and proceeded to use the already considerable number of trained United States and friendly Dominican workers in the country. The policy seemingly was approved in Washington and most of the Dominicans cooperated well. About a year later Rear-Admiral Snowden was placed in control and he changed the program, apparently without protest from Washington, and largely ignored Dominicans by an increasingly detailed and strict military control. Only a nominal supervision of Dominican affairs was maintained by the Navy Department in Washington and officials there appear to have been essentially ignorant of what was happening in the Island.[175] The State Department had practically withdrawn from the picture [176] so there was all the more reason to consider that the nation of Santo Domingo was non-existent, even though the legal fiction was still maintained.[177]

Admiral Knapp had been interested in a fundamental program which included the settlement of claims against the government, the definition of land claims and the establishment of police and civil service systems.[178] There were some complaints of harsh conduct of marines but they were few. After the sterner Snowden program was adopted

[174] Martin, p. 485.
[175] Welles, *Naboth's Vineyard*, II, 818-20.   [176] *Ibid.*, II, 827.
[177] Memorandum of Office of Solicitor for the Department of State, March 18, 1918, *Foreign Relations*, 1918, pp. 382-9.
[178] Annual Report of Military Governor, July 21, 1917, *ibid.*, 1917, pp. 709-20. See also Welles, *op. cit.*, II, 805-15; Kelsey, p. 168.

and the Dominicans felt that they had no voice in their own affairs friction became more serious, especially as the occupation seemed to be making its plans for more or less permanent control. Beyond doubt revenue collections improved [180] steadily so there was apparent justification for general satisfaction in the United States over the situation. Unfortunately this was partially fictitious due to war conditions and to the fact that the United States Government was bearing part of the expenses of government. However, the maintenance of law and order, school expansion and miscellaneous internal reforms should also be noted even though an unfortunately rigid censorship brought about the arrest of prominent Dominicans and created much criticism.[182]

By 1919 a strong movement for resumption of self-government had resulted in sending the Provisional President at the time of the intervention to consult the State Department with the active endorsement of certain agents of the Department.[183] However, the Military Governor was convinced that such projects " for the restoration of Dominican Civil Government, would result in anarchy and early ruin of this country, as there have been so many factions of divergent views taken for power rendering task [sic]. Dominican Government election impossible [184] [sic]." Ad-

[179] For example see Hearings on Sen. Res. 112, II, 1119-22.

[180] Quarterly Report of Military Governor, October 18, 1918, Foreign Relations, 1918, p. 369; Kelsey, cir. p. 188.

[181] Knight, Americans in Santo Domingo, pp. 98-107; Stuart, p. 293.

[182] Schoenrich in Blakeslee, op. cit., pp. 212-3; 245; Knight, pp. 116-7.

[183] Foreign Relations, 1919, II, 98 ff.

[184] Roosevelt to Secretary of State, August 27, 1919, ibid., 1919, II, 120-1.

miral Snowden was convinced that the control should continue for twenty years and the systematic ignoring of
Dominican recommendations caused even cooperationists
among them to give up hope.[185]

But the State Department and the American public were
beginning to wake up on the subject.[186] Wilson's program
called for self-government so to the great surprise of the
officers of the Occupation who frankly considered themselves agents of the United States and not of the Dominican [187] Republic, in December, 1920, orders were received
to proclaim throughout Santo Domingo that military control was to end.[188] Beyond doubt there had been mistakes
and blunders committed by an absolutist government intrusted with controlling the minute details of everyday life
of a strange people.[189] Also it is likely that individual
officers had not been above reproach in their personal conduct. However, this order was certainly sudden and
unexpected.

[185] Welles, II, 826-7.
[186] For pressure on State Department see *ibid.,* II, 822-9.
[187] Secretary of the Navy Daniels wrote the Secretary of State
on November 29, 1920:
. . . it is my conclusion . . . that the Military Government by
armed forces of the United States in the Dominican Republic
should not be regarded as " administering affairs for the Government of the Republic " by virtue of any authority derived from the
sovereign people of Santo Domingo, but as administering the
affairs of the Government of that Republic for, on account of, and
by authority of the Government of the United States whose agent
it, the Military Government, is; the Government of the United
States having taken over in their entirety the Governmental functions of Santo Domingo, the Dominican Republic. (*Foreign Relations,* 1920, II, 144.)
[188] Davis to Russell, December 4, 1920, *ibid.,* 1920, II, 145-6.
[189] Kelsey, p. 189; Schoenrich in Blakeslee, pp. 210-1.

Just why this was done has been the subject of much debate. Certainly the Department of State was worried about the Latin American attitude toward the Dominican program of the United States and was trying to offset this by publicity secured in Latin American periodicals.[190] Some stated that the announcement of the withdrawal in December, 1920, after the Democrats had been defeated at the polls was for the specific purpose of putting the Republicans in a difficult position. These felt that the new administration should have had the right to announce its own policy and that it was unfair for it to come into office committed to a program that had been announced by the old administration after it had been repudiated. To the sick and disappointed man in the White House this probably appeared to be a last act in vindication of the principles for which he had stood and to which he was truly devoted. If their application at this time in concrete form tended to complicate the path of those who had just defeated him in a bitter mud-slinging campaign, a somewhat ironical smile would be all that could be expected of him. The Republicans had complained of his domineering in the Caribbean; very well, he would withdraw United States troops. Thinking Dominicans had expected to wait until the new party took office for any major policy change but the disconcerting announcement at once set the Dominican political pot to bubbling merrily.[191] Kelsey found himself at a loss to explain or justify the intervention in the first place, and then at a loss to justify the offer to withdraw in the second.[192]

[190] Davis to Diplomatic Officers of the United States in Latin America, October 2, 1920, *Foreign Relations,* 1920, II, 132.
[191] Kelsey, p. 192.   [192] *Ibid.,* pp. 177-8; 197-8.

However, using the vantage point of additional distance and considering the Caribbean as a whole, and Santo Domingo as part of that whole, much of the difficulty is removed. Military defense of the Canal and of the Caribbean demanded occupation or control in war time; therefore control was secured even at the expense of a real enthusiasm for self-government on the part of Wilson. As soon as the war was over and the military need had passed, self-government as a principle was once more followed as the basis of the administration's actions wherever practicable. Complicating details had developed during the occupation due to the fact that the paternal direction was no longer in the kindly hands of Wilson but in those of subordinates who were not actuated by his high idealism. The question may be asked why the same thing was not done in Haiti. Probably because the control of the United States was much more recent and local leaders less well trained, and because that country as a result could not yet be relieved of some military supervision.

Still farther to the east lay Puerto Rico. During the war there was an excellent spirit of cooperation and young men of the island readily entered the armies of the United States under the Selective Service Act, while those at home supported Liberty Loans, Red Cross drives and the like most cordially. The Jones Bill had greatly increased the base of the suffrage and extended principles of self-government but now there was a rising unrest and a demand for further consideration. Many of the people wanted statehood but others felt the proposal unwise.[193] The one thing most Puerto Ricans were agreed on was the need for further

[193] Pedro Capo Rodriguez in Blakeslee, pp. 337-8; 358-60.

recognition in some form or other. That, however, was a problem for the coming decade to face.

Those new possessions, the Virgin Islands, acquired as a war measure, were now by way of becoming a problem too. Reasons for acquisition were one thing but how to handle them was another. As early as December 31, 1917, Rear-Admiral James H. Oliver, Governor of the islands, wrote that he feared they would be an increasing burden financially.[194] In his reply of February 11, 1918, headed "Personal and Confidential," Lansing agreed that the islands had no immediate strategic value and should be transferred from the Navy Department to civil control as soon as possible unless the navy planned some use for them. He repeated that they had been acquired as a kind of insurance against possible foreign aggression. Reasoning from Haiti and Liberia as examples the Secretary was convinced the government must come from without the islands for he felt that while the African race had produced many exceptions still it was "devoid of any capacity for political organization" and lacked "genius for government." [195] Here the matter rested.

And so the study of individual regions of the Caribbean during the War is brought to a close. What about the picture as a whole? In spite of contradictions people with a perspective can feel that the program was harmonious. Major European powers were sufficiently aware of the problems of defense and of economic needs to know that the United States would dominate the region so there was no further debate or protest. Whether this country entered into the League of Nations or not, was, so far as the

---

[194] LC., Lansing MS.　　　　[195] *Ibid.*

Caribbean was concerned, an academic point. The few contradictory Europeon expressions merely reflected wishful thinking with regard to the small remaining European colonies there and the thinly disguised wish that some of the riches of the sparsely occupied New World possessions might be acquired.

In Latin America the Caribbean policy was likewise recognized as a very real thing. However, as such it had not been professed, acknowledged officially, or sponsored by Washington so there was no uniform thinking in connection with it. The result was often an unreasoning fear that the United States would sooner or later dominate, or attempt to dominate, the whole New World. Almost everything that had ever been done by the United States in the New World had by some, and usually by Washington, been ascribed to the Monroe Doctrine. That Doctrine simply referred to the New World as a whole so what was more logical than to suppose that the recent procedure in the Caribbean would soon be the policy applied to the wole hemisphere? Visits by Root, Knox and Colby to the contrary, repeated professions of Root and Wilson to the contrary, self-denying action in Mexico and proclamations of withdrawal from Santo Domingo to the contrary, the fact remained that with tacit European and world approval the United States was dominating the Caribbean when and how it wished. It was doing it in the name of the Monroe Doctrine but the wording of that Doctrine included the whole hemisphere. So popular arguments and thinking always rounded back to the same point—the hemisphere was in danger.

Thus, fear reached a crescendo as Pan-Americanism was declared to be suicidal for Latin America since it was the sheep's clothing that covered the wolf of expansion and imperialism so long as the United States dominated and directed the movement.[196] The Latin-American was held to be the world's ideal race [197] and every effort should be made to develop it. When the United States was felt to sponsor the Treaty of Versailles and the League of Nations, Latin American nations at first hesitated to enter the League, which they felt the powerful nation of the north would dominate so far as New World affairs were concerned. Then when the United States declined to join they rather felt that they should do so as an insurance against United States aggression. If they stood together at Geneva they might well be able to invoke the aid and sympathy of Europe in their own behalf.

To offset this there was a rarely questioned appreciation of the idealism of Woodrow Wilson and of what he had stood for. This was shown in the development of his idea for an " American League " or Concert of the Western World that was discussed somewhat generally.[198] Scholars of real ability were beginning to discriminate in judging United States actions, and efforts to bring about a better understanding of what had happened were fostered by such able men as Alejandro Alvarez and others.[199]

[196] Alvarez, The Monroe Doctrine, pp. 224-6.

[197] F. García Calderón, " Latin America, Europe and the U. S.," Foreign Affairs, VII, 196-7.

[198] W. R. Shepherd, " The Monroe Doctrine Reconsidered," Pol. Sc. Quar., XXXIX, 64. Also Julius Klein, " The Monroe Doctrine as a Regional Understanding," Hisp. Amer. Hist. Rev., IV, 252-3.

[199] For articles in a single learned journal see those of Alejandro Alvarez, S. G. Inman and W. E. Dunn in Hisp. Amer. Hist. Rev., Vols. I-IV.

In the United States the confusion was almost as great though certain facts were emerging into national consciousness. The public feeling was that the Canal was national property and anything in that general neighborhood ought to be under control if needed for defense. Beyond that the average man had the vaguest of notions as to whether the region included half a dozen or a score of countries. But leaders were very conscious of weaknesses in the national program and were sincerely desirous of remedying them. Many admitted the confusion in the meanings that had been attached to the Monroe Doctrine and called for clarifications.[200] Calls were made for a central administrative organization to handle colonies so that differing programs would not be adopted simultaneously and so that untrained men would not be placed in responsible positions.[201] The new Secretary of State Hughes stated specifically that his nation had varying policies for varying regions and that they could not all be denominated " Monroe Doctrine " but should be distinguished from each other. At the very least, said others, if the old name was to be retained it should be an international policy, internationally adopted throughout the Americas, and jointly applied.

Obviously there still remained much to be done in the way of clarifying national thinking, but the people had come a long way since 1890. At that time the man in the street knew little or nothing of any region beyond the continental borders of his own nation. Appealed to by

[200] Charles E. Hughes, " Centenary of the Monroe Doctrine," *The Annals,* III, supplement, *cir.* pp. 18-9; W. R. Shepherd, *op. cit.,* p. 62.

[201] Major General Frank McIntyre, "American Territorial Administration," *Foreign Affairs,* X, 301.

imperialists he endorsed their program in order to secure, as he thought, rights for Cubans and blessings of civilization for downtrodden peoples in the Far East. When he became aware that this program had been prostituted at times on behalf of business men and that the blessings of civilization given to the other fellow brought serious difficulties to the giver, he reacted vigorously. From that time forward expansionist moves had to be justified on special grounds in order to secure endorsement. Dollar Diplomacy was repudiated and held up to scorn even though the dollar diplomats were simply following the program of expansionist nations through the centuries.

Then there came to the White House a man who expressed the conscience of the American people as he called for democracy and self-government as fundamental principles and as he denounced dictatorship and land-grabbing by force. He honestly endeavored to carry out his principles and gave the world a splendid lesson in patience and went far to prove his principles in practice in Mexico. Left in peace the world might have been able to applaud his program as an outstanding success even though forcible disapproval of revolutions and of dishonestly elected officials in other countries might have caused no little pondering on the situation by outsiders. But he was not left in peace and the pressure of war forced, with or without his active planning, the military occupation and control of strategic points throughout the Caribbean. Imperialists, strategists, and "practical" politicians could boast that idealism was dead and their ideas triumphant.

Not so with the American people. They might be lulled to sleep by the anaesthetic of prosperity for a few years and during that time might again be blind to the evils of Dollar Diplomacy, but indiscriminate expansion had been stopped and a rising clamor demanded the withdrawal of marines from Haiti, Santo Domingo, Nicaragua, Cuba, and Panama. A national conscience had been created, largely in this thirty years, which would again adopt " democracy " as its watchword and cooperation in the New World as its slogan, even while it insisted on supporting absolute domination of key military objectives in the Caribbean as a very minimum and was ready to include others when they appeared to be essential. And further this conscience demanded that the two fundamentals of self-respect and respect for one's neighbors so ably pled for by both Elihu Root and Woodrow Wilson should be retained as basic. The program was no longer spasmodic and unknown with a people to be whipped into excitement by a Blaine, or a Cleveland and an Olney. It was a national consciousness and an educated public that had to be considered. Wilson's Pan-American Pact did not get beyond the stage of discussion but F. D. Roosevelt's Consultative Pact was to secure practical results.

Thus the Caribbean had forced itself on a national consciousness and on the international stage. It was the crystallizing factor in the New World foreign policy of the United States in the period from 1890 to 1920. After that date new responsibilities, new means of communication, and new international complications were to broaden the Washington program to one of true hemisphere significance but even so the Caribbean was to remain a strategic unit in the foreign policy of the United States as it had been the actual dominating factor for upwards of a quarter of a century in the policy of the State Department.

BIBLIOGRAPHY

I. MANUSCRIPT COLLECTIONS

Chandler Parsons Anderson Papers. Library of Congress. (Diary of seven volumes especially valuable.)

William Jennings Bryan Papers. Library of Congress. (A heterogeneous collection poorly organized.)

Philippe Bunau-Varilla Papers. Library of Congress. (Six letter boxes on Panama Affair. Valuable.)

Walter Q. Gresham Papers. Library of Congress. (Three letter boxes only.)

Edward Mandell House Papers. Sterling Memorial Library, Yale University. (Extensive and valuable.)

Philander Chase Knox Papers. Library of Congress. (Extensive and valuable.)

Robert Lansing Papers. Library of Congress. (Good.)

Richard Olney Papers. Library of Congress. (Incoming letters good. Letter books badly mutilated.)

Elihu Root Papers. Library of Congress. (Excellent and extensive.)

William Howard Taft Papers. Library of Congress. (Large collection, chiefly used for 98 out-going letter books and for Orders Issued as Secy. War.

Woodrow Wilson Papers. Library of Congress. (Excellent. Consulted freely. Direct quotations limited in quantity but not in quality.)

II. GOVERNMENT DOCUMENTS

A. UNITED STATES

C[lark], J[oshua] R[euben]. Right to protect citizens in foreign countries by landing forces. Memorandum of the Solicitor for the Department of State, October 5, 1912. Washington, 1929 and 1934.

Clark, Joshua Reuben. Memorandum on the Monroe Doctrine. Washington, 1930.

Correspondence relating to wrongs done to American citizens by the Government of Venezuela. . . . (Sen. Doc. No. 413, 60th cong., 1st sess.) Washington, 1908.

Department of State. Report of the United States Commission on education in Haiti, October 1, 1930. Washington, 1931.

——, ——. Response to resolution, correspondence between Nov. 5, 1875, and . . . 1878, relating to intervention by United States in . . . Cuba (Sen. Exec. Doc. No. 213, 54th cong., 1st sess.) Washington, 1896.

——, ——. The United States and Nicaragua, a survey of the relations from 1909 to 1932. Washington, 1932.

Diplomatic History of the Panama Canal. Correspondence relating to the negotiation and application of certain treaties on the subject of the construction of an interoceanic canal, and accompanying papers. (Sen. Doc. No. 474, 63d cong., 2d sess.) Washington, 1914.

Inquiry into occupation and administration of Haiti and Santo Domingo. Hearings before a select committee on Haiti and Santo Domingo. U. S. Senate, 67th cong., 1st and 2d sess. pursuant to S. Res. 112. . . . Washington, 1922. 2 vols.

Inquiry into occupation and administration of Haiti and the Dominican Republic. . . . Report [pursuant to S. Res. 112]. (Sen. Report No. 794, 67th cong., 2d sess.) Washington.

Investigation of Mexican Affairs. Hearings before a sub-committee of the Committee on Foreign Relations, United States Senate, Sixty-sixth Congress, first session, pursuant to S. Res. 106 directing the Committee on Foreign Relations to investigate the matter of outrages on citizens of the United States in Mexico. Washington, 1919, 3 vols.

Knox, Philander Chase, Relations between the United States and the Republic of Colombia. (House Doc. No. 1444, 62d cong., 3d sess.) Washington, 1913.

——, ——. Speeches incident to the visit of . . . , Secretary of State of the United States of America to the countries of the Caribbean, February 23 to April 17, 1912. Washington, 1913.

Moore, John Bassett. A Digest of International Law. Washington, 1906. 8 vols.

Papers relating to the Foreign Relations of the United States with the Annual Message of the President (Also published as House Document No. 1, of the various sessions of the Congress). Washington, 1862—.

Richardson, James D. A compilation of the messages and papers of the presidents, 1789-1897. Washington, 1896-9. 10 vols. plus two supplementary.

Sale of government bonds or securities in the United States. Hearings before the Senate Committee on Finance, 1931-32. Washington, 1932. 4 parts.

Senate Document No. 166, 54th cong., 1st sess. Washington, 1896. (On U. S.-Cuban relations; belligerent rights.)

Senate Document No. 166, 54th cong., 1st sess. Washington, 1896. (On filibustering and efforts to stop it.)

United States Tariff Commission. Reciprocity and commercial treaties. Washington. 1919.

Use by the United States of a military force in the internal affairs of Colombia, . . . (Sen. Doc. No. 143, 58th cong., 2d sess.) Washington, 1904.

The Venezuelan arbitration before the Hague Tribunal, 1903. Proceedings of the Tribunal under the protocols between Venezuela and . . . signed at Washington, May 7, 1903. (Sen. Doc. No. 119, 58th cong., 3d sess.) Washington, 1905.

Weitzel, George T. American Policy in Nicaragua. Memorandum on convention . . . relative to an interoceanic canal and a naval station . . . signed . . . February 8, 1913. (Sen. Doc. No. 334, 64th cong., 1st sess.) Washington, 1916.

B. FOREIGN

Documents Diplomatiques Français (1871-1914). 2e Série (1901-1911). Paris, 1934-7, vols. V-VII.

British and foreign State papers, compiled by the librarian and keeper of the papers. London, 1841—. (Vols. 84 (1891)-114 (1921) valuable.)

British documents on the origins of the war, 1898-1914 (G. P. Gooch and Harold Temperley, editors). London, 1926-1936. 11 vols. in 13 parts.

III. MEMOIRS, COLLECTED WORKS AND BIOGRAPHIES

Adams, Henry. The Education of Henry Adams. An autobiography. Boston and New York, 1918. (Good for personal contacts.)

Alvarez, Alejandro. The Monroe Doctrine, its importance in the international life of the States of the New World. New York, 1924. (Excellent set of articles.)

Atkins, Edwin F. Sixty Years in Cuba. Reminiscences of Edwin F. Atkins. Cambridge, 1926. (Views of a conservative sugar planter.)

Baker, Ray Stannard. Woodrow Wilson, life and letters. Garden City, 1929-39. 8 vols. (The official biography, vols. iv-viii contain material of value for this study.)

Bemis, Samuel Flagg, editor. The American Secretaries of State and their diplomacy. New York, 1928-9. (Vols. vii-x contain short sketches of men of this period. Of varying value.)

Bunau-Varilla, Philippe. The great adventure of Panama. Garden City, 1920. (Memoirs of the Panama affair.)

——, ——. Panama, creation, destruction, and resurrection. London, 1913. (Autobiographical and memoirs.)

Bernstorff, Memoirs of Count. Eric Sutton, translator. New York, 1936. (German viewpoint.)

Bernstorff, Count. My three years in America. New York, 1920. (German view of New World diplomacy.)

Bigelow, John. Retrospections of an active life. Garden City, 1909-13. 5 vols. (Good on early part of study.)

Bishop, Joseph Bucklin, and Bishop, Farnham. Goethals: genius of the Panama Canal, a biography. New York and London, 1930. (On Canal policy.)

Bishop, Joseph Bucklin. Theodore Roosevelt and his time. Shown in his own letters. New York, 1920. 2 vols. (View of a personal friend and literary executor.)

Blaine, James G. The foreign policy of the Garfield Administration (pamphlet), Chicago Weekly Magazine, Sept. 16, 1882. (Personal apology.)

Blakeslee, George H., editor. Mexico and the Caribbean (Clark University addresses.) New York, 1920. (A variety of opinions.)

Bryan, William Jennings, and Bryan, Mary B. Memoirs of William Jennings Bryan. Philadelphia, 1925. (Of moderate value only.)

Bulnes, Francisco. Dora Scott, translator. The whole truth about Mexico, President Wilson's responsibility. New York, 1916. (Semi-autobiographical, interesting Mexican viewpoint.)

Callcott, Wilfrid Hardy. Santa Anna, the story of an enigma who once was Mexico. Norman, 1936. (Deals with middle of the century.)

Cecil, Lady Gwendolyn. Life of Robert Marquis of Salisbury. London, 1921-1932. 4 vols. (British viewpoint.)

Clark, Champ. My Quarter Century of American Politics. New York and London, 1920. 2 vols. (Of moderate value only.)

Cleveland, Grover. Presidential problems. New York, 1904. (Cleveland's own account.)

——, ——. The Venezuela Boundary Controversy. Princeton Univ. Press, 1913. (Controversy as seen by Cleveland in 1913.)

Coolidge, Louis A. An old-fashioned senator; Orville H. Platt of Connecticut. New York, 1910 (Biography of a man prominent in the new colonial policy of the U. S.)

Daniels, Josephus. The Life of Woodrow Wilson, 1856-1924. Chicago, Philadelphia and Toronto, 1924. (Ardent admirer of Wilson; discursive.)

Dennett, Tyler. John Hay, from poetry to politics. New York, 1934. (Good work on an important man.)

Dennis, Alfred L. P. Adventures in American diplomacy, 1896-1906 (From unpublished documents.) New York, 1928. (An enthusiast, interesting and valuable.)

Duffy, Herbert S. William Howard Taft. New York, 1930. (Fairly good.)

Dugdale, Blanche E. C. Arthur James Balfour, First Earl of Balfour, K. G., O. M., F. R. S, Etc. New York, 1937. 2 vols. (British view.)

Echanove Trujillo, Carlos. La vida pasionel e inquieta de Don Crecencio Rejón. Mexico, 1941. (Bitterly critical of 19th century U. S.)

Fisher, H. A. L. James Bryce (Viscount Bryce of Dechmont, O. M.). New York, 1927. (A careful study of the British statesman.)

Foster, John Watson. Diplomatic memoirs. Boston, 1909. 2 vols. (Some good material.)

Garvin, J. L. Life of Joseph Chamberlain. London, 1932-4. 3 vols. (Little on U. S. except for Canadian affairs.)

Gonzales, N. G. In darkest Cuba. Columbia, 1922. (Son of Cuban patriot of middle of century returns in the 1890s.)

Gonzales, William E. Concerning Dollar Diplomacy, crooks and grafters—incidents. . . . [Columbia, 1937 (?)]. (Recollections of war-time minister to Cuba.)

Gresham, Matilda. Life of Walter Quintin Gresham, 1832-1895. Chicago, 1919. 2 vols. (A wife's account. Some good interpretations.)

Viscount Gray of Fallodon, K. G. Twenty-five years 1892-1916. New York, 1925. 2 vols. (Autobiographical. Good.)

Griscom, Lloyd C. Diplomatically speaking. Boston, 1940. (Prepared for Root's trip in 1906 as Ambassador to Brazil.)

Gwynn, Stephen, editor. The Letters and friendships of Sir Cecil Spring-Rice. Boston and New York, 1929. 2 vols. (A good friend of Roosevelt and Lodge. Did not understand Wilson.)

Hammond, John Hays. The autobiography of John Hays Hammond. Murray Hill, N. Y., 1935. vols. (A " big-business " conservative in Mexico and elsewhere.)

Hendrick, Burton J. Life and letters of Walter Hines Page. New York, 1922-5. 3 vols. (Some good material.)

Houston, David F. Eight years with Wilson's Cabinet. Garden City, 1926. 2 vols. (A man in a position to know.)

James, Henry. Richard Olney and his public service. With documents including unpublished diplomatic correspondence. Boston and New York, 1923. (Good. 135 pages of documents.)

Jessup. Philip C. Elihu Root. New York, 1938. 2 vols. (Excellent biography with emphasis on legal work of the subject.)

The Lansing Papers, 1914-1920. (Published as a supplement to the *Foreign Relations of the United States.*) Washington, 1940. 2 vols. (Excellent material.)

Levine, Isaac Don, copyist and editor. Letters from the Kaiser to the Czar, copied from government archives in Petrograd, unpublished before 1920. New York, 1920. (A few references to the U. S.)

Lodge, Henry Cabot, editor. Selections from the correspondence of Theodore Roosevelt and Henry Cabot Lodge, 1884-1918. New York and London, 1925. 2 vols. (Excellent.)

McElroy, Robert. Grover Cleveland, the man and the statesman. New York, 1923. 2 vols. (Rather good.)

Marett, R. H. K. An eye-witness of Mexico. London, New York and Toronto, 1939. (A British conservative in Mexico.)

Márquez Sterling, M. Los últimos días del presidente Madero (Mi gestión diplomática en México). Habana, 1917. (Cuban diplomat in Mexico, bitterly critical of U. S. policy to 1913.)

Muzzey, David Saville. James G. Blaine, a political idol of other days. New York, 1934. (A good estimate.)

Nevins, Allan. Grover Cleveland. A study in courage. New York, 1932. (Laudatory but an estimate by a scholar.)

———, ———. Henry White. Thirty years of American diplomacy. New York and London, 1930. (Little on New World.)

O'Shaughnessy, Edith. A diplomat's wife in Mexico. New York, 1916 (Reminiscences of the Mexican Revolution.)

Pringle, Henry F. The Life and Times of William Howard Taft. New York and Toronto, 1939. 2 vols. (Excellent, by a scholar.)

——, ——. Theodore Roosevelt. London, 1932 and 1934. (Rather critical of Roosevelt. Much valuable material.)

Puleston, Captain W. D. Mahan. The life and work of Captain Alfred Thayer Mahan. New Haven, 1939. (Interprets the man in the spirit of his time and his profession.)

Robinson, Edgar Eugene, and West, Victor J. The Foreign Policy of Woodrow Wilson. New York, 1918. (A handy collection of Wilson papers and addresses.)

Root, Elihu. Addresses on International Subjects (Collected and edited by Robert Bacon and James Brown Scott). Cambridge, 1916. (Valuable.)

——, ——. Latin America and the United States, addresses by Elihu Root (Robert Bacon and James Brown Scott, editors). Cambridge, 1917. (Addresses of good-will tours.)

Roosevelt, Theodore. An autobiography. New York, 1919. (As the man would have himself seen.)

Sanso, Aro. Policarpo Bonilla, algunos apuntes biográficos. México, 1936. (Laudatory biography of a prominent Central American.)

Scott, James Brown, editor and author of introduction. The International conferences of the American States, 1889-1928. (Excellent reference work.)

——, ——. President Wilson's Foreign Policy. Messages, addresses, papers, edited with introduction and notes. New York, 1918. (A handy reference set.)

Seymour, Charles. The intimate papers of Colonel House. Boston and New York, 1926-8. 4 vols. (First two volumes most important for New World affairs. Valuable.)

Smith, Arthur D. Howden. Mr. House of Texas. New York and London, 1940. (Journalistic and laudatory. Impressions probably accurate in many cases. No documentation.)

Spender, J. A. Weetman Pearson, First Viscount Cowdray, 1856-1927. London, etc., 1930. (Weak on international relations.)

Thayer, William Roscoe. The life and letters of John Hay. Boston and New York, 1915. 2 vols. (Heroizes the hero. Quite good.)

Trevelyan, George Macaulay. Grey of Fallodon. The life and letters of Sir Edward Grey, afterwards Viscount Grey of Fallodon. Boston, 1937. (Good work; brief on New World affairs.)

Voight, F. A., translator. Memoirs of Prince Von Bülow. Vol. I from Secretary of State to Imperial Chancellor. Boston, 1931. (Little on New World affairs.)

Volweiler, Albert T., editor. The Correspondence between Benjamin Harrison and James G. Blaine, 1882-1893. Philadelphia, 1940 (Good.)

Von Tirpitz, Grand Admiral. My Memoirs. New York, 1919. 2 vols. (German view. Little on New World.)

White, Andrew Dickson. Autobiography of . . . , with portraits. New York, 1905. 2 vols. (Has facts on Venezuela and Santo Domingo.)

White, T. R., and Tower, Charlemagne. Our duty concerning Panama Tolls. Boston, 1913. (An argument by men involved.)

Williams, Charles Richard. The life of Rutherford Birchard Hayes, nineteenth President of the United States. Boston and New York, 1914. 2 vols. (Little on foreign policy.)

Wilson, Henry Lane. Diplomatic episodes in Mexico, Belgium and Chile. New York, 1927. (A Dollar Diplomat's apology on Mexico.)

IV. PERIODICALS

It is to be noted that no effort is made here to list a very large number of separate articles in scattered periodicals. With one exception, indicated below by special volume numbers, the following journals have been followed number by number for the years indicated.

Foreign Affairs; an American quarterly review. New York, 1922-1941.

American Historical Review. New York, 1895-1942.

American Journal of International Law. New York and Concord, N. H., 1907-1941.

The Annals. American Academy of Political and Social Science, Philadelphia, 1890-1926.

Atlantic Monthly. Boston, 1911 and 1913. (Two articles on the Monroe Doctrine by Hiram Bingham and F. García Calderón.)

Hispanic American Historical Review. Baltimore and Durham, 1918-1922; 1926-1942.

Political Science Quarterly. Lancaster, Pa., and New York, 1886-1941.

V. SECONDARY

Ackerman, Carl W. Mexico's Dilemma. New York, 1918. (Notes of a shrewd reporter.)

Aikman, Duncan. All-American Front. New York, 1940. (Another shrewd reporter at a later date.)

Arias, Harmodio. The Panama Canal, a study in international law and diplomacy. London, 1911. (Critical and rather pro-British. (Careful work.)

Balch, Emily Greene, editor. Occupied Haiti, being the report of a committee of . . . Americans, who . . . favor the restoration of the independence of the Negro republic. New York, 1927. (Uncritical denunciation of U. S. but has some facts.)

Beals, Carleton. The crime of Cuba. Philadelphia, 1933. (Journalistic denunciation of U. S. Some facts.)

Beard, Charles A. The idea of national interest, an analytical study in American foreign policy. New York, 1934. (Suggestive.)

Bell, Edward I. The political shame of Mexico. New York, 1914. (One of the first books to face facts on Mexico.)

Benton, Elbert J. International law and diplomacy of the Spanish-American War. Baltimore, 1908. (Technical study. Good.)

Bingham, Hiram. The Monroe Doctrine, an obsolete shibboleth. New Haven, 1913 (A plea for cooperation. Significant.)

Blakeslee, George H. The recent foreign policy of the United States. New York, 1925. (A good statement by a great admirer of Secretary of State Hughes.)

Blanco-Fombona, Horacio. Crimenes del imperialismo norteamericano. México, 1927. (A violent denunciation of the United States.)

Bonsal, Stephen. The American Mediterranean. New York, 1913. (An advocate of U. S. imperialism.)

Bryce, James. The American Commonwealth. New York, 1910. 2 vols. (A master's interpretation of U. S. government, by a kindly foreigner.)

Buell, Raymond Leslie. The American occupation of Haiti (Foreign Policy Association Information Service, V, Nos. 19-20). New York, 1929. (Impartial and critical.)

——, ——. American supervision of elections in Nicaragua (F.

P. A. Information Service, VI, No. 21). New York, 1930.
(Impartial.)

——, ——. Cuba and the Platt Amendment (F. P. A. Information
Service, V, No. 3). New York, 1929. (Critical and impartial.)

——, ——. Isolated America. New York, 1940. (A recent set of
lectures by a scholar. Good.)

——, ——, and others. Problems of the New Cuba, report of the
Commission on Cuban Affairs. New York, 1935. (Special
studies on phases of Cuban life and politics. (Not to be
ignored.)

——, ——. Reconstruction in Nicaragua (F. P. A. Information
Service, VI, No. 18). New York, 1930. (Critical.)

Callahan, James Morton. American foreign policy in Mexican relations. New York, 1932. (Careful study by a scholar.)

——, ——. Cuba and international relations. A historical study
in American diplomacy. Baltimore, 1899. (One of early critical studies of Cuban relations with U. S.)

——, ——. Evolution of Seward's Mexican Policy. Morgantown,
1908. (Interesting but somewhat forced.)

Callcott, Wilfrid Hardy. Liberalism in Mexico, 1857-1929. Stanford University Press, 1931. (Interpretation of Mexico and
its relations against the Mexican background.)

Carter, John. Conquest; America's painless imperialism. New
York, 1928. (Shows needs and development of economic
imperialism.)

Chadwick, French Ensor. Relations of the United States and
Spain. Diplomacy. New York, 1909. (Good but not exhaustive.)

Chapman, C. E. A history of the Cuban Republic, a study in Hispanic American politics. New York, 1927. (A good hand-
book. Good on internal affairs in Cuba by an Anglo-Saxon
egotist.)

Clark, Victor S., and associates. Porto Rico and its problems.
Washington, 1930. (Emphasizes economic conditions.)

Coolidge, Archibald Cary. The United States as a world power.
New York, 1909. (Lecture material given at the Sorbonne.
Interesting.)

Cox, Isaac Joslin. Nicaragua and the United States, 1909-1927.
Boston, 1927. (Many documents.)

Creel, George. The people next door, an interpretative history of

Mexico and the Mexicans. New York, 1926. (Suggestive and general.)

Crowther, Samuel. The romance and rise of the tropics. Garden City, 1929. (By a financial imperialist.)

Davis, Harold Palmer. Black Democracy. New York, 1928. (Very good survey.)

Dawes, Charles G., and others. Report of Dominican Economic Commission. Chicago, 1929. (Good economic survey made at invitation of Dominican President.)

Dealey, James Quayle. Foreign policies of the United States, Their bases and development. Boston, 1926. (Lectures on phases of U. S. policy.)

Dillon, E. J. Mexico on the Verge. New York, 1921. (Pro-British and quite critical of U. S.)

Dunn, Frederick Sherwood. Diplomatic protection of Americans in Mexico. New York, 1933. (Good, especially for questions of claims.)

Dunning, William Archibald. The British Empire and the United States. A review of their relations during the century of peace following the Treaty of Ghent. New York, 1914. (General.)

DuVal, Miles P., Jr. Cadiz to Cathay. The story of the long struggle for a waterway across the American Isthmus. Stanford University Press, 1940. (Good. Makes use of Herrán Papers.)

Estrada, Genaro, editor and author of prologue. La Doctrina de Monroe y el fracasado de una conferencia panamericana en México. México, 1937. (Good for the 1890s.)

Ferrara, Orestes (William E. Shea, translator). The last Spanish war. Revelations in " diplomacy." New York, 1937. (Good on effort of Spain to secure European support in 1890s.)

Fitzgibbon, Russell H. Cuba and the United Stattes, 1900-1935. Menasha, 1935. (A careful piece of work.)

Flack, Horace Edgar. Spanish-American relations preceding the war of 1898. Baltimore, 1906. (Fair but not exhaustive.)

Foster, John W. A Century of American diplomacy, being a brief review of the foreign relations of the United States, 1776-1876. Boston and New York, 1900. (Suggestive.)

Froude, James Anthony. The English in the West Indies, or, the bow of Ulysses. New York, 1888. (Caribbean interpretations of a shrewd British traveller.)

García Calderón, Francisco. Latin America: its rise and progress. London, 1919 (sixth edition). (An excellent interpretation.)

Gregg, Robert Danforth. The influence of border troubles on relations between the United States and Mexico, 1876-1910. Baltimore, 1937. (Careful study based largely on U. S. Government documents.)

Gruening, Ernest. Mexico and its heritage. New York and London, 1928. (An able commentator on current affairs.)

Guggenheim, Harry F. The United States and Cuba; a study in international relations. New York, 1934. (A strong plea for U. S. investors in Cuba.)

Hackett, Charles Wilson. The Mexican Revolution and the United States, 1910-1926. Boston, 1926. (An excellent survey.)

Hall, Arnold Bennett. The Monroe Doctrine and the Great War. Chicago, 1920. (A popular treatment of value.)

Haring, Clarence H. South America looks at the United States. New York, 1929. (To be considered. A good interpretation.)

Hart, Albert Bushnell. The Monroe Doctrine: an interpretation. Boston, 1920. (An excellent survey of varying opinions to 1915).

Henríquez Ureña, Max. La Liga de Naciones Americanas y la conferencia de Buenos Aires. . . . Nueva York, 1937. (Some good documents.)

——, ——. Los Yanquis en Santo Domingo. Madrid, 1929. (Severely critical of U. S. in Santo Domingo.)

Hill, Howard C. Roosevelt and the Caribbean. Chicago, 1927. (Very good.)

Holt, W. Stull. Treaties defeated by the Senate, a study of the struggle between President and Senate over the conduct of foreign relations. Baltimore, 1933. (A glance behind the scenes.)

Hughes, Charles Evans. Our relations to the nations of the Western Hemisphere. Princeton, 1928. (Lectures at Princeton. Good.)

Hunt, Gaillard. The Department of State of the United States, its history and functions. New Haven, 1914. (Excellent on subject; not a diplomatic history of the U. S.)

Jenks, Leland H. Our Cuban Colony, a study in sugar. New York, 1928. (Anti-imperialistic. Has some good material.)

Jones, Chester Lloyd. Caribbean backgrounds and prospects. New York, 1931. (Economic emphasis.)

Jones, Chester Lloyd. Caribbean interests of the United States. New York, 1916. (Excellent economic summary.)

——, ——. The Caribbean since 1900. New York, 1936. (Economic study by countries. Omits Mexico.)

——, ——. Guatemala, past and present. Minneapolis, 1940. (A general survey.)

Jones, Chester Lloyd; Norton, H. K., and Moon, Parker T. The United States and the Caribbean. Chicago, 1929. (Good contrasting views.)

Kelsey, Carl. The American intervention in Haiti and the Dominican Republic. . . . *The Annals*, C, 109-202. (A special report of outstanding merit.)

Knight, Melvin M. The Americans in Santo Domingo. New York, 1928. (Severely critical of the U. S.)

Latané, John Holladay. America as a World power, 1897-1907. New York and London, 1907. (An excellent ground-breaking study.)

——, ——. Diplomatic relations of the United States and Spanish America. Baltimore, 1900. (First of the Shaw Lectures. Good interpretations now better substantiated by later research.)

——, ——. The United States and Latin America. Garden City, 1920. (Earlier lectures amplified and brought up to date.)

Lewis Cleona, assisted by Schlotterbeck, Karl T. America's Stake in international investments. Washington, 1938. (A mass of statistical information.)

Lockey, Joseph Byrne. Pan-Americanism, its beginnings. New York, 1926. (Emphasis on early period.)

Logan, Rayford W. The diplomatic relations of the United States with Haiti, 1776-1891. Chapel Hill. (Detailed research.)

McCain, William D. The United States and the Republic of Panama. Durham, 1937 (Good material.)

MacCormac, John. Canada: America's problem. New York, 1940. (Good to keep the Canadian side of picture balanced.)

Mahan, Alfred Thayer. The interest of America in sea power, present and future. Boston (1897), 1918. (A collection of the Mahan articles.)

Malin, James C. The United States after the World War. Boston, 1930. (Partisan. Good suggestive interpretations.)

Martin, Percy Alvin. Latin America and the War. Baltimore, 1925. (An excellent preliminary survey.)

Mathews, John Mabry. The conduct of American foreign relations. New York, 1922. (Text-book type of survey. Good to 1920).

Millis, Walter. The Martial Spirit; a study of the War with Spain. Boston and New York, 1931. (A good de-bunking effort.)

Millspaugh, Arthur C. Haiti under American control, 1915-1930. Boston, 1931. (Very critical of Democrats and not too pleased with Republicans in Haiti.)

Miner, Dwight Carroll. The fight for the Panama Route. The story of the Spooner Act and the Hay-Herrán Treaty. New York, 1940. (Probably definitive.)

Moon, Parker Thomas. Imperialism and World Politics. New York, 1926. (General interpretations of world imperialism.)

Moore, John Bassett. Candor and Common Sense. (Address before the Association of the Bar of the City of New York, December 4, 1930). n. p., n. d. (Interesting criticism of novel practices in diplomacy.)

Mowat, R. B. The diplomatic relations of Great Britain and the United States. London, 1925. (Excellent material by a Britisher who is anxious for good relations and pulls his punches a little.)

———, ———. Life of Lord Pauncefote, first ambassador to the United States. Boston and New York, 1929. (Good.)

Munro, Dana G. The five republics of Central America. New York, 1918. (A good analysis of relations.)

———, ———. The United States and the Caribbean Area. Boston, 1934. (Well balanced; good.)

Nearing, Scott, and Freeman, Joseph. Dollar Diplomacy. New York, 1925. (Severe criticism of Dollar Diplomacy.)

Nerval, Gaston (pseudonym for Raul Díez de Medina). Autopsy of the Monroe Doctrine; the strange story of inter-American relations. New York, 1934. (Indictment of the U. S. To be considered.)

Nogales, Rafael de. The Looting of Nicaragua. New York, 1928. (Title indicates material.)

Notter, Harley. Origins of the foreign policy of Woodrow Wilson. Baltimore, 1937. (A careful study based on Wilson Papers and other correspondence.)

Offutt, Milton. Protection of citizens abroad by the armed forces of the United States. Baltimore, 1928. (A good check list of incidents.)

Paxson, Frederick L. Independence of the South American repub-

‹lics, a study in recognition and foreign policy. Philadelphia, 1916 (1903). (An early study. Suggestive.)

Perkins, Dexter. Hands off: a history of the Monroe Doctrine. Boston, 1941. (A general treatment.)

——, ——. The Monroe Doctrine, 1823-1826. Cambridge, 1927. (With the two following volumes, the best treatment of the Doctrine.)

——, ——. The Monroe Doctrine, 1826-1867. Baltimore, 1933. (See above.)

——, ——. The Monroe Doctrine, 1867-1907. Baltimore, 1937. (See above.)

Portell Vilá, Herminio. Historia de Cuba en relaciones con los Estados Unidos y España. Havana, 1938-9. 3 vols. (Best research by a Cuban on the subject. Critical of the U. S.)

Pratt, Julius W. Expansionists of 1898. The acquisition of Hawaii and the Spanish islands. Baltimore, 1936. (Shaw Lectures for 1936. A good study of public opinion.)

Rippy, J. Fred. The Capitalists and Colombia. New York, 1931. (Strongly anti-imperialistic.)

——, ——. The Caribbean Danger Zone. New York, 1940. (General.)

——, ——. Latin America in World politics; an outline survey. New York, 1928. (Some good suggestions.)

——, ——. The United States and Colombian oil (Foreign Policy Association Information Service, V, No. 2). New York, 1929. (A good summary. Anti-imperialistic.)

——, ——. The United States and Mexico. New York, 1931. (A good survey for period since 1845.)

Robertson, William Spence. Hispanic-American relations with the United States. New York, 1923. (Essays on special topics.)

Rojas, Luis Manuel. La culpa de Henry Lane Wilson en el gran desastre de México, vol. I, México, 1928. (Subject indicated by title.)

Roosevelt, Theodore. Fear God and take your own part. New York, 1916. (A collection of essays and articles chiefly attacking the Wilson administration.)

Rubens, Horacio S. Liberty, the story of Cuba. New York, 1932. (Partisan and interesting account of Cuban juntas in the U. S. in 1890s.)

Salmon, C. S. The Caribbean Confederation . . . a plan for the union of the . . . British West Indian colonies . . . a refutation of . . . statements by Mr. Froude in . . . " The British in the West Indies." London and New York, [1888]. (Title indicates contents.)

Schoenrich, Otto. Santo Domingo, a country with a future. New York, 1918. (More interested in possibilities than history.)

Stevens, Guy. Current controversies with Mexico. Addresses and writings. n. p., n. d. (Advocate of protection of financial investments.)

Stolberg-Wernigerode, Count Otto zu. Germany and the United States during the era of Bismarck. Reading, [1937?]. (Based on careful use of German and U. S. documents.)

Stuart, Graham H. Latin America and the United States. New York, 1938 (1922). (Good discussion of special topics.)

Taft, William H. The United States and peace. New York, 1914. (A set of four addresses. One on Monroe Doctrine.)

Tansill, Charles Callan. The foreign policy of Thomas F. Bayard, 1885-1897. New York, 1940. (Work of a partisan of Bayard and Gersham, and critic of Olney and Cleveland.)

——, ——. The Purchase of the Danish West Indies. Baltimore, 1932. (Best study of subject available.)

Temperley, Harold, and Penson, Lillian. Foundations of British foreign policy from Pitt (1792) to Salisbury (1902). . . . Cambridge University Press, 1938. (Interesting.)

Thomas, D. Y. One hundred years of the Monroe Doctrine. New York, 1927. (Some good interpretations.)

Tyler, Alice Felt. The foreign policy of James G. Blaine. Minneapolis, 1927. (Heroizes Blaine. Some good material.)

Ugarte, Manuel (J. Fred Rippy, editor). The Destiny of a continent. New York, 1925. (Bitter criticism of the U. S.)

Uribe, Antonio José. Colombia y los Estados Unidos de América. Bogotá, 1926. (Many documents on recent relations.)

The United States and the Nicaraguan Canal (Foreign Policy Association Information Service, IV, No. 6). New York, 1928. (Indictment of Bryan-Chamorro treaty.)

Viallate, Achille. Economic imperialism and international relations during the last fifty years. New York, 1923. (European scholar sets U. S. in the world scene. General.)

Weinberg, Albert K. Manifest destiny, a study of nationalist expansionism in American history. Baltimore, 1935. (Suggestive.)

Welles, Sumner. Naboth's Vineyard, the Dominican Republic,

1844-1924. New York, 1928. 2 vols. (A study by a man who knew his facts.)

Whitaker, Arthur Preston. The United States and the Independence of Latin America, 1800-1830. Baltimore, 1941. (An excellent study.)

Williams, Benjamin H. American diplomacy, policies and practice. New York, 1936. (Title is descriptive.)

——, ——. Economic foreign policy of the United States. New York, 1929. (Excellent study of motives.)

Winkler, Max. Investments of United States capital in Latin America. Boston, 1929. (A mass of statistical information.)

Wriston, Henry Merritt. Executive agents in American foreign relations. Baltimore, 1929. (Shaw Lectures for 1923. An immense amount of detailed work. Valuable.)

INDEX

A

ABC Powers, Pan-American Pact, 323-325, 326-328, 330; Mexico, 326-327, 344, 364, 365; Niagara Falls Conference, 358; House wishes to use, 363.

Adams, John Quincy, purpose in Monroe Doctrine, 6, 8; Cuba, 7; Colombia, 7-8, 10; Panama Conference, 11.

Adee, Alvey A., 59, 209.

Atkins, Edwin F., 80, 98.

Alvarez, Alejandro, 262.

Anderson, Chandler P., 436-437, 462.

B

Blaine, James G., as a party man, 45; foreign policy, 45-48; return as Secretary of State, 59-60; presides at Pan-American conference, 60; Venezuelan boundary, 63-64; expansionism, 64-67; mentioned, 118.

Bonilla, Policarpo, 454-456.

Bryan, William Jennings, as Secretary of State, 310-311; relations with Woodrow Wilson, 311; 332-333; Bryan peace treaties, 322, 388,n.; resignation, 325, 363-364; Caribbean problems, 332, 375-376; personal, 332-333; opinon of Carnegie, 333; Bryan peace plan, 334,n., 335; scheme for Caribbean loans, 335-337; aid to investors in Haiti, 337; opinion of Spring-Rice, 354,n.; disagrees with Wilson on Mexico, 363-364; Panama tolls, 376-377; urges treaty with Colombia, 383; Bryan-Chamorro Treaty, 384-390; lack of policy on islands, 396, 406; Santo Domingo, 396-397; 399, Haiti, 405-406; Dollar Diplomacy in Cuba, 423-424; confusion of, 431.

Bryan-Chamorro Treaty, mentioned, 54, 321; Nicaraguan proposals, 385; Platt Amendment idea, 385-386; Treaty in U. S. Senate, 386-388; action of Peace Court concerning, 388-390; Cleveland Award, 390.

Bunau-Varilla, Philippe, connection with French in Panama, 141; in U. S., 142 ff.; preparing Panama revolt, 149-154, 158; threatens Colombia, 150; relations with U. S., State Department, 153-154; relations with Roosevelt, 154,n.; Minister of Panama, 155, 159-160; relations with the press, 160-161; Hay-Bunau-Varilla Treaty, 163.

Bureau of American Republics, 110-111:

C

Cacos, 414-415, 420, 478.

Canada, boundary dispute, 118-119.

Caperton, Admiral W. B., intervenes in Haiti, 413-415; Cacos, 414-415; elections in Haiti, 415-417; treaty with Haiti, 417-419; trouble over new constitution, 419-420.

Caribbean, colonial interest, 1; U. S. on revolutions against Spain, 3-4; piracy, 1, 5; reception of Monroe Doctrine, 8-9; rising interest in islands, 21; fear of U. S., 1850s, 26; Seward's expansionism, 36-37; German interest, 41-42, 107-108; no policy formed for, 42; Blaine to reduce European influence, 46; a policy evolves, 57-58, 209-210; a confederation of British possessions, 69; importance of, 71, 73; area, 73; fear of U. S., 1890s, 74-75, 95, 113, 135; Cleveland policy, 95-96; influence of U. S. policy to 1900, 115; recognition of U. S. priority, 117, 138; major problems in, 117, 124; British withdrawal of naval squadron, 134-135; the problem of 1901, 138; influence of canal, 157; recognition of Panama, 162; pattern evolves, 166, 188; opinions on constitutional rights, 168; U. S. economic influence, 202; U. S. to dominate, 206-207; opinions on, 209-210; Root's economic policy, 214; Knox tour, 269, 275-276, 278-279, 306-307; as U. S. barnyard, 278; British colonies at opening of Canal, 305; Dollar Diplomacy, 309; approach of Woodrow Wilson, 311-312; investments and trade, 312; Wilson considers as a special sphere, 317; Bryan and Caribbean problems, 332, 375-376; hails Bryan peace treaties, 335; a distinctive region, 335; Bryan's financial proposals, 335-336, 337; Lansing for a definite policy, 339; pig-in-a-poke request, 379; effect of intervention in Santo Domingo,